The Bilingual A...

BILINGUAL EDUCATION & BILINGUALISM

Series Editors: **Nancy H. Hornberger**, (*University of Pennsylvania, USA*) and **Colin Baker** (*Bangor University, Wales, UK*)

Bilingual Education and Bilingualism is an international, multidisciplinary series publishing research on the philosophy, politics, policy, provision and practice of language planning, global English, indigenous and minority language education, multilingualism, multiculturalism, biliteracy, bilingualism and bilingual education. The series aims to mirror current debates and discussions.

Full details of all the books in this series and of all our other publications can be found on http://www.multilingual-matters.com, or by writing to Multilingual Matters, St Nicholas House, 31-34 High Street, Bristol BS1 2AW, UK.

BILINGUAL EDUCATION & BILINGUALISM: 99

The Bilingual Advantage

Language, Literacy and the US Labor Market

Edited by

**Rebecca M. Callahan
and Patricia C. Gándara**

MULTILINGUAL MATTERS
Bristol • Buffalo • Toronto

Library of Congress Cataloging in Publication Data
A catalog record for this book is available from the Library of Congress.
The Bilingual Advantage: Language, Literacy and the US Labor Market/Edited by
Rebecca M. Callahan and Patricia C. Gándara.
Bilingual Education & Bilingualism: 99
Includes bibliographical references and index.
1.English language—Study and teaching (Higher)—United States. 2.English language—
Study and teaching (Higher)—Foreign speakers. 3.English language—Technical
English—Study and teaching. 4.English language—Business English—Study and
teaching. 5.Interdisciplinary approach in education—United States. 6.Vocational
education—United States. 7.Career education—United States. 8.Literacy—United
States. 9.Education, Bilingual—United States. I.Callahan, Rebecca M., editor. II.Gandara,
Patricia C., editor.
PE1068.U5B55 2014
428.0071'073–dc23 2014016752

British Library Cataloguing in Publication Data
A catalogue entry for this book is available from the British Library.

ISBN-13: 978-1-78309-242-0 (hbk)
ISBN-13: 978-1-78309-241-3 (pbk)

Multilingual Matters
UK: St Nicholas House, 31-34 High Street, Bristol BS1 2AW, UK.
USA: UTP, 2250 Military Road, Tonawanda, NY 14150, USA.
Canada: UTP, 5201 Dufferin Street, North York, Ontario M3H 5T8, Canada.

Website: www.multilingual-matters.com
Twitter: Multi_Ling_Mat
Facebook: https://www.facebook.com/multilingualmatters
Blog: www.channelviewpublications.wordpress.com

The policy of Multilingual Matters/Channel View Publications is to use papers that
are natural, renewable and recyclable products, made from wood grown in sustainable
forests. In the manufacturing process of our books, and to further support our policy,
preference is given to printers that have FSC and PEFC Chain of Custody certification.
The FSC and/or PEFC logos will appear on those books where full certification has been
granted to the printer concerned.

Typeset by Deanta Global Publishing Services Limited.
Printed and bound in Great Britain by Short Run Press Ltd.

To all those young English learners who struggle to maintain their home languages in the face of restrictive school policies that often make this difficult: May you prosper in your multilingualism, and benefit from the fruits of your labor!

We wish to express our gratitude to the Educational Testing Service for their finanical support of much of the research presented in this volume, with special thanks to Michael Nettles and Jonathan Rochkind for their belief in the project and their unwavering support as it came to fruition.

Contents

Contributors

Orhan Agirdag (PhD, Sociology) is an assistant professor of education at the University of Amsterdam. Formerly, he worked at Ghent University and he was a Fulbright Fellow at the Civil Rights Project (UCLA). His main research interests include (in)equalities in education, multilingualism and teacher education. His doctoral thesis on school segregation has won multiple awards. His work is published in more than 20 American and European journals.

Amado Alarcón (PhD, Sociology, Universitat Autònoma de Barcelona) is an associate professor of sociology at the Departament de Gestió d'Empreses at the Universitat Rovira i Virgili. His research focuses on relations between migration, language and economic activity. He has directed various research projects for the Ministerio de Educación, Cultura y Deporte and Ministerio de Economía y Competitividad of the Government of Spain, and the Secretaria de Joventut and the Secretaria per a la Immigració of the Generalitat de Catalunya. In addition, he is president of the Research Committee 25 on Language and Society of the International Sociological Association.

Ursula S. Aldana's research focuses on education reform, particularly with regard to issues of equity and access for historically underserved students. She has conducted a range of education studies focused on language policy and practice; Catholic schools; and the sociocultural competencies of teachers and students. Dr Aldana received her PhD in Education with a concentration on urban schooling from UCLA's Graduate School of Education and Information Studies; she holds an MA in Elementary Education from Loyola Marymount University, a multiple-subject and single-subject teaching credential in social science; and a BS in International Politics from the School of Foreign Service at Georgetown University. Dr Aldana is currently an assistant professor of education at the University of San Francisco.

M. Beatriz Arias is an associate professor in the Department of English Education at Arizona State University and director of development and the division of K-12 professional development at the Center for Applied Linguistics. She is the author and editor of several books and more than 30 scholarly articles and chapters on issues of language policy, bilingual education, school desegregation and equity for Latino students. She is a recognized national expert in the area of school desegregation, having served as a court-appointed expert in the Los Angeles, San Jose, Denver and Chicago desegregation cases.

Rebecca M. Callahan is an assistant professor of education at the University of Texas at Austin, and a faculty research affiliate with the Population Research Center. Her primary research interests center on the academic and civic preparation of immigrant, language minority adolescents as they transition from high school into young adulthood. Recent publications, including her book, *Coming of Political Age: American Schools and the Civic Development of Immigrant Youth* (Russell Sage Press, 2013), have focused on the educational and linguistic experiences of immigrant language minority adolescents. Her research has been funded by the Russell Sage Foundation, the National Science Foundation, the American Educational Research Association and the Texas Higher Education Opportunity Project/Spencer Foundation.

Antonio Di Paolo holds an MA in Economics from the University of Bologna and a PhD in Economics from the Autonomous University of Barcelona. After completing his PhD, he worked as a postdoctoral researcher at the Rovira i Virgili University. Currently, he is a visiting professor at the Department of Econometrics at the University of Barcelona. Previously, DiPaolo has been a visiting researcher at the Institute for Social and Economic Research (ISER), the Center of European Economic Research (ZEW) and the German Institute for Economic Research (DIW). His main research interests are education economics, labor economics, language economics and applied microeconometrics.

Jongyeon Ee is a graduate student researcher with the Civil Rights Project/ Proyecto Derechos Civiles at the University of California at Los Angeles, where she is also a PhD student in the Graduate School of Education. Her research interests include English language learners (ELLs), language minority students, immigrant students and school segregation by race, poverty and language. Ms Ee studies the effects of a variety of policies on language and integration and the role of education in urban areas, focusing on ways in which greater opportunities can be created for language minority students and ELLs.

Molly Fee is a research assistant at the Center for Applied Linguistics where she conducts research, presents at national and international conferences and coauthors papers for CAL's Language Policy Research Network (LPReN). Additionally, she assists in the management of the English for Heritage Language Speakers Program, a federally funded program that provides advanced English training for native speakers of critical languages in preparation for careers in the federal government. She holds an MA in International Affairs, Conflict Resolution and Civil Society Development and an MA in Cultural Translation, both from the American University of Paris.

Patricia Gándara is research professor in the Graduate School of Education and Information Studies and co-director of the Civil Rights Project/Proyecto Derechos Civiles at UCLA. She received her PhD in Educational Psychology from UCLA. She has directed education research in the California State Legislature and served as a Commissioner of Postsecondary Education for the state of California. She currently serves on the White House Commission for Educational Excellence for Hispanics. Her research focuses on educational equity, Latino students and language policy.

Josiah Heyman is professor of Anthropology, endowed professor of Border Trade Issues and chair of Sociology and Anthropology at the University of Texas El Paso. His work focuses on borders, states, power, migration and engaged social sciences. He is the author or editor of three books and over 140 scholarly articles, book chapters and essays. Two recent publications are 'Culture Theory and the US–Mexico Border' in *A Companion to Border Studies* (Wiley-Blackwell, 2012) and (with John Symons) 'Borders' in *A Companion to Moral Anthropology* (Wiley-Blackwell 2012). He also participates in community initiatives, addressing public policy and human rights at the US–Mexico border. He can be contacted at jmheyman@utep.edu.

Reynaldo F. Macías is a faculty member and former chair of the UCLA Department of Chicana and Chicano Studies and the César E. Chávez Center for Interdisciplinary Instruction. He is the author, coauthor and editor of six books and over three dozen research articles and chapters on such topics as bilingual education, teacher supply and demand, Chicanos and schooling, adult literacy, language choice, analyses of national language survey data, population projections, language policies and media research. His work has appeared in such journals as the *NABE Journal*, the *International Journal of the Sociology of Language* and the *Annual Review of Applied Linguistics*. His current research activities are in language policy/politics/demography, adult literacy and teacher studies.

Anysia P. Mayer is an associate professor of educational leadership in the College of Education at California State University Stanislaus, where she arrived after five years on faculty at the University of Connecticut. Dr Mayer's work examines education policy with a specific focus on understanding how schools can advance students of color and immigrant students to high academic achievement, with the goal of participation in a four-year college. Dr Mayer is currently researching issues related to urban schooling, namely, classroom instructional quality, tracking and programs for ELLs. In addition, she previously worked as a classroom teacher and a college counselor.

Sarah Catherine K. Moore is program director at the Center for Applied Linguistics where her work focuses on teacher preparation, educator professional development, virtual learning, language minority schooling, language policy and education policy implementation. She also manages projects and oversees activities under CAL's Language Policy Research Network (LPReN). Dr Moore's recent publications and edited volumes include *Language Policy, Processes and Consequences: Arizona Case Studies* (editor, Multilingual Matters, 2014) and *Handbook of Heritage, Community, and Native American Languages: Research, Policy, and Practice* (coeditor, Routledge, 2014).

María Cristina Morales (PhD Sociology, Texas A&M University) is an associate professor of sociology at the University of Texas El Paso. Her research investigates issues of race, ethnicity, citizenship/ nationality and class; US Latinos; migration; labor markets; informal economies; demography and research methods.

Diana A. Porras is a PhD student in the Urban Schooling Division of the Graduate School of Education and Information Studies at UC Los Angeles. A native of Salinas, CA, Diana received her BA degree in Native American Studies from the University of California at Berkeley and her MA in Public Administration from California State University at Long Beach. Previously, Ms Porras worked as the Education Field Deputy for Congresswoman Lucille Roybal-Allard in the Los Angeles area. Her research interests are in understanding the relationships shared between elected officials and their constituents, with a focus on collaborative decision-making efforts.

Joseph P. Robinson-Cimpian's research focuses on the use and development of novel and rigorous methods to study equity and policy, particularly concerning sexual minorities, women and language minorities. With colleagues, he has recently examined how bullying relates to psychological disparities between sexual minority and heterosexual youth, how teachers' expectations of girls' and boys' math abilities predict growth in the gender gap and how well-intentioned education policies may hinder ELL achievement. He has received research funding from the AERA Grants Board and IES. He serves on the editorial boards of the *American Educational Research Journal* and *Developmental Psychology*. Dr Robinson-Cimpian is a former Spencer Dissertation Fellow and a current Spencer/National Academy of Education Postdoctoral Fellow (PhD, Stanford University, 2009).

Rubén G. Rumbaut is professor of sociology at the University of California Irvine. Over the past three decades, he has directed seminal empirical studies of immigrants and refugees in the United States, including the landmark *Children of Immigrants Longitudinal Study* (with Alejandro Portes). Among other books, he is the coauthor of *Immigrant America: A Portrait* and *Legacies: The Story of the Immigrant Second Generation*, which won the American Sociological Association's top award for Distinguished Scholarship. He is the founding chair of the International Migration Section of the American Sociological Association, and an elected member of the National Academy of Education. For more information and links to publications: http://www.faculty.uci.edu/profile.cfm?faculty_id=4999.

Lucrecia Santibañez (PhD Education, MA Economics, Stanford University) is an education economist at the RAND Corporation. She has studied how to increase education quality and access of opportunity for low-income populations in the United States and abroad. Her research focuses on school-based management, parental involvement, school leadership and teacher labor markets. Her academic research has been published by *Economics of Education Review, Teachers College Record, Review of Educational Research, Well-Being and Social Policy* and *Revista Mexicana de Investigacion Educativa*. As principal investigator or co-principal investigator, she has received research grants from the Kellogg Foundation, the Hewlett Foundation, the Strategic Impact Evaluation Fund and the Bill and Melinda Gates Foundation.

Terrence G. Wiley is president of the Center for Applied Linguistics in Washington DC; special professor, Department of Teaching and Learning, Policy and Leadership and Graduate School, University of Maryland, College Park; and professor emeritus at Arizona State University. His recent publications include: *Handbook of Heritage, Community, and Native American Languages: Research, Policy, and Practice* (coeditor, Routledge, 2014). His editorial service includes cofounding the *Journal of Language, Identity and Education* (Routledge), the *International Multilingual Research Journal* (Routledge) and most recently coediting AERA's *Review of Research in Education, Vol. 38,* 'Language Policy, Politics, and Diversity in Education' (2014).

Maria Estela Zárate is an associate professor of educational leadership at California State University Fullerton. Her research primarily focuses on the educational trajectories and experiences of Latino students and other students of color in US schools. To investigate how students fare in schools, she examines the structural forces that limit and expand students' access to equitable education and family's strategies for supporting education. Prior to joining CSUF, she was assistant professor of education at the University of California Irvine, where she taught both undergraduate and doctoral students. She was formerly director of educational policy research at the Tomas Rivera Policy Institute (TRPI) where she led the institute's educational research agenda.

Section 1

Bilingualism in the US Labor Market

1 Contextualizing Bilingualism in the Labor Market: New Destinations, Established Enclaves and the Information Age

Rebecca M. Callahan and
Patricia C. Gándara

One of the ironies of the United States is that although it is a self-proclaimed 'nation of immigrants', it has been less welcoming of the linguistic diversity with which it is so richly endowed than many countries that have not historically been immigrant-receiving nations. Lieberson and colleagues (1975) first called attention to the rapid rate of language loss in the US, referring to the nation, albeit tongue-in-cheek, as a linguistic cemetery, and Rumbaut (2009) later identifies the loss of home languages within one generation, labeling the US 'a graveyard for languages'. Some have argued that *because* the US is an immigrant-receiving nation, it must eschew other-than-English languages and impose a single national language – in practice if not in law – in order to bind together many disparate national identities (Schlesinger, 1991). While actual evidence does not support this notion, it nonetheless carries great cultural cachet in the US. At times, English-only sentiments prevail and shape public ideas and ideologies (see Macias, Chapter 2, this volume), driving state and national policy with respect to the education of children from immigrant families (Kloss, 1977; MacSwan & Rolstad, 2003). The societal dominance of English cannot help but shape economic trends; scholars have consistently found that in the past, being bilingual in the US held little, if any, economic advantage. In fact, being bilingual may even carry a penalty in the US labor market; at least some bilinguals have been shown to earn less than their monolingual counterparts (Chiswick & Miller, 2007; see Alarcón *et al.*, Chapter 5, this volume). Nevertheless, today it is impossible to live and work in many parts of the US without encountering languages other than English on a daily basis.

Considerable research has investigated the cognitive (Bialystok, 2009; Bialystok & Majumder, 1998; Peal & Lambert, 1962), social (Cho, 2000; Church & King, 1993), psychosocial (Colzato *et al.*, 2008; Portes & Hao, 2002), sociocultural (Zhou & Bankston, 1998) and academic (Mouw & Xie, 1999; Umansky & Reardon, forthcoming) effects of bilingualism, finding quite remarkable benefits in every area. However, research investigating its economic returns remains inconclusive at best. Despite the empirical evidence suggesting social, cognitive and psychological benefits to bilingualism, a broad swath of American society has remained unconvinced as to the value of bilingualism, as evidenced in the powerful political force embodied in the English-only movement (Marschall *et al.*, 2011; Wiley & Wright, 2004). The studies in this volume provide new methodological and theoretical approaches to investigating the economic value of bilingualism in US society. To do so requires understanding the complicated history of language(s) in a historically English-dominant context, while also taking into account the current linguistic landscape. While these studies focus on the US context, the themes and theories discussed and the arguments made apply well beyond the nation's borders. Multilingual societies by definition must decide whether to address language as a problem to be rectified, or as human capital, a resource rich among its citizenry (Ruiz, 1984).

A New Age of Linguistic Diversity

Languages other than English are growing in use across the US, moving the nation away from the myth that only English is spoken here. The US Census Bureau's recent mapping of languages in the US underlines this perception. Nearly 60 million people, more than one in five Americans, speak a language other than English at home. Of those, almost two-thirds (62%) speak Spanish, while another 15% speak one of several Asian languages, the most commonly spoken being Chinese (approximately 5%). Growth in other-than-English language speakers has been dramatic over the last three decades: from about 23 million persons in 1980 to nearly 60 million today. The Census Bureau estimates that the US will continue to add more other-than-English speakers to the population in the future, though it anticipates that the growth will be slower than in the last few decades (Ryan, 2013).

While most of these 60 million speakers of other languages also speak English, many prefer to carry on their day-to-day interactions in their native language. When queried, it is common to hear that communicating with others in one's native language creates a sense of personal 'understanding' among the speakers; a common language can fortify the identity of the individual as part of a larger, socially connected community (Gumperz, 1982; Norton, 1997). These other-than-English speakers often feel a greater sense of confidence in others who speak their language (see Porras *et al.*, Chapter 10, this volume). And, as Madison Avenue knows, linguistic diversity not only represents potential bridges to diverse groups and cultures, both foreign and domestic, but also new markets.

In 2014, more than 25,000 graduating seniors in California received the State Seal of Biliteracy on their diplomas – meaning that they had met very high standards of proficiency in both English and a second language – in spite of the fact that in 1998, the state had all but banned bilingual education in its public schools (González, 2008).[1] This astounding number raises obvious questions: How might this matter for the students with these language skills? Would their bilingualism provide them with any advantage either in the labor market or in postsecondary studies? Is it still the case that being bilingual (and biliterate) in the US carries more of a penalty than a reward in the labor market? Is it time to reframe the learning and maintenance of languages other than English as an asset rather than a deficit? Could it be that immigration and globalization have changed the basic calculus that we had come to take for granted? This book attempts to answer this series of questions.

Three sites in American life have been at the center of the English-only movement: the schools, the voting booth and the workplace. Macias (Chapter 2, this volume) recounts legal initiatives over time that have sought to bar the teaching of other languages in public schools, as well as the use of the students' primary language to provide access to the general curriculum. The most recent of these laws were passed in California, Arizona and Massachusetts in 1998, 2000 and 2002, respectively. The Voting Rights Act (VRA), part of the massive civil rights legislation passed in the mid-1960s, was designed to ensure access to the vote by minorities, including language minorities. Nationally, however, threats to remove bilingual ballots from the provisions of the VRA constantly surface, led by congressional members aligned with the English-only movement. Despite evidence to the contrary, these legislators argue that bilingual ballots are costly and unnecessary inasmuch as citizens are supposed to be able to speak English (Loo, 1985). The fact that the level of English used in ballot arguments is far above the reading comprehension level of the average citizen who is still developing a strong command of English[2] (Tucker, 2009) proves of little interest to these policymakers. The cost to society of the disenfranchisement of the growing language minority population has yet to be measured. In the workplace, English-only rulings have shaped how language may be used and how bilingual workers are viewed. A societal orientation to other-than-English languages and speakers of those languages frames multilingualism and its accordant languages as either a right, a problem or a resource (Ruiz, 1984). Drawing from this perspective allows for a richer understanding of the economic value attributable to bilingualism, not only in the context of the labor market, but also of the educational system that prepares the workforce.

Bilingualism and the workplace: Language as a right?

As the Latino population has grown and dispersed throughout most states in the nation, both law and practice have had to confront the use and desirability of employees who speak a language other than English in the workplace. While employers have increasingly sought workers who can interact with clients and customers who speak Spanish, at the same time a number of cases have been brought by employees who allege discrimination in the workplace when punished for using their primary language. Despite the fact that the bilinguals in these cases were hired for their language skills, most of these cases have been decided in favor of the employers (Gibson, 2004). For example, in the case of *Garcia v Gloor* (1980), a precedent in many subsequent language rights cases, the court found that while seven of eight employees of the company were Hispanic and had been hired for the purpose of communicating with customers in Spanish, the use of Spanish between employees could be prohibited by the employer without violating Title VII national origin law. In this decision, the court reasoned that the English-only rule applies 'to a person who is fully capable of speaking English and chooses not to do so in deliberate disregard of his employer's rule'. Thus, if a person is capable of speaking English, they must speak English if the employer requires it. The *Garcia v Gloor* decision presents the odd situation in which an employee may be hired expressly because of his or her Spanish (or other) language skills to be used with customers or clients, but if the employee then speaks to a coworker in the same language, he or she may be fired for 'deliberately disregarding the employer's rule'.

As a result of *Garcia v Gloor*, in 1980 the Equal Employment Opportunity Commission (EEOC) created guidelines that spelled out how Title VII legislation should be applied. According to the guidelines, English-only rules are discriminatory if applied at all times, including breaks and lunch. However, if the employer can show a business justification for it, the employer can prohibit the use of a language other than English during working hours (29 C.F.R. §1606.7). Gibson (2004) points out that many courts have disregarded the EEOC guidelines entirely and even those that recognize them have commonly cited two justifications for disallowing languages other than English in the workplace: to promote harmony among employees and the need for supervisors to monitor employees. Nonetheless, the EEOC has insisted that employees should be able to use their primary language during nonwork times such as breaks and lunch, and that employers must demonstrate that there is a need for any restrictive language policies that they impose. This was reaffirmed in the more recent 2000 case of *EEOC v Premier Operator Services, Inc.*

Gibson (2004) notes that there was a 600% increase in EEOC investigations into cases involving English-only rules in the workplace between 1996 and 2002, suggesting increasing tensions over the use of languages other than English in the workplace. To address these tensions, a briefing held by the US Commission on Civil Rights in 2010 resulted in the recommendation that EEOC guidelines be withdrawn, allowing employers to designate English-only workplace policies except in the case where 'it can be shown by a preponderance of evidence that the policy was adopted for the purpose of harassing, embarrassing or excluding employees' (US Commission on Civil Rights, 2010: 5). None of the many civil rights organizations invited to provide testimony chose to appear before the Commission, evidently believing that their testimony would be fruitless. Clearly, this is a contentious issue reflecting a deep irony. With the growth in the other-than-English, especially Spanish, language markets, increasing numbers of people are hired *because of their ability to communicate in Spanish* (and other languages) with customers, clients, and business associates, attitudes toward those employees – and how and when they are allowed to speak Spanish – will almost inevitably shift with time.

Educational policy and costs: Language as a problem

The schizophrenic nature of America's relationship with bilingualism is codified in California's education code. California is arguably the most linguistically, ethnically and economically diverse state in the US, yet in 1998 it adopted one of the most draconian approaches to the education of its 2.7 million[3] language minority students. California's current education code not only prohibits bilingual instruction in most cases, consequently limiting societal bilingualism (González, 2008), but also attempts to link bilingualism and economic loss. Specifically, the code states that

> *the public schools of California* currently do a poor job of educating immigrant children, *wasting financial resources on costly experimental language programs* whose failure over the past two decades is demonstrated by the current high drop-out rates and low English literacy levels of many immigrant children. (*California Education Code: Chapter 3, Article 1, 300(d)*, emphasis added)

With the passage of Proposition 227 in 1998, a popular, though largely untested[4] preconception about the cost of bilingual instruction registered as part of the state education code, linguistic diversity was framed not as a resource, but as an expensive waste of taxpayer funds, reflective of a *language as a problem* orientation (Ruiz, 1984).

It is unclear whether developing bilingualism in public schools might actually pose an excessive economic cost, as Proposition 227 would suggest, or if instead California has spent the last 15 years limiting its economic potential. In fact, as Agirdag notes (Chapter 7, this volume), little research has studied bilingualism from the perspective of language loss, i.e. the cost to the individual and society of the shift to English monolingualism within one or two generations (Rumbaut, 2009). Understanding the value of all aspects of bilingualism in a capitalist economy demands consideration of both supply (bilinguals) and demand (need and value of linguistic services) simultaneously, as well as individual and community characteristics. The authors of this volume not only problematize the conflicting American perceptions of bilingualism, but they do so while attempting to expand the empirical discourse in this area beyond economic returns, income and wages (Chiswick, 2009; Fry & Lowell, 2003). This volume aims to introduce new theoretical and empirical approaches to investigate the market value of bilingualism.

Dual language education: Language as a resource

Increasing interest in dual language programs among monolingual English-speaking families raises the question: Why do increasing numbers of English-speaking parents spend uncomfortable nights in sleeping bags to secure enrollment for their children in dual language programs and schools? A primary motivation among some knowledgeable parents may be their familiarity with the research showing that students in dual immersion programs tend to outperform their peers on a host of academic measures (Genesee *et al.*, 2006). In general, better academic outcomes lead to better postsecondary options, which in turn lead to better earnings. Additionally, seemingly every other day a new study is published that shows significant cognitive advantages to being bilingual. A secondary, but no less significant motivation may be parents' perception that speaking another language, especially one as prevalent as Spanish, will benefit their children in the labor market as adults. Bilingualism, especially Spanish–English bilingualism, emerges as a 'marketable' skill in the eyes of these parents, begging the questions: To what extent are they right? Does this only hold for native English speakers? What benefits exist for language minority children already on the path to bilingualism?

Latinos, language and the labor market

Language, however, is not a simple, neutral economic commodity; in a racially stratified society like the US, language use is delicately interwoven with questions of class, status, culture and identity. The studies reported in this book deal primarily, though not exclusively, with the Spanish-speaking population. Latinos comprise the overwhelming majority of other-than-English speakers in the US. Considerable research has studied the social, educational and cultural integration of the growing Latino population. In fact, the growth in the foreign-born population today is due largely to increases in the Latino population over the past three decades. Latinos are expected to account for nearly one in four residents by the year 2050 (US Census Bureau, 2006). In addition, the Latino population is younger than the national average, with a higher birth rate (Durand *et al.*, 2006). Ultimately, Latinos will comprise a growing segment of not only the school-age population, but also the labor force. Moore *et al.* (Chapter 3, this volume) deconstruct this population to show the very different levels of language proficiency – both English and Spanish – and literacy among the various subgroups and argue that these differences should be taken into account in considering labor market outcomes. Their analyses spotlight the importance of literacy in considering labor market advantages and foreshadow a discussion that will run through the rest of the chapters about the importance – and difficulty – of measuring literacy in both (or all) languages to truly gauge the value of multilingualism in the workforce.

Questions of measurement and analysis also come into play; combining all 'Hispanics' into one group for analytic purposes may obscure important differences in labor market advantages and disadvantages among the subgroups. Moreover, while English proficiency may affect the value of the bilingual individual in the marketplace, primary language literacy is increasingly emerging as a sought-after trait in employees, although the impact may vary by gender (Hernández-León & Lakhani, 2013). However, few data sets employ specific, detailed measures of language proficiency, much less literacy skills. Moore *et al.* (Chapter 3, this volume), Rumbaut (Chapter 8, this volume) and Santibañez and Zárate (Chapter 9, this volume) all employ innovative techniques in their attempts to capture bilingual proficiency constructs. The struggle to adequately define and measure the abstract concepts of language proficiency, bilingualism and literacy emerges as the analyses in this volume unfold. In the field, an understanding of the role and value of bilinguals and bilingualism is constrained by the ability to accurately and robustly identify the construct being measured. Most language proficiency measures in large-scale survey data are self-reports, limited by nature in the ability of individuals to accurately report their proficiency in relation to others (Oscarson, 1989). Changing our empirical lens, adapting to the measures available for analyses and addressing the context of bilingualism and how its value is measured all allow us to better understand variation in trends by gender, occupational sector, region and age. These questions are increasingly pressing in an era of unprecedented racial, ethnic and linguistic diversity.

Looking Forward: Globalization, Research and Practice

Bilingualism in an era of globalization brings with it additional considerations of context. American youth coming of age today look outward to multinational corporations and global enterprises for their economic futures. Fortune 500 companies target bilingual and bicultural college graduates (Cere, 2012) who are able to navigate an international workplace. Looking to K-12 education, state- and district-wide implementation of dual language programs is occurring nationally at an unprecedented rate[5] with considerable growth in elementary schools in Utah, California and Texas (Palmer, 2007; Palmer et al., 2015). The popularity of dual language programs for young students draws on the promise of bilingualism in preparation for a future in a global economy.

The societal changes of the past half-century of immigration (Fix & Passel, 2003) combined with the onset of the online era (Suárez-Orozco, 2007) have created a new and different context for bilingualism. The immediacy of communication and access to information in digitally driven societies have changed not only the social, cultural and linguistic integration of immigrant youth, but also the linguistic expectations of both the home and host cultures. Immigrant youth coming of age today can expect to keep in touch with friends and families via Skype, email and chats, keeping the lines of communication open to a degree never before experienced. At the same time, this external flood of information flows in English, the lingua franca of the internet, and also in other global languages, giving youth ample opportunities to develop their proficiency in both English and their primary language.

Real-time access to communication not only facilitates the maintenance and development of primary languages, but does so with an audience that is broader than prior generations were able to reach. In an increasingly global economy, the bilingualism of new immigrant youth has the potential to develop as a social, educational and economic asset to the economy and to their communities – human capital if we may (Agirdag, Chapter 7, this volume). However, while it is easier than ever to maintain communication in the primary language, children of immigrants are losing their heritage languages faster than ever before. It is at this critical juncture that we situate these studies, aware of the patterns of the past, but looking toward the context of the future. As the immigrant population grows, we suggest that businesses will begin to recognize the value of employee bilingualism in increasing the trust that consumers experience with individuals who speak their language and understand their culture while facilitating negotiations and opening new markets.

Interrogating the Returns to Bilingualism in a Changing Linguistic Landscape

While the studies in the first section of this volume (Chapters 2 and 3) present a picture of the broader bilingual landscape, both historically and contemporaneously, the research presented in the second section of the book grapples with how to best contextualize bilingualism in the workforce; which covariates of bilingualism matter most? In Chapter 4, Robinson-Cimpian finds, as have others, that when earnings are analyzed for bilinguals vs monolinguals without controlling for age or gender, there is no apparent advantage for bilinguals in the labor market. However, in Robinson-Cimpian's work, not only do males and females demonstrate different levels of bilingualism, but its effects may vary by gender as well. He argues that the economic returns of bilingualism cannot be understood without taking gender into account, suggesting that it is a critical variable for future research. In Chapters 5 and 6, Alarcón and his colleagues test assumptions about the importance of both the occupational sector and region in determining whether or not bilinguals experience a labor market advantage. They study the US–Mexico border region, hypothesizing that this area would have a high demand for bilinguals, especially in public service occupations like health and criminal justice. In theory, an area experiencing relatively high demand for bilinguals would be more likely to compensate employees for this skill than other regions of the country. Here, Alarcon and colleagues find that although the desirability of bilingualism varies according to employees' location in the workplace hierarchy, no differences in compensation emerged based on regional linguistic composition. Together, these studies suggest a delicate balance in the labor market between supply and demand that we do not fully understand. In Chapter 7, Agirdag turns the analytic lens around to consider the economic and social *costs* associated with the *loss* of the primary language. Like Robinson-Cimpian, Agirdag also finds differences by gender. Overall, however, he concludes that the high cost to linguistic assimilation should be considered in instructional planning for students who arrive at school already conversant in a language other than English; to date, no clear metrics exist to understand the economic scope of this loss of linguistic resources, though he estimates the annual monetary costs to those individuals who lose their primary language. Rumbaut (Chapter 8) culminates this section with an extensive analysis of two unique longitudinal data sets that allow him to examine the sociocultural benefits in the workforce for a new generation of bilinguals on the US coasts. He concludes, as does Agirdag, that there are substantial benefits in the labor market for young bilinguals in the early stages of their careers and these include both a salary premium as well as better positioning in the employment hierarchy.

The final section of this volume presents a set of studies that explore bilingualism from different educational and economic perspectives: its relationship to schooling outcomes, how it factors in to hiring decisions and how it can be acquired at high levels. Santibañez and Zárate (Chapter 9) frame bilingualism as not only a cognitive factor, but also a resource that promotes college going in a contemporary cohort of young adults. Their models find that Spanish speakers who maintain their bilingual capabilities are more likely to go to college than those who do not, signaling an important future labor market asset. Linguistic skills improve educational outcomes and ultimately, college education provides a huge economic payoff relative to a high school diploma (Baum *et al*., 2013). From an economic perspective, Porras and her colleagues (Chapter 10) survey a wide range of employers throughout California to determine if there are perceived preferences for bilinguals in employment. They also interview bilingual employees to understand how they use their multiple languages in the workplace, and how those skills can be advantageous, whether or not they are officially compensated for them. And finally, returning to the educational context, Aldana and Mayer (Chapter 11) explore the possibility of supporting bilingual development through the reframing of International Baccalaureate programs, as a tool through which bilingualism may not only flourish, but also meet the dual academic and linguistic needs of the particularly at-risk population of immigrant, English learner (EL) adolescents. They argue that these programs, normally reserved for high-achieving, middle-class students, can be effectively repurposed to provide a rigorous college preparatory education for immigrant students. In the final chapter, we take a moment to summarize and reflect on the collected studies. At this point, we consider the implications of the findings as a whole, as well as the theoretical and empirical innovations employed across the various sections. Understanding the value of bilingualism in any society requires considering the ideological space occupied by language in the national psyche, as well as the relationships between language, identity and power (Mertz, 1982; Pavlenko, 2002; Spolsky, 2004). The final chapter serves as a springboard for future research, focused closely on possible directions in a new global economy.

Cumulatively, these studies build upon the prior literature by foregrounding the context of bilingualism. These authors consider not only the bilingual individual, but also the market into which he or she enters – both geographically and temporally. The current immigrant, language minority population has changed not only the market, but also the consumer base. Immigrants no longer exist only in gateway communities and enclaves, but increasingly in new suburban, rural, Midwestern and southern destinations (Millard & Chapa, 2004; Wortham *et al.*, 2002). Ultimately, the demographic and technological changes of the past decades may make the contextual *when* matter more than ever before; a bilingual entering today's labor market can expect to encounter a very different reception than his or her father did in 1982.

Notes

(1) As this book was going to press, New York, Illinois and New Mexico also joined the State Seal of Biliteracy bandwagon with legislation of their own.
(2) In the debate in the House on amendments to Section 203 of the Voting Rights Act, July 13, 2006, it was entered into the record that Mr Chris Norby, Supervisor of Elections for Orange County, California, testified that the June 6, 2006 California ballot was written for a reading comprehension level of between 12th and 14th grade English. Hence, the average English as a second language speaker would have difficulty understanding the ballot initiatives in English. Volume 152, Part 11, Page 14287.
(3) See http://dq.cde.ca.gov/dataquest/lc/NumberElState.asp?Level=State&TheYear= 2012-13.
(4) While there is much rhetoric about the costs of providing bilingual instruction, only two studies, now quite old, have actually used district cost data to answer the question. In both cases, the researchers found that bilingual instruction was no more costly than other forms of instruction for ELs, and often actually cost less (see Carpenter-Huffman & Samulon, 1981; Chambers & Parrish, 1992).
(5) See http://www.cal.org/twi/directory/growth.gif.

References

Baum, S., Ma, J. and Payea, K. (2013) *Education Pays 2013: The Benefits of Higher Education for Individuals and Society.* New York: The College Board.

Bialystok, E. (2009) Bilingualism: The good, the bad, and the indifferent. *Bilingualism: Language and Cognition* 12 (1), 3–11.

Bialystok, E. and Majumder, S. (1998) The relationship between bilingualism and the development of cognitive processes in problem solving. *Applied Psycholinguistics* 19 (1), 69–85.

Cere, R.C. (2012) Foreign language careers for international business and the professions. *Global Advances in Business Communication* 1 (1), 6.

Chiswick, B.R. (2009) The economics of language for immigrants: An introduction and overview. In T.G. Wiley, J.S. Lee and R.W. Rumberger (eds) *The Education of Language Minority Immigrants in the United States* (pp. 72–91). Bristol: Multilingual Matters.

Chiswick, B.R. and Miller, P.W. (2007) *The Economics of Language: International Analyses.* New York: Taylor & Francis.

Cho, G. (2000) The role of heritage language in social interactions and relationships: Reflections from a language minority group. *Bilingual Research Journal* 24 (4), 369–384.

Church, J. and King, I. (1993) Bilingualism and network externalities. *The Canadian Journal of Economics/Revue canadienne d'Economique* 26 (2), 337–345.

Colzato, L.S., Bajo, M.T., van den Wildenberg, W., Paolieri, D., Nieuwenhuis, S., La Heij, W. and Hommel, B. (2008) How does bilingualism improve executive control? A comparison of active and reactive inhibition mechanisms. *Journal of Experimental Psychology: Learning, Memory, and Cognition* 34 (2), 302–312.

Durand, J., Telles, E. and Flashman, J. (2006) The demographic foundations of the Latino population. In M. Tienda and F. Mitchell (eds) *Hispanics and the Future of America* (pp. 66–99). Washington DC: National Academies Press.

Fix, M. and Passel, J.S. (2003) *US Immigration: Trends and Implications for Schools.* Washington, DC: Urban Institute.

Fry, R. and Lowell, B.L. (2003) The value of bilingualism in the US labor market. *Industrial and Labor Relations Review* 57 (1), 128–140.

Garcia v Gloor 609 f.2d 156 US Court of Appeals, 5th Circuit (1980).

Genesee, F., Lindholm-Leary, K., Saunders, W. and Christian, D. (2006) *Educating English Language Learners: A Synthesis of Research Evidence.* New York: Cambridge University Press.

Gibson, K. (2004) English only court cases involving the US workplace: The myths of language use and the homogenization of bilingual workers' identities. *Second Language Studies* 22 (2), 1–60.

González, J. (2008) California Proposition 227. In J. González (ed.) *Encyclopedia of Bilingual Education* (p. 110). Thousand Oaks, CA: Sage Publications.

Gumperz, J.J. (1982) *Language and Social Identity* (Vol. 2). Cambridge: Cambridge University Press.

Hernández-León, R. and Lakhani, S.M. (2013) Gender, bilingualism, and the early occupational careers of second-generation Mexicans in the South. *Social Forces* 92 (1), 59–80.

Kloss, H. (1977) *The American Bilingual Tradition.* Rowley, MA: Newbury House Publishers.

Lieberson, S., Dalto, G. and Johnston, M. E. (1975). The course of mother tongue diversity in nations. *American Journal of Sociology,* 81 (1), 34–61.

Loo, C.M. (1985) The 'biliterate' ballot controversy: Language acquisition and cultural shift among immigrants. *International Migration Review* 19 (3), 493–515.

MacSwan, J. and Rolstad, K. (2003) Linguistic diversity, schooling, and social class: Rethinking our conception of language proficiency in language minority education. In C.B. Paulston and R. Tucker (eds) *Sociolinguistics: The Essential Readings* (pp. 329–340). Oxford: Blackwell.

Marschall, M.J., Rigby, E. and Jenkins, J. (2011) Do state policies constrain local actors? The impact of English only laws on language instruction in public schools. *Publius: The Journal of Federalism* 41 (4), 586–609.

Mertz, E. (1982) Language and mind: A 'Whorfian' folk theory in united states language law. *Sociolinguistics Working Paper* (Vol. No. 93). Austin, TX: Southwest Educational Development Laboratory.

Millard, A.V. and Chapa, J. (2004) *Apple Pie and Enchiladas: Latino Newcomers in the Rural Midwest.* Austin, TX: University of Texas Press.

Mouw, T. and Xie, Y. (1999) Bilingualism and the academic achievement of first and second-generation asian americans: Accommodation with or without assimilation? *American Sociological Review* 64 (2), 232–252.

Norton, B. (1997) Language, identity, and the ownership of English. *TESOL Quarterly* 31 (3), 409–429.

Oscarson, M. (1989) Self-assessment of language proficiency: Rationale and applications. *Language Testing* 6 (1), 1–13.

Palmer, D. (2007) A dual immersion strand programme in California: Carrying out the promise of dual language education in an English-dominant context. *International Journal of Bilingual Education and Bilingualism* 10 (6), 752–768.

Palmer, D., Zuñiga, C. and Henderson, K. (2015) A dual language revolution in the United States? From compensatory to enrichment bilingual education in Texas. In W. Wright, S. Boun and O. García (eds) *Handbook of Bilingual and Multilingual Education*. Malden, MA: Wiley-Blackwell.

Pavlenko, A. (2002) 'We have room for but one language here': Language and national identity in the US at the turn of the 20th century. *Multilingua* 21, 163–196.

Peal, E. and Lambert, W.E. (1962) The relation of bilingualism to intelligence. *Psychological Monographs: General and Applied* 76 (27), 1–23.

Portes, A. and Hao, L. (2002) The price of uniformity: Language, family and personality adjustment in the immigrant second generation. *Ethnic and Racial Studies* 25 (6), 889–912.

Ruiz, R. (1984) Orientations in language planning. *NABE: The Journal for the National Association of Bilingual Education* 8 (2), 15–34.

Rumbaut, R.G. (2009) A language graveyard? The evolution of language competencies, preferences and use among young adult children of immigrants. In T.G. Wiley, J.S. Lee and R.W. Rumberger (eds) *The Education of Language Minority Immigrants in the United States* (pp. 35–71). Bristol: Multilingual Matters.

Ryan, C. (2013) *Language Use in the United States: American Community Survey Reports* (Vol. ACS-22). Washington DC: US Census Bureau.

Schlesinger, Jr., A.M. (1991) *The Disuniting of America: Reflections on a Multicultural Society.* New York: W.W. Norton.

Spolsky, B. (2004) *Language Policy: Key Topics in Sociolinguistics.* Cambridge: Cambridge University Press.

Suárez-Orozco, M. (ed.) (2007) *Learning in the Global Era: International Perspectives on Globalization and Education.* Berkeley and Los Angeles, CA: University of California Press.

Tucker, J.T. (2009) *The Battle Over Bilingual Ballots: Language Minorities and Political Access Under the Voting Rights Act.* Burlington, VT: Ashgate Publishing Company.

US Census Bureau. (2006) *Hispanics in the United States.* Washington DC: US Census Bureau.   See   http://www.census.gov/population/www/socdemo/hispanic/hispanic_pop_presentation.html (accessed 1 March 2009).

US Commission on Civil Rights. (2010) *English in the Workplace. A Civil Rights Commission Briefing.* Washington, DC: US Commission on Civil Rights.

Umansky, I. and Reardon, S.F. (forthcoming) Reclassification patterns among Latino English learner students in bilingual, dual immersion, and English immersion classrooms. *American Educational Research Journal.*

Wiley, T.G. and Wright, W.E. (2004) Against the undertow: Language-minority education policy and politics in the 'age of accountability'. *Educational Policy* 18 (1), 142–168.

Wortham, S., Murillo, E. and Hamann, E.T. (2002) *Education in the New Latino Diaspora: Policy and the Politics of Identity.* Westport, CT: Ablex Publishing.

Zhou, M. and Bankston, C.L. (1998) *Growing Up American: How Vietnamese Children Adapt to Life in the United States.* New York: Russell Sage Foundation.

2 Benefits of Bilingualism: In the Eye of the Beholder?

Reynaldo F. Macías

Introduction

'What, if any, are the advantages to bilingualism and/or biliteracy?' is a question that has been asked in sociolinguistics, economics and other disciplines for several decades. It has been asked specific to the US; it has been asked of specific languages in the US; it has been asked of bilingualism or multilingualism in the US. The answers have been mixed, often depending on how the questions were asked; which disciplines asked the questions; which languages were involved; whether individual or social (group) benefits were the focus; and whether monetary or nonmonetary benefits were of concern. My colleagues in this volume take up the question again with respect to the economic benefits, but this time with new data, new methods of analysis and a new demographic reality. This chapter contextualizes the questions about the economic benefit of bi/multilingualism within a historical context in the US. How languages have been viewed and regulated historically in the US is intimately linked to their economic value both in the past and in the present.

About 7000 natural oral languages are spoken in the world (with a similar estimate for signed languages), in about 200 organized political units (e.g. nation-states, kingdoms), within increasingly globalized political-economic networks and systems. While there are speech communities for each of these single languages, the majority of the world's population is bilingual rather than monolingual. Whether the result of language contact between neighboring speech communities, or migration, or language impositions, or economic/political interactions, many of us are in contact with naturally occurring and modal language diversity. No country is without language diversity. The questions regarding the benefits (or costs) and advantages (or disadvantages) of languages are about how we, as human communities, have organized ourselves into social and political groups and have accommodated our language diversities within them, reflecting our valuations of those languages and that diversity in political and economic policies and practices.

It is useful to note the need for interdisciplinarity in exploring this topic (Grin, 2008), especially those disciplines that deal with language, political economy and human collectivities. The study of the covariation between language variables and social or economic variables in the context of language diversity has been used as a way to view and study those accommodations, often more descriptively and polemically than explanatorily at a micro level. At a macro level, the study of language policy and politics has been viewed as an explicit societal expression of our accommodations to language diversity and their concomitant valuations. The subfields of critical sociolinguistics, critical applied linguistics or critical linguistics place 'power' as a central element in the study of language and society, implicating notions of inequalities in social structures and group relations that are reflected in language uses, functions, varieties, ideologies, attitudes and status. Official social (and language) policies adopted by the state are framed as often reflecting the dominant values of a society – that is, the values of the dominant group(s) rather than the majority of the polity – including the political-economic value of languages.

The rise of disciplines organized around human collectivities (e.g. Chican@ Studies, African American Studies, Women's Studies) is not new if we accept the epistemological notion of the humanities as being organized around (language) groups (e.g. French and Francophone Studies, English Language and Literature). While the centrality of language, speech or linguistics in these disciplines may vary, research on these groups (especially in the US) over the last 45 years has provided us with conceptual tools and much empirical research on these groups, qua speech communities, that inform our exploration of the questions posed on language, (in)equalities and benefits (González, 2002; Romero, 1979).

Lastly, the discipline most concerned with 'value' is economics. A subdisciplinary area called the economics of language has developed over the last 20 years and this provides important conceptual and methodological tools to explore the values of language(s) to individuals (private) and groups (social) (Grin, 2008; Grin & Vallaincourt, 1997). Economics, then, is also the discipline that can inform us about the economic structures and activities that may underlie the valence (positive–negative; advantages–disadvantages; benefits–costs) and salience (importance; intensity) of individual languages or multilingualism. This chapter focuses on the US economy, understanding that economies today are hardly constrained by political national limits and borders, and that politics, policy and governance are often about economic regulation, trade and commerce, material conditions and surplus allocation (Wolff & Resnick, 2012). For example, the US has a large and variegated capitalist economy with formal, informal, public and private 'sectors' (Weinberg, 2002). For our purposes, it is important to understand how the economy is organized and how different ethnolinguistic groups participate in it, whether there is an 'ethnic economy' and the language(s) in which these economic activities are undertaken. Since racial, ethnic and language groups occupy different positions/spaces in the social, economic and political structures of the society, it is also important to take into account the intersectionalities of race, ethnicity, national origin, gender and age with language abilities and economic participation.

The focus of this chapter, then, is to briefly belabor the social- and political-economic relationships, accommodations and valuations across time of people with different language abilities in this society. This heuristic exploration provides us with a picture of how language resources have been variously valued within this political economy to be better able to answer whether and why there may be economic benefits to bilingualism or to specific languages within the US.

Language Practices and Policies in the Political Economy

How do the language policies of, and the institutional practices in, the US affect our questions about the benefits of bilingualism? Language demography, population growth, geographic expansion, political consolidation and economic development across time within the US provide a political-economic frame of reference for understanding the relationship between language diversity and language policies in the nation, and should provide a more substantive frame of reference for the analyses of our questions.

Planting the seeds: The prenational period

The language diversity of the North American continent on the eve of contact with Europeans in 1492 has been estimated at over 500 languages. The number of these languages that survived 500 years later, was less than half. Over the same time period, colonial languages – Spanish, Portuguese, English and French – became regionally hegemonic throughout the hemisphere.

Spanish was the first European language to take root in what became known as the Americas. Unlike colonial languages in other parts of the world, Spanish in the 'Americas' became the native language of much of the indigenous, native-born majority over time. The overwhelming majority of people in early 21st-century 'Latin America' were monolingual Spanish speakers with a smaller proportion of bilinguals and monolingual speakers of indigenous languages (e.g. in 2007, Mexico estimated that 10% of its national population spoke indigenous languages). As independence from colonialism took hold in the western hemisphere, nearly two dozen of the new nations adopted Spanish, their colonial language, as their national political-linguistic legacy (Macías, 2014).

English was the legacy of the British colonies in North America. No specific language policy for the British colonies was formulated by England during the colonial period. According to Heath (1976a), in England, language choice and style was a matter of individual choice, something that was not to be legislated by the state. This attitude toward language use was paralleled in the colonies. The language contacts of colonists with American Indians tended to be limited during the colonial period, with some schooling provided to the indigenous for religious conversion and diplomatic purposes, and trading jargons developed for hunting and bartering. Few colonists learned or valued indigenous languages.

By the time of the colonial revolution against the English crown, the economic structures of these colonies were primarily mercantile trade, subsistence agriculture with limited agricultural products and human slavery. The colonial population was primarily rural (and remained so until about 1900, when the majority of the population shifted to city living). They lived in cohesive European-language speech communities throughout the colonies. There was significant language diversity, then, within the British colonies on the eve of the revolution.

> Inside the colonies at the time, there were not so many native English speakers as generally assumed. First, non-English European settlers made up one quarter of the total white population. (Two-fifths of Pennsylvania's population alone spoke German.) Second, the languages of the Amerindian populations–called 'Aborigines' by George Washington– were numerous and widespread. Third were the blacks, mostly slaves, with their many African languages, who numbered more than one-fifth of the total population. (Had a slave the courage to speak his native language, punishment was sometimes severe; there are reports of blacks having their tongues removed.) (Shell, 1993: 105)

The compact language communities were principally German, French and Dutch (Kloss, 1998/1977). In fact, the German language was so widely spoken in the new colonies that in 1751, Benjamin Franklin was reported as bemoaning the possibility that Pennsylvania 'in a few years [would] become a German colony' (Schmid, 2001: 15). German was the most commonly spoken non-English language in the British colonies and in the young nation. By 1850, Germans also constituted one-third of all immigration to the US (Schlossman, 1983). As a result, during the 1800s, the German language and German bilingual schools flourished throughout large swaths of the country, particularly the Midwest. Especially in rural areas, there was a strong inclination to teach only in German, as this was the first language of both the students and the teachers. Moreover, many newspapers were printed in German, providing jobs for German speakers and reinforcing the German language among the literate classes. Most of the arguments for German language education were cultural and practical – maintaining the German culture and community ties and providing an education in a language that students understood (Schlossman, 1983). The social, political and economic structures of these compact communities, townships and farms linguistically operated in German, maintaining a local economic value for the language.

There was also impressive language diversity prior to the British colonies, in territories that would eventually become part of the new nation-state.

> Outside the colonies, too, there were mostly non-English speakers, principally the various Amerindians and next the French and Spanish. Hence Thomas Jefferson suggested that Americans should travel to Canada in order to acquire a knowledge of French, and he emphasized that Spanish was an important influence in the New World. (Shell, 1993: 105–106)

The official 'tolerance' of languages other than English within the British colonies, however, was group and language specific. The exception was enslaved black Africans, who were brought to these British colonies (and later to the US) from the beginning of the English colonization of North America until 1808, when the importation of slaves was made illegal in the US. Even though the importation of slaves continued illegally until the Civil War, the number of foreign-born African people diminished after 1808 in the US in favor of native-born African Americans. These 'Africans' were transported to the British colonies, speaking many languages but not knowing English. They were forced to develop a limited proficiency in English speech (enough to understand commands in English) during a 'seasoning' process (lasting as long as three years) to socialize them as forced labor (cf. Gómez [1998], especially Chapter 7, 'Talking Half African'). White slavers and slaveholders were suspicious of the use of African languages, fearing organized revolts by the enslaved Africans.

These peculiar institutional language domestication practices had broader social, political and even legal support. Colonies (and, later some states) adopted policies and laws prohibiting the teaching of reading or writing to the black population (any language, but specifically English) and/or the schooling of blacks altogether. Widely adopted, these laws were collectively named the 'compulsory ignorance laws' (Weinberg, 1995). The first of these 'compulsory ignorance' laws was adopted by South Carolina colony in 1740.

These language policies and practices were specifically designed for the economic control of this population, and went hand in hand with other socially constructed rationales that maintained human slaves as a form of property, as unfree labor, a status that gave them few or no political, civil or language rights, and for whom learning only a 'limited English' was considered economically 'valuable'. Human development (literacy instruction or schooling) of this population was criminalized, the speech of Africans and African Americans became stigmatized and devalued, and English was promoted as the key to 'success', all in the name of a productive economy and the social order.

At the same time, American Indian languages were overwhelmingly ignored as being 'outside' the colonial polity, with limited colonial settler contact, primarily through the use of interpreters.

Setting up a new nation: Incorporating language diversity into the body politic (1776–1898)

The political and demographic expansion of the new nation in its first century is important to understanding its linguistic diversity and political economy. No official language was designated in the 1789 Constitution (nor had there been in the Articles of Confederation), even though the members of the Continental Congress were predominantly British, and English speakers. One could argue that this was a reflection of the English cultural and political legacy that an individual's languages were to be respected, and not for government to impose. One could also argue that this was a social policy for the individual states to consider if desirable; language was not the province of a central authority since it was not explicitly defined as a federal responsibility. Alternatively, one could propose that on a practical basis, the political leadership of the new nation needed to persuade as many of the linguistically diverse settler population as possible about the wisdom of the new politics, and exclusionary language policies would be detrimental to this realpolitik. Selected founding documents were printed in German to inform and persuade the large German-speaking populations in Pennsylvania, Maryland, Virginia and other areas about the desirable nature of the revolution and the new republic.

However, there was a continuing discussion, if not debate, about the role of language, as part of the new nation building. Some proposals advocated distinguishing an American English from British English by standardizing it on the basis of the particular speech varieties used in the former colonies with the help of a language academy (Heath, 1976b) or independent dictionaries (Lepore, 2002). Other proposals rejected anything associated with England, even language, and advocated substituting another language, such as Hebrew, Greek or French, as a common, national or official language; and prognostications were also made that a new language would develop in the new nation given its linguistic diversity (Shell, 1993). All in all, no official language proposal was officially adopted.

The 19th century was dominated by population growth and territorial expansion, political reunification, consolidation and reorganization, economic integration and restructuring, and sociopolitical assimilation. In the first half of the century (1803–1853), the territorial jurisdiction tripled, adding the Gulf of Mexico and Pacific Ocean coastlines to the new nation. In 1803, the US purchased the Louisiana Territory from France (explored by the Spanish in the early 1500s, under French colonial administration between 1699 and 1763 and again under Spain's rule between 1763 and 1803). This purchase was a total of 1 million square miles, doubling the jurisdiction of the US. The purchase treaty maintained that the liberties (cultural and language rights), properties and (the Catholic) religion of the persons remaining in the sold territory were to be respected (Klotz, 1968: 24). However, when the US military governor began governing this new territory only in English the local popular leadership challenged this policy and so it was revised to include the use of both the English and French languages in legislative deliberations and the administration of government, setting a critical practice and precedent that English be required as a language of government in any new territory or political unit (Fedynskyj, 1971). More broadly, the territory included many and various indigenous communities, provided unfettered access to the length of the Mississippi River as a major transportation and commercial waterway and solidified jurisdictional control of all lands east of the Mississippi River, in part by catalyzing the transfer to the US of other Gulf Coast territories claimed by Spain (including the Floridas in 1819).

In 1848, the US acquired 945,000 square miles of land as spoils of the war against Mexico (1846–1848). This included the recognition of Texas independence from Mexico (1836) and its subsequent annexation by the US (1845). This cession added to the national US population about 100,000 Spanish-speaking Mexicans and another 100,000 indigenous persons of various tribes and nations who had already collectively developed transportation routes and several important settlements (Martínez, 1975: 55). In 1853, the US acquired another 45,000 square miles of land from Mexico, known as the Gadsden Purchase, along the southern edge of what are now the states of Arizona and New Mexico, for a southern railroad route to the Pacific Ocean.

According to the Treaty of Guadalupe Hidalgo (1848), those Mexicans who stayed on the ceded lands for one year automatically became US citizens (Griswold del Castillo, 1990). Language rights in the treaty, however, were not explicitly mentioned; Mexicans who remained in the territory, according to the treaty, 'shall be maintained and protected in the free enjoyment of their liberty and property, and secured in the free exercise of their religion without restriction'. The treaty's statements on liberty, property and religion were apparently based primarily on those in the treaty for the Louisiana Territory between France and the US (Klotz, 1968: 22–24, 108). The similarity of the terms (and, one would expect, definitions) between the Treaty of 1803 and the Treaty of Guadalupe Hidalgo of 1848 is of interest if 'liberty' and 'religion' were understood to include not only unfettered use of the (non-English) language, but public access and support for its use.

In recognition of the prior sovereign, and of the predominantly Spanish-speaking legacy populations of the ceded areas, the federal government of the US recognized an official status for Spanish for varying periods of time and for various purposes, in areas organized as territories, and even after the statehood of some areas. Despite the dominant Mexican-origin population of the new southwestern territories and their new status as US citizens, as areas became more Euro-American, political power shifted from Mexicans to Anglos, and Spanish was often officially tossed aside and only English was officially embraced, favoring the newcomers politically and economically with commerce tied to the predominantly English-speaking East of the country. The new territories, especially California, were an economic boon to the new country, especially after gold and silver were found in Sutter's Mill in 1848. The mining of these precious metals in northern California attracted over 300,000 miners, half from other parts of the US and the other half from around the world, generating much wealth that was transferred to the northeast and catalyzing the second industrial revolution in the country in the second half of the 19th century.

In the mid-western part of the country, the federal government's population and settlement policies similarly 'opened up the Plains to white settlers' by adopting the Homestead Act in 1862, and promoting ecological warfare against the buffalo to overwhelm the various indigenous populations and their livelihoods. In 1867, Congress established the Indian Peace Commission, with the purpose of investigating and making recommendations on the 'permanent removal of the causes of Indian hostility'. Leibowitz (1971) quoted the following passage from the Commission's 1868 report.

> in the difference of language today lies two-thirds of our trouble. Schools should be established which children would be required to attend; their barbarous dialects would be blotted out and the English language substituted. (Leibowitz, 1971: 67)

This position that language was 'two-thirds of our trouble' should be placed in the context of the purpose of the Commission: 'the permanent removal of the causes of Indian hostility', which was seen as the principal obstacle, after the civil war and reconstruction, to national unity and security. So, in 1871, Congress included a rider that unilaterally ended the

Treaty Period between the US government and the Indian nations in the Appropriation Act for that year. It read in part:

> Hereafter, no Indian nation or tribe within the territory of the United States shall be acknowledged or recognized as an independent tribe or power with whom the United States may contract by treaty. (Quoted in Leibowitz, 1971: 68)

The same year that the rider was passed, the federal government began establishing English language schools for the purposes of domesticating Indian children and displacing the religious, missionary, bilingual schools. These government schools displaced the Indian-created and Indian-run schools that had previously flourished. Initially, the government schools were run as day schools; however, in 1873, the Board of Indian Commissioners objected to the lack of progress in domesticating the children. So, 'in 1879, the first off-reservation boarding school–the institution which was to dominate Indian education for the next 50 years–was established at Carlisle, Pennsylvania' (Leibowitz, 1971: 69). It was not long before greater coercion, force and violence were used to promote the English-only language policy, forcing the assimilation (domestication) of the children and further denigrating the value and utility of indigenous languages.

In the Caribbean at the end of the 19th century, the US intervened in the Cuban war of independence from Spain (the Spanish-American War), and in the process gained the former Spanish colonies of Cuba, Puerto Rico, the Philippines and Guam. Under the Teller Amendment (1898), the US was forbidden to annex Cuba, but it acquired Puerto Rico and occupied the Philippine Islands and Guam in the South Pacific. The US gave the Philippine Islands their qualified political independence as of 4 July 1946. The US still includes Guam and Puerto Rico within its jurisdiction, the latter having its political relation changed from colony to commonwealth in 1952.

The occupation of Puerto Rico alone resulted in the addition of over 950,000 Spanish speakers to the US population, with limited US citizenship granted *en masse* in 1917, through an act of Congress known as the Jones Act (Castro, 1977: 93). A few English language policies were included in the 1900 Territorial Organic Act (known as the Foraker Act), including that the Resident Commissioner for Puerto Rico to the US Congress be literate in English, the members of the legislative lower house be literate in English *or* Spanish and that the federal courts on the island operate exclusively in English. Spanish and English became the official languages of government in Puerto Rico by an act of its legislature on 21 February 1902. This 1902 Act provided that in the government and in the courts 'the English language and the Spanish language shall be used indiscriminately; and, when necessary, translations and oral interpretations shall be made from one language to the other so that all parties interested may understand any proceedings or communications made therein' (Alvarez-González, 1999: 365). The 1902 law was in effect until 1991, when it was repealed in favor of Spanish as the only official language for the island's government by the procommonwealth Popular Democratic Party to stress its support for autonomy. When the prostatehood New Progressive Party returned to power in 1993, it reinstated the 1902 bilingual policy (Alvarez-González, 1999: 366–367).

More generally, the official purposes of these English-only policies and laws throughout the 19th century were to reaffirm an (Anglo) 'American identity', provide a privilege to Anglo-Americans and wipe away the 'native' language and culture of the 'foreign' populations altogether. Despite no constitutional or official federal language policy, Congress and the Executive branch promoted English throughout their territorial and statehood policies as well as strategically in their immigration, population and settlement policies, all of which reinforced English as the favored, privileged and valued language in the economy and the nation.

Legal segregation and English-only: 1890–1960

At the beginning of the 20th century, reflecting the nativism of the period, most states: (1) had officially subjugated non-English languages, including Spanish; (2) had made English the exclusive and official language of instruction in schools; (3) operated *de jure* and *de facto* segregated schools; (4) required English fluency for immigration and English literacy for naturalization and voting; and (5) used English exclusively as the language for the administration of government.

European immigration increased dramatically in 1880, but from southern and eastern Europe, peaking between 1900 and 1910, when over six million people immigrated to the US. The percentage of foreign–born during this decade reached a peak of 15% of the total population in 1910. Between a quarter and one-third of these European immigrants who came between 1880 and 1930 returned to Europe after having made and sent monies to their European towns and families, or having saved enough money to restart their economic livelihood back home (cf. Wyman, 1993: 6). These immigrants left Europe to escape droughts, poverty and severe social and economic conditions, came and found jobs in the northeastern, eastern and Midwestern US cities as these places became urban centers of manufacturing and industrial factory work.

At the turn of the century then, large southern and eastern European immigrant populations dominated US language diversity. It was concentrated in cities and urban areas, which meant that language contact was greater between these different ethnolinguistic groups, requiring a lingua franca (often English) and other means of social accommodations (Fishman *et al.*, 1966). These groups settled in ethnolinguistic concentrations, i.e. neighborhoods, where they could carry out their daily life in the languages they knew with family and friends of similar backgrounds. And, some of them began to learn English.

> Immigrants had been highly resourceful in hiring themselves out as groups working under an interpreter in foundries, stockyards, and construction projects. 'Gang work' in employment and efforts to learn about city transportation systems, labor laws, and union practices had provided means by which immigrants were cushioned through group efforts to acquire English for necessary function. (Heath, 1977: 42)

The increased, linguistically diverse, European immigrant population, particularly as it concentrated in single-ethnic urban neighborhoods in eastern and Midwestern cities with the political ward boss and similar electoral mechanisms, threatened the political dominance, and hence the public sector economic power, of white, English-speaking natives in many states. The view of these foreigners was filtered through language. White nativist protectionists throughout the country adopted laws that restricted voting to those who could read and write English, as a way to politically neutralize their non-English-speaking (NES) brethren. Nativists aggressively promoted their antiforeigner policies as linguistic and cultural diversity increased throughout the nation from southeastern European immigration, such that 'rioting directed against various national origin groups occurred, and nativists called for more restrictive immigration laws and the expulsion of the foreign born' (Piatt, 1993: 10; also see Bustamante (1972) for a social history of undocumented immigrant treatment in the US).

In the southeastern states, English literacy requirements for voting were adopted by politically dominant whites to exclude blacks, who by this time were largely monolingual English speakers, from voting. Mississippi political bosses were well aware, for example, that 60% of blacks and only 10% of Anglos could not read English, as they promoted English literacy requirements in order to vote (Leibowitz, 1974: 29–36). The voting booth converted into political power for whites who used it to maintain their privileges and advantages in the political economy and to regulate labor, work conditions and public budgets, often discriminatingly, as with the Black Codes after the Civil War and the Jim Crow Laws after Reconstruction.

These restrictive language policies were complemented by prohibitory language policies. When the US entered World War I in 1917, in the third year of fighting, Anglo-American nativists took advantage of the war context by promoting fear, stereotypes and questions about the political loyalties of German Americans, and foreigners residing in the US who did not speak English natively, as a threat to national security (Wiley, 1998).

The federal government adopted war measures regulating and censoring the non-English press, requiring English translations before publication. In the burgeoning radio broadcast industry, initially involving many languages, the federal government required English-speaking engineers as monitors and censors during broadcasts. Local governments responded likewise, adopting laws outlawing the use of German in public. These measures, and others, dealt a near fatal blow to the widespread German-language private and public schools and the study of German as a second and foreign language and to many German language businesses (e.g. printing), and caused the unemployment of many German-speaking Americans. The government and others promoted the acquisition of English as a patriotic activity. English-speaking and literacy abilities were adopted as requirements for employment (e.g. to practice as a barber in New York City) and to pass certification and licensing examinations for various professions (e.g. medical competency examinations). The US government even created a 'mother tongue' question on the decennial census to track the size of the white and European immigrant populations, and their English language (linguistic) incorporation into the body politic (cf. Leeman, 2004).

Congress engaged the issue of racial and language diversity by adopting immigration laws requiring English-speaking ability to enter the country and to naturalize, and then established the national quota system in 1924 that favored northern and western Europeans. At this point, the Chinese Exclusion Act (1882) and the 'Gentlemen's Agreement' between the US government and Japan (1907) already excluded worker immigration from China and Japan, respectively, to protect white workers from labor competition. Defining who was a citizen qua 'American' became a central public policy issue after the *Dred Scott v Sandford* (1857) decision holding that African Americans were not and could not be citizens, resulting in the adoption of the 1866 Civil Rights Act and of the 14th Amendment to the Constitution (1868) providing for birthright citizenship. It was reignited as a popular concern on the heels of massive southern and eastern European immigration at the turn of the century; the 1917 grant of citizenship to the people of 'Porto Rico'; and the Indian Citizenship Act of 1924 (P.L. 175), which granted full US citizenship to America's indigenous peoples, in partial recognition of the thousands of American Indians who served in the armed forces in World War I.

The western hemisphere, however, was exempted from the national quota system of 1924, because agricultural and railroad construction interests wanted to maintain a free cross-national flow of Mexican labor. Many Mexicans also moved north to the US to escape the civil war in Mexico between 1910 and 1917 (Délano, 2011). Native and foreign-born Mexicans diversified their occupations and the industries in which they worked, and consequently the regions of the US in which they resided.

'Soon Mexicans were to be found in steel mills, mines, meat packing plants, canneries, brick-yards, construction sites, dry cleaning establishments, and restaurants' (Piatt, 1993: 15), in Chicago, New York and other parts of the US.

> By 1910 the superintendent of the Boston public schools observed that of the estimated thirteen million immigrants in the US, three million spoke no English. Yet, in noting that the public schools could not be the sole agent of immigrant education, he warned against forcing language-acquisition programs upon immigrants. (Piatt, 1993: 9)

Industrial owners and management responded to this consequent language diversity, as well.

> The industrial response to a linguistically diverse work force was neither to refuse employment to the foreign born nor to those who spoke a language other than English, nor was the response to prohibit immigrant workers from speaking their own languages on the job. ... Rather, American industry realized that immigrant workers were a necessary component of industrial society and that immigrant workers ultimately needed knowledge of the English language not only for their own benefit but also for the sake of industry. Rather than rely on legislation to make English official and attempt to coerce people into conformity, American industry generally concluded that it, and not government, bore initial responsibility for educating and training its workers, including English instruction. (Piatt, 1993: 10–11)

However, the owners and management of agriculture and the railroads did not share the attitude of manufacturing industry leaders. Consequently, employer responsibility for educating and training its workers did not extend to Mexicans or blacks.

> One obvious explanation for the disinterest in educating these [Mexican] workers is that agricultural work required less training than in many industrial settings. Less need seemingly existed for them to acquire English language and other skills. Another explanation is that these workers and their children were the victims of the same educational discrimination aimed at African-American and Asian workers and their families. Apparently, no formal language or other training programs were organized for agricultural workers of these ethnic groups, either. In fact, because skin color was central to the image that white Americans had of these Mexican workers, many of the discriminatory practices whites had established against African-Americans were transferred to the Mexicans. (Piatt, 1993: 14–15)

Of course, the fact that lack of ability to speak English could impede union organizing and official redress of illegal treatment in the workplace could not be discarded as factors in 'tolerating' NES workers in the agricultural and railroad industries.

Civil society also engaged this immigrant language diversity much more widely than ever before, leading to the Americanization Movement of the early 20th century. The teaching of English and government or 'civics' in settlement houses were components of this movement (Bale, 2008). Schools were also important for adults as well as children and youth, although adult education could not and did not meet the English language instructional needs of the population.

Nonetheless, state curriculum requirements began to include the teaching of a political patriotism and civics (limited often to government) in elementary and secondary schools. Civil War (Union) and then World War I veterans promoted patriotism by distributing US flags to every school, and developing a required public pledge, in English, of political allegiance to the national government was instituted in schools as a way of integrating the reconstructed former confederate states, foreigners and their progeny, as well as socializing the youth of the nation as 'Americans' (cf. Ellis, 2005).

By the beginning of the 20th century, public elementary schooling was secular and near universal and secondary schooling was dramatically expanded. Mandatory school attendance together with child labor laws filled the public schools. Greater state-level control of the curricula and language of instruction in private as well as public schools became a major English-only offensive of states in response to the linguistic diversity of immigrants during this period. For example, beginning in the 1880s, the teaching of German in the rapidly growing urban public schools of the East and Midwest came under severe attack. In several cities, including St Louis (Missouri), Louisville (Kentucky), St Paul (Minnesota) and San Francisco (California), public schools discontinued their use of German.

As a result of the legislation requiring English as the only medium of instruction in public schools in the late 19th century, and the subsequent antialien German feelings, German Americans developed large numbers of private and religious schools (especially Catholic and Lutheran) that taught in German or bilingually with English, with German language textbooks and curricular materials. In places where Germans were settled in large numbers, this practice all but displaced the public schools (Leibowitz, 1971: 11).

The five states that were admitted into the Union between 1875 and 1889 (Colorado, North Dakota, South Dakota, Montana, Washington) included constitutional provisions that prohibited sectarian (read Catholic) schooling; banned sectarian books from the classrooms and school libraries; or prohibited state fund allocations to church schools. By 1903, a total of

39 states had some form of these provisions (Leibowitz, 1971: 12–13). This undermined the various language groups' capacity to develop and maintain non-English private and religious schools.

In addition to the laws against sectarian schooling, states engaged in controlling and standardizing the curriculum (cf. Wright, 1980) and the language of instruction in the public and private secular schools. The study of the English language became a universal, mandatory part of the school curriculum from elementary to secondary and tertiary schooling, and also became increasingly dominant as the required medium of instruction in elementary and secondary schools. In 1903, 14 states had laws requiring that instruction in elementary schools be conducted in English. By 1923, 34 states required English as the medium of instruction in the schools (Leibowitz, 1971: 15).

These English-only laws were coercive, not just symbolic or regulatory, by criminalizing language behaviors, and they were often harshly enforced in some areas and for some groups, reminiscent of the compulsory ignorance laws of earlier years and the federal government's Indian boarding school policies of the time. For example, Texas passed a stringent English-only law in 1918, which made it a criminal offense for teachers, principals, superintendents and other school personnel to teach in a language other than English. The following year, Nebraska adopted a law that imposed restrictions and criminal penalties on both the use of a foreign language as a medium of instruction and on foreign languages as a subject of study, unconstitutionally affecting the livelihood of German language teachers and their work conditions, and parents' abilities to direct their children's education (*Meyer v Nebraska*, 262 US 390, 1923; Luebke, 1980).

The English-only school laws that directed the language of instruction (and the subject of English language study as well) were also enforced on the students in cruel ways. For decades, Spanish-speaking children in the Southwest were punished for speaking Spanish in school, even at recess or lunch. Oral histories relate instances of corporal punishment and abuse for speaking Spanish or having their mouths washed out with soap. And yet, school districts used Mexican students' alleged lack of English-speaking ability as a subterfuge to racially segregate them into 'Mexican schools' and racially segregated tracks that provided inferior schooling (Weinberg, 1995). These language practices reinforced in dramatic, coercive and violent ways that English was a required valuable language and that the Spanish language or other non-English speech was not only less valued, but also a detriment to physical, social, economic and mental health.

From 1875 to 1930, through statehood constitutions and new state legislation, the principal source of linguistic diversity of the period, immigration, was addressed with language policies that required English in public and private schooling, as a condition for employment, professional licensing and political participation. These policies also censored the non-English language press, and even criminalized the speaking of German in public. Federal policies extended English language requirements to statehood proposals, the administration of government, territorial and Indian schooling, immigration, naturalization and other areas (Leibowitz, 1984). Many of these policies were coercive and criminalized language and speech behaviors. Through political and institutional policies and practices, the recruitment of immigrant labor pools, access to jobs, work conditions and economic value were promoted for English and restricted for non-English languages. These English-only laws dominated through most of the 20th century.

The Cold War, civil rights, education and languages: Federal initiatives (1960–1990)

At the close of the 1950s, with the Cold War at its height, global and regional international organizations like the United Nations were taking root and expanding, language capacities in the US were associated with national security (Brecht & Rivers, 2012), and the dominance of US prestige and power in the world was well established. The US reaction to the successful launch of Sputnik by the Soviet Union in 1957 and the continuation of the Cold War led to concern about the ability of US schools to train students in mathematics, the sciences and foreign languages, reaffirming the notion that there were critical languages for the purposes of national defense and security. The 1958 National Defense Education Act (P.L. 85-864; 72 Stat. 1580) provided for language learning for high school and college instructors, and promoted the teaching and learning of foreign languages, albeit within the legal restrictions adopted in the early part of the 20th century in which foreign languages were generally taught in secondary schools and not in elementary schools, with a great bias toward teaching these languages in English or in contrast to English.

Other world events also influenced language diversity and language teaching. The Cuban Revolution of 1959 caused major changes on the island, especially after Fidel Castro declared Cuba a socialist state in 1960. Many Cuban political elites, professionals and members of the upper class left the island and settled in southern Florida. The US federal government provided financial and other support to these expatriates by expanding a little-known category in the immigration laws – the refugee. The policies developed in local Florida communities in response to the arrival of Cuban refugees in the early 1960s differed from the Americanization and 'English-only' policies directed at turn-of-the-century southern and eastern European, Japanese and Chinese immigrants, Hawaiians, American Indians and other native Americans, or even other Spanish-speaking children in the Southwest and Puerto Ricans. Situated within the context of Cold War politics, school policies toward the Cuban refugees were more flexible, open and supportive of Spanish maintenance. The Cubans saw themselves and were seen by others as temporary visitors. A good number of these adult refugees were bilingual, and many were provided with English-language assistance and recertification of their Cuban professional credentials as teachers, doctors and lawyers, so that they could practice in the US.

As early as 1961, Miami's public schools offered Cuban students a variety of separate 'pull-out' English as a second language (ESL) programs. In 1963, with funding from the Ford Foundation and Dade County Schools, and the availability of recertified bilingual Cuban teachers, Coral Way Elementary School in Miami, Florida, became the first two-way bilingual, bi-ethnic public school in the post-World War II era. In 1973, the growth and robustness of bilingual schools and the resulting social and economic structures led Dade County to adopt an ordinance declaring it officially bilingual in English and Spanish. The economic power of an educated and capitalized population that had fled Cuba with significant resources was a factor in the acceptance of their language. After all, the first wave of Cuban immigrants had produced an economic boon for the southern Florida region, albeit in Spanish. Along with new research on the cognitive benefits of bilingualism in Canada and success in achieving civil rights in the US, there came a renewed support for, and promotion of, bilingual education to improve the schooling of language minority groups in other parts of the country.

The civil rights movement of the 1950s and 1960s caused the federal passage of the Civil Rights Act (1964), the Voting Rights Act (1965), the Elementary and Secondary Education Act (1965) and its 1968 amendment and the Bilingual Education Act. The Economic Opportunity Act of 1964 (P.L. 88-452) was the basis of the national war to end poverty. Immigration policies were also changed dramatically in 1965, extending the national quota system to all countries of the world, eliminating the bias in favor of northern and western Europe, ending the racial exclusion of Asians and removing the exemption of the western hemisphere established in 1924. This immigration reform opened the door to an extensive change in the cultural and linguistic diversity of the nation, allowing it to become more like the rest of the world than just its white and European imagined community legacy.

A new era was in play. The Civil Rights Act and the Voting Rights Act were concerned with the protection of the rights of individuals and equality for members of minority groups. The Civil Rights Act led to identifying language discrimination by defining language as a characteristic of the protected class of 'national origin'. The Voting Rights Act codified several federal court decisions in suspending the use of English literacy tests as a basis for voting registration and exercising one's franchise. It also eliminated state laws requiring voter literacy in English by incorporating schooling in US flag schools in which the language of instruction was a language other than English, a nod to Puerto Rico and the Spanish language medium of instruction of the island's schools and the native citizenship of its population. In 1975 amendments to the Voting Rights Act, Congress found prior language-based discrimination used by states to exclude or discourage voter registration and the voting of Chicanos, American Indians and Asian language citizen groups. Congress required relief and provided for bilingual ballots and bilingual electoral services as remedies in selected jurisdictions where this discrimination had occurred.

The Elementary and Secondary Education Act (ESEA) of 1965 provided formula-driven funding for programs for all poor children, early childhood education, migrant education, adult education and teacher preparation. The Bilingual Education Act, a 1968 amendment to the ESEA, however, was only intended to demonstrate the effectiveness and utility of using two languages (one of which had to be English) for instruction to acquire English and improve the academic achievement of language minorities who were limited in their English-speaking abilities. It was funded as a voluntary, discretionary, competitive program. It would take litigation and civil rights laws to get school districts to provide bilingual education more widely (San Miguel, 2004).

On 25 May 1970, the Office of Civil Rights in the US Department of Health, Education and Welfare issued a memorandum to school districts throughout the country indicating that in order to be in compliance with the 1964 Civil Rights Act regarding its prohibition of national-origin discrimination, they must take affirmative steps to address the language needs of national-origin students who are limited in English ability, stop high-stakes testing of these students in the English language and communicate with their parents in a language they can understand. Using this memorandum as a standard for school services, Chinese-origin parents brought a lawsuit against the San Francisco Unified School District for national-origin discrimination. In *Lau v Nichols* (1974), the US Supreme Court affirmed the legality of the May 25th memorandum, and indicated that such instruction would make a mockery of education. The consent decree between the San Francisco Unified School District and the parent-plaintiffs selected bilingual education as the remedy for this national-origin discrimination. In the 1974 Equal Educational Opportunity Act (§ 1703(f)), Congress echoed the *Lau* decision and required that states take 'appropriate action to overcome language barriers that impede equal participation by its students'.

It took almost a decade for these programs to be widely implemented and to develop a functional infrastructure and a theoretical and research base. This infrastructure included a bilingual teacher, paraprofessional and counselor workforces, teacher credential standards, bilingual curricular materials and textbooks and relative language proficiency tests, all of which can be seen as language-based economic activities. The issues raised by the bilingual instruction of limited English proficient (LEP) students influenced the development of bilingual special education and bilingual vocational education as well.

Even with the tremendous growth in efforts to address the language needs of LEP students, bilingual education was available to only a fraction of those K-12 students who needed it, seldom reaching 10% nationally during the 1980s and 1990s. Most LEP students received, and still receive, some form of ESL instruction, 45 years after the adoption of the 1968 Bilingual Education Act. In fact, since the onset of the 21st century, fewer and fewer LEP students each decade have had access to bilingual instruction (Gándara & Hopkins, 2011; Zehler et al., 2003).

The adoption of these federal laws caused several things to happen: (1) it encouraged states to amend or repeal laws that prohibited the use of non-English languages, or that mandated English as a restrictive condition, or as a required language for specific functions, like the medium of instruction in public schools, most of which were adopted between 1890 and 1920; (2) it signaled that it was alright for government to use the non-English language in service to the public, or to teach language minority students, particularly Chicanos in the Southwest and Puerto Ricans in the Northeast of the country, as a transitional process for a limited time with the goal of English acquisition; and (3) it made nationally visible the conditions and problems of Mexicans, Puerto Ricans, other Latin@s and other language minorities, and revived the notion of an NES or a limited English-speaking (LES) community.

In other areas, language issues were being raised with a similar concern about discrimination. Language policies were developed to protect individual rights and liberties. In 1973, the Equal Employment Opportunity Commission (EEOC), for example, announced that it had instituted proceedings against a union that published its constitution, collective bargaining agreement and bylaws only in English and conducted its meetings solely in English (Leibowitz, 1974), indicating that the individual rights of national-origin union members who were limited in their English abilities were being violated. The EEOC issued regulations on English-only rules in the workplace in 1980, allowing them only with a business necessity rationale, and with a limited application of the rule to working hours (e.g. not breaks, lunch) (Macías, 1997).

California adopted the Bilingual Services Act in 1974, to guide the provision of bilingual state government workers to meet the needs of constituents who spoke a language other than English and were limited in their English. While the execution of the law has been much criticized, it was used as a blueprint for President Clinton's Executive Order

13166 (2000), which directed the federal government to seek the same goals by requiring departments and agencies to develop plans to serve LEP Americans.

In 1978, Congress enacted the Court Interpreters Act, providing interpreters for deaf, hard-of-hearing as well as language minority criminal defendants in federal court who could not understand English well enough to participate effectively in those proceedings, to protect their Fifth Amendment constitutional rights and to meet their needs, as well as the court's needs. The Act also provided funds for the training of translators and interpreters.

Reflecting these changing language policies, the US Census Bureau substituted its decennial census mother tongue question in 1980 with three questions on whether a non-English language was currently used in the home, and if so, what that language was and how well English was spoken by each person in that home (e.g. to be able to identify persons of LES ability, their location and concentrations).

By 1990, there were several federal language laws and policies intended to remedy prior language-based discrimination, or secure protections of fundamental rights. In addition, many of the restrictive English-only language policies established at the beginning of the 20th century by the states were eliminated in the name of an expanded understanding of civil rights.

Challenges to language diversity and retrenchment: 1980–2013

Even while the official bilingual education goals were benign and transitionally assimilationist, debates raged over the purposes and uses of bilingual education, the roles of non-English languages, especially Spanish, in schooling, government and society. In the last two decades of the 20th century, a nativist English-only movement reemerged that made bilingual education the controversial centerpiece of its political agenda to eliminate the use of all non-English languages in the country. This movement attempted to make English the official language of the states and the nation, to eliminate the use of non-English languages in economic activities (e.g. protested the use of bilingual menus at McDonalds restaurant in Miami, Florida), schools, public libraries and government, and sought to return to the English-only policies of the early 20th century. It had some success. Seventeen states declared English their official language between 1981 and 1990. By 2010, 31 states had some new form of official English.

In 1989, the District Court for the Northern District of California in *Teresa P. v Berkeley Unified School District*, found that the all-ESL program of the school district was theoretically sound and constituted 'appropriate action' under the Equal Education Opportunity Act of 1974. This provided a boost for the English-only movement to push for such English-only programs against a bilingual instruction option. The English-only movement later successfully reversed the bilingual education policies of California (1998), Arizona (2000) and Massachusetts (2002), replacing them with a form of ESL called structured English immersion as the default instructional program for all LEP students. The consequence of these policy changes was that language minorities, especially Latin@ LEP students, had even fewer bilingual education services available to them in public schools, even though almost all of these programs had been transitional (designed to move students to English-only instruction as quickly as possible) in nature.

At the beginning of the 21st century, with the executive and congressional branches of the federal government in Republican Party control, the federal government withdrew its support for bilingual education and put considerable pressure on state and local educational agencies to move away from bilingual education toward English-only instruction. While LEP enrollments increased across the country, federal policies echoed the restrictive educational language policies of the early 20th century with the passage of the conservative No Child Left Behind Act (NCLB) (2002), which: (1) expanded the use of English-only instruction for LEP students; (2) eliminated the use of the term 'bilingual education' from government offices and programs; and (3) required greater participation of LEP students in state and federal accountability systems, especially English-only standardized testing, regardless of students' English proficiency level or the ecological validity of such testing. Of course, prior to NCLB many districts paid little attention to how their LEP students were doing and failed to evaluate their programs at all. One principle of educational policy reflected in the early calls for bilingual instruction was that a student who was not yet English proficient had a right to be taught in a language that he or she could understand, or it would make a 'mockery of education'. While the implementation of this principle left much to be desired, it guided much of the educational policy, teacher education and program standards for 30 years. Recently, the English-only movement successfully overturned this principle in several states, replacing it with mandatory, coercive anglicization.

Leaders of English-only organizations have been appointed to various government bodies, on which they continue to advocate for retrograde language policies. Appointees to the US Commission on Civil Rights held hearings and issued reports on the constraints to free enterprise that are represented by the EEOC rules on English-only policies in the workplace as presumptive violations of law (cf. US Commission on Civil Rights, 2011).

These English-only policies in schooling, commerce, the workplace and US society in general, are steeped in a propaganda-like discourse of tough love that frames non-English languages as the source of educational and economic problems and English monolingualism as the solution.

This rhetoric ideologically frames English as the key to success in schools, the workplace, society and the body politic, as if it was, has been, and forever shall be in the US.

A Historical Perspective on the Economic Value of Languages

This brief historical survey informs our inquiry on the benefits of bilingualism in several ways. We note that (1) there has been a long history of policies and practices attempting to and actually influencing the language abilities and uses of the domestic population favoring English acquisition and use, often in coercive ways; (2) there have been several political-economic rationales or justifications for these various policies and practices, with the dominance of an English-only ideology in the 20th century that 'protected' the white, English-speaking and literate population in the labor market, the workplace and other economic and political spheres; (3) language diversity has been part of the history of the country, and this reality has often clashed with the ideological desires of these official policies and institutional practices, even while many immigrant language groups have not maintained their immigrant languages across generations (see Rumbaut, this volume).

Historical excavation of language politics

There is little question anymore that there is an 'American bilingual tradition' (see Kloss, 1977, 1998) of language diversity and a history of language politics, policies and practices that echo the national valuation of that diversity. Yet, there are seemingly disparate descriptions of that language policy history on how or whether specific languages (including English) or bilingualism have borne positive value, advantages or benefits within the political economy of the US.

In the 19th century, language policies were differentially tailored for specific languages. The degree of political consolidation of the federal government over a particular new land area as the country expanded from the Atlantic to the Pacific coasts and beyond to Alaska, the Caribbean and the South Seas, also made a difference as to whether and what types of language policies were adopted. With only a tenuous hold over an area, there was little prohibitory language legislation and even an official recognition of the language of the prior sovereign or of a significant portion of the population speaking the language. As the federal government drew tighter reins of geopolitical control, there seemed to be a concomitant increase in migration to the area by Euro-American English speakers, rural to urban population shifts and explicit English language legislation, facilitating the transfer of power, wealth, property and other economic resources from local populations to Anglo Americans. This geopolitical consolidation by the federal government was reinforced when statehood was granted by Congress to those parts of the country designated as territories, by often requiring English as the language of state government administration, even while nominally allowing Spanish, or French, to be used for limited periods of time in recognition of the prior sovereign of those territories, or the significance of the legacy populations speaking those languages within those jurisdictions. Issues of national identity became intertwined with the economic interests of the dominant Anglo, white population. Access to governmental and administrative power could be controlled and regulated via the English language, and economic enclaves dominated by non-English speakers could be marginalized, exploited, dismantled and transferred to Anglo Americans.

The 20th century was different from the 19th century in both language diversity and language policies. The urbanization of the population, the spread of the public school systems and mandatory attendance laws, antichild labor laws forcing children into schools, the rise of the mass media industries and the debates over immigration, citizenship and American identity, all affected the formation of language policies and their configuration in the 20th century.

English language laws, policies and practices were adopted much more widely throughout society, making it an English-only era for most of the 20th century. This English legal adoption and use was so widespread that it created a normative social expectation of accommodation to English-only as the valued language, almost exclusively, and gave substance and body to an English language ideology rationalizing the anglicization of all non-English language (LEP) speakers and communities, associating them with foreignness, and with immigrants or nonnatives, and so with lesser rights than 'citizens'. Non-English languages, indigenous, colonial and immigrant, were devalued, 'minoritized' (García & Mason, 2009; Hill, 2008), made invisible by being lumped together and conflated as the 'non-English proficient' (NEP or LEP).

If we were to broadly paint modal types, patterns or 'streams' of language policies in the 19th and 20th centuries, we might say that there were at least two fragmented streams in the 19th century, tied to the social and political relations between groups: a 'tolerant' stream involving German and French, Dutch and other Western and Northern European-origin settler language groups; and a 'repressive' stream involving American Indians, Mexicans, Puerto Ricans, Chinese, Hawaiians, Afro-Americans and others. The two streams mixed into a 'restrictive' stream that dominated the first three quarters of the 20th century by conditioning social, political and economic benefits on English language abilities, thus differentially valuing English over other languages, and advantaging white English speakers.

Language ideologies and economic control

The ideological rationales for English-only language policies and legislative and executive language policy strategies changed until they were consistent with the legal framework of the country. When anti-immigrant language legislation was drafted in the 19th century, it initially prohibited the use of non-English languages in various institutional settings (not unlike the earlier legal prohibitions on the use of the non-English languages of racialized groups, indigenous, blacks and militarily conquered populations). As these laws were legally challenged in the late 19th century and early 20th century, the courts declared prohibitory language policies as unconstitutional on equal protection, liberty and other constitutional grounds. At the same time, they developed a legal and ideological rationale that allowed the states to reach the same objective, but with a legally approved means. Legislative acts that universally mandated English, say as a medium of instruction in schools or a prerequisite for voting, were approved by the courts as being within authorized and appropriate state interests, and within their state police powers. With legal support, then, many states in their search for standardization mandated English abilities as a condition for the exercise of many rights, access to benefits and services and even participation in the economy and society. It became a small policy extension to then make these English language requirements exclusive, and increase the language proficiency threshold of these laws by adding English literacy requirements to English oral fluency.

The general promotion of English was rationalized to secure Anglo 'American' identity dominance, used to develop and maintain white privilege, thus minoritizing, dismissing and devaluing non-English languages as part of the policies of social control between groups, even 'blaming' the non-English language, accent or inability to speak English as the reason for economic subordination (De La Zerda & Hopper, 1979; Lippi-Green, 2012). Both official language policies and social ideologies contributed to the affirmative valuation and privileging of English and the devaluation of all other languages and the resultant or concomitant differential participation and status of groups in the political-economic structures of the nation.

Language diversity in the US today

Another note that arises from our brief historical summary is the change in the language diversity of the country over time. Through the 19th century, most of these language communities were compact in rural communities and small townships without intense language contacts with other language groups. By 1900, the majority of the national population lived in cities and the language contact among newly arrived immigrant communities was much greater and more intimate. As we know from Fishman *et al.*'s (1966) major study of the language loyalty of these groups between 1900 and 1960, most of the European immigrant language groups shifted to English monolingualism over three generations, reducing the number of immigrant heritage language speakers, and the consequent language diversity of the nation. Yet, unlike these European language groups, during the 20th century the Spanish-speaking population grew at a higher rate than the rest of the country and benefitted from a continuous stream of in-migration of Spanish speakers, primarily from Mexico, and other parts of the western hemisphere. It became possible to maintain compact Spanish-speaking communities in which native–born Chican@s, Boricuas, refugee Cubans and other immigrants primarily from the western hemisphere could live and work in Spanish without knowing much, if any English. These communities were and are the legacy of historical Spanish colonial settlements and the wide-ranging and long-lasting racial and ethnic segregation of these peoples.

In 1850, there were an estimated 118,000 Spanish speakers, who represented about 0.5% of the total national population of about 23 million. In 1900, the Spanish-speaking population was estimated at 2% of the national population, while in 2011, there were 34.7 million Spanish speakers in the country, representing 12.3% of the total national population of 308.7 million. Not only was there an increase in the absolute numbers of Spanish speakers, but there was also an increase proportionately to the national population as well.

Ethnic and racial projections of the national population from 2012 to 2060 indicate a large increase in the 'Hispanic' population (Toosi, 2012; US Census Bureau, 2012). After 2020, within one generation, Latin@s may contribute more net growth to the US population than all other groups combined. The Latin@ population would more than double, from 53.3 million in 2012 to 128.8 million in 2060. Consequently, by the end of the period, nearly one in three US residents would be Latin@, up from about one in six today. The US is projected to become a non-white majority nation for the first time in 2043. The US national population will be more like the rest of the hemisphere, if not the rest of the world, than it has been in the dominant American imagination. Non-whites were 37% of the US population in 2012, and are projected to comprise 57% of the population in 2060.

If we assume a similar language distribution among Latin@s in 2060 as in 2011, when 75% spoke Spanish (25% as Spanish monolinguals and 50% as bilinguals), then the number of Spanish speakers could be as large as 96 million in 2060, nearly tripling in size from 2011 (even if we assume 50% of the national Latin@ population will speak Spanish, there will be almost a doubling in the number of Spanish speakers). The number of Spanish speakers has increased for over 150 years in the US at a rate that is faster than the national population, the ethnic base of the Spanish-speaking population has become bilingual and there is every indication that the growth of Spanish speakers will continue into the near future.

The Latin@ demographic growth is reflected in language practices throughout the country. In commerce, for example, 98.9% (14,325,928) of the companies that responded to the 2007 business survey undertaken by the US Census Bureau used English in their customer transactions (receipts, sales and shipments), representing $21.8 billion, while 7.4% (1,079,350) of them also used Spanish in these transactions, representing $6.3 billion, with all other languages each being used by less than 1% of these companies. Among the 2,260,269 respondent firms owned by Hispanics, 90.1% of them transacted exchanges in English (representing $221.8 million), while 56.1% of them also used Spanish (representing $129.4 million).

Spanish language print, broadcast and digital media have also reflected the growth of the Latin@ populations. In 2010, the number of Spanish language newspapers in the country remained stable over the previous year, with 832 publications, including 25 dailies and 428 weeklies. Television and radio both grew in audience and value, and often competed successfully in local markets against the English language media companies (Guskin & Mitchell, 2011). In July 2013, Univision, the largest Spanish language television network in the country won the network sweeps. *Daily Finance* reported 'This summer, there's a new No. 1 among television viewers aged 18-49: For the fourth week in a row, the Spanish-language network Univision has won the primetime ratings contest for this coveted demographic, as well as the 18-34 cohort. It's Univision's first top finish in a sweeps month; the network previously beat NBC to come in fourth in the critical February sweeps period' (Murphy, 2013). The economic activity in business and employment in this language industry continues to be important (Valenzuela & Hunt, 2004).

Will the changes in the racial/ethnic composition of our national population and the multiple Spanish language economic practices throughout society affect the valuation of our language diversity? Would this valuation change require a reconsideration of or at least a challenge to the English assimilation goals of the current language policies that predicate abandonment of non-English languages as a condition of political, economic and social participation in the US? European national language policies are accommodating their regional political reorganization (the European Union) and more intimate linguistic diversity with multiple languages in their school policies and other social, political and economic structures, challenging the 'one nation, one language' political principle of the 19th century. The US currently has the fourth-largest Spanish-speaking population in the world. Global Spanish has the second-largest number of native speakers behind Chinese and slightly ahead of English. With a greater number of second language speakers of English than Spanish, it is still the third most spoken language in the world. So, in the future, whither the US? As other chapters of this book make clear: the times they are a-changing.

As we explore the value of bilingualism or single languages within the US economy, we should keep in mind this history of language diversity and language policies and practices as well as the ideological forces that affect the organization of the economy, social relations between groups and the participation of people with different ethnolinguistic characteristics and talents in these political economies. Demography and the dollar may yet trump ideology. Ultimately, we should bear in mind that the social, political or economic value, benefit or advantage of bilingualism or of specific languages may very well lie in the eye of the beholder.

References

Álvarez-González, J. (1999) Law, language and statehood: The role of English in the great state of Puerto Rico. *Law and Inequality* 17, 359–443.

Bale, J. (2008) Americanization by schooling. In J. González (ed.) *Encyclopedia of Bilingual Education* (pp. 32–38). London: Sage Publications.

Brecht, R. and Rivers, W. (2012) US language policy in defence and attack. In B. Spolsky (ed.) *The Cambridge Handbook of Language Policy* (pp. 262–275). Cambridge: Cambridge University Press.

Bustamante, J. (1972) The historical context of the undocumented immigration from Mexico to the United States. *Aztlán-Chicano Journal of the Social Sciences and the Arts* 3 (2, Fall), 257–282.

Castro, R. (1977) The Bilingual Education Act – A historical analysis of Title VII. In R.F. Macías (ed.) *Perspectivas en Chicano Studies* (pp. 81–122). Los Angeles: NACCS & UCLA Chicano Studies Center.

De La Zerda, N. and Hopper, R. (1979) Employment interviewers' reactions to Mexican American speech. *Communication Monographs* 46 (2), 126–134.

Délano, A. (2011) *México and Its Diaspora in the United States: Policies of Emigration since 1848*. Cambridge: Cambridge University Press.

Ellis, R. (2005) *To the Flag: The Unlikely History of the Pledge of Allegiance*. Lawrence, KS: University Press of Kansas.

Fedynskyj, J. (1971) State session laws in non-English languages: A chapter of American legal history. *Indiana Law Journal* 46 (4), 463–478.

Fishman, J.A., Nahirny V.C., Hofman, J.E., and Hayden, R.G.(1966) *Language Loyalty in the United States: The Maintenance and Perpetuation of Non-English Mother Tongues by American Ethnic and Religious Groups*. The Hague: Mouton Publishers.

Gándara, P. and Hopkins, M. (2011). *Forbidden Language: English Learners and Restrictive Language Policies*. New York: Teachers College Press.

García, O. and Mason, L. (2009) Where in the world is US Spanish? Creating a space of opportunity for US Latinos. In W. Harbert, S. McConnell-Ginet, A. Miller and J. Whitman (eds) *Language and Poverty* (pp. 78–101). Bristol: Multilingual Matters.

Gómez, M. (1998) *Exchanging Our Country Marks: The Transformation of African Identities in the Colonial and Antebellum South*. Chapel Hill, NC: University of North Carolina Press.

González, A. (2002) *Mexican Americans and the US Economy*. Tucson, AZ: University of Arizona Press.

Grin, F. (2008) Economics and language policy. In M. Hellinger and A. Pauwels (eds) *Handbook of Language and Communication: Diversity & Change* (pp. 271–297). Berlin: Mouton de Gruyter.

Grin, F. and Vallaincourt, F. (1997) The economics of multilingualism: Overview and analytical framework. *Annual Review of Applied Linguistics* 17, 43–65.

Griswold del Castillo, R. (1990) *The Treaty of Guadalupe Hidalgo: A Legacy of Conflict.* Norman, OK: University of Oklahoma Press.

Guskin, E. and Mitchell, A. (2011) Hispanic media: Faring better than the mainstream media. *The State of the News Media, An Annual Report on American Journalism.* Pew Research Center's Project for Excellence in Journalism. See http://stateofthemedia.org/2011/ (accessed 1 September 2011).

Heath, S. (1976a) Colonial language status achievement: Mexico, Peru and the United States. In A. Verdoodt and R. Kjolseth (eds) *Language in Sociology* (pp. 49–92). Louvain: Éditions Peeters.

Heath, S. (1976b) A national language academy? Debate in the new nation. *International Journal of the Sociology of Language* 11, 9–43.

Heath, S. (1977) Our language heritage: A historical perspective. In J. Phillips (ed.) *The Language Connection: From the Classroom to the World* (pp. 21–51). Vol. 9 of the ACTFL Foreign Language Education Series. Skokie, IL: National Textbook Co.

Hill, J. (2008) *The Everyday Language of White Racism.* Malden, MA: Wiley-Blackwell.

Kloss, H. (1998, 1977) *The American Bilingual Tradition.* Rowley, MA: Newbury House Publishers.

Klotz, E. (1968) Honest and glorious. In G.E. Frakes and C.B. Solberg (eds) *El Tratado de Guadalupe Hidalgo/The Treaty of Guadalupe Hidalgo 1848* (pp. 10–28). Sacramento, CA: Telefact Foundation.

Leeman, J. (2004) Racializing language: A history of linguistic ideologies in the US Census. *Journal of Language and Politics* 3 (3), 507–534.

Leibowitz, A. (1971) *Educational Policy and Political Acceptance: The Imposition of English as the Language of Instruction in American Schools.* ERIC document no. ED 047321 (March). Washington DC: ERIC Clearinghouse for Linguistics, Center for Applied Linguistics.

Leibowitz, A. (1974) Language as a means of social control: The United States experience. Paper delivered at the VIII World Congress of Sociology, Committee on Sociolinguistics. University of Toronto, Toronto, Canada (August).

Leibowitz, A. (1984) The official character of English in the United States: Literacy requirements for immigration, citizenship, and entrance into American life. *Aztlán* 15 (1), 25–70.

Lepore, J. (2002) *A is for American: Letters and Other Characters in the Newly United States.* New York: Alfred A. Knopf.

Lippi-Green, R. (1997, 2012) *English with an Accent: Language, Ideology, and Discrimination in the United States* (2nd edn). London and New York: Routledge.

Luebke, F. (1980) Legal restrictions on foreign languages in the Great Plains States, 1917–1923. In P. Schach (ed.) *Languages in Conflict: Linguistic Acculturation on the Great Plains* (pp. 1–19). Lincoln, NE: University of Nebraska Press.

Macías, R.F. (1997) Bilingual workers and language use rules in the workplace: A case study of a non-discriminatory language policy. *International Journal of the Sociology of Language* 127, 53–70.

Macías, R.F. (2014) Spanish as the second national language of the United States: Fact, future, fiction, or hope? *Review of Research in Education* 38 (1 March), 56–80.

Martínez, O. (1975) On the size of the Chicano population: New estimates, 1850–1900. *Aztlán* 6 (1), 43–68.

Murphy, E. (2013) Univision bests the big four in July sweeps ratings contest. *Daily Finance,* 26 July. See www.dailyfinance.com/on/univision-number-one-nielsen-tv-ratings-july/ (accessed 26 February 2014).

Piatt, B. (1993) *Language on the Job: Balancing Business Needs and Employee Rights.* Albuquerque, NM: University of New Mexico Press.

Romero, F. (1979) *Chicano Workers: Their Utilization and Development.* Monograph No. 8. Los Angeles: UCLA Chicano Studies Research Center.

San Miguel, Jr., G. (2004) *Contested Policy: The Rise and Fall of Federal Bilingual Education in the United States, 1960–2001.* Denton, TX: University of North Texas Press.

Schlossman, S. (1983) Is there an American tradition of bilingual education? German in the public elementary schools, 1840–1919. *American Journal of Education* 91 (2), 139–186.

Schmid, C. (2001) *The Politics of Language: Conflict, Identity, and Cultural Pluralism in Comparative Perspective.* New York: Oxford Press.

Shell, M. (1993) Babel in America; or, the politics of language diversity in the United States. *Critical Inquiry* 20 (1), 103–127.

Toosi, M. (2012) Employment outlook: 2010–2020. Labor force projections to 2020: A more slowly growing workforce. *Monthly Labor Review* (January), 43–64.

US Census Bureau. (2012) US Census Bureau projections show a slower growing, older, more diverse nation a half century from now. *Press release.* CB12-243 (12 December).

US Commission on Civil Rights. (2011) *English Only Policies in the Workplace.* Washington, DC: Author. See http://www.usccr.gov/pubs/English_Only_Policies_Report-July2011.pdf (accessed 21 April 2013).

Valenzuela, A. and Hunt, D. (2004) Labor and Spanish-language broadcasters. *Working USA* 7 (4, Spring), 78–102.

Weinberg, M. (1995) *A Chance to Learn: The History of Race and Education in the United States* (2nd edn). Long Beach, CA: California State University Press.

Weinberg, M. (2002) *Short History of American Capitalism.* New History Press. See http://www.newhistory.org/AmCap.pdf

Wiley, T.G. (1998) The imposition of World War I era English-only policies and the fate of German in North America. In T. Ricento and B. Burnaby (eds) *Language Policies in the United States and Canada: Myths and Realities* (pp. 211–241). Mahwah, NJ: Lawrence Erlbaum Associates.

Wolff, R. and Resnick, S. (2012) *Contending Economic Theories: Neoclassical, Keynesian, and Marxian.* Cambridge, MA: MIT Press.

Wright, E. (1980) School English and public policy. *College English* 42 (4 December), 327–342.

Wyman, M. (1993) *Round-Trip to America: The Immigrants Return to Europe, 1880–1930.* Ithaca, NY: Cornell University Press.

Zehler, A., Fleischman, H., Hopstock, P., Stephenson, T., Pendzick, M. and Sapru, S. (2003) *Descriptive Study of Services to Limited English Proficient Students.* Washington, DC: Development Associates.

3 Exploring Bilingualism, Literacy, Employability and Income Levels among Latinos in the United States

Sarah Catherine K. Moore,
Molly Fee, Jongyeon Ee,
Terrence G. Wiley and M. Beatriz Arias[1]

This chapter focuses on the association between language, literacy, employability and income levels for the Latino-origin population in the United States. The study uses data from the 2007–2011 American Community Survey (ACS) and demonstrates its utility for exploring characteristics of the major Latino subgroups of Mexican, Puerto Rican, Cuban, Dominican, Central American and South American origin. In addition, we suggest possible associations among self-reported English proficiency, years of schooling, employment and levels of income.

Introduction

Discussions regarding language use among immigrants in the US frequently revolve around the extent and development of their English proficiency (Bleakley & Chin, 2010). English in the US and global contexts, particularly among labor markets, has been largely deemed the 'language of opportunity' and the world's lingua franca (Maurais & Morris, 2003; Spolsky, 2004) for international businesses and industries. In part due to this role and the position of English as the dominant language spoken in the US for formal processes and systems, as discussed in the previous chapter, the role of languages other than English in business and trade is often overlooked. However, nearly a fifth of children in the US grow up in a household where a language other than English is spoken (US Census/ACS, 2012), suggesting that among immigrant families, communities and workers, languages other than English offer a potential resource for individuals and employers.

Languages other than English may have economic value that affects both the employability and income of heritage speakers and their families, as Chapters 5, 6 and 10 in this volume suggest. In order to assess the role of languages other than English within the US labor force and different segments of society, this chapter provides a preliminary description of the language and literacy characteristics of Latino immigrant and heritage language populations. We briefly review the role of multilingualism among immigrant groups and the association between language and literacy characteristics, employment status and income level across subgroups.

For the purposes of the study, the Latino population is divided into seven subgroups: those of Mexican, Puerto Rican,[2] Cuban, Dominican, Central American, South American and Other Spanish/Latino origin. The overarching research aims driving this chapter involve identifying the economic benefits of bilingualism and literacy. The specific research questions we address are:

(1) What is the extent of English proficiency, English and Spanish literacy, employment and income levels among Latino subgroups in the US?
(2) How are bilingualism, English and Spanish literacy, employment and income levels related to one another among Latinos in the US?

Scholars have addressed the purported cognitive and/or social benefits of literacy in general (Kintgen *et al.*, 1988) and with respect to languages other than English within the US context (Spolsky, 2004; Garcia, 2009). In addition, considerable literature has investigated the benefits of English oral and literacy abilities (Kroskrity, 2000; Wiley, 2005). A basic assumption reflected in the literature is that literacy counts; it is important for its cognitive, social and economic benefits. In the US and other multilingual/multiliterate societies, concerns exist regarding the extent to which literacy is important, regardless of language; the importance of literacy in the dominant language; and the extent to which literacy and oral proficiency in other languages relate to employability and economic well-being.

Methodology

Data and sample

To investigate our research questions, we use 2007–2011 ACS five-year estimates data, which allow us to include a substantial period of data. With respect to using survey data, however, a key issue often affecting research on bilingualism and biliteracy is the tendency to confound limited English oral proficiency with overall illiteracy (Macías,

1988; Macías & Spencer, 1984). It is important to distinguish between becoming literate in a second language, learning to speak a second language and developing initial literacy in a first or second language (Wiley, 2005). De Klerk and Wiley (2008) provide an example of the construction of composite language and literacy variables, drawing on methodologies previously used for analyses of US Census data (Castro & Wiley, 2007; Macías, 1988; Wiley, 2005). In our study, the ACS data provide an opportunity to assess multiple characteristics of both the general population in the US, as well as specific language minority groups – in this case, the Latino population.

One caveat to the reader, however, is that with any secondary data analysis, it is important to note the limitations of the original survey items from which data are drawn. For example, the ACS did not ask questions specific to either literacy abilities or proficiency in languages other than English. Respondents were asked to self-assess their English 'speaking' abilities, but no data were collected regarding respondents' ability to read or write in either English or in languages other than English (de Klerk & Wiley, 2008). In order to deal with the limited literacy information available in the ACS survey data, we follow a long-standing approach and use years of schooling as an indicator of literacy. Specifically, we develop a surrogate indicator employing years of school (eight or more) as a minimal equivalent to literacy (see de Klerk & Wiley, 2008; Macías, 1988, 1993, 1994, 2000; Wiley, 2005, for further discussion.)

We focus our inquiry on the Latino population, a key demographic in terms of its participation in and impact on the US economy. In addition, as our models estimate employment and income, we limit our ACS sample to respondents aged 16–65, the typical working age range in the US.

Dependent variables

Our overarching research aim explores the economic benefits of bilingualism and literacy among Latino-origin ACS respondents. In order to investigate how and to what degree bilingualism and literacy are associated with economic benefits, we identify two separate outcomes: employment status and income level.

Employment status was recoded as a binary variable (0 = unemployed, 1 = employed) from the employment status (ESR) variable in the ACS.

Income level was recoded from total personal earnings in the ACS. This measure represents individual as opposed to family income. Given the research emphasis on labor markets, earnings of zero were removed from analyses. In addition, we identified three separate income ranges, namely, lower-income, middle-income and upper-income levels. They ranged from greater than zero to less than $19,428; from $19,428 to less than $57,994;

and from 57,994 to $99,999,999, respectively.[3] While recoding income from a continuous to a categorical variable loses some power in the analyses, in turn it grants comparability across studies (please see Note 3 for further discussion and greater detail).

Independent variables

Gender was derived from the ACS data and coded 1 for males and 2 for females.

Age upon entry (US) was created for the foreign-born respondents using two indicators in the ACS: (1) respondent's age when the survey was being administered, and (2) year of entry into the US. Age upon entry was thus calculated: Age upon entry = Age−(2011−Year of entry into the US).

Country/region of origin was derived from the 24 detailed responses to the ACS item regarding Hispanic origin; we recoded the variable by combining labels based on geographical locations. Ultimately, we created seven subgroups based on region of origin: Mexican, Puerto Rican, Cuban, Dominican, Central American, South American and all Other Spanish/ Latino.

Language grouping: Bilingualism

'Bilingualism' was estimated based on the presence of Spanish spoken in the home[4] combined with English proficiency. Although this approach is far from ideal, there is substantial precedent based on previous research drawing on census data (e.g. see Alba, 2004; Fry & Lowell, 2003; Wiley, 2005).

Spanish–English Bilingual was established based on self-reports of speaking Spanish in the home and speaking English *well* or *very well* (i.e. *English proficient*).

Spanish Dominant was established based on self-reports of speaking Spanish in the home and speaking English *not well* or *not at all* (i.e. *not English proficient*).

English Dominant was created based on self-reports of speaking only English at home. Respondents who reported speaking only English were excluded from the *English Proficiency* follow-up question; thus, this variable is not correlated with the *Spanish-English Bilingual* and *Spanish Dominant* variables above.

Literacy

Over the past century, the use of years of schooling as a surrogate indicator of literacy has gradually increased. At one time, the US military used four years as a basic threshold; since then, six years has been used based on the assumption that completion of primary school generally results in basic literacy (Wiley, 2005). Following de Klerk and Wiley (2008), we employ a Grade 8 threshold, labeled 'Grade 7 or Grade 8' in response to an ACS educational attainment question. Given our emphasis on the bilingual Latino population, we include two different indicators of literacy: English Literacy and Spanish Literacy. The two literacy indicators allow us to examine how bilingualism is related to economic benefits while addressing both English and Spanish literacy simultaneously.

English Literacy. English literacy was created from three indicators: years of schooling, place of birth and age upon arrival in the US. We created an *English Literacy* binary variable as (0 = *not English literate*, 1 = *English literate*); if a person was born in the US *and* obtained over eight years of schooling, the person was considered *English literate*. Respondents who migrated from non-English-speaking countries before age 7 *and* received over eight years of schooling in the US were also considered *English literate*. All remaining respondents were coded to *not English literate*.

However, we are also cognizant of the fact that English literacy is not solely based on years of schooling. In the US labor market in particular, English literacy tends to be assessed in multifaceted ways, such as education level (years of schooling), formal and/or informal English-language tests (e.g. *Test of English as a Foreign Language* [TOEFL], *Test of English for International Communication* [TOEIC]), references, entrance exams, artifacts and so forth. Given these complex factors that influence how the construct of literacy is understood, we admit the limitation of our current binary distinction of English literacy. In an ideal world, large-scale surveys like the Current Population Survey (CPS) and ACS would gather information specific to literacy abilities as measured by employers and by educational institutions, allowing for a more precise literacy indicator.

Spanish Literacy. Spanish literacy was determined through three indicators: place of birth, years of schooling and age upon arrival in the US. Like English literacy, Spanish literacy was coded as a binary variable (0 = *Literacy Unknown*, 1 = *Spanish literate*). If a person migrated from a non-English-speaking region after age 14 *and* received over eight years of schooling in a home country, she or he was coded to *Spanish literate*. Respondents who migrated after age 7 and before age 14 *or* who completed less than eight years of schooling were coded to *Literacy Unknown*.[5] Again, we are cognizant of the limits of the literacy indicator. We acknowledge that for the purposes of employment, especially in jobs that require a high level of literacy (i.e. ability to translate documents, read complex text with good comprehension), our Spanish literacy indicator may be too imprecise to pick up meaningful differences. As Alarcón and colleagues (Chapter 5, this volume) note with respect to their own findings, the lack of specific information regarding literacy in the ACS data may obscure the advantages of higher levels of literacy. Rumbaut also argues in Chapter 8 (this volume) that the greater precision of his data with respect to the language ability of respondents allows him to detect differences that do not emerge from other, less-detailed data.

Age Groups. Considering the impact of work experience by age on employment status and income levels, we created three age groups to understand our inferential results more accurately: 16–29 (youth cohort), 30–49 (middle cohort) and 50–65 (oldest cohort). Age group functioned not as an independent variable, but rather as a domain, allowing us to run models separately for each age group.

Analytic plan

Inferential analyses

ACS sample weights were utilized to produce national estimates, and all subpopulation analyses (three age groups) were conducted using the domain analyses procedure in SAS 9.3. In addition, a series of multivariate logistic and multinomial logistic regression analyses were performed using the SAS survey procedure.

First, we ran descriptive statistics to illustrate trends in the Latino population by language proficiency, followed by region of origin to illustrate additional variation in the population. Inferential analyses were then conducted using logistic regression models to determine the association between employment status and bilingual abilities, English literacy, Spanish literacy, gender, age upon entry into the US and country/regions of origin. A series of analyses were performed based on each age domain in order to obtain more accurate odds ratios for different age groups. Next, we employed multinomial logistic regression models, which allow for multiple categories of the outcome variable to be considered in a single analysis, to predict *income level* (lower, middle, upper) using the same independent variables listed above. Reference coding was used for all dichotomous predictor variables, requiring that results be interpreted in comparison to the relevant reference group.

Background: Latino Subgroups

Immigration trends

The sections outlined below provide background and contextual information for the seven major subgroups and regions of origin used to categorize the Latino population for the purposes of data analysis. The review of the literature draws on sociohistorical, political, economic and other factors that relate to immigration trends among the seven major subgroups and regions of origin. The composition of the foreign-born population in the US has changed markedly over the past 40 years. The

US Census reported that 19.4% of the foreign-born population originated in Latin America in 1970; this figure jumped to 44.3% by 1990 (US Bureau of the Census, 1999) and reached 53.1% by 2010 (Grieco, 2012). The Immigration and Nationality Act of 1965 is one of the major policies that have contributed to these changes. The Act ended a national-origin quota system for immigrant access, while emphasizing economic and labor migration alongside family reunification (McBride, 1999). Over the past 40 years, numerous economic and political 'push' factors from major Latin American-sending countries have coupled with economic and social 'pull' factors in the US that encourage migration. Estimates of future demographic and immigration patterns suggest that this trend will not change; between 2000 and 2010, growth of the Latino population made up more than 50% of total population growth in the US (National Council of La Raza, n.d.). As more first-generation immigrants of working age come to the US and as the second and third generations approach working age, the impact of the Latino population on the US labor force will likely continue to grow in importance.

The US Latino-origin population, in particular the foreign-born, represents a key demographic in terms of its participation in and impact on the economy; importantly, however, it is not monolithic. This study disaggregates the Latino-origin population in the US into seven subgroups, based on region of origin, as well as nativity, literacy and language proficiency. Understanding the characteristics of the Latino population is important, because the non-Latino white population in the US labor force is expected to decline by 1.6 million by 2020, while Latino-origin workers will increase by 7.7 million, representing 74% of the workers that will join the US labor force over the next decade (Kochhar, 2012). Therefore, it is imperative to have a better understanding of the professional background, education, language proficiency and literacy of such an important part of the US economy among the foreign-born and their US-born children. Many in the Latino population speak Spanish as a heritage or immigrant language (Valdés, 2001), suggesting that, given the dominance of English, these individuals are largely bilingual, while some may also be English/Spanish biliterate. Despite some commonalities across the population of Spanish-speaking immigrants and heritage speakers, the larger population is quite diverse. It is valuable to acknowledge their varied characteristics, immigration patterns and context, and to conduct an analysis by major subgroups.

The following sections provide brief overviews of the Latino subgroups identified for this study. Any conclusions drawn from data analysis must take into consideration the distinct sociohistorical, sociopolitical and sociocultural factors that contribute to US immigration across the various subgroups. Due to the broad nature of this research, in which we attempt to investigate language, literacy, employability and income level profiles by Latino subgroup, issues surrounding historical immigration trends and the factors motivating immigration are relevant. Scholars from diverse disciplines have explored the range of issues and patterns at play in the context of immigration, assimilation and integration. Theories related to immigration have moved away from traditional approaches that assumed straight-line assimilation (Alba & Nee, 1997) and take into account the many societal factors that may shape an immigrant's experience (Gordon, 1964), such as segmented assimilation (Portes & Zhou, 1993; Rumbaut, 1994). For example, higher socioeconomic status subgroups may have more choices regarding immigration and may be less affected by push-pull factors, or the challenges of border crossings.

Mexican-origin population

Accounting for almost two-thirds of the Latino population in the US, the Mexican-origin population makes up the largest national-origin immigrant group in the country. Among the nearly 48 million people who self-identified as Latino in the 2010 ACS, almost 31 million were of Mexican origin, including both those who are either Mexican-born or US-born. When compared with other Latino subgroups, the Mexican-origin population is weighted toward a younger demographic, with more than half under the age of 30 (Dockterman, 2011c).

Mexican immigration to the US became a more formalized pattern of labor migration during World War II when the US government invited Mexican workers into the country through the *bracero* program to fill temporary jobs in the agriculture industry. This guest worker program brought several waves of workers into the country before officially ending in 1964. After approximately 4.5 million Mexicans had come to the US to support the agriculture industry, both the US and Mexican economies had come to rely on mutually beneficial 'pull' and 'push' factors to sustain the continued movement of workers across their common border. Following the *bracero* program, many single, male Mexicans participated in a pattern of circular labor migration in response to changing economies and seasonal demand. This pattern began to change in the 1980s, when immigration began to stabilize through a more permanent relocation and settlement of legal permanent residents and unauthorized immigrants in the US (Brick et al., 2011; Rosenblum & Brick, 2011).

Among the Mexican-origin population, the close economic relationship between the US and Mexico has created an open environment for trade, which includes the movement of labor both within and across international borders. It is important to note that emigration is frequently motivated not by a desire to earn more money for a life in the US, but rather to be able to send more back to Mexico during periods of economic downturn (Hanson & Spilimbergo, 1996). Additionally, during the 1960s, significant numbers of Mexicans moved from rural to industrial areas near the US–Mexico border, facilitating more [people] crossing into the US (Andreas, 1996). Research suggests that when wages in Mexico decrease, more people attempt to immigrate to the US (Chiquiar & Salcedo, 2013).

Since the 1970s, the Mexican-origin population in the US has grown significantly each decade. The foreign-born Mexican population in the US was approximately 760,000 in 1970, but by 1980, it had grown to 2.2 million; by 1990, it had nearly doubled to 4.3 million; in 2000, it doubled again to nearly 9.2 million. As the number of arriving Mexican-origin immigrants has skyrocketed over the past 40 years, so has its share of US immigration. In recent years, the proportion of Mexican-origin entrants among overall immigrants has hovered at around 30% (Terrazas, 2010). Employment has been the primary motivating, or 'pull', factor for Mexican entry into the US. In comparing earnings for manual and semiskilled jobs, wages in the US have maintained a ratio of 10 to 1 as compared with the same industries in Mexico. Since the 1970s, the employment industries most common among Mexican immigrant workers have expanded from primarily those in agriculture to include the service industry, manufacturing and construction. Furthermore, while Mexican immigrants previously came from rural parts of central Mexico, new entrants draw from both rural and urban areas across the country. Current Mexican immigrants to the US are more diverse in their experience, education and skill level, contributing to the brain drain in Mexico as well. By 2008, it was estimated that 7% of Mexican professionals with at least a bachelor's degree were living and working in the US (Alba, 2010).

The rapid growth in immigrant arrivals from Mexico has slowed in recent years because of a decrease in unauthorized immigration, in part the result of increased border enforcement and the recent global recession, which constrained opportunities for employment. Mexican arrivals hit their peak in 2007 and remained steady for two years before starting to slowly decline. Since much of Mexican immigration has historically been associated with the pull of available jobs in the US, the recent economic recession can be linked to the decline in new immigration (Passel et al., 2012).

Puerto Rican-origin population

Those of Puerto Rican origin make up the second-largest Latino subgroup in the US, representing 9.3% of the total US Latino population in 2009 (Dockterman, 2011d). Puerto Rican immigration is not easily comparable to immigration from other regions. Puerto Rico became a US territory in 1917, and Puerto Ricans are US citizens, which sets them apart from other Latino immigrant groups (see Macías, this volume). Due to their US citizenship, Puerto Ricans move easily between Puerto Rico and the continental US; Puerto Ricans in the continental US now outnumber those living in Puerto Rico (Dockterman, 2011d). Since 1970, the Puerto Rican-origin population in the continental US has grown from 1.4 million to 4.6 million while the population living in Puerto Rico has only increased from 2.7 million to 3.7 million (Dockterman, 2011d).

Among those of Puerto Rican origin, the education level of those living in the continental US is lower than that of those living in Puerto Rico, but their annual earnings are markedly higher. Among those in Puerto Rico, 22% have a bachelor's degree compared to only 16% in the continental US; yet, the annual earnings for those of Puerto Rican origin who are 16 years and older in Puerto Rico and the continental US are $14,400 and $25,000, respectively (Lopez, 2011). Sixty-one percent of all Latinos in the US have at least a high school diploma compared to 73% of Latinos of Puerto Rican origin (Dockterman, 2011d). Puerto Ricans self-report higher English proficiency than do other Latino subgroups in the US. Eighty-one percent report either speaking only English in the home or speaking English very well, compared to 63% of all Latinos (Dockterman, 2011d). Higher levels of English proficiency reflect the mandatory schooling in English in Puerto Rico, and may also be attributable in part to patterns of circular migration, as Puerto Rican migrants are likely to develop bilingual abilities moving between the two contexts (Duany, 2003). The division of the population between the continental US and Puerto Rico reinforces the need for greater functional bilingualism (Duany, 2002).

This ease of migration has also created a pattern of circular labor migration that facilitates 'mobile livelihood practices' within the transient diaspora which is not characteristic of other Latino subgroups (Duany, 2003). Called el vaivén, or 'coming and going', this pattern of circular migration gained momentum in the 1970s as many immigrants returned to Puerto Rico following a raise in the minimum wage in the commonwealth that coincided with reforms in the industrial labor market in New York City. During the 1980s, emigration increased alongside continued return migration, generating 'a sustained bilateral movement of people' (Duany, 2003: 431–432). Because of US citizenship, Puerto Rican labor migrants more easily pursue opportunities in the changing economy (Duany, 2002), relative to other immigrant groups.

The Puerto Rican government has not discouraged this continual movement of people, and at some points, has encouraged it to avoid high levels of local unemployment and overpopulation within the commonwealth (Duany, 2003). A 2002 survey found that more than 13%

of return migrants residing in Puerto Rico had already made this circular move at least twice (Duany, 2003). While it may be easier for Puerto Rican migrants to follow economic opportunities, frequent movement interrupts schooling and limits Puerto Ricans to low-skilled jobs and the service industry (Duany, 2002), which may explain the relatively low socioeconomic status of the Puerto Rican diaspora (Duany, 2002). Figures for the net migration from Puerto Rico take into account the simultaneous outflow of those returning to the island.

Cuban-origin population

According to the 2010 ACS, Latinos of Cuban origin represent 3.5% of US Latinos. Among the 1.7 million of Cuban origin in the US, 59% are foreign-born (53% of these arrived prior to 1990). Compared to the overall Latino population in the US, those of Cuban origin are on average older, have higher levels of education, have higher educational attainment and have lower poverty levels (Dockterman, 2011a).

Much of Cuban migration to the US has been politically motivated and has followed three main historical waves. In response to Fidel Castro's 1959 Cuban Revolution, those who were affiliated with or who had prospered under the prior regime began to flee to the US. These largely educated, middle-class refugees received a welcome reception upon arrival. At a time when only 4% of the Cuban population had a high school or college education, a disproportionate 36% of these arriving refugees did (Torres, 2004). This first wave of Cuban immigration has been termed the 'golden exile' due to this combination of education, wealth and positive reception. Cuban immigration was halted by the Cuban missile crisis in 1962 and did not pick up again until 1965 when the Cuban government permitted those already with family in the US to leave (Torres, 2004). This second major wave of immigration was characterized by family reunification. From 1965 to 1973, the Cuban government allowed those with relatives in the US to leave and join family who had already settled in the US. These immigrants were less likely to be professionals and instead were mostly skilled workers (Torres, 2004; Wasem, 2009). By 1969, about 1 in every 21 Cubans (approximately 380,000) had fled to the US (Portes, 1969). Over six months in 1980, the Mariel boatlift brought another 125,000 Cubans seeking political asylum or family reunification, most with occupational and educational backgrounds similar to the two prior waves (Torres, 2004; Wasem, 2009). By 1985, the total Cuban-origin population in the US had reached 900,000 (Desbarats, 1985).

Following a decline in Cuban immigration from the late 1980s to the early 1990s, Cuban immigration shifted again in 1994. Riots in

Havana sparked by threats from Castro fueled an increase in the number of Cubans fleeing by boat. The US has since attempted to regularize Cuban immigration, beginning with the Cuban Migration Agreement in September 1994. As a result of this law, Cubans intercepted by the US Coast Guard are not allowed entry into the US (Wasem, 2009). Between 1995 and 2006, the US Coast Guard estimates that it has interdicted and returned approximately 15,000 Cubans who attempted to migrate (Wasem, 2007).

Despite this long-term shift in its approach to Cuban arrivals, the US still accepts a limited number of Cuban refugees each year who are processed in Cuba and arrive in the US with refugee status (Wasem, 2007). In addition, the US has held three separate visa lotteries under the Special Cuban Migration Program in 1994, 1996 and 1998. In order to be eligible for this visa lottery, applicants were required to fulfill two of the following three criteria: completion of secondary school or higher, at least three years of work experience and having relatives in the US (Wasem, 2007). While this visa lottery program provides more Cubans with a legal pathway for entry into the US, the required levels of education, work experience and family ties reflected a desire by the US to maintain the higher level of education, professional work experience and community support that was characteristic of the Cuban immigrant population over the previous several decades. Based on 2000 Census data, 73% of those of Cuban origin in the US have at least a high school education, which is higher than the Puerto Rican-origin, Central American-origin and South American-origin population. In addition, a higher proportion of Cubans enrolled in undergraduate higher education (42%) than other Latino subgroups (Torres, 2004).

Dominican Republic-origin population

The Dominican-origin population is one of the fastest growing Latino subgroups in the US; it grew by 89% between 1990 and 2000 (Migration Policy Institute, 2004). Much of the Dominican-origin population in the US is the result of recent immigration; according to 2010 data, just under two-thirds of the foreign-born Dominican population arrived in the US after 1990. A larger percentage of the Dominican-origin population is foreign-born (57%) as compared to the general Latino population (37%) (Dockterman, 2011b).

As a result of this more recent migration, the US-born second generation of Dominican-origin people has grown, resulting in population characteristics that differ from those of its first-generation predecessors. While the Dominican foreign-born population in the US is characterized by low income, high rates of unemployment, low rates of participation in more highly skilled jobs and low educational attainment, the second-generation has achieved remarkably high educational levels when compared to their parents or other Latino subgroups. For example, in 2000, 49% of foreign-born Dominicans age 25 and older had not received a high school diploma, whereas 60% of the second-generation age 25 and older had completed some college (Hernández & Rivera-Batiz, 2003).

Dominican migration to the US was first prompted in the mid-1960s, following an era of political unrest. To calm internal unrest, the US government and the Dominican government agreed to allow oppositional members to come to the US, with most settling in the New York metropolitan area (Itzigsohn, 2000). The immigrants who arrived in this early wave were mostly political activists of the left and members of the rural and urban lower and middle class. The next wave of Dominican migration was prompted by economic decline in the Dominican Republic during the 1980s and 1990s, which has continued steadily ever since. Those leaving for the US tend to come from the working-class middle sectors of society and do not include highly qualified professionals or the least-skilled workers (Reynoso, 2003). Recently though, Dominicans with higher levels of education have begun to leave for the US and have found success as small business owners (Reynoso, 2003).

Central American-origin population

The Central American-origin population in the US consists of several national groups from Costa Rica, El Salvador, Guatemala, Honduras, Nicaragua and Panama. Combined, these immigrant groups make up 8.2% of the Latino population in the US. Though Mexico is technically considered part of Central America, it merits a separate analysis in the context of US immigration due to both its sheer numbers and the myriad of factors setting it apart from other Central American migration (including, but not limited to, the shared border).

The Central American-origin population in the US is comprised predominantly of El Salvadorans and Guatemalans. Both groups began arriving in the 1980s as a result of political instability resulting from civil wars and weak economies, as did Nicaraguan immigrants. These two push factors encouraged both legal and unauthorized labor migration in addition to refugee migration. Certain parts of Central America experienced slow economies and employment levels that did not match the growth in working adults; thus, many followed preexisting pathways for labor migration to the US that fed a continual demand for low-skilled workers. What began as seasonal or circular labor migration developed into more permanent migration after border crossings became more costly and dangerous in the 1980s (Brick et al., 2011). Between 1984 and

1990, Nicaraguans experienced considerable success in the approval of their asylum applications, likely attributable to their plight of escaping a communist government. The flight from communism appealed to US political ideology at the time. Similar patterns of migration continued in the wake of several natural disasters in the region, including Hurricane Mitch in 1998, Hurricane Stan in 2005 and two earthquakes that struck El Salvador in 2001.

Among the foreign-born Central American population in the US, approximately 40% lack legal authorization and 10% have been approved temporarily for humanitarian protection. Central American immigrants generally have low levels of education and English proficiency. In addition, they display higher levels of poverty compared to other immigrants (Terrazas, 2011). Recent migration from Central America has been most common among working-age adults who have gained an active role in the US workforce, most often in construction, manufacturing and services, i.e. employment sectors adversely affected by the economic downturn.

Throughout the 1990s, several pieces of legislation regularized, or legalized, certain groups of Central American immigrants living in the US without authorization. A 1991 class-action suit claimed that the US asylum system discriminated against Salvadorans and Guatemalans, allowing any who had entered the US prior to 1 October 1990, a new asylum interview. Additionally, President Clinton provided protection to many Central American immigrants through the Nicaraguan Adjustment and Central American Relief Act in 1997, which protected many Central Americans from the potential threat of deportation. Many Central American immigrants also fall under the category of 'Temporary Protected Status', being granted work authorization as a result of certain natural disasters.

South American-origin population

The South American-origin population represents a small proportion of the Latino-origin population in the US, yet this group has seen growth over the past few decades with migration from Argentina, Bolivia, Chile, Colombia, Ecuador, Paraguay, Peru, Uruguay and Venezuela. Among the foreign-born from Spanish-speaking countries, Colombians, Ecuadoreans and Peruvians have the largest populations in the US. However, in recent years, Venezuelan and Paraguayan immigration have produced the largest percentage of new arrivals.

There are noticeable differences in the unemployment rates and annual income levels by South American region, as well as the push factors related to migration to the US (Dixon & Gelatt, 2006). Despite relatively low out-migration, the foreign-born Argentinian population in the US has grown in recent years as the young and educated seek better economic opportunities abroad (Jachimowicz, 2006). Immigration from Colombia has been the result of a mixture of political and economic motivations as the political and humanitarian situation began to worsen along with the economy in the 1990s. Unemployment and shelter from the war continue to motivate Colombian immigration today (Bérubé, 2005). Migration from Ecuador has followed a different pattern over the past several decades; the early waves in the 1970s consisted of young subsistence farmers who arrived without documentation to work in low-skilled employment sectors. Economic decline in Ecuador in the 1980s spurred another wave of migration that persisted through the 1990s and early 2000s and continues today (Jokisch, 2007).

The discussion to this point provides the backdrop for our analysis regarding the major Latino subgroups in the US. In the forthcoming sections, we illustrate the current status of each of the subgroup populations, with particular emphasis on the extent of bilingualism, literacy, employment status and income level.

Descriptive Findings

The previous sections provided context and background demographics for the overall Latino population and the identified subgroups. Table 3.1 provides a detailed breakdown of information regarding the subgroups and key characteristics as they relate to the research questions guiding this study. The careful reader will note that the English-dominant group is markedly older than the other two cohorts, while Spanish–English bilinguals are significantly younger on average. In addition, among the first-generation, those who remain Spanish dominant in adulthood arrived on average at age 28, compared to the other two cohorts who arrived on average at 18 or 19 years of age. Among the English dominant, over half also report Spanish literacy, e.g. eight-plus years of schooling prior to immigration; while only 7% of the Spanish dominant report English literacy, reflecting the strength of years of education in the US.

In turn, Table 3.2 shows information regarding the breakdown of the subgroups within the Latino population by region of origin. We note first that for working-age respondents (16–64 years), the majority of Latino ACS respondents are of Mexican origin (65%), and that Dominican-origin immigrants claim the smallest share (3%). Similarly, respondents aged 30–49 are most highly represented across regions of origin. Central Americans and South Americans are most likely to be in the middle range (30–49), and Cubans and South Americans hold the fewest workers in the youngest age range (16–29). Among Latino ACS respondents, women slightly outnumber men in all subgroups with the exception of those from Mexico and Central America. Among Cubans, the numbers are evenly split between men and women.

Table 3.1 Means and proportions of Latino population by linguistic group: ACS 2007–2011

	Total population	Spanish-English bilingual	Spanish dominant	English dominant	
n (in millions)	286	45	14	228	
Gender					
Female	0.51	0.50	0.53	0.51	a,b,c
Age cohort					
16–29	0.30	0.36	0.23	0.29	a,b,c
30–49	0.42	0.44	0.51	0.41	a,b,c
50–64	0.28	0.19	0.26	0.30	a,b,c
Age upon arrival (first-generation only n=40M)	21.6	19.3	27.8	18.1	a,b,c
Literacy					
English	0.73	0.45	0.07	0.82	a,b,c
Spanish	0.54	0.58	0.49	0.54	a,b,c
Origin (n=39M)					
Mexican	0.64	0.63	0.67	0.64	a,b,c
Puerto Rican	0.09	0.10	0.04	0.14	a,b,c
Cuban	0.04	0.04	0.05	0.03	a,b,c
Dominican	0.03	0.03	0.04	0.01	a,b,c
Central American	0.09	0.09	0.13	0.04	a,b,c
South American	0.06	0.07	0.06	0.03	a,b,c
Other Latino	0.05	0.04	0.01	0.11	a,b,c
Employment status (n=156M)					
Employed	0.91	0.92	0.91	0.90	a,b,c
Income level					
Lower	0.36	0.36	0.57	0.34	a,b,c
Middle	0.44	0.44	0.39	0.44	a,b,c
Upper	0.21	0.19	0.04	0.22	a,b,c

Source: 2007–2011 five-year American Community Survey (ACS) Public Use Microdata sample data.
[a]Difference between Spanish-English bilingual and Spanish dominant significant at $p < 0.05$.
[b]Difference between English dominant and Spanish-English bilingual significant at $p < 0.05$.
[c]Difference between English dominant and Spanish dominant significant at $p < 0.05$.

We now discuss English proficiency as it relates to establishing bilingualism among the subgroups via self-reports of English ability among both US and foreign-born Latinos. Regardless of region of origin, Latino respondents were likely to self-report English proficiency, from 87% of Puerto Ricans to 62% of Central Americans. Differences in

Table 3.2 Means and proportions of Latino population by regions of origin: ACS 2007–2011

	Mexico	Puerto Rico	Cuba	Dominican Republic	Central America	South America	Other
n = 39 millions	0.65	0.09	0.04	0.03	0.09	0.06	0.05
Gender							
Female	0.48	0.51	0.50	0.54	0.48	0.52	0.51
Age cohort							
16–29	0.40	0.36	0.28	0.38	0.38	0.31	0.36
30–49	0.45	0.43	0.46	0.42	0.47	0.48	0.42
50–64	0.15	0.20	0.26	0.20	0.15	0.21	0.23
English proficient	0.70	0.87	0.67	0.68	0.62	0.76	0.88
Language skills							
Spanish-English bilingual	0.53	0.57	0.55	0.62	0.55	0.66	0.42
Spanish dominant	0.23	0.08	0.27	0.29	0.34	0.20	0.06
English dominant	0.24	0.35	0.18	0.09	0.11	0.14	0.53
Literacy							
English	0.45	0.70	0.39	0.34	0.26	0.29	0.64
Spanish	0.35	0.49	0.57	0.48	0.44	0.65	0.54
Employment status							
Employed	0.90	0.87	0.90	0.87	0.90	0.92	0.90
Male income level							
Lower	0.42	0.34	0.33	0.40	0.43	0.31	0.35
Middle	0.48	0.48	0.46	0.48	0.49	0.50	0.44
Upper	0.10	0.18	0.21	0.11	0.08	0.19	0.21
Female income level							
Lower	0.57	0.43	0.44	0.54	0.58	0.47	0.47
Middle	0.37	0.46	0.44	0.40	0.37	0.43	0.42
Upper	0.06	0.11	0.13	0.06	0.05	0.10	0.11

Source: 2007–2011 five-year American Community Survey (ACS) Public Use Microdata sample data.

English proficiency across the seven regions may be due to variation in socioeconomic status and national educational systems. The considerable English proficiency of Puerto Ricans reflects the unique position of Puerto Rico as a US territory where English has been used as a medium of instruction.

English proficiency is only part of bilingualism in the US; we now take a moment to discuss the three domains of bilingual abilities identified across the subgroups. Spanish–English bilingualism was most prevalent among South American (66%), Dominican (62%) and Puerto Rican (57%) respondents. The Other Spanish/Latino group had the highest proportion of respondents categorized as English dominant (53%). Central Americans and Dominicans were most likely to report Spanish dominance, and the lowest levels of English proficiency.

We now consider schooling, language and literacy. Latino ACS respondents overwhelmingly reported English literacy. English literacy rates were relatively high among Puerto Rican (70%), and all Other Spanish/ Latino (64%). Spanish literacy rates were equally high among most other groups, with the highest levels of Spanish literacy among Central American and South American respondents. In turn, the rates of Spanish literacy and literacy unknown were roughly split in half for several populations (Puerto Ricans and Dominicans in particular). South Americans showed the highest levels of Spanish literacy (65%) and Mexicans showed the highest levels of literacy unknown (65%).

Finally, we turn to our outcome indicators: employment status and income. In 2011, overall unemployment in the US was 8.9% according to the CPS (Bureau of Labor Statistics, n.d.), while unemployment rates among Latino ACS respondents ranged from 8.4% (South Americans) to 13.2% (Puerto Ricans). Puerto Rican and Dominican-origin respondents reported the highest levels of unemployment, and South American-origin respondents reported the lowest. In regard to the relationship between income levels and bilingual abilities, most Spanish–English bilinguals and English-dominant respondents (44% for both) were represented in the middle-income level. On the contrary, Spanish-dominant respondents showed the highest levels of low income (57%), which was substantially lower than their Spanish-English (19%) and English-dominant (22%) counterparts.

With respect to the income levels of Latino males, Central American respondents (43%) reported the highest levels of being in the lower income bracket, whereas South American respondents showed the lowest levels of being in the same category. Approximately half of Latino males were in the middle-income group with the exception of Other Spanish/Latino (44%) and Cuban-origin (46%) respondents. Being in the upper income bracket rates ranged from 8% (Central American males) to 21% (Cuban and Other Spanish/Latino males).

As opposed to their male counterparts, a substantial number of Latino females were in the lower income bracket, ranging from 43% (Puerto Rican) to 58% (Central American). In the middle-income category, Puerto Rican females showed the highest levels (46%), while Mexican and Central American females (both 37%) reported the lowest levels. As for the upper-income level, Cuban (13%), Puerto Rican (11%), South American (10%) followed by Dominican (6%), Mexican (6%) and Central American (5%) females comprised the upper-income category.

Inferential Analyses and Results

The following discussion reviews findings from additional analyses of data on Latino subgroups with an emphasis on the extent to which levels of Spanish–English bilingualism, English and Spanish literacy, gender and age upon arrival seem to impact employment and income levels. The following discussion is in reference to the tables in the Appendix, which are organized around three groups within the larger working-age population: 16–29, 30–49 and 50–65 years old.

Employment

Youth cohort: In investigating the relationship between bilingualism, English and Spanish literacy and employment for the youngest age group (ages 16–29, Appendix: Table A1), our analysis showed no significant differences between Spanish–English bilinguals and English-dominant respondents; but a significant positive association for Spanish–English bilinguals over the Spanish-dominant group did emerge. In particular, Spanish-dominant individuals experienced an 8% decrease in the odds of employment compared to Spanish–English bilinguals. Females in this age bracket were also 40% less likely to be employed than males. In addition, Mexican-origin youth in this cohort were significantly more likely to be employed than most other groups, with the exception of South Americans and Other Spanish/Latinos.

Middle cohort: Our models predicting employment for the middle cohort (ages 30–49, Appendix: Table A2) showed no significant differences between Spanish–English bilinguals and English-dominant individuals with regard to employment. However, we found a significant positive association for Spanish–English bilinguals relative to Spanish-dominant respondents. More specifically, Spanish-dominant respondents were 29% less likely to be employed than Spanish–English bilinguals, and we found a 14% increase in the likelihood of being employed with Spanish literacy abilities than without. In addition, females in this group demonstrated 38% lower odds of being employed than males.

Oldest cohort: Models predicting employment among the oldest cohort (ages 50–65, Appendix: Table A3) showed a strong, positive advantage among Spanish–English bilinguals over both English-dominant and Spanish-dominant respondents. Specifically, we found a 12% increase in the odds employment for Spanish–English bilinguals compared to English-dominant respondents, and a 28% increase over the Spanish-dominant group. In addition, models demonstrated a significant positive employment advantage associated with literacy, both English and Spanish, relative to those with less than eight years of schooling. English literacy results in a 19% increase in the likelihood of being employed, and respondents with Spanish literacy were 16% more likely to be employed than those with less than eight years of schooling. Regarding gender, females in this age group had a 5% lower chance of being employed than males.

Income level

Youth cohort: Our models investigating the relationship of these factors with income level for the youngest cohort (Appendix, Table A4) showed a clear benefit for Spanish–English bilinguals over Spanish-dominant respondents in predicting income (upper vs lower and middle vs lower). However, we found no significant differences between the English-dominant group and Spanish–English bilinguals. In addition, a significant, positive association emerged between English literacy and income (upper vs lower) and Spanish literacy and income (middle vs lower *and* upper vs lower).

Here, Spanish-dominant respondents were 42% less likely to be middle income (vs lower) than Spanish–English bilinguals, and 70% less likely to be upper income (vs lower). In addition, those with Spanish literacy were 34% more likely to be middle income (vs lower) than those with less than eight years of schooling and had 2.3 times higher odds of being upper income (vs lower). English literacy was also associated with 3.3 times higher odds in the likelihood of being upper income (vs lower). Among this youth cohort, women were 54% less likely to be middle income (vs lower) and were 62% less likely to be upper income (vs lower) than men. As for age upon arrival, there was a 1% decrease in the odds of being middle (vs lower) income, with one unit (=year) increase in one's age when one migrated to the United States. However, there was a 4% increase in the odds of being upper (vs lower) income level for the same factor.

Middle cohort: Among 30–49 year olds (Appendix, Table A5), Spanish–English bilinguals demonstrated a clear advantage over English-dominant (middle vs lower) and Spanish-dominant respondents (middle vs lower *and* upper vs lower). A positive association existed between English literacy and middle/upper (vs lower) income and between Spanish literacy and middle/upper (vs lower) income. For this middle cohort, English-dominant respondents demonstrated 8% lower odds of being middle (vs lower) but 18% higher odds of being upper (vs lower) income than Spanish–English bilinguals. Among this middle cohort, there was a 51% decrease in the odds of being middle (vs lower) income among Spanish-dominant respondents relative to Spanish–English bilinguals and an 82% decrease in the odds of being upper (vs lower) income level.

In addition, English literacy resulted in 38% higher odds of being middle (vs lower) income, and those with English literacy had 4.8 times higher odds of being upper (vs lower) income than those with less than eight years of schooling. Spanish literacy also resulted in 42% higher odds of being middle (vs lower) income and 2.5 times higher odds of being upper (vs lower) income levels. Like the young cohort, females were 65% less likely to be middle (vs lower) income and were 78% less likely to be upper (vs lower) income than their male counterparts. In regard to age upon arrival, one unit increase in one's age when one immigrated to the United States was associated with a 3% decrease and a 2% decrease in the odds of being middle (vs lower) income and upper (vs lower) income, respectively.

Oldest cohort: Among the oldest cohort (Appendix, Table A6), a clear benefit emerged for Spanish–English bilinguals over both English- and Spanish-dominant respondents, as well as a positive association between both Spanish and English literacy and higher income levels. Specifically, English-dominant respondents were 12% less likely to earn middle (vs lower) income levels than Spanish–English bilinguals, but there was no statistically significant difference between the English-dominant group and the Spanish-English bilingual group in terms of being in the upper (vs lower) income group. Spanish-dominant respondents were 46% less likely to earn middle (vs lower) income levels than Spanish–English bilinguals and had 79% lower odds of being upper (vs lower) income.

As the results for the other age cohorts showed, both English literacy and Spanish literacy were positively associated with economic benefits. Those with English literacy had 23% higher odds of being in the middle (vs lower) income bracket than those without. The magnitude was greater in the upper (vs lower) income bracket; those with English literacy were 3.4 times more likely to be in the upper (vs lower) income category. In addition, those with Spanish literacy had 1.6 times higher odds of being middle (vs lower) income; they were 3.6 times more likely to be in the upper (vs lower) level than those without. Among the oldest cohort, women were disproportionately underrepresented in both the middle and the upper income brackets. Latino females were 62% less likely to earn middle (vs lower) incomes and had 77% lower odds of being in the upper (vs lower) income group than their male counterparts. The age upon arrival factor was negatively associated with earnings in the oldest cohort. As one unit increased in age when one entered the United States, there was a 2% and a 4% decrease in the odds of being in the middle (vs lower) and the upper (vs lower) income brackets, respectively.

Discussion and Conclusions

The overarching foci of this chapter involved first, exploring the differences among Latino subgroups with regard to their levels of bilingualism, literacy, employment and region of origin; and next, developing a better understanding of the relationships of Spanish–English bilingualism and literacy to employment and income levels across the US Latino population. The Latino population and its regional subgroups are diverse; certain factors affect each group differently, including cultural and ethnic backgrounds, economic matters, political alliances and other issues of identity construction related to the decision to immigrate to (and perhaps emigrate from) the US.

A key issue raised in the investigation of the relationships among language, literacy, employability and income levels regards the extent to which bilingualism and literacy count for Latino workers in the US labor market. With regard to language characteristics, high proportions of respondents across all subgroups (67%–88%) reported being English proficient, with Spanish–English bilingualism highest among South American, Dominican and Puerto Rican-origin respondents. Not surprisingly, English literacy was highest among respondents of Puerto Rican-origin, and Spanish literacy was greatest among respondents of Central American and South American-origin. As literacy reflects years of schooling, our findings demonstrate that more schooling does translate to economic advantages, suggesting that literacy counts. Within the oldest age cohort (50–65 years old), there was a positive employment advantage regardless of literacy in Spanish or English. More notably, the middle age cohort (30–49 years old) had a higher likelihood of being employed with Spanish literacy than without. Similarly, all three age brackets demonstrated a positive income advantage for both Spanish and English literacy.

With regard to employment status, there was no significant difference in the employment of Spanish–English bilinguals and English-dominant respondents for the youth and middle cohorts, while Spanish–English bilinguals in the oldest cohort did have an employment advantage over both English-dominant and Spanish-dominant respondents. When comparing income levels, the youth cohort again shows no significant difference between Spanish–English bilinguals and English-dominant respondents. However, Spanish–English bilinguals did have a clear income advantage over English-dominant and Spanish-dominant respondents in both the middle and oldest cohorts, a finding that will resonate in different ways in Chapters 5, 6 and 10 of this volume. Therefore, while respondents aged 30–49 may have the same likelihood of being employed as English-dominant respondents, their earnings are greater compared to English-dominant respondents. Thus, while Spanish–English bilinguals and English-dominant respondents may be employed at the same rate, it appears as though there is a bilingual advantage at the middle-income level.

Furthermore, when age upon arrival in the US was examined with regard to income level, all three age cohorts demonstrated a 1%–3%

decrease in the odds of being middle vs lower income with each year increase at age of migration. In other words, within each cohort, income levels decreased the older the individual was upon arrival in the US. This finding raises several questions as to which factors are leading to a uniformly decreased income that comes with each year added to their age of migration (for further discussion of this topic, both Chapters 7 and 8, this volume, address language and the educational preparation of younger immigrants to the US).

Although women are more represented than men in all subgroups except for those of Mexican and Central American-origin, women are uniformly less employed and earn less than their male counterparts. Across subgroups for female respondents, Cubans are the most likely to be upper income; Puerto Ricans, middle income; and Mexican and Central Americans, low income. Furthermore, when predicting employment, females in both the youth and middle cohorts are less likely to be employed than men in those age groups. This discrepancy is even more striking when examining income levels by age cohorts. Females in the middle and oldest cohorts are discernibly less likely than men to be middle income vs lower income and upper income vs lower income. While multiple factors likely contribute to this gender differential, it is important to note that Latina females are employed less, and are earning comparatively less, than Latino-origin men in the US. In Chapter 4 of this volume, Robinson-Cimpian furthers the investigation of the complex relationships between gender, language and income.

Essentially, the ACS findings suggest that Spanish-English bilingual ability does in some instances improve both the likelihood of employability, as well as higher levels of income for the Latino population. In addition, both Spanish and English literacy are positively associated with not only employability, but also income level, and Spanish literacy, in some cases, demonstrated a significant, positive relationship with employment (for greater inquiry into this matter, see Chapters 4–6 of this volume). The scope of our analysis was limited to – and focused on – the greater Latino population; future research might investigate the extent to which bilingualism and English and Spanish literacy play a role in employability and income levels within each of the major subgroups and within various job sectors. Moreover, there may be regional differences across the US that might make individuals who are Spanish-English bilingual or Spanish dominant more desirable in the labor market than individuals who are English dominant. In addition, research that moves beyond census survey analysis, and incorporates interviews and other sources of data that are collected to examine these kinds of language questions, might better illustrate the complex portrait of the immigrant experience for Latinos from various regions and other diverse backgrounds.

Notes

(1)   The authors would like to acknowledge Casey O'Hara for his preliminary data analysis.

(2)   For the Puerto Rican population included in this analysis, there may be instances of self-reporting errors for foreign-born vs US-born, since all Puerto Ricans are US citizens by birth.

(3)   Income levels were determined based on a method used by the Pew Research Center (2012): middle income = 67–200% of the median income; lower income = less than 67% of the median income; upper income = more than 200% of the median income. Values regarding the median earnings of workers were calculated using the variable of total persons' earnings in the ACS data that included part-time and full-time workers, after excluding earnings of zero. Given the focus of the ACS data on both part-time and full-time workers, the median values calculated in this chapter are relatively lower than publicly available income values in which only full-time workers are included.

(4)   Some of these countries or regions of origin, particularly Mexico and Central America, have indigenous languages that are spoken instead of or in addition to Spanish. Due to the restrictions of the question in the ACS, this study was unable to analyze the extent to which indigenous languages were used as language of instruction or are spoken in the home. Therefore, we understand that other languages may have been used in schooling or may be spoken in the home.

(5)   Although the counterpart to 'English literate' is 'Not English literate', due to the two separate indicators here, age upon immigration *and* years of schooling, we labeled the counterpart to 'Spanish literate' as 'Literacy Unknown', as it could refer to either 'Not Spanish literate' or 'Uncertainty remains regarding Spanish literacy'.

References

Alba, F. (2010) Mexico: A crucial crossroads. *The Migration Information Source*. Migration Policy Institute. See http://www.migrationinformation.org/feature/display.cfm?ID=772 (accessed 14 June 2012).

Alba, R. (2004) *Language Assimilation Today: Bilingualism Persists More Than In the Past, But English Still Dominates*. Albany, NY: Lewis Mumford Center for Comparative Urban and Regional Research.

Alba, R. and Nee, V. (1997) Rethinking assimilation theory for a new era of immigration. *International Migration Review* 31 (4), 826–874.

Andreas, P. (1996) US-Mexico: Open markets, closed borders. *Foreign Policy* 103, 51–69.

Bérubé, M. (2005) *"Colombia: In the Crossfire."* *The Migration Information*. Migration Policy Institute. Accessed 01 August 2012. See http://www.migrationinformation.org/Profiles/display.cfm?ID=344.

Bleakley, H. and Chin, A. (2010) Age at arrival, English proficiency, and social assimilation among US immigrants. *American Economic Journal: Applied Economics* 2 (1), 165–192.

Brick, K., Challinor, A.E. and Rosenblum, M.R. (2011) *Mexican and Central American Immigrants in the United States*. Washington DC: Migration Policy Institute.

Bureau of Labor Statistics. (n.d.) Labor force statistics from the Current Population Survey. *United States Department of Labor*. See http://data.bls.gov/timeseries/LNS14000000 (accessed 26 September 2013).

Castro, M. and Wiley, T.G. (2007) Adult literacy and language diversity: How well do national data inform policy? In K.M. Rivera and A. Huerta-Macías (eds) *Adult Biliteracy: Sociocultural and Programmatic Responses* (pp. 29–55). Mahwah, NJ: Lawrence Erlbaum Associates.

Chiquiar, D. and Salcedo, A. (2013) *Mexican Migration to the United States: Underlying Economic Factors and Possible Scenarios for Future Flows*. Washington, DC: Migration Policy Institute.

de Klerk, G. and Wiley, T.G. (2008) Using the American Community Language Survey to investigate bilingualism and biliteracy among immigrant communities. *Journal of Southeast Asian Education and Advancement* 3, 68–78.

Desbarats, J. (1985) Indochinese resettlement in the United States. *Annals of the Association of American Geographers* 75 (4), 522–538.

Dixon, D. and Gelatt, J. (2006) Detailed characteristics of the South American born in the United States. *The Migration Information Source*. Migration Policy Institute. See http://www.migrationinformation.org/usfocus/display.cfm?ID=400 (accessed 8 June 2012).

Dockterman, D. (2011a) Hispanics of Cuban origin in the United States, 2009. *Pew Research Center*. See http://pewhispanic.org/files/factsheets/73.pdf (accessed August 2012).

Dockterman, D. (2011b) Hispanics of Dominican origin in the United States, 2009. *Pew Research Center*. See http://pewhispanic.org/files/factsheets/75.pdf (accessed August 2012).

Dockterman, D. (2011c) Hispanics of Mexican origin in the United States, 2009. *Pew Research Center*. See http://pewhispanic.org/files/factsheets/71.pdf (accessed August 2012).

Dockterman, D. (2011d) Hispanics of Puerto Rican origin in the United States, 2009. *Pew Research Center*. See http://pewhispanic.org/files/factsheets/72.pdf (accessed August 2012).

Duany, J. (2002) Mobile livelihoods: The sociocultural practices of circular migrants between Puerto Rico and the United States. *International Migration Review* 36 (2), 355–388.

Duany, J. (2003) Nation, migration, identity: The case of Puerto Ricans. *Havens Center*. See http://www.havenscenter.org/files/Nation,Migration,Identity.pdf (accessed August 2012).

Fry, R. and Lowell, B.L. (2003) The value of bilingualism in the US labor market. *Industrial and Labor Relations Review* 57 (1), 128–140.

Gándara, P.C. and Contreras, F. (2009) *The Latino Education Crisis: The Consequences of Failed Social Policies*. Cambridge, MA: Harvard University Press.

García, O. (2009) *Bilingual Education in the 21st Century: A Global Perspective*. Malden, MA and Oxford: Basil/Blackwell.

Gordon, M. (1964) *Assimilation in American Life*. New York: Oxford University Press.

Grieco, E.M., Acosta, Y.D., de la Cruz, G.P., Gambino, C., Gryn, T., Larsen, L.J., Trevelyan, E.N. and Walters, N.P. (2012) The foreign-born population in the United States: 2010. *American Community Survey*. United States Census Bureau. See http://www.census.gov/prod/2012pubs/acs-19.pdf (accessed August 2012).

Hanson, G.H. and Spilimbergo, A. (1996) Illegal immigration, border enforcement, and relative wages: Evidence from apprehensions at the US–Mexico border. *National Bureau of Economic Research, Working Paper 5592*.

Hernández, R. and Rivera-Batiz, F. (2003) *Dominicans in the United States: A Socioeconomic Profile, 2000*. Dominican Research Monographs: The CUNY Dominican Studies Institute. See http://www.columbia.edu/~flr9/documents/Dominicans_in_the_united_states_2003.pdf (accessed August 2012).

Itzigsohn, J. (2000) Immigration and the boundaries of citizenship: The institutions of immigrant's political transnationalism. *International Migration Review* 34 (4), 1126–1153.

Jachimowicz, M. (2006) *Argentina: A new era of migration and migration policy. The Migration Information Source.* Migration Policy Institute. See http://www.migrationinformation. org/Profiles/display.cfm?ID=374 (accessed 1 August 2012).

Jokisch, B. (2007) *Ecuador: Diversity in migration. The Migration Information Source.* Migration Policy Institute. See http://www.migrationinformation.org/Profiles/ display.cfm?ID=575 (accessed 1 August 2012).

Kintgen, E.R., Kroll, B.M. and Rose, M. (eds) (1988) *Perspectives on Literacy.* Carbondale, IL: Southern Illinois University Press.

Kochhar, R. (2012) Labor force growth slows, Hispanic share grows. *Pew Hispanic Center.* Pew Research Center. See http://www.pewhispanic.org/2012/02/13/labor-force-growth-slows-hispanic-share-grows (accessed 1 August 2012).

Kroskrity, P.V. (ed.) (2000) *Regimes of Language: Ideologies, Polities, and Identities.* Santa Fe, MN: SAR Press.

Lopez, M. and Velasco, G. (2011) A demographic portrait of Puerto Ricans, 2009. *Pew Research Center.* See http://pewhispanic.org/files/reports/143.pdf (accessed 1 August 2012).

McBride, M.J. (1999) Migrants and asylum seekers: Policy responses in the United States to immigrants and refugees from Central American and the Caribbean. *International Migration* 37 (1), 289–314.

Macías, R.F. (1988) *Latino Illiteracy in the United States.* Claremont, CA: Tomás Rivera Center.

Macías, R.F. (1993) Language and ethnic classification of language minorities: Chicano and Latino students in the 1990s. *Hispanic Journal of Behavioral Sciences* 15 (2), 230–257.

Macías, R.F. (1994) Inheriting sins while seeking absolution: Language diversity and national statistical data sets. In D. Spener (ed.) *Adult Biliteracy in the United States* (pp. 15–45). Washington DC and McHenry, IL: Center for Applied Linguistics and Delta Systems.

Macías, R.F. (2000) The flowering of America: Linguistic diversity in the United States. In S. McKay and S. Wong (eds) *New Immigrants in the United States: Readings for Second Language Educators* (pp. 11–57). Cambridge: Cambridge University Press.

Macías, R.F. and Spencer, M. (1984) *Estimating the Number of Language Minority and Limited English Proficient Persons in the US: A Comparative Analysis of the Studies.* Los Alamitos, CA: National Center for Bilingual Research.

Maurais, J. and Morris, M.A. (2003) *Languages in a Globalising World.* Cambridge: Cambridge University Press.

Migration Policy Institute (2004) The Dominican population in the United States: Growth and distribution (2004). See http://www.migrationpolicy.org/pubs/MPI_Report_Dominican_Pop_US.pdf (accessed 11 June 2012).

National Council of La Raza. (n.d) 20 FAQs about Hispanics. *National Council of La Raza.* See http://www.nclr.org/index.php/about_us/faqs/most_frequently_asked_questions_about_hispanics_in_the_us/ (accessed October 2013).

Ortman, J. and Shin, H.B. (2011, August) Language projections: 2010 to 2020. Paper presented at the 106th Annual Meeting of the American Sociological Association, Las Vegas, NV.

Passel, J., Cohn, D. and Gonzalez-Barrera, A. (2012) Net migration from Mexico falls to zero—and perhaps less. *Pew Hispanic Center.* See http://www.pewhispanic. org/2012/04/23/net-migration-from-mexico-falls-to-zero-and-perhaps-less (accessed August 2012).

Pew Research Center (2012) Fewer, poorer, gloomier. The lost decade of the middle class, 2012. *Pew Research Center.* See http://www.pewsocialtrends.org/files/2012/08/pew-social-trends-lost-decade-of-the-middle-class.pdf (accessed 12 February 2014).

Portes, A. (1969) Dilemmas of a golden exile: Integration of Cuban refugee families in Milwaukee. *American Sociological Review* 34 (4), 505–518.

Portes, A. and Zhou, M. (1993) The new second generation: Segmented assimilation and its variants. *The Annals of the American Academy of Political and Social Sciences* 530, 74–96.

Reynoso, J. (2003) Dominican immigrants and social capital in New York City: A case study. *Encrucijada/Crossroads: An Online Academic Journal* 1 (1), 57–78.

Rosenblum, M.R. and Brick, K. (2011) *US Immigration Policy and Mexican/Central American Migration Flows: Then and Now.* Washington, DC: Migration Policy Institute.

Rumbaut, R. (1994) The crucible within: Ethnic identity, self-esteem and segmented assimilation among children of immigrants. *International Migration Review* 18, 748–794.

Spolsky, B. (2004) *Language Policy.* Cambridge: Cambridge University Press.

Terrazas, A. (2010) Mexican immigrants in the United States. *The Migration Information Source.* Migration Policy Institute. See http://www.migrationinformation.org/usfocus/display.cfm?ID=767 (accessed 1 August 2012).

Terrazas, A. (2011) Central American immigrants in the United States. *The Migration Information Source.* Migration Policy Institute. See http://www.migrationinformation.org/usfocus/display.cfm?ID=821 (accessed 1 August 2012).

Torres, V. (2004) The diversity among us: Puerto Ricans, Cuban Americans, Caribbean Americans, and Central and South Americans. *New Directions for Student Services* 105, 5–16.

US Bureau of the Census (1999) Tech paper 29: Table 2. Region of birth of the foreign-born population: 1850 to 1930 and 1960 to 1990. See http://www.census.gov/population/www/documentation/twps0029/tab02.html (accessed 1 August 2012).

Valdés, G. (2001) Heritage language students: Profiles and possibilities. In J.K. Peyton and S. McGinnis (eds) *Heritage Languages in America.* Washington DC: Center for Applied Linguistics.

Wasem, R.E. (2007) Cuban migration policy and trends. *Congressional Research Service.* See http://www.ilw.com/immigrationdaily/news/2007,1029-crs.pdf (accessed 8 June 2012).

Wasem, R.E. (2009) Cuban migration to the United States: Policy and trends. *Congressional Research Service.* See https://www.fas.org/sgp/crs/row/R40566.pdf (accessed 28 June 2012).

Wiley, T.G. (2005) *Literacy and Language Diversity in the United States.* Washington DC and McHenry, IL: Center for Applied Linguistics and Delta Systems.

Appendix

Table A1 Coefficients, odds ratio estimates and standard errors from logistic regression models predicting employment ($16 \leq$ Ages < 30)

	Coeff	Odds ratio	SE	Pr>ChiSq	
Linguistic group (reference: Spanish-English bilingual)					
English dominant	0.004	1.004	0.204	0.652	
Spanish dominant	−0.085	0.919	0.036	0.018	*
Literacy (reference: less than eight years of schooling)					
English literacy	−0.248	0.781	0.061	<0.0001	***
Spanish literacy	0.150	1.162	0.037	<0.0001	***
Female	−0.506	0.603	0.033	<0.0001	***
Age upon arrival	0.004	1.004	0.004	0.296	
Ethnic origin (reference: Mexican origin)					
Puerto Rican	−0.559	0.572	0.053	<0.0001	***
Cuban	−0.381	0.683	0.089	<0.0001	***
Dominican	−0.436	0.646	0.067	<0.0001	***
Central American	−0.106	0.899	0.041	0.010	**
South American	0.013	1.013	0.062	0.839	
Other Latino	−0.015	0.986	0.106	0.891	

Source: 2007–2011 five-year American Community Survey (ACS) Public Use Microdata sample data.
$*p < 0.05$; $**p < 0.01$; $***p < 0.001$.

Table A2 Coefficients, odds ratio estimates and standard errors from logistic regression models predicting employment (30≤Ages<50)

	Coeff	Odds ratio	SE	Pr>ChiSq	
Linguistic group (reference: Spanish-English bilingual)					
English dominant	−0.031	0.969	0.050	0.529	
Spanish dominant	−0.350	0.705	0.021	<0.0001	***
Literacy (reference: less than eight years of schooling)					
English literacy	0.046	1.047	0.046	0.319	
Spanish literacy	0.133	1.143	0.020	<0.0001	***
Female	−0.475	0.622	0.018	<0.0001	***
Age upon arrival	−0.006	0.994	0.002	<0.0001	***
Ethnic origin (reference: Mexican origin)					
Puerto Rican	−0.453	0.636	0.034	<0.0001	***
Cuban	−0.272	0.762	0.045	<0.0001	***
Dominican	−0.145	0.865	0.057	0.011	*
Central American	−0.019	0.981	0.025	0.447	
South American	0.119	1.126	0.036	0.001	***
Other Latino	0.111	1.118	0.077	0.149	

Source: 2007–2011 five-year American Community Survey (ACS) Public Use Microdata sample data.
*$p<0.05$; **$p<0.01$; ***$p<0.001$.

Table A3 Coefficients, odds ratio estimates and standard errors from logistic regression models predicting employment (50≤Ages<65)

	Coeff	Odds ratio	SE	Pr>ChiSq	
Linguistic group (reference: Spanish-English bilingual)					
English dominant	−0.124	0.884	0.054	0.022	*
Spanish dominant	−0.334	0.716	0.035	<0.0001	***
Literacy (reference: less than eight years of schooling)					
English literacy	0.177	1.193	0.069	0.011	*
Spanish literacy	0.146	1.157	0.036	<0.0001	***
Female	−0.048	0.953	0.022	0.031	*
Age upon arrival	−0.007	0.993	0.001	<0.0001	***
Ethnic origin (reference: Mexican origin)					
Puerto Rican	−0.164	0.849	0.059	0.005	**
Cuban	−0.256	0.775	0.063	<0.0001	***
Dominican	0.046	1.047	0.071	0.513	
Central American	−0.088	0.916	0.048	0.064	†
South American	0.065	1.067	0.046	0.162	
Other Latino	−0.049	0.952	0.089	0.583	

Source: 2007–2011 five-year American Community Survey (ACS) Public Use Microdata sample data.
†$p<0.10$; *$p<0.05$; **$p<0.01$; ***$p<0.001$.

Table A4 Coefficients, odds ratio estimates and standard errors from multinomial logistic regression models predicting income level (reference: lower-income group) (16≤Ages<30)

	Middle income				Upper income			
	Coeff	Odds ratio	SE	Pr>ChiSq	Coeff	Odds ratio	SE	Pr>ChiSq
Linguistic group (reference: Spanish-English bilingual)								
English dominant	-0.014	0.986	0.049	0.781	0.168	1.183	0.115	0.142
Spanish dominant	-0.546	0.579	0.021	<0.0001 ***	-1.198	0.302	0.087	<0.0001 ***
Literacy (reference: less than eight years of schooling)								
English literacy	0.005	1.005	0.042	0.899	1.195	3.303	0.175	<0.0001 ***
Spanish literacy	0.292	1.339	0.026	<0.0001 ***	0.816	2.262	0.124	<0.0001 ***
Female	-0.777	0.460	0.019	<0.0001 ***	-0.963	0.382	0.061	<0.0001 ***
Age upon arrival	-0.011	0.990	0.003	<0.0001 ***	0.035	1.035	0.010	0.0003 ***
Ethnic origin (reference: Mexican origin)								
Puerto Rican	0.137	1.147	0.038	0.0003 ***	0.470	1.600	0.128	0.0002 ***
Cuban	0.031	1.031	0.066	0.643	0.533	1.705	0.178	0.003 **
Dominican	0.029	1.030	0.056	0.601	0.524	1.688	0.156	0.001 ***
Central American	0.097	1.102	0.026	0.0002 ***	0.293	1.341	0.082	0.0003 ***
South American	0.324	1.383	0.040	<0.0001 ***	0.979	2.663	0.087	<0.0001 ***
Other Latino	0.074	1.077	0.073	0.308	0.862	2.368	0.191	<0.0001 ***

Source: 2007–2011 five-year American Community Survey (ACS) Public Use Microdata sample data.
$*p<0.05$; $**p<0.01$; $***p<0.001$.

Table A5 Coefficients, odds ratio estimates and standard errors from multinomial logistic regression models predicting income level (reference: lower-income group) (30≤Ages<50)

	Middle income				Upper income			
	Coeff	Odds ratio	SE	Pr>ChiSq	Coeff	Odds ratio	SE	Pr>ChiSq
Linguistic group (reference: Spanish-English bilingual)								
English dominant	-0.081	0.922	0.031	0.010 **	0.163	1.177	0.036	<0.0001 ***
Spanish dominant	-0.708	0.493	0.012	<0.0001 ***	-1.697	0.183	0.026	<0.0001 ***
Literacy (reference: less than eight years of schooling)								
English literacy	0.325	1.384	0.029	<0.0001 ***	1.558	4.751	0.050	<0.0001 ***
Spanish literacy	0.348	1.416	0.015	<0.0001 ***	0.906	2.474	0.029	<0.0001 ***
Female	-1.060	0.347	0.010	<0.0001 ***	-1.535	0.215	0.022	<0.0001 ***
Age upon arrival	-0.029	0.972	0.001	<0.0001 ***	-0.023	0.978	0.002	<0.0001 ***
Ethnic origin (reference: Mexican origin)								
Puerto Rican	0.279	1.322	0.029	<0.0001 ***	0.670	1.954	0.041	<0.0001 ***
Cuban	0.352	1.422	0.033	<0.0001 ***	0.845	2.328	0.047	<0.0001 ***
Dominican	0.240	1.272	0.031	<0.0001 ***	0.491	1.634	0.058	<0.0001 ***
Central American	0.148	1.159	0.015	<0.0001 ***	0.277	1.320	0.030	<0.0001 ***
South American	0.437	1.548	0.019	<0.0001 ***	1.162	3.195	0.031	<0.0001 ***
Other Latino	0.239	1.270	0.041	<0.0001 ***	1.185	3.271	0.054	<0.0001 ***

Source: 2007–2011 five-year American Community Survey (ACS) Public Use Microdata sample data.
*$p<0.05$; **$p<0.01$; ***$p<0.001$.

Table A6 Coefficients, odds ratio estimates and standard errors from multinomial logistic regression models predicting income level (reference: lower-income group) (50≤Ages<65)

	Middle income				Upper income			
	Coeff	Odds ratio	SE	Pr>ChiSq	Coeff	Odds ratio	SE	Pr>ChiSq
Linguistic group (reference: Spanish-English bilingual)								
English dominant	-0.131	0.877	0.044	0.003 **	0.096	1.101	0.055	0.080 †
Spanish dominant	-0.612	0.542	0.019	<0.0001 ***	-1.572	0.208	0.040	<0.0001 ***
Literacy (reference: less than eight years of schooling)								
English literacy	0.204	1.226	0.045	<0.0001 ***	1.223	3.396	0.066	<0.0001 ***
Spanish literacy	0.440	1.553	0.023	<0.0001 ***	1.277	3.586	0.050	<0.0001 ***
Female	-0.973	0.378	0.016	<0.0001 ***	-1.490	0.225	0.031	<0.0001 ***
Age upon arrival	-0.025	0.975	0.001	<0.0001 ***	-0.040	0.961	0.002	<0.0001 ***
Ethnic origin (reference: Mexican origin)								
Puerto Rican	0.171	1.186	0.035	<0.0001 ***	0.378	1.459	0.052	<0.0001 ***
Cuban	0.060	1.061	0.033	0.073 †	0.726	2.066	0.049	<0.0001 ***
Dominican	0.114	1.121	0.047	0.015 *	0.256	1.292	0.070	0.0003 ***
Central American	0.098	1.103	0.031	0.002 **	0.142	1.153	0.048	0.003 **
South American	0.318	1.375	0.035	<0.0001 ***	0.881	2.414	0.043	<0.0001 ***
Other Latino	0.244	1.277	0.061	<0.0001 ***	1.013	2.754	0.073	<0.0001 ***

Source: 2007–2011 five-year American Community Survey (ACS) Public Use Microdata sample data.
†p<0.10; *p<0.05; **p<0.01; ***p<0.001.

Section 2

Are There Really Economic Benefits to Bilingualism in the US Labor Market?

4 Labor Market Differences Between Bilingual and Monolingual Hispanics

Joseph P. Robinson-Cimpian

Introduction

This chapter uses five years of data from the 2006–2010 American Community Survey (ACS) to explore how labor market participation, employment rates and wages differ between bilingual and monolingual Hispanic individuals aged 24–64 years. Analyses accounting for variation across locations revealed little difference in average labor market outcomes between bilingual and English monolingual Hispanic males and females. Bilingual males were slightly less likely to participate in the labor market than monolingual males, but bilingual females were more likely to participate than monolingual females. Among those individuals who participated in the labor market, there were no differences in employment rates. Bilingual males earned slightly lower wages than did monolingual males, but there was no bilingual wage differential among females. Subsequent analyses explored whether labor market differentials varied depending on the concentration of Spanish speakers in a local area. Most notably from these analyses, bilingual individuals were significantly more likely to participate in the labor market when the concentration of Spanish speakers in the area was higher. Overall, this study suggests that future research should broaden the scope of the outcomes explored beyond a singular focus on wage differentials, especially as some of the more interesting patterns in these data lie in the participation rates. Moreover, labor market research on bilingualism should not exclude females from analyses. Before discussing the details of the analyses, results and implications of this research, the next section provides a review of the relevant literature on the topics studied in this chapter.

Background

Bilingualism has been associated with improved cognitive performance in children (Bialystok, 2001) and in older adults (Bialystok *et al.*, 2004). Some of the apparent advantages of bilingualism, such as a greater ability to multitask, may be attractive to employers as well. Moreover, speaking more than one language could conceivably confer other comparative advantages on individuals in the labor market, especially in an increasingly globalized economy (Portes & Rumbaut, 2001). All else equal, bilingual individuals have the ability to converse with a greater (and more varied) pool of individuals, and employers may be willing to pay a premium for employees with these skills.

Quantifying the wage returns to bilingualism, however, is difficult because it is nearly impossible to isolate the effect of bilingualism. For this reason, although researchers have claimed to study the 'wage returns to bilingualism' (e.g. Fry & Lowell, 2003; Shin & Alba, 2009), it is more appropriate to represent that prior research as examining the difference between the wages of bilinguals and monolinguals after statistically conditioning on individual and sometimes locational factors – this difference is referred to as the marginal differential (MD).

The present study will continue in this tradition of studying these MDs, but with some important modifications: First, prior research has focused on *wage* differentials but has ignored whether differentials exist in terms of other labor market outcomes, such as simply participating in the labor market or in employment rates among those who participate. This study will examine three labor market outcomes: civilian labor market participation, employment and annual wages. Second, much research on bilingual wage differentials has focused on *males* and ignored the labor market outcomes of females. The labor market outcomes of both genders will be studied here. Third, although there are some exceptions that will be discussed later, prior research tends to present bilingual *average* marginal differentials (AMDs), but does not explore whether these differentials vary as a function of the location that individuals are embedded in and, more specifically, as a function of the concentration of the heritage language spoken in the location. The present study explores whether labor market differences vary with the concentration of the heritage language spoken. Finally, it is important to note that this study is concerned with comparisons between similar individuals who speak only English and those who speak English and Spanish. Thus, unlike other studies focusing on the value of *English* in the labor market (see Chiswick & Miller, 2002, 2010), all participants in the current study are assumed to be fluent in English.

Several studies exploring the bilingual–monolingual wage differential have used data from the US Census Bureau (Chiswick & Miller, 2002, 2010; Portes & Rumbaut, 2001; Shin & Alba, 2009), as does the present study.[1] The census-based study that is perhaps closest to the current research was conducted by Shin and Alba (2009), who estimated bilingual wage differentials from 2000 Census data for Hispanic and Asian individuals. In one analysis, the authors found that bilingual individuals of Mexican descent earned 5.6% less than their English monolingual peers. In subsequent analyses, they found that the concentration of Spanish speakers in a metropolitan statistical area is associated with higher earnings for Mexican-descent individuals, but that there is no evidence that bilinguals earn any additional wages in areas with higher concentrations. However, it is important to note that census-based data are limited in three significant respects: First, the data are self-reported. Second, census questions ask respondents whether they speak a language other than English in the home but do not in any way gauge proficiency in the non-English language. Third, individuals report how well they speak English, responding either *poor, fair, well* or *very well*, and the interpretations of these categories likely vary across respondents. Thus, the reliability and validity of whether an individual is bilingual may be questionable.

Addressing some of these limitations, Fry and Lowell (2003) took a different approach to studying bilingual marginal differences. Their analysis used the 1992 National Adult Literacy Survey (NALS), which asked adults not only about their English proficiency, but also about their non-English proficiency. When compared to census-based studies, however, this language-information-rich NALS data set has its own drawbacks, including a substantially smaller sample (5742 English monolingual males and 560 bilingual males between ages 18 and 64 with positive weekly earnings in Fry and Lowell's study) and a dated sample (NALS data were gathered in 1992).[2] These features of NALS are less than ideal given the goals of the current study, especially the current study's focus on systematic variation in MDs across locations. Nevertheless, Fry and Lowell's (2003) study using NALS informs our expectations of bilingual marginal differences in wages. Fry and Lowell (2003) found no MD for bilingualism once other factors were accounted for in their statistical models, and they found no consistent evidence that living in a self-reported, linguistically isolated enclave predicted bilingual MDs (but see Chiswick & Miller, 2002; McManus, 1990). Thus, they concluded that bilingualism was not rewarded by employers in 1992.

In a related study focusing on labor market outcomes in ethnic enclaves, Edin *et al.*, (2003) estimated the effect of living in an ethnic enclave among refugee immigrants in Sweden. Between 1985 and 1991, the Swedish government placed immigrants in a locale, rather than allowing the immigrants to choose where they wanted to locate. As Edin *et al.* discuss, this policy increased the dispersion of immigrants throughout the country by reducing the concentrations of immigrants in some areas with low housing availability (e.g. Stockholm), while increasing their concentrations in areas with housing availability. Because this Swedish immigration policy made the government (not the individual immigrant) the agent that decided the initial location for the immigrant, Edin *et al.* could capitalize on as-if random variation in whether one lived in an ethnic enclave to estimate the effects of living in an ethnic enclave. They found that living in an ethnic enclave resulted in higher earnings; moreover, they found that because lower-skilled immigrants self-sorted into ethnic enclaves, not accounting for the self-sorting selection bias produced downwardly biased estimates of the effects of enclaves. Damm (2009) used a similar approach with more recent data from Denmark and found results consistent with Edin *et al*. The findings of Edin *et al*. and Damm suggest that living in an ethnic enclave leads to increased wages, and that correlational analyses estimating ethnic enclave effects may underestimate the true benefits. But it is important to note that these studies did not examine the interaction between ethnic enclave and language, and thus they do not speak to whether bilinguals may fare better in ethnic enclaves than monolinguals. Moreover, these studies by Edin *et al*., (2003) and Damm (2009) were conducted in European countries, and thus the findings may not generalize to the US context. Indeed, in contrast to research in the US that has failed to show a bilingual wage advantage, Ginsburgh and Prieto-Rodriguez (2011) provide evidence that multilingualism may result in higher wages, but their research was conducted on a European sample and the nonnative language was in many cases *English*, the lingua franca of commerce. In short, we should be cautious about drawing conclusions from European studies regarding bilingualism or the effects of ethnic enclaves in the US.

The present study uses five years of data from the 2006–2010 ACS to examine labor market outcomes of bilingual and monolingual Hispanic individuals. This study asks: (1) Do bilingual and monolingual individuals experience different levels of labor market participation, employment rates and annual wages? (2) Do these bilingual MDs change when we account for individual characteristics, such as educational attainment? (3) Do these MDs vary depending on the concentration of Spanish speakers in the area? These questions will be explored separately for males and females.

Method

Data

The current study uses data from the ACS, collected annually by the US Census Bureau on a random 1% sample of all individuals in the US. Among other factors, the ACS asks individuals about demographics (e.g. race, ethnicity, education, gender, nativity, language spoken in the home) and recent employment (e.g. employment status, hours and weeks worked, earnings, place of employment, occupation).

Analyses are restricted to only Hispanic individuals who are monolingual English speakers or who speak Spanish and report speaking English 'very well'.

Because individuals on visas have employment conditions that they must meet, analyses are restricted to US citizens (there was no indicator for permanent residents). Moreover, the ACS contains data on whether individuals are currently enrolled in school. As school enrollment can affect labor market outcomes, analyses are restricted to only individuals not currently enrolled in school.

In sum, all analyses presented here were estimated on Hispanic individuals who are US citizens, between the ages of 24 and 64 and not currently enrolled in school. The final analytic sample pooled across the five years included 192,840 males and 204,616 females.

Dependent variables

Civilian labor market participation. This is a dichotomous variable, taking on a value of 1 for individuals with reported employment status records of *civilian employed, at work; civilian employed, with a job but not at work*[3]; *unemployed.* Values of 0 were assigned to individuals with employment status records of *not in labor force.* Individuals with records of *armed forces* were excluded; thus, this variable refers to participation in the *civilian* labor market.

Employed. This is a dichotomous variable with values of 0 or 1 for individuals in the civilian labor market. Values of 1 were assigned to those with reported employment status records of *civilian employed, at work* or *civilian employed, with a job but not at work.* Values of 0 were assigned to individuals with records of *unemployed.*

Logged annual wages. This is a continuous variable with values only for employed individuals with nonzero wages. The original variable of annual wages was log-transformed to adjust for the positively skewed distribution and to facilitate interpreting the wage differentials as percentage differences.

Independent variables

Bilingual. For these analyses, 'bilingual' is defined as someone who (a) speaks Spanish at home and (b) self-reports speaking English *very well.* Note that this means that individuals who self-report speaking English less than *very well* are excluded from these analyses. Individuals who speak only English are coded as 0 (for 'monolingual').

Percent Spanish speaking. Individuals who speak Spanish (regardless of how well they speak English) are counted as Spanish speakers. Within each Public Use Microdata Area (PUMA), this count is divided by the total sample. Weights are applied, so that the proportions reflect the population. Note that this variable is based on all individuals aged 5 and older, and thus is intended to reflect the broader community (e.g. school-age children, senior citizens) and not simply those of traditional working age.

Age. Individuals with values of this continuous variable between 24 and 64 were retained for analyses. In all analyses, age, age squared and age cubed are included to allow for flexibility in the relationships between age and the outcomes.

Educational attainment. Only individuals not currently in school were retained for analyses. Individuals were then coded by their highest level of degree into one of the following five categories: *less than a high school diploma; high school diploma; some college with no degree, or an associate's degree, bachelor's degree, master's degree, professional degree (e.g. JD) or a doctorate degree.* Analyses include indicator variables for each category, which is more flexible than treating educational attainment as an ordinal variable.

Citizenship. Only US citizens were retained for analyses, but the place of birth and process of citizenship vary across individuals. This variable has four categories: *born in the US; born in Puerto Rico, Guam, US Virgin Islands or the Northern Marianas; born abroad of American parent(s); US citizen by naturalization.* Each category is entered as an indicator in analyses.

Marital status. Marital status takes on five different values: *married; widowed; divorced; separated; never married.* Just as with educational attainment, indicators are included for each category.

Race. Individuals who reported only one were retained for analyses (this represented over 98% of the sample). Race is coded as: *white only; black only; American Indian, Alaska Native, Native Hawaiian or Pacific Islander; Other.* Indicators for each category are included in analyses.

Year of US entry. The final analytic data set includes only US citizens; however, some are citizens by birth and others through naturalization. Those who are citizens through naturalization entered the US at different times, and the length of time since arrival may correlate with labor market outcomes. The variable takes on five values: *N/A, born in US; 1919–1979; 1980–1989; 1990–1999; 2000–2010.* Just as with other categorical variables used here, each value has its own indicator in the analyses.

Class of worker. This variable refers to the general type of employer/ business the employee works for. The eight values include: *employee of a private for-profit business; employee of a private not-for-profit business; local government employee; state government employee; federal government employee; self-employed in own nonincorporated business; self-employed in own incorporated business; working without pay in family business or farm.* Indicators for each category are included in some analyses predicting annual wages.

Weeks worked in the past 12 months. This variable takes on six values: *50–52 weeks; 48–49; 40–47; 27–39; 14–26; less than 14 weeks.* Indicators for each category are included in some analyses predicting annual wages.

Statistical analyses

For each outcome (i.e. participation, employment and annual wages), a baseline/unconditional random-intercepts model was estimated with two levels – Level 1 was the individual level and Level 2 was the PUMA code level (a PUMA is an area with a population of 100,000+). The baseline model has a Level-2 random error because, for example, some locations may have generally high wages, while others may have generally lower wages. Model 1 predicts outcome y for individual i in PUMA j as a function of whether the individual is bilingual (vs monolingual), allowing for individual (ε) and PUMA (v) random errors:

$$y_{ij} = \alpha + \beta bil_{ij} + \varepsilon_{ij} + v_j$$

Thus, β in Model 1 is the average labor market outcome MD between bilinguals and monolinguals after accounting for random variation across locations. Model 2 builds on Model 1 to include covariates for age, race and educational attainment. This model intends to account for demographic differences (other than language) that may vary between bilingual and monolingual individuals and that may be related to labor market outcomes. Model 3 adds covariates for year of US entry,[4] and (in the wage model only) class of worker and weeks employed in the past year. Where $\mathbf{X}$ is a vector of covariates (e.g. age, year of US entry), Models 2 and 3 take the general form of:

$$y_{ij} = \alpha + \beta bil_{ij} + \mathbf{X'_{ij}\Gamma} + \varepsilon_{ij} + v_j$$

Although Models 1–3 allow for random variation in outcomes across locations, they do not explore whether the bilingual–monolingual differentials vary systematically as a function of the characteristics of the locations. Model 4 changes this by exploring whether labor market differentials vary as a function of the concentration of Spanish speakers in the location. In Model 4, linear, quadratic and cubic terms for the proportion of Spanish speakers are added, as are the interactions of these terms with whether the individual is bilingual:

$$y_{ij} = \alpha + \beta bil_{ij} + \sum_k^3 [\pi_k sp_j^k + \phi_k (sp_j^k \times bil_{ij})] + \mathbf{X'_{ij}\Gamma} + \varepsilon_{ij} + v_j$$

Because the AMD is not reflected in a single coefficient in Model 4, the AMD is calculated by integration following the regression analysis. In addition, MDs are calculated for each proportion of Spanish speakers, thereby demonstrating the levels of Spanish speaker concentrations where significant differentials exist.[5]

Results

Descriptive statistics and simple differences

Table 4.1 presents results separately by gender. But it is worth noting that there are disproportionately more bilinguals among females than

Table 4.1 Descriptive statistics

Variable	Male				Female			
	Bilingual (n=143,255)	Monolingual (n=93,454)	Std. Diff.	p value	Bilingual (n=152,874)	Monolingual (n=93,749)	Std. Diff.	p value
In labor market	0.78	0.79	-0.02	<0.0001	0.71	0.71	0.00	0.6771
Employed (if in LM)	0.91	0.90	0.04	<0.0001	0.92	0.92	0.00	0.4439
Logged annual wages (if employed)	10.37	10.42	-0.05	<0.0001	10.08	10.09	-0.00	0.3887
	(0.91)	(0.95)			(0.93)	(0.97)		
Prop. PUMA Spanish speaking	0.34	0.22	0.52	<0.0001	0.34	0.22	0.52	<0.0001
	(0.24)	(0.19)			(0.24)	(0.19)		
Age	40.67	39.76	0.06	<0.0001	41.72	40.69	0.07	<0.0001
	(14.24)	(13.83)			(14.23)	(13.85)		
Educational attainment				<0.0001				<0.0001
Less than high school diploma	0.22	0.18	0.11		0.18	0.14	0.09	
High school diploma	0.33	0.34	-0.02		0.31	0.32	-0.02	
Some college or AA	0.28	0.31	-0.05		0.32	0.34	-0.03	
Bachelor's degree	0.11	0.12	-0.04		0.13	0.14	-0.02	
Master's, professional or PhD	0.06	0.06	0.00		0.07	0.06	0.01	
Marital status				<0.0001				<0.0001
Married	0.55	0.49	0.11		0.55	0.52	0.06	
Widowed	0.01	0.01	-0.01		0.04	0.03	0.02	
Divorced	0.09	0.10	-0.03		0.13	0.13	0.00	
Separated	0.03	0.02	0.03		0.04	0.03	0.05	
Never married	0.32	0.37	-0.10		0.24	0.28	-0.09	

Race			<0.0001				<0.0001
White	0.63	0.69	-0.13		0.64	0.70	-0.13
Black	0.01	0.03	-0.11		0.02	0.03	-0.10
Other	0.35	0.25	0.21		0.33	0.24	0.21
American Indian/Alaska Native/ Native Hawaiian/ Pacific Islander	0.01	0.03	-0.13		0.01	0.03	-0.15
Year of US entry			<0.0001				<0.0001
N/A – born in US	0.68	0.91	-0.58		0.67	0.91	-0.59
1919–1979	0.16	0.05	0.33		0.17	0.05	0.35
1980–1989	0.09	0.02	0.30		0.09	0.02	0.29
1990–1999	0.05	0.01	0.23		0.05	0.01	0.23
2000–2010	0.02	0.00	0.12		0.02	0.00	0.12
Citizenship process			<0.0001				<0.0001
Born in US	0.65	0.91	-0.64		0.66	0.92	-0.64
Born Puerto Rico/ Guam/ US Virgin Islands/ North Marianas	0.06	0.02	0.23		0.07	0.01	0.25
Born abroad of American parents	0.01	0.01	0.00		0.01	0.01	0.00
Citizen by naturalization	0.27	0.06	0.57		0.26	0.05	0.56
Class of worker (if employed)			<0.0001				<0.0001
Private for-profit company	0.75	0.75	-0.01		0.65	0.67	-0.05
Private not-for-profit company	0.04	0.04	0.00		0.09	0.09	0.00
Local government	0.08	0.08	0.01		0.14	0.12	0.07
State government	0.04	0.04	-0.01		0.06	0.06	0.01

(Continued)

Table 4.1 (Continued)

Variable	Male				Female			
	Bilingual (n=143,255)	Monolingual (n=93,454)	Std. Diff.	p value	Bilingual (n=152,874)	Monolingual (n=93,749)	Std. Diff.	p value
Federal government	0.04	0.04	0.00		0.03	0.03	-0.01	
Self-employed, not incorporated	0.00	0.01	-0.02		0.00	0.00	-0.02	
Self-employed, incorporated	0.04	0.04	0.03		0.02	0.02	0.02	
Family business, without pay	0.00	0.00	0.01		0.00	0.00	-0.01	
Weeks worked in the past 12 months (if employed)				<0.0001				0.0017
50–52	0.84	0.83	0.02		0.79	0.78	0.02	
48–49	0.03	0.03	-0.01		0.03	0.03	0.00	
40–47	0.04	0.05	-0.02		0.06	0.06	-0.01	
27–39	0.04	0.04	-0.02		0.05	0.05	-0.02	
14–26	0.03	0.03	0.00		0.04	0.03	0.00	
Less than 14	0.03	0.03	0.02		0.03	0.03	-0.01	

among males – this can be seen by simply comparing the sample sizes in the top row. This may also suggest that the focus of prior literature on only *male* bilingual–monolingual labor market differences is missing a large piece of the puzzle, namely, differences among *females*, the disproportionate share of bilinguals in this sample. Importantly, basic descriptive statistics also suggest that the labor market differences observed between bilingual and monolingual males may not hold for females. For example, 78% and 79% of bilingual and monolingual civilian males participate in the labor market, respectively (a difference of 0.02 SDs favoring monolingual males, $p < 0.0001$); but there is no difference among females, with 71% of both groups participating in the labor market ($p = 0.68$).

Although the labor market outcome differences (shown at the top of Table 4.1) are relatively small for both males and females, there are larger differences between bilinguals and monolinguals in terms of their demographic characteristics in the lower portion of the table. Most notably, among both males and females, the mean percentage of Spanish speakers in the PUMA of bilinguals is 34%, while the mean percentage is 22% for monolinguals – this translates into a difference of 0.52 SDs (ps < 0.0001). This suggests two things: (1) bilinguals and monolinguals live in areas that are linguistically very different; and (2) given this large difference, the concentration of Spanish speakers in an area may be an important dimension to explore as a predictor of bilingual–monolingual labor market differences.

Small but significant differences between bilinguals and monolinguals exist in terms of other variables. Bilinguals are on average one year older, less likely to have a high school diploma, more likely to be married and more likely to racially identify as 'other' (i.e. not one of the listed race categories, such as white or black, even though a separate question asks about Hispanic ethnicity). But the biggest difference between bilinguals and monolinguals concerns nativity ($p \leq 0.0001$): about 68% of bilinguals and 91% of monolinguals were born in the US. Importantly, recall that these numbers reflect Hispanic US citizens, and the proportions not born in the US would be higher if noncitizens were included.

Average marginal differentials

We now turn to the results of the statistical analyses that account for the clustering of individuals in locations (i.e. PUMAs) and account for the random variation in outcomes across these locations.

Civilian labor market participation. Model 1 in Table 4.2 demonstrates that bilingual and monolingual males participated in the labor market at statistically similar rates before accounting for demographic differences. Model 2 accounts for differences in age, educational attainment, marital status, citizenship process and race, and finds that 1.1% more monolingual

Table 4.2 Average within-PUMA, bilingual–monolingual labor market differences, by gender, outcome and model

	Male			Female		
	Model 1	Model 2	Model 3	Model 1	Model 2	Model 3
Civilian labor market participation						
Estimate	-0.004	-0.011***	-0.011***	0.010***	0.019***	0.019***
Standard error	(0.003)	(0.003)	(0.003)	(0.003)	(0.002)	(0.002)
Std. difference	-0.011	-0.030	-0.030	0.023	0.044	0.044
Employment (if in the civilian labor market)						
Estimate	0.008***	0.003	0.002	0.001	-0.001	-0.001
Standard error	(0.001)	(0.002)	(0.002)	(0.002)	(0.002)	(0.002)
Std. difference	0.031	0.012	0.008	0.004	-0.004	-0.004
Logged annual wages (if employed)						
Estimate	-0.022***	-0.025***	-0.020***	-0.019***	-0.001	0.000
Standard error	(0.005)	(0.004)	(0.004)	(0.006)	(0.005)	(0.004)
Std. difference	-0.027	-0.031	-0.025	-0.022	-0.001	0.000
Models also include:						
Age (lin., quad., cubed)		X	X		X	X
Educational attainment		X	X		X	X
Marital status		X	X		X	X
Race		X	X		X	X
Citizenship process		X	X		X	X
Year of US entry			X			X
Class of worker[1]			X			X
Weeks worked[1]			X			X

***p<0.001.

[1]Only included in models predicting logged annual wages.

Note: Table presents only the bilingual–monolingual average marginal differential, but the Appendix tables present all coefficient estimates.

than bilingual males participated in the labor market ($p < 0.001$). When differences in year of entry are also taken into account in Model 3, the participation gap remains the same. This 1.1% difference in participation amounts to a 0.03 SD within PUMAs, which is shown in the row labeled 'Std. difference'.[6]

Among females, 1% more bilinguals than monolinguals participate in the labor market in the unconditional model ($p < 0.001$). This participation gap grows to about 2% in Models 2 and 3 ($ps < 0.001$), and this translates into a within-PUMA standardized difference of 0.044 SDs.

Employment. Bearing in mind that participating in the labor market includes both employed and unemployed outcomes, we now turn to the employment rates *among* civilian labor market participants. Model 1 of Table 4.2 demonstrates that male bilinguals were significantly more likely to be employed (vs unemployed) than monolingual males, but this significant difference goes away once other factors are accounted for in Models 2 and 3. There are no significant differences in employment rates among females.

Annual wage (natural log). Among employed males with nonzero annual wages, bilingual males earn about 2% less than monolingual males – this is consistent across Models 1–3 ($ps < 0.001$). However, there is no evidence of a wage gap among observationally similar bilingual and monolingual females. For example, Model 3 shows that there is no average discrepancy in wages between bilingual and monolingual, conditional on age, educational attainment, marital status, race, citizenship process, year of US entry, class of worker and number of weeks worked in the past year.

Marginal differentials throughout the range of Spanish speaker concentrations

The results presented above come from models that do not consider variation in outcomes systematically related to the concentration of Spanish speakers in a location. We now review the results of models that explore these systematic differences.

Civilian labor market participation. Panel A of Figure 4.1 shows that after accounting for all factors included in Model 3, bilingual–monolingual labor market participation gaps are strongly related to the concentration of Spanish speakers in the area. At lower concentrations of Spanish speakers, bilinguals are less likely than monolinguals to participate; but at higher concentrations, bilinguals are more likely to participate. For example, when 10% of the PUMA is Spanish speaking, about 2.5% more monolingual than bilingual males participate, other factors held constant; when 70% of the PUMA is Spanish speaking, about 2.5% more bilingual than monolingual males participate. Each of these concentration-specific MDs is statistically significant (i.e. $p < 0.05$), as can be seen in the graphic showing that the 95% confidence interval does not contain zero.

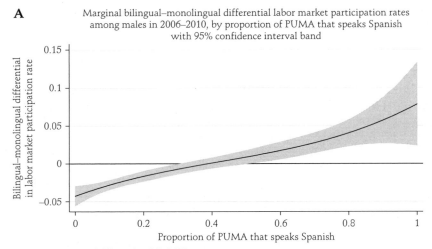

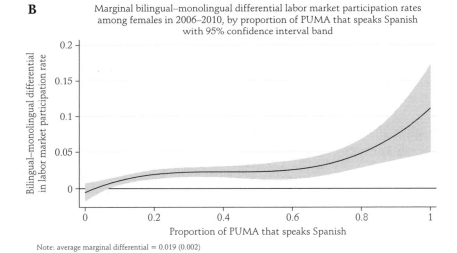

Figure 4.1 Labor market participation rate bilingual–monolingual marginal differences by proportion of Spanish speakers in PUMA, for males (Panel A) and females (Panel B). 95% CIs appear in gray bands

For females (Panel B), the concentration of Spanish speakers is also a significant predictor of the participation gap, but there are some distinct differences from the male results: At no Spanish speaker concentration level do monolingual females participate significantly more than bilingual females. That is, at the lowest levels, there is no significant difference in participation rates. When 30% of the PUMA is Spanish speaking, about 2.5% more bilinguals than monolinguals participate ($p < 0.05$), other factors held constant. At the highest concentration of Spanish speakers, about 10% more bilinguals than monolinguals participate ($p < 0.05$). What is also different between the male and female patterns is that the relationship between the bilingual–monolingual MDs for males is relatively linear (i.e. at every higher concentration level, the estimated MD is more positive than at the concentration level just below); but among females, there is a large range of the concentration distribution (from about 25% to 60%) where the bilingual–monolingual MDs remain relatively constant at about 2.5% more bilinguals than monolinguals participating. This may suggest that male bilinguals are somewhat more sensitive to the concentration of Spanish speakers in the area, at least in the middle range of Spanish-speaking concentrations.

Employment. Turning to the employment rate bilingual–monolingual MDs for males in Panel A of Figure 4.2, there is no evidence that employment rate MDs vary significantly by concentration of Spanish speakers for males. For females (Panel B), there is some evidence that about 1% more monolingual than bilingual females are employed when the concentration of Spanish speakers is low (around 0%–15%). Between concentrations of 40%–55% Spanish speakers, this disparity reverses, and about 1% more bilingual than monolingual females are employed. At all other concentration levels, there is no significant difference.

Annual wage (natural log). As shown in Panel A of Figure 4.3, significant wage disparities among males are found when the concentration of Spanish speakers is between 5% and 50%. In this range, monolinguals report higher wages, with the peak disparity found at about 25% Spanish speakers; at this concentration level, monolinguals earn about 3% more annually, other factors held constant. No significant wage disparities are found at concentrations above 50% Spanish speakers.

For females (Panel B of Figure 4.3), bilinguals earn significantly lower wages when the concentration of Spanish speakers is between 20% and 55%. The peak of the female disparity is found at around 40% Spanish speakers, where monolinguals earn about 2.5% more annually. No significant disparities are found at concentrations above 60%, but significant disparities favoring bilinguals are found at Spanish speaker concentrations below 10%.

Discussion

Prior research has found that bilingual males earn equal or lower wages than English monolingual males do (e.g. Chiswick & Miller, 2002; Fry & Lowell, 2003; Shin & Alba, 2009). Importantly, this prior literature focused exclusively on wages and did not examine other labor market outcomes

A

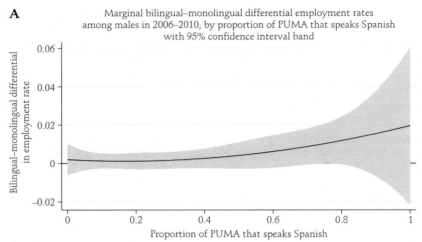

Note: average marginal differential = 0.003 (0.002)

B

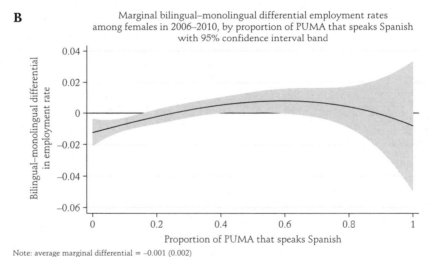

Note: average marginal differential = –0.001 (0.002)

Figure 4.2 Employment rate bilingual–monolingual marginal differences by proportion of Spanish speakers in PUMA, for males (Panel A) and females (Panel B). 95% CIs appear in gray bands

(e.g. participation in the labor market, employment). Moreover, the literature largely ignored females' labor market outcomes (but see Shin & Alba, 2009). Examining a wider variety of labor market outcomes for both males and females, this chapter presents evidence that bilingual–monolingual labor market disparities are on average very small or practically nonexistent.

A

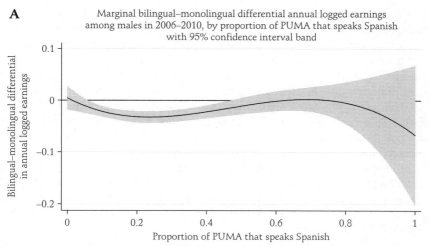

Marginal bilingual–monolingual differential annual logged earnings among males in 2006–2010, by proportion of PUMA that speaks Spanish with 95% confidence interval band

Note: average marginal differential = –0.019 (0.004)

B

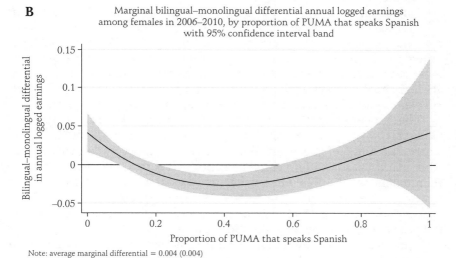

Marginal bilingual–monolingual differential annual logged earnings among females in 2006–2010, by proportion of PUMA that speaks Spanish with 95% confidence interval band

Note: average marginal differential = 0.004 (0.004)

Figure 4.3 Logged annual wages bilingual–monolingual marginal differences by proportion of Spanish speakers in PUMA, for males (Panel A) and females (Panel B). 95% CIs appear in gray bands

Consistent with prior studies in the US that explored bilingual–monolingual wage differences among Hispanic males, the current study finds evidence that male bilinguals earn slightly lower wages, other factors held constant. In the current study, bilingual Hispanic males earned 2% lower wages than observationally similar monolingual Hispanic males, and there was no evidence of a wage gap between observationally similar bilingual and monolingual Hispanic females. These findings lie somewhere in the middle of prior studies. For example, Shin and Alba (2009) found a gap of about 5.6% (favoring monolinguals) among Mexican males and females.[7] Fry and Lowell (2003) found no gap among Hispanic males, and they did not examine the female bilingual–monolingual wage differential.

The present study also finds some evidence that bilingual males participate in the labor market at slightly lower rates. However, this and the male wage gap are the extent to which there is any evidence of lower average bilingual outcomes once other factors are taken into account. That is, on average bilingual and monolingual males are employed at the same rates, and there is no average difference between bilingual and monolingual females in employment rates or in annual wages. Importantly, there are positive correlates of bilingualism: there is significant evidence that female bilinguals participate in the labor market at higher rates than do observationally similar monolingual females; this difference is the largest standardized difference found in this study (0.044 SDs).

One should note that all average bilingual–monolingual MDs found in this chapter – whether for males or females, and regardless of which outcome was examined – were extremely small. Moreover, most of these differences were not statistically significant, even with sample sizes of more than 130,000 individuals. Thus, the most consistent finding across all of the analyses presented in Table 4.2 is that bilingual and monolingual Hispanic individuals have remarkably similar labor market outcomes.

The present study found virtually no evidence of lower outcomes for bilinguals when the concentration of Spanish speakers exceeded 50%, a point Chapters 5 and 6 of this volume investigate further. In fact, in the case of labor market participation, bilingual males participated significantly more than monolingual males when the concentration was above 50%. Among females, the participation gap favored bilinguals throughout most of the concentration distribution, and the gap increasingly favored bilinguals as the percentage of Spanish speakers in the area neared 100%.

These results may have implications for whether the loss of bilingualism is inevitable. Some authors have concluded that because there are no obvious wage returns to bilingualism in the US and because bilingualism is difficult to maintain across generations, assimilation will occur (see, e.g. Fry & Lowell, 2003; Shin & Alba, 2009). However, this research has ignored an important piece of the puzzle: the concentration of individuals in a location speaking a non-English language with respect to the total labor market bundle, not just wages. If the labor market differentials overall favor bilinguals in these locations and if a heritage language is easier to maintain in the presence of many heritage language speakers, then perhaps the loss of bilingualism is not inevitable. (Chapters 9–11 of this volume look toward the future in examining this question of labor market differentials for the younger generation.) Although the question of assimilation cannot be answered with these cross-sectional data, we can explore whether or not the labor market disparities differ depending on the concentration of Spanish speakers in the location, which may be an important factor in assimilation.

We saw that the higher participation rates for bilinguals at higher concentrations of Spanish speakers are not accompanied by any marked decrements in employment rates or wages. Thus, observationally similar bilinguals fared *better* overall than monolinguals at these higher concentrations – concentrations where it is also presumably easier to maintain bilingualism. The wage differential component of this labor market experience is largely consistent with prior studies (e.g. Fry & Lowell, 2003; Shin & Alba, 2009; but see Chiswick & Miller, 2002). However, and importantly, those prior studies did not explore participation differentials and thus they may have overlooked significant relationships between bilingual participation differentials and Spanish speaker concentrations.

The present research suggests that scholars should consider a broader set of labor market outcomes, expanding beyond the traditional focus on wages. Although the current study, as well as prior research, finds that bilingual individuals in the US do not earn more than monolingual individuals once other factors are taken into account, the current study suggests that a singular focus on wages may miss important differences between bilinguals and monolinguals in participation and employment rates. Importantly, these analyses do not suggest any 'bilingual advantage' in participation in a causal sense – just as they do not suggest a male 'bilingual disadvantage' in wages in a causal sense – but rather they are a reflection of the existing labor market differences between bilingual and monolingual Hispanic US citizens not currently enrolled in school. Moreover, as with other studies using census-based data, the estimates in this study are based on self-reported data and should be interpreted cautiously. Nevertheless, the participation differentials – and, in particular, participation with respect to the interaction between bilingualism and the concentration of Spanish speakers – point to a new area for researchers to explore. For example, why do we see higher participation rates among female bilinguals? Does speaking two languages lead women to perceive that they have a more marketable skill set, and thus to participate in the labor market more, or do other circumstances in these women's lives compel them to seek out employment opportunities at higher rates? While these questions remain unanswered, one thing is clear in this study: among females, bilingualism is not associated with lower labor market outcomes, and in fact may be associated with positive outcomes.

Notes

(1)   The current study uses data from the American Community Surveys of 2006 to 2010, which are 1% samples of the population collected by the US Census Bureau each year.

(2)   But note that a comparable, more recent data set, the 2003 National Assessment of Adult Literacy (NAAL) exists.

(3)   The group 'civilian employed, with a job but not at work' accounts for less than 2% of all individuals. Individuals in this group report a variety of occupations, including occupations characterized by seasonal work such as teachers (who are not at work during the summer, if the survey is administered during the summer) or occasional work such as freight truck drivers. Other individuals in this group may be on temporary leave from their jobs but do not consider themselves to be unemployed.

(4)   I added year of US entry because I suspected that recent immigrants who self-identify as speaking English 'very well' may not be as well versed in American colloquialisms and that this may affect their labor market outcomes. In addition, recent immigrants may not navigate the labor market as well as individuals who have lived in the US for longer periods. Interestingly, it turns out that conditioning on year of US entry results in reducing the bilingual–monolingual disparity (which *favored* bilinguals) because bilinguals are more likely to be foreign-born and foreign-born individuals participate in the labor market at higher rates and have higher levels of employment among those in the labor market.

(5)   Without estimating MDs, this would be difficult to see because the MD is a cubic function of the concentration of Spanish speakers. The margins command in Stata was used to calculate all MDs and AMDs.

(6)   This standardized difference is calculated by dividing the bilingual–monolingual estimate by the standard deviation of the Level-1 residual in the unconditional model (i.e. Model 1).

(7)   Although there are many similarities between Shin and Alba's (2009) analyses and the analyses in this chapter (e.g. age 25–64 in Shin and Alba, and 24–64 here; accounting for location factors to some extent), there is one noticeable difference that may explain the difference in results. Shin and Alba include only 1.5-generation individuals and those who are born in the US. My analyses are limited to US citizens. If bilingual individuals who immigrated later in life and became naturalized US citizens earn higher wages, then this could partially explain why the wage gap is smaller here. Shin and Alba also combine males and females into a single analysis, and this could also partially explain the difference in results.

References

Bialystok, E. (2001) *Bilingualism in Development: Language, Literacy, and Cognition.* Cambridge: Cambridge University Press.

Bialystok, E., Craik, F.I., Klein, R. and Viswanathan, M. (2004) Bilingualism, aging, and cognitive control: Evidence from the Simon task. *Psychology and Aging* 19 (2), 290–303.

Chiswick, B.R. and Miller, P.W. (2002) Immigrant earnings: Linguistic concentrations and the business cycle. *Journal of Population Economics* 15 (1), 31–57.

Chiswick, B.R. and Miller, P.W. (2008) Why is the payoff to schooling smaller for immigrants? *Labour Economics* 15 (6), 1317–1340.

Chiswick, B.R. and Miller, P.W. (2010) Occupational language requirements and the value of English in the U.S. labor market. *Journal of Population Economics* 23 (1), 353–372.

Damm, A.P. (2009) Ethnic enclaves and immigrant labor market outcomes: Quasi-experimental evidence. *Journal of Labor Economics* 27 (2), 281–314.

Edin, P.-A., Fredriksson, P. and Åslund, O. (2003) Ethnic enclaves and the economic success of immigrants—Evidence from a natural experiment. *Quarterly Journal of Economics* 118 (1), 329–357.

Fry, L. and Lowell, B.L. (2003) The value of bilingualism in the U.S. labor market. *Industrial and Labor Relations Review* 57 (1), 128–140.

Ginsburgh, V.A. and Prieto-Rodriguez, J. (2011) Returns to foreign languages of native workers in the European Union. *Industrial and Labor Relations Review* 64 (3), 599–618.

McManus, W.S. (1990) Labor market effects of language enclaves: Hispanic men in the United States. *Journal of Human Resources* 25 (2), 228–252.

Portes, A. and Rumbaut, R. (2001) *Legacies: The Story of the Immigrant Second Generation.* Berkeley, CA: University of California Press.

Shin, H.-J. and Alba, R. (2009) The economic value of bilingualism for Asians and Hispanics. *Sociological Forum* 24 (2), 254–275.

Appendix

Table A1 In civilian labor market

	Male			Female		
	Model 1	Model 2	Model 3	Model 1	Model 2	Model 3
Bilingual	-0.004	-0.011***	-0.011***	0.010***	0.019***	0.019***
	(0.003)	(0.003)	(0.003)	(0.003)	(0.002)	(0.002)
Standardized difference	*-0.011*	*-0.030*	*-0.030*	*0.023*	*0.044*	*0.044*
Age		-0.098***	-0.098***		-0.082***	-0.082***
		(0.004)	(0.004)		(0.004)	(0.004)
Age squared		0.003***	0.003***		0.002***	0.002***
		0.000	0.000		0.000	0.000
Age cubed		-0.000***	-0.000***		-0.000***	-0.000***
		0.000	0.000		0.000	0.000
2007		-0.006*	-0.006*		0.000	0.000
		(0.003)	(0.003)		(0.003)	(0.003)
2008		0.021***	0.020***		0.025***	0.025***
		(0.003)	(0.003)		(0.003)	(0.003)
2009		0.014***	0.014***		0.027***	0.027***
		(0.003)	(0.003)		(0.003)	(0.003)
2010		0.013***	0.013***		0.022***	0.023***
		(0.003)	(0.003)		(0.003)	(0.003)
HS diploma		0.108***	0.108***		0.165***	0.165***
		(0.004)	(0.004)		(0.004)	(0.004)
Some college		0.158***	0.158***		0.237***	0.237***
		(0.004)	(0.004)		(0.004)	(0.004)

Bachelor's	0.204***	0.204***	0.285***	0.285***
	(0.005)	(0.005)	(0.004)	(0.004)
Master's, professional, PhD	0.218***	0.218***	0.333***	0.333***
	(0.005)	(0.005)	(0.005)	(0.005)
Black	−0.080***	−0.080***	−0.007	−0.007
	(0.008)	(0.008)	(0.006)	(0.006)
Other	−0.005	−0.005	0.009***	0.009***
	(0.003)	(0.003)	(0.002)	(0.002)
Native American/Alaska Native/Native Hawaiian/Pacific Islander	−0.021**	−0.021**	−0.019**	−0.019**
	(0.006)	(0.006)	(0.007)	(0.007)
Born in Puerto Rico/Guam/US Virgin Islands/North Marianas	−0.026***	−0.028***	−0.039***	−0.032***
	(0.005)	(0.005)	(0.005)	(0.005)
Born abroad of American parents	0.019**	0.017**	−0.012	−0.008
	(0.006)	(0.007)	(0.008)	(0.008)
Naturalized	0.064***	0.062***	0.028***	0.032***
	(0.003)	(0.004)	(0.003)	(0.003)
Married	0.140***	0.140***	−0.061***	−0.061***
	(0.004)	(0.004)	(0.003)	(0.003)
Widowed	−0.004	−0.004	−0.052***	−0.051***
	(0.012)	(0.012)	(0.007)	(0.007)
Divorced	0.050***	0.050***	0.042***	0.042***
	(0.004)	(0.004)	(0.003)	(0.003)

(Continued)

Table A1 (Continued)

	Male			Female		
	Model 1	Model 2	Model 3	Model 1	Model 2	Model 3
Separated		0.022***	0.022***		0.005	0.005
		(0.006)	(0.006)		(0.005)	(0.005)
US entry: 2000–2010			−0.001			−0.043***
			(0.007)			(0.009)
US entry: 1990–1999			0.004			−0.023***
			(0.004)			(0.005)
US entry: 1980–1989			0.007			0.005
			(0.004)			(0.004)
Constant	0.830***	1.877***	1.879***	0.746***	1.534***	1.533***
	(0.003)	(0.052)	(0.052)	(0.002)	(0.058)	(0.058)
Level-1 error						
Ln(sd_epsilon)	−1.014***	−1.072***	−1.072***	−0.842***	−0.888***	−0.888***
	(0.007)	(0.007)	(0.007)	(0.003)	(0.003)	(0.003)
Level-2 error						
Ln(sd_upsilon)	−2.194***	−2.387***	−2.387***	−2.976***	−3.344***	−3.344***
	(0.039)	(0.046)	(0.046)	(0.039)	(0.065)	(0.065)
Sample size	192,840	192,840	192,840	204,616	204,616	204,616
No. of PUMAs	2,069	2,069	2,069	2,069	2,069	2,069

*p<0.05; **p<0.01; ***p<0.001.

Table A2 Employment

	Male			Female		
	Model 1	Model 2	Model 3	Model 1	Model 2	Model 3
Bilingual	0.008***	0.003	0.002	0.001	-0.001	-0.001
	(0.001)	(0.002)	(0.002)	(0.002)	(0.002)	(0.002)
Standardized difference	*0.031*	*0.012*	*0.008*	*0.004*	*-0.004*	*-0.004*
Age		0.013***	0.012***		0.018***	0.018***
		(0.003)	(0.003)		(0.003)	(0.003)
Age squared		-0.000***	-0.000***		-0.000***	-0.000***
		0.000	0.000		0.000	0.000
Age cubed		0.000**	0.000**		0.000***	0.000***
		0.000	0.000		0.000	0.000
2007		0.000	-0.001		0.005*	0.005*
		(0.002)	(0.002)		(0.002)	(0.002)
2008		-0.001	-0.001		0.005*	0.005*
		(0.002)	(0.002)		(0.002)	(0.002)
2009		-0.043***	-0.043***		-0.022***	-0.022***
		(0.002)	(0.002)		(0.002)	(0.002)
2010		-0.052***	-0.052***		-0.033***	-0.033***
		(0.002)	(0.002)		(0.002)	(0.002)
HS diploma		0.046***	0.046***		0.060***	0.060***
		(0.003)	(0.003)		(0.003)	(0.003)
Some college		0.069***	0.069***		0.074***	0.074***
		(0.003)	(0.003)		(0.003)	(0.003)

(Continued)

Table A2 (Continued)

	Male			Female		
	Model 1	Model 2	Model 3	Model 1	Model 2	Model 3
Bachelor's		0.088***	0.088***		0.098***	0.098***
		(0.003)	(0.003)		(0.003)	(0.003)
Master's, professional, PhD		0.095***	0.095***		0.109***	0.109***
		(0.003)	(0.003)		(0.003)	(0.003)
Black		-0.029***	-0.029***		-0.033***	-0.033***
		(0.006)	(0.006)		(0.005)	(0.005)
Other		0.001	0.001		0.001	0.001
		(0.001)	(0.001)		(0.002)	(0.002)
Native American/Alaska Native/ Native Hawaiian/Pacific Islander		-0.019***	-0.019***		-0.020***	-0.020***
		(0.005)	(0.005)		(0.005)	(0.005)
Born in Puerto Rico/Guam/US Virgin Islands/North Marianas		-0.004	-0.009*		-0.011**	-0.010**
		(0.005)	(0.005)		(0.005)	(0.004)
Born abroad of American parents		0.011*	0.007		0.007	0.007
		(0.005)	(0.005)		(0.005)	(0.006)
Naturalized		0.020***	0.016***		0.011***	0.011***
		(0.002)	(0.002)		(0.002)	(0.002)
Married		0.064***	0.064***		0.018***	0.018***
		(0.002)	(0.002)		(0.002)	(0.002)
Widowed		0.041***	0.041***		0.004	0.004
		(0.010)	(0.010)		(0.005)	(0.005)

Divorced		0.021***	0.021***		0.006*	0.006*
		(0.003)	(0.003)		(0.002)	(0.002)
Separated		0.004	0.004		-0.015***	-0.015***
		(0.006)	(0.006)		(0.004)	(0.004)
US entry: 2000–2010			0.011*		-0.018**	
			(0.006)		(0.007)	
US entry: 1990–1999			0.007*		0.003	
			(0.003)		(0.003)	
US entry: 1980–1989			0.009***		0.002	
			(0.003)		(0.003)	
Constant	0.921***	0.654***	0.657***	0.929***	0.578***	0.578***
	(0.001)	(0.042)	(0.042)	(0.001)	(0.044)	(0.044)
Level-1 error						
Ln(sd_epsilon)	-1.344***	-1.362***	-1.362***	-1.366***	-1.376***	-1.376***
	(0.007)	(0.007)	(0.007)	(0.006)	(0.006)	(0.006)
Level-2 error						
Ln(sd_upsilon)	-3.639***	-3.883***	-3.886***	-3.889***	-4.142***	-4.141***
	(0.049)	(0.057)	(0.058)	(0.059)	(0.070)	(0.070)
Sample size	159,604	159,604	159,604	153,205	153,205	153,205
No. of PUMAs	2,067	2,067	2,067	2,064	2,064	2,064

*p<0.05; **p<0.01; ***p<0.001.

Table A3 Logged annual wage

	Male			Female		
	Model 1	Model 2	Model 3	Model 1	Model 2	Model 3
Bilingual	-0.022***	-0.025***	-0.020***	-0.019***	-0.001	0.000
	(0.005)	(0.004)	(0.004)	(0.006)	(0.005)	(0.004)
	-0.027	*-0.031*	*-0.025*	*-0.022*	*-0.001*	*0.000*
Age		0.126***	0.112***		0.135***	0.110***
		(0.010)	(0.009)		(0.011)	(0.009)
Age squared		-0.002***	-0.002***		-0.002***	-0.002***
		0.000	0.000		0.000	0.000
Age cubed		0.000***	0.000***		0.000***	0.000***
		0.000	0.000		0.000	0.000
2007		0.052***	0.053***		0.050***	0.052***
		(0.006)	(0.006)		(0.007)	(0.006)
2008		0.058***	0.025***		0.064***	0.004
		(0.006)	(0.006)		(0.007)	(0.006)
2009		0.061***	0.031***		0.074***	0.007
		(0.007)	(0.006)		(0.007)	(0.006)
2010		0.020**	0.008		0.078***	0.012
		(0.007)	(0.006)		(0.007)	(0.006)
HS diploma		0.211***	0.162***		0.311***	0.233***
		(0.007)	(0.006)		(0.009)	(0.007)
Some college		0.415***	0.342***		0.521***	0.430***
		(0.007)	(0.006)		(0.009)	(0.008)
Bachelor's		0.710***	0.628***		0.863***	0.774***

	(1)	(2)	(3)	(4)
	(0.009)	(0.008)	(0.011)	(0.010)
Master's, professional, PhD	0.980***	0.915***	1.134***	1.060***
	(0.011)	(0.011)	(0.012)	(0.011)
Black	-0.140***	-0.103***	-0.02	-0.015
	(0.017)	(0.014)	(0.016)	(0.013)
Other	-0.028***	-0.026***	-0.017**	-0.023***
	(0.005)	(0.004)	(0.005)	(0.004)
Native American/Alaska Native/Native Hawaiian/Pacific Islander	-0.070***	-0.053***	-0.079***	-0.027*
	(0.014)	(0.013)	(0.017)	(0.014)
Born in Puerto Rico/Guam/US Virgin Islands/North Marianas	-0.035***	0.007	-0.039***	0.009
	(0.010)	(0.009)	(0.011)	(0.010)
Born abroad of American parents	0.028	0.050***	-0.022	0.024
	(0.016)	(0.014)	(0.022)	(0.018)
Naturalized	0.021***	0.053***	-0.023***	0.016*
	(0.005)	(0.006)	(0.006)	(0.006)
Married	0.337***	0.273***	-0.002	0.035***
	(0.006)	(0.005)	(0.006)	(0.005)
Widowed	0.101***	0.067*	-0.090***	-0.048***
	(0.030)	(0.027)	(0.017)	(0.014)
Divorced	0.147***	0.126***	0.062***	0.073***
	(0.009)	(0.007)	(0.008)	(0.006)
Separated	0.082***	0.082***	-0.124***	-0.071***
	(0.006)	(0.007)	(0.008)	(0.006)

(Continued)

Table A3 (Continued)

	Male			Female		
	Model 1	Model 2	Model 3	Model 1	Model 2	Model 3
		(0.015)	(0.013)		(0.012)	(0.009)
US entry: 2000–2010			-0.151***			-0.174***
			(0.015)			(0.018)
US entry: 1990–1999			-0.094***			-0.108***
			(0.010)			(0.011)
US entry: 1980–1989			-0.072***			-0.063***
			(0.008)			(0.008)
COW: Employee of not-for-profit			-0.132***			-0.060***
			(0.009)			(0.007)
COW: Employee of local government			0.019*			-0.018**
			(0.008)			(0.006)
COW: Employee of state government			-0.023*			0.014
			(0.010)			(0.008)
COW: Employee of federal government			0.184***			0.301***
			(0.010)			(0.010)
COW: Self-employed, not incorporated			-0.595***			-0.927***
			(0.059)			(0.068)
COW: Self-employed, incorporated			0.054***			-0.048*
			(0.012)			(0.019)
COW: Working w/o pay, family bus./farm			-0.823***			-0.851***
			(0.127)			(0.096)
Weeks worked: 48–49			-0.113***			-0.160***
			(0.010)			(0.011)

Weeks worked: 40–47			-0.317***			-0.365***
			(0.010)			(0.008)
Weeks worked: 27–39			-0.701***			-0.748***
			(0.013)			(0.012)
Weeks worked: 14–26			-1.152***			-1.295***
			(0.018)			(0.016)
Weeks worked: <14			-2.150***			-2.345***
			(0.028)			(0.024)
Constant	10.544***	7.556***	8.040***	10.182***	7.166***	7.935***
	(0.007)	(0.127)	(0.114)	(0.007)	(0.143)	(0.114)
Level-2 error						
Ln(sd_upsilon)	-1.451***	-1.900***	-1.963***	-1.429***	-1.758***	-1.876***
	(0.022)	(0.027)	(0.026)	(0.023)	(0.026)	(0.024)
Level-1 error						
Ln(sd_epsilon)	-0.219***	-0.322***	-0.459***	-0.152***	-0.224***	-0.420***
	(0.004)	(0.005)	(0.004)	(0.004)	(0.005)	(0.004)
Sample size	139,371	139,371	139,371	136,677	136,677	136,677
No. of PUMAs	2,061	2,061	2,061	2,062	2,062	2,062

$*p<0.05; **p<0.01; ***p<0.001.$

5 The Occupational Location of Spanish–English Bilinguals in the New Information Economy: The Health and Criminal Justice Sectors in the US Borderlands with Mexico

Amado Alarcón, Antonio Di Paolo,
Josiah Heyman and
María Cristina Morales

Introduction

Globalization and the new information economy are having profound effects on communication across cultural and linguistic groups. Globalization implies more contact among different languages while linguistically coded information and knowledge have become crucial to productivity. Many service production processes are characterized by medium- to high-intensity communication. These processes have, of course, existed throughout modern history, but are rapidly increasing in scale and importance in the contemporary world, together with other forms of accumulation, management and transfer of information. This has been termed the 'new information economy', characterized by a more complex and intensive use of language in the workplace (Grin *et al.*, 2010: 47–50; Heller, 2003, 2010). In some ways these processes have brought about more carefully controlled and scripted communication, but in other ways they have required greater flexibility and sophistication of both oral and written messages. Given the importance of language in this new context, it is surprising that the role of bi- and multilingualism is so poorly studied.

In this context, extensive immigration (e.g. Spanish speakers to the United States) has increased the need for the provision of services in multiple languages. This chapter addresses three key issues: (1) What role does bilingualism play in occupational sectors that serve a multilingual public? (2) How frequently does workplace bilingualism occur? and (3) How is bilingualism distributed across occupational roles? In a workplace context, we hypothesize that bilingualism will occur in services provided to a multilingual public as a labor skill that adds productive value in the new information economy. In this study, we focus on Spanish–English bilingualism, specifically in the US borderlands with Mexico, a vast area of bilingual, binational individuals that allows us to look at bilingualism in perhaps its most intense form. Our framework, though not necessarily our findings, is relevant to many social and geographical sites of language contact.

Literature Review

Since the 1970s, researchers in United States reported a persistent, unidirectional, intergenerational transition from Spanish to English (Bills, 1989; Bills *et al.*, 1995; Mills, 2005; Rivera-Mills, 2001; Silva Corvalán & Lynch, 2009; Veltman, 1981). Some might argue that the loss of Spanish reflects the higher perceived market value of English; however, evidence has also emerged to counter this pattern, especially with reference to the instrumentality of bilingualism within the economy of the US Southwest (Villa & Villa, 2005). Spanish maintenance is no longer solely associated with the lowest economic returns (Jenkins, 2009), and even when it is, the association is weaker than it has been in the past (Martínez, 2009; McCullough & Jenkins, 2005; Mora *et al.*, 2006). Hidalgo (2001) identified a linguistic change favorable to Spanish –language shift reversal (LSR) – evident in the use of Spanish in the public domain as a consequence of several factors. Demographic attributes (growth of the Hispanic population) and market factors, particularly 'consumer demands for goods and services in the ancestral language, and the ready response to these demands on the part of providers of goods and service' (Hidalgo, 2001: 63), stand out as relevant factors.

Spanish can be viewed as a production resource in service interactions and sales, especially in roles dealing with an exclusively Spanish-speaking public (i.e. ethnic enclaves). Isolated Spanish-language markets (e.g. Spanish-language media) or technologically routed Spanish-only interactions (e.g. call centers, after a caller has requested Spanish) also exist. In such cases, bilingualism may not be necessary, although we have found that it adds to workplace flexibility (e.g. ability to shift from Spanish to English as needed) (Alarcón & Heyman, 2013). However, in service and sales situations open to the randomness customers, the service provider needs to be able to respond rapidly and flexibly with multiple language options. In many areas of the United States, this means responding competently in English and Spanish. An inability to communicate in the client's language of choice may result in delays, miscommunication and errors, frustration, lost business and reduced public services (such as public safety or health). Our prior work (Alarcón & Heyman, 2013) suggests that both bilingualism and multilingualism increase productivity, and monolingualism reduces it.

Bilingualism alone does not necessarily ensure a favorable status for Spanish speakers. According to Villa and Villa (2005):

> there may exist a certain resistance to promote a bilingual employee to management, as that employee is most valuable to the institution in a contact job. At the same time, there is relatively little need for bilingual managers, who tend not to be in direct contact with monolingual Spanish-speaking public (...) as there is little need for bilingual skills at administrative levels, the employment edge created by bilingual skills would appear to be nullified. (Villa & Villa, 2005: 181)

We are not altogether in agreement with the latter half of this statement, as our qualitative findings suggest that managers and professionals may also need Spanish skills, but it does accurately describe how bilingualism is *perceived* as a useful, but limited, workplace resource.

In the Taylorist–Fordist industrial context that began in the first quarter of the past century, work was typically manual and routine, incorporating immigrants relatively easily and with few training costs. By contrast, in the new economy where production is based on information and knowledge, workers' cultural and linguistic competencies are transformed into mechanisms of productivity and competition (Boutet, 2001; Castells, 1998; Cohen, 2009; Heller, 2003, 2010; Reich, 1991). Organizational tendencies toward more decentralized and independent structures, supported by new, more linguistically intensive technologies, imply a greater volume and complexity of linguistic exchanges involving a higher percentage of employees across different levels of organizational hierarchies (Charles & Marschan-Piekkari, 2002; O'Hara-Devereaux & Johansen, 1994). This combination of factors suggests that bilingualism may enhance workplace productivity in sectors of the new economy involving interactions between a multilingual workforce and a multilingual public that have not been channeled into one specific language by pre-arranged options (i.e. choosing a preferred language on a service call).

Studies investigating the economic value of Spanish in general and of bilingualism in particular focus on aggregate rates of return to language under the human capital approach. These studies struggle to explain why bilingualism in immigrant-receiving countries is associated with low, if not negative, rates of return and effects on wages (Chiswick, 2008; Cortina *et al.*, 2008: 1; Shin & Alba, 2009; Tubergen & Kalmijn, 2009). In addition, these studies do not investigate language use and change; in our case, the specific communicative activities in production processes and the role of bilingualism in work productivity (Gal, 1979; Grin *et al.*, 2010; Villa & Villa, 2005). The current chapter and Chapter 6 begin to address this gap in the literature.

In recent years, studies investigating linguistic variables in labor performance suggest that language differences between native and immigrant workers are following a pattern of specialization, via self-selection or employer selection or both. Aldashev *et al.*, (2009) find that the relationship between language and earnings among immigrants is mostly indirect, working through the occupational channel as immigrants with better language skills move into better-paid occupations (also see Chapter 6, this volume). Using the O*NET classification of occupations, Chiswick and Miller (2010) find that people self-select into occupations that better match their language skills. Peri and Sparber (2009: 136) report that 'less educated natives respond to immigration by leaving physically demanding occupations for language-intensive ones'. Peri and Sparber imply that the native-born are monolingual English speakers, and thus do not address native-born bilinguals. Also, the O*NET classification of occupational skills matches poorly with the role of bilingualism in the new information economy. For example, given 862 occupations, farm contractors rank fourth in the importance of foreign language (63/100 points) while financial service sales drops to 755th (5/100) and door-to-door sales ranks 762nd (4/100).[1] An issue with this data set is that such language skills are conceptualized as 'foreign language' skills, meaning that the domestic value of bilingualism in the workplace is neglected.

Our long-term research trajectory addresses the 'black box' of language in workplace activity and productivity, though we certainly cannot claim to reveal it in its entirety. While selection processes are interesting, we also broach the question of what comes next, the differential distribution of linguistic skills in linguistically sensitive work roles. Our qualitative work, described below and in Alarcón and Heyman (2012, 2013, n.d.), not only points to the productivity advantages of bilingualism in actual work activities, but it also suggests that the advantages of bilingualism were not distributed consistently across occupations where communication with a multilingual public could contribute to such productivity. In particular, we found less bilingualism in managerial and professional jobs despite their public roles.

In this chapter, we build on Villa and Villa's (2005) local study of employer practices in which the authors characterize employer selection for bilingualism in a highly multilingual area, possibly in response to work productivity dynamics. In a sample of both private and public institutions at Mesilla Valley (within the US–Mexico border region we study), Villa and Villa found that 61.71% of employers required or preferred bilinguals when hiring, but only 4.11% provided a differential pay for bilinguals. Villa and Villa examine hiring processes, while we look at occupational distribution, which are clearly related though not identical, and both their study and our much larger one (see Chapter 6) look at compensation for bilinguals. Our current study seeks to investigate whether our previous qualitative findings and those of Villa and Villa can be generalized across a large regional (US–Mexico border) population in a highly multilingual area. We approach this by asking if bilinguals disproportionately occur in occupations that involve communication with a multilingual public. However, due to the nature of the American Community Survey (ACS) data, we suffer from the 'black box' limitation with respect to work processes themselves. We know the at-home speaking skills of job holders and the general nature of the work duties in those occupations, but not the actual activities, language skills or language use required in the workplace of ACS job holders. Nevertheless, the triangulation of previous qualitative findings and the current quantitative findings suggest that the work productivity value of bilingualism is an important topic for future research.

Workplace productivity is important as it indicates an economic and societal case for multilingualism, especially in the new information economy. Examination of the role of multilingualism in workplace productivity challenges English-only policies and documents as well as educational policies that suppress bilingualism and biliteracy. Research investigating the workplace presence of multilingual communication can illuminate the role of multilingualism in the new economy.

Research Focus

We examine two specific sectors, health care and criminal justice, in the US borderlands with Mexico; the focus on these two sectors provides greater clarity about the role of language in production. Health care and criminal justice represent employment sectors with considerable presence and future growth potential; in addition, these sectors are central to organizational and public policy. Both involve a wide range of linguistic-occupational roles, supporting our cross-sectional analysis, and capture the dynamics of the contemporary service economy where information exchange (and thus language use) with a multilingual public is crucial to production. They are sites where we expect to discern key issues with monolingualism and bilingualism in the new information economy.

We focus on the border region because it provides a good example of a Spanish–English bilingual public and because it is home to millions of bilingual individuals along its 2000-mile span. In particular, Spanish–English bilingualism is a daily part of social interactions with border residents and cross-border commerce. The possibility of Spanish maintenance is greater in the border region (Anderson-Mejías, 2005;

Hidalgo, 1993; Jenkins, 2009), which represents an ideal site to explore whether occupational productivity will favor bilinguals in interactive job roles. Employing a border sample allows us to look for a bilingual effect where it should be clearest and most intense. We certainly expect that this effect may occur in the interior US as well; this study offers one step toward a national analysis.[2] We do not present the occupational location of bilinguals as a unique border phenomenon, but the border is a good setting for an initial examination.

Our earlier qualitative work generated possible patterns of language use in the workplace, which motivated the present quantitative study. The following section provides an overview of the qualitative findings that informed our current analyses.

Qualitative Background and Research Propositions

In a study of language and work in El Paso, Texas (Alarcón & Heyman, 2012, 2013, n.d.), using both interviews and ethnographic observation, we investigated four occupational sectors according to their linguistic intensity in the production process: janitorial and maintenance services; call centers; health services; and translation and interpretation (Alarcón & Heyman, 2012, n.d.). We supplemented this large qualitative study with a small exploratory study of a public safety organization in El Paso.[3] We briefly summarize our findings from the health and public safety sectors. Occupations involving formal educational certification (such as lawyers or medical professionals) require either an advanced skill set, advanced testing in English, or both. Even middle- to upper-management positions, without a formal professional certification, generally function in business and government roles dominated by English in the higher levels of the hierarchy. Of course, workers in these occupations can be bilingual, multilingual or monolingual English; however, the occupational filter for entry into their jobs does not require multilingualism. For example, we observed a workplace where the head physical therapist (MS degree) and one other licensed therapist were monolingual English speakers, while two other licensed therapists spoke Spanish as their first language as well as fluent English. In this case, the occupational filter was the certification as therapists, and this appeared to favor the individual with the highest level of education.

The broader reasons for racial and ethnic disparities are access to those credentials; the selective process affected by them is beyond the range of this chapter, but were evident in our qualitative data. Differences in credential access resulted in a concentration of non-Spanish speakers (monolingual in English or bilingual in non-Spanish languages) in these occupations. These occupations broadly have the highest pay rates, the most occupational prestige and the highest levels of intraorganizational power, which occur despite the lack of Spanish language skills needed in some cases to communicate in work processes (with members of the public, with Spanish-dominant workers). For example, an important public safety leader in our study was monolingual in English, despite frequently presenting major policy and information issues to a multilingual public; he reported seeking grant funds to hire interpreters to overcome this job limitation.

Lower-ranking, lower-paid personnel become *de facto* interpreters; in the same workplace, Hispanic Spanish–English bilingual therapy technicians (AA degrees) often interpreted between the two English monolingual therapists and their clients who spoke little or no English. Interestingly, one Hispanic therapy technician spoke only English, but the therapy center director pointed to his more advanced education (BS degree, kinesiology) as compensation for his lack of bilingualism. The expectation of bilingualism among the other technicians was explicit in the mind of the unit director. In a doctor's office, the staff nurse (BSN degree, MS coursework) spoke very little Spanish, despite intensive, health-affecting interactions with a multilingual public, but interpretation support was provided by a medical technician (AA degree). In both case studies, billing and appointment clerks who had extensive interaction with the public were all bilingual.

Data from our qualitative case studies suggest that Spanish–English bilingualism was an inconsistent criterion for hiring and promotion. In the therapy center (a small, semi-autonomous unit of a medium-sized private firm), the hiring director indicated that bilingualism was an employment criterion for technicians and office staff, but not for therapists (reportedly very scarce). In a large public safety agency, a governmental office potentially constrained by employment law, the human resource director reported that bilingualism was specifically not a hiring criterion; however, language skill was, as hiring was based on a written exam that tested high school, graduate-level verbal and math skills in English. Promotion could be affected by language skill, since the ability to carry out investigations factors into individual's professional advancement along the way e.g. from sergeant to detective. More importantly, it is possible (though difficult to prove qualitatively) that continued employment in public safety jobs depends on the ability to use English or Spanish or a mix of both in everyday policing tasks. Interviews with both English monolingual and Spanish–English bilingual officers revealed that the ability to conduct public safety work in Spanish was important (monolinguals had to call for bilingual officers), a lack of Spanish was perceived to be a limitation to carrying out a valued mission.

Hence, in occupations that require both modest but real educational preparation (e.g. high school diploma, AA degree), as well as considerable communication with the public (e.g. police, medical assistants, front office staff), many processes favor bilingualism. People in these occupations must be able to communicate effectively in both English and Spanish with a linguistically diverse public. At the same time, there are few if any credentialing processes such as an MD, JD, MPT, and so forth that eliminate less-educated bilinguals, even if such people also have multilingual needs for communication in service to a multilingual public (as doctors, lawyers and other professionals often do). Such credentialed persons sometimes have bilingual skills, which serve them well in the workplace (as we found for bilingual physical therapists and a bilingual doctor), but the mandatory need for the credential 'trumps' the linguistic skill that a potential employee brings to the situation. The senior physical therapist in charge of hiring decisions stressed this point in our interview.

The most complex case that we identified in our qualitative research was nurses. Nurses, in many instances, have intensive and vital spoken interaction with a multilingual public. They likewise have moderate to high need for understanding and producing written and numerical materials. They are employed under a vast and complex range of credentials and educational degrees; for example registered nurses have at least an associate's degree and have passed a registered nurse examination. Because of these multidimensional workplace considerations, we pay specific attention to nurses in the quantitative study reported here.

In our qualitative research, we found few formal hiring, promotion or training processes that actively selected bilinguals; rather, we found that the relative concentration of bilinguals emerges from wider social processes at play in border society (and likely applicable to other heavily post-immigrant regions). The capacity of local speech communities to produce untrained speakers of Spanish with middle-range education in English; the informal advantages of bilinguals in work functions that encourage bilinguals to remain in a current positions, in contrast to either Spanish or English monolinguals; and broad social factors, e.g. the education levels of second- and third-generation Latinos.

We also identified two kinds of occupations with relatively high concentrations of people with limited English skills. The first set involves relatively simple interpersonal tasks involving language, with minimal need for precision, and few written products (e.g. home health-care aides). The second set involves mainly physical work activities and skills (e.g. janitors), traditionally called 'silent jobs'[4] as communication is often internal to the work organization, and interaction with the wider world occurs via bilingual supervisors and middle managers. In both instances, broader social processes (Mexican immigrants' low educational levels, barriers to alternative jobs for non-English speakers, networks within workplaces) tend to channel monolingual Spanish speakers into these occupations. It is important to note that there is no productivity advantage to a specific language, but rather a selective bias for English speakers, monolingual or bilingual, to exit such occupations.

We also find few explicit labor market rewards for bilingualism (also see Chapter 6, this volume, for a quantitative examination of earnings), with the rare exception of formal interpreters or translators. Human capital theory would suggest that bilingualism would be an asset (specifically in these social-economic environments where important work activities need to be done flexibly in English and Spanish). Yet, we found that hiring practices favoring bilinguals are inconsistent (as opposed to educational credentials), and there is rarely promotion, extra pay or training for bilinguals. Indeed, we found in national corporate jobs that advancement in organizations (e.g. intracorporate transfers) often requires a shift from multilingualism toward English monolingualism. As a result, there is little cultivation of bilingualism in the labor-supplying community (recently, dual language education has gained popularity, but most Spanish-speaking parents see Spanish as a cultural good but not an economic asset and sometimes as an economic detriment [Velázquez, 2009]). Instead, bilinguals – who in fact are crucial to many production processes in the information-rich service economy – are provided free of cost through speech community processes (e.g. being second- or third-generation immigrants) that produce and maintain the heritage language.

Hypotheses

Building on our qualitative work, we offer the following hypotheses:

(1) *Fluent bilinguals* (native Spanish speakers who speak English very well) will:
   (a) have a reduced probability of holding professional and managerial occupations;
   (b) have an elevated probability of occupations with intensive oral interaction with the public;
   (c) have a reduced probability of holding positions as nurses, despite their oral interactions with the public, due to educational certification constraints.
(2) *Monolingual English* speakers will have an elevated probability of holding professional and managerial occupations.
(3) *Limited English proficient* speakers will have an elevated probability of holding service jobs with minimal written and limited oral skills, and physical labor jobs.

We also offer a more general research proposition that cannot be tested with our data but provides important context for our study:

• There will be indirect evidence of the work productivity role of Spanish–English bilingualism through its high presence in occupations involving interaction with a multilingual public.

Quantitative Study: Data and Methods

Following grounded theory tradition (Glaser & Strauss, 1967), the qualitative findings described above drove the development of research hypotheses for the quantitative portion of this project and assisted with the interpretation of that data. The quantitative phase enabled us to examine aggregate evidence to determine whether the findings would hold true across a representative sample.

We use data from five years (2006–2010) of the Public Use Microdata Set (PUMS) of the ACS. Collected by the US Census Bureau, the ACS is the largest household survey in the US that gathers data on demographic and socioeconomic information in a reliable and timely manner. The ACS-PUMS has a wide range of variables of interest, including the economic sector, occupation and language skills, as well as many other contextual variables.

The ACS-PUMS data set was drawn from the US borderlands with Mexico. In that geographic sample, we selected individuals working in the health (industry codes 7970 to 8290 in the ACS survey) and criminal justice (industry code 9470) systems. We dropped observations of individuals who were not in the labor force (i.e. unemployed and inactive individuals), as well as those who were aged less than 17 and more than 70. Self-employed individuals were also excluded from the empirical analysis, to avoid complications for the analysis of earnings in Chapter 6. After cleaning for missing values of relevant variables, we obtained a final sample of $n = 7695$.[5]

Dependent variable

The dependent variable is a category of occupations clustered by language use. Based on our qualitative analyses, we present a novel classification of occupations by the role of language in production that is relatively intuitive and consistent with other classifications (e.g. by skill and/or workplace hierarchy), and by the concept of linguistic intensity of the production process (Alarcón, 2007; Grin et al., 2010; Reich, 1991). In categorizing occupations,[6] we followed two classificatory axes: (1) the reliance of productive roles on written, numerical and other comparable communications (symbolic analysis) vs production relying on oral interaction with the external public; and (2) the degree of linguistic intensity (high vs low) in those production processes. Following this framework, we have constructed the occupational classifications shown in Table 5.1.

We considered the following occupational categories based on the degree of symbolic analysis and language intensity: (A) high symbolic analysts, (B) low symbolic analysts, (C) high intensity oral interaction with public (high public service), (D) low intensity oral interaction with public (low

Table 5.1 Classification of occupations by language use

Major occupational classification	Linguistic characteristics of occupation	Subclassification	Example of occupation
A: High symbolic analysts	Produce/consume long or complex written communications, with variable but often important oral communication	A1. Upper management	Chief executive, human resource executive
		A2. Professionals	Lawyer, doctor
		A3. Lower management	First line manager/supervisor
		A4. High symbolic analysts, not managers	Public relations specialists, computer systems specialists
B: Low symbolic analysts	Produce/consume short or simple written communications, with variable but often important oral communication	B1. Low symbolic analysts with low likelihood of public interaction	File clerks
		B2. Low symbolic analysts with high likelihood of public interaction	Receptionists, billing/appointment clerks
C: High in-person service workers	Important oral communication, high public interaction, some written skills	C1. Nurses	Nurses
		C2. Assistants and technicians in public service settings	Medical technicians
		C3. Police, etc.	Police, detectives, investigators
		C4. Firefighters, emergency medical technicians	Firefighters, emergency medical technicians
D. Low in-person service workers	Simple oral communication and public interaction, very limited or no writing	C5. Miscellaneous (no subcategories in our study)	Counselors, dispatchers home health care-aides, security guards
E. Manual workers	Limited oral and written consumption and production	E1. Skilled manual work	Plumber
		E2. Unskilled manual work	Janitor

public service) and (E) manual labor occupations with limited symbolic and oral demands. Since we are interested in the relationship between fluent bilingualism and interaction with a multilingual public, we divided the low symbolic analyst occupations, many of whom also serve the public, into two subgroups, (B1) those whose work is generally inside the organization (such as file clerks) and (B2) those whose work includes interacting with the public (such as receptionists). In addition, we separated the occupational category of nurses (C1) for reasons grounded in our qualitative research, as discussed above, permitting us to test Hypothesis 1(c). This resulted in creating an occupation by language category from the remainder of the high public service occupations (C2–5), henceforth simply called high public service. In summary, we use one dependent variable (occupation by language use) with seven mutually exclusive categories listed in Table 5.1.[7]

Main independent variable: Language background

Language background is measured with three mutually exclusive categories[8]: (1) likely *monolingual English* (home language = English)[9]; (2) *limited English proficient* (home language = Spanish with English either [a] not at all, [b] not well or [c] well)[10]; and (3) *fluent bilingual* (home language = Spanish with English very well).[11] These categories are determined by the structure of the questions in the ACS; justifications and limitations of specific categories are discussed in the notes.

Several caveats should be mentioned about the data on language background. The ACS questions concern language spoken at home, and not at work; there is a reasonable inference that people who speak Spanish at home have at least some ability to use it at work, plus the levels of English which the ACS does identify. The ACS asks about spoken language, but not written language. Hence, our approach to workplace language skills and performance is indirect. Finally, language skills in the ACS are self-described, a limitation that we partially address with our more linguistically sensitive (direct interview/observation) data from the qualitative study.

Control variables

In our model, we included control variables for demographic, human capital and labor market attributes. We included age, gender, marital status and the number of children, allowing for gender-specific effects through interaction terms. Educational attainment addressed the value of educational certificates and their strong influence on occupation segmentation. We included nativity and region of origin premigration as well as years since migration to capture immigrants' assimilation. Labor market factors included full-time vs part-time employment, sector (health vs public safety) and government vs non-government jobs. We excluded self-employed workers from the analysis to align with Chapter 6.[12] We also controlled for state, due to uneven economic factors along the border (poor toward the east, relatively prosperous to the west).[13]

Results and Discussion of Hypotheses

Table 5.2 shows the frequencies of language speakers (columns) for each of the seven occupations (rows). Bivariate statistical tests of each occupational category[14] allow us to reject (at the 0.05 level of probability) the null hypothesis that those categories are independent of language ability. Hence, proceeding with the analysis of the relationship between

Table 5.2 Language and occupation counts and descriptives

Occupation by linguistic intensity	Monolingual English	Fluent bilinguals	Limited English proficient	Totals
A. High symbolic analysts	731	568	124	1423
	51.37	39.92	8.71	100
	26.1	16.64	8.38	18.49
B1. Low symbolic analysts with low public contact	161	203	38	402
	40.05	50.5	9.45	100
	5.75	5.95	2.57	5.22
B2. Low symbolic analysts with high public contact	230	366	81	677
	33.97	54.06	11.96	100
	8.21	10.72	5.47	8.8
C1. Nurses	433	345	67	845
	51.42	40.83	7.93	100
	15.46	10.11	4.53	10.98
C2–5. High in-person service workers	796	1139	207	2142
	37.16	53.17	9.66	100
	28.42	33.36	13.99	27.84
D. Low in-person service workers	360	692	792	1844
	19.52	37.53	42.95	100
	12.85	20.27	53.51	23.96
E. Manual workers	90	101	171	362
	24.86	27.90	47.24	100
	3.21	2.96	11.55	4.70
Total	2801	3414	1480	7695
	36.40	44.37	19.23	100
	100	100	100	100

Note: First percentage is row (% of occupation with that language background): second is column (% of each language background in that occupation).

occupation and language is appropriate. Table 5.3 reports the basic demographic characteristics of our sample, including the key control variables.

In order to more accurately assess the hypotheses, we turn to multivariate analysis. It is important to emphasize the role of multivariate analysis: we examine the effects of language background on the probabilities of being in each occupational category, controlling for other factors that characteristically affect occupational placement, including many social and human capital characteristics, such as age, gender, education, nativity and so forth. While we cannot remove possible confounding factors, we can increase the extent to which we are able to control for them, and thus to focus more clearly on the effect of language background on occupational placement. Because we were working with categorical variables, a multinomial logistic technique was used.

Our reference group is fluent bilinguals. This is grounded in our theoretical focus, which is the role of Spanish–English bilingualism in work processes in services to a multilingual public, and our qualitative research that suggested that occupations with oral interactions with a multilingual public are often filled with fluent bilinguals. The results are expressed as the change in probability from fluent bilinguals of persons in each language background group having an occupation in each occupational group.[15] Therefore, a positive probability in Table 5.4 indicates that such language speakers have an increased likelihood of holding that occupation over fluent bilinguals; a negative sign on the probability means that they are less likely to hold such jobs. The row below the probability is the 'standard error'. We also include information about the probability of these results occurring randomly, or conversely the 'significance' of the results, with low probabilities of random occurrences indicated by the asterisks (the key is at the bottom of the table).

Here, we discuss only those results that are of interest to our hypotheses (see the section Hypotheses). Hypotheses 1(a) and 2, taken together, suggested that English-only speakers were more likely to hold high symbolic analysis (A) occupations than fluent bilinguals. This is supported, though at a relatively weak level of probability ($p < 0.1$). Such jobs are an occupational language use proxy for professional and managerial positions (see Table 5.1), so English-only speakers have an elevated probability over fluent bilinguals of holding such positions with organizational power and societal prestige, even after controlling for many demographic and human capital variables that might seem to offer alternative explanations (we say this with caution due to the significance level).

Hypothesis 1(b) posited that fluent bilinguals would have a greater probability of holding jobs with significant oral interaction with the public. We can operationalize this hypothesis in two occupational categories,

Table 5.3 Other descriptive statistics

Variable	All the sample		A. High symbolic analysts		B1. Low public contact		B2. Possibility of public contact		C1. Nurses		C2–C5. High in-person service workers		D. Low in-person service workers		E. Manual workers	
	Mean	SD	Mean	SD	Mean	SD	Mean	SD	Mean	SD	Mean	SD	Mean	SD	Mean	SD
Sociodemographic variables																
Age	41	12	43.4	10.9	39.4	12.0	38.8	13	42.4	11.2	37.3	11.1	42.8	12.6	46.1	11.1
Males	0.34	0.47	0.48	0.50	0.17	0.38	0.10	0.30	0.20	0.40	0.48	0.50	0.23	0.42	0.43	0.50
Females	0.66	0.47	0.52	0.50	0.83	0.38	0.90	0.30	0.80	0.40	0.52	0.50	0.77	0.42	0.57	0.50
No. of children	0.88	1.14	0.82	1.11	0.85	1.10	0.80	1.11	0.79	1.08	0.98	1.17	0.90	1.20	0.77	1.07
Married	0.57	0.49	0.66	0.47	0.50	0.50	0.49	0.50	0.58	0.49	0.57	0.50	0.54	0.50	0.64	0.48
Educational attainment																
Less than high school	0.13	0.34	0.02	0.13	0.04	0.19	0.06	0.24	0.00	0.06	0.03	0.17	0.38	0.48	0.46	0.50
High school	0.19	0.39	0.10	0.30	0.30	0.46	0.29	0.46	0.04	0.19	0.17	0.37	0.28	0.45	0.31	0.46
Some college	0.42	0.49	0.32	0.47	0.54	0.50	0.55	0.50	0.55	0.50	0.52	0.50	0.29	0.46	0.20	0.40
Bachelors	0.16	0.37	0.24	0.43	0.09	0.29	0.08	0.27	0.31	0.46	0.21	0.41	0.04	0.19	0.02	0.13
Above bachelors	0.10	0.29	0.33	0.47	0.03	0.16	0.01	0.12	0.09	0.29	0.07	0.25	0.01	0.10	0.01	0.10
Origin variables																
US-born	0.74	0.44	0.82	0.38	0.85	0.36	0.81	0.39	0.81	0.39	0.82	0.39	0.55	0.50	0.50	0.50
Latin America	0.23	0.42	0.13	0.34	0.13	0.34	0.16	0.37	0.14	0.35	0.16	0.36	0.44	0.50	0.48	0.50
Puerto Rico, US Islands and other developed countries	0.02	0.12	0.03	0.16	0.01	0.09	0.01	0.09	0.03	0.16	0.02	0.13	0.01	0.08	0.01	0.07
Other developing countries	0.01	0.12	0.02	0.13	0.02	0.13	0.02	0.13	0.02	0.16	0.01	0.10	0.01	0.10	0.01	0.10

Years since migration (= 0 for natives)	6.70	13	4.71	11.9	4.67	12.1	5.02	11.9	4.96	11.8	4.61	11	11.3	14.9	12.6	14.8
Job-related variables																
Criminal justice	0.25	0.43	0.32	0.47	0.18	0.39	0.19	0.40	0.02	0.13	0.40	0.49	0.17	0.38	0.14	0.35
Health–government	0.09	0.28	0.10	0.30	0.09	0.29	0.06	0.24	0.11	0.31	0.06	0.25	0.10	0.30	0.11	0.31
Health–private	0.67	0.47	0.58	0.49	0.73	0.45	0.74	0.44	0.87	0.33	0.54	0.50	0.72	0.45	0.75	0.43
Full-time worker	0.28	0.45	0.82	0.39	0.78	0.42	0.74	0.44	0.90	0.30	0.73	0.44	0.52	0.50	0.72	0.45
Part-time worker	0.28	0.45	0.18	0.39	0.22	0.42	0.26	0.44	0.10	0.30	0.27	0.44	0.48	0.50	0.28	0.45
State																
Arizona	0.12	0.32	0.13	0.34	0.12	0.32	0.11	0.31	0.13	0.33	0.14	0.34	0.09	0.28	0.11	0.31
California	0.25	0.43	0.32	0.47	0.33	0.47	0.29	0.45	0.25	0.43	0.24	0.43	0.18	0.38	0.24	0.43
New Mexico	0.05	0.22	0.05	0.22	0.05	0.22	0.05	0.23	0.05	0.22	0.05	0.22	0.05	0.22	0.05	0.21
Texas	0.58	0.49	0.50	0.50	0.50	0.50	0.55	0.50	0.57	0.50	0.57	0.50	0.69	0.46	0.60	0.49
No. of observations	7695		1423		402		677		845		2142		1844		362	

Table 5.4 Multinomial regression model of language background/occupation relationship with additional control variables

	A. High symbolic analysts Δ Prob.	B1. Low public contact Δ Prob.	B2. Possibility of public contact Δ Prob.	C2-5. High in-person services Δ Prob.	C1. Nurses Δ Prob.	D. Low in-person service workers Δ Prob.	E. Manual workers Δ Prob.
English only	0.020*	-0.002	-0.018**	-0.030**	0.035***	-0.019*	0.015**
	(0.010)	(0.006)	(0.008)	(0.012)	(0.008)	(0.011)	(0.007)
Fluent bilingual	Reference group						
Limited English proficiency	-0.018	-0.011	-0.019*	-0.063***	-0.024**	0.110***	0.024***
	(0.014)	(0.009)	(0.011)	(0.016)	(0.010)	(0.015)	(0.007)
Age	0.016***	-0.001	-0.010***	-0.010***	0.006***	-0.006**	0.004***
	(0.003)	(0.002)	(0.002)	(0.003)	(0.002)	(0.002)	(0.002)
Age (squared)	-0.001***	0.001	0.001***	0.001	-0.001***	0.000***	-0.000**
	(0.000)	(0.000)	(0.000)	(0.000)	(0.000)	(0.000)	(0.000)
Female (ref. male)	-0.060***	0.033***	0.084***	-0.052***	0.028***	0.022	-0.054***
	(0.016)	(0.008)	(0.009)	(0.017)	(0.011)	(0.016)	(0.013)
Children	-0.011*	-0.017**	-0.017	0.010	0.018***	0.024***	-0.007*
	(0.006)	(0.007)	(0.012)	(0.008)	(0.007)	(0.008)	(0.004)
Married (ref. single or other situations)	0.047***	0.007	-0.028	0.047***	-0.036***	-0.059***	0.022**
	(0.014)	(0.013)	(0.021)	(0.017)	(0.016)	(0.018)	(0.009)
Female* children	0.017**	0.018**	0.014	-0.005	-0.025***	-0.024***	0.004
	(0.008)	(0.008)	(0.012)	(0.009)	(0.007)	(0.009)	(0.004)
Female* married	-0.011	-0.010	0.034	-0.067***	0.055***	0.024	-0.025**
	(0.018)	(0.014)	(0.023)	(0.021)	(0.018)	(0.021)	(0.010)

Education: Twelfth grade with no diploma or less	Reference group						
Education: high school	0.054***	0.055***	0.062***	0.117***	0.016***	-0.206***	-0.098***
	(0.012)	(0.010)	(0.013)	(0.018)	(0.005)	(0.023)	(0.018)
Education: some college	0.089***	0.038***	0.046***	0.193***	0.140***	-0.353***	-0.154***
	(0.011)	(0.009)	(0.012)	(0.018)	(0.007)	(0.022)	(0.017)
Education: bachelor's	0.215***	0.005	-0.018	0.236***	0.211***	-0.471***	-0.176***
	(0.016)	(0.009)	(0.013)	(0.021)	(0.011)	(0.022)	(0.017)
Education: master's, professional schools or PhD	0.525***	-0.010	-0.048***	0.123***	0.097***	-0.509***	-0.177***
	(0.022)	(0.009)	(0.012)	(0.023)	(0.011)	(0.022)	(0.017)
Latin America	-0.041*	-0.047***	-0.033**	-0.001	0.005***	0.082***	0.034***
	(0.020)	(0.013)	(0.016)	(0.026)	(0.018)	(0.023)	(0.013)
Puerto Rico, US Islands and other developed countries	0.021	-0.052***	-0.033	0.030	0.046***	-0.017	0.005
	(0.036)	(0.016)	(0.027)	(0.047)	(0.031)	(0.044)	(0.028)
Other developing countries	-0.047	-0.031	0.010	-0.083**	0.014***	0.112**	0.025
	(0.029)	(0.019)	(0.033)	(0.042)	(0.026)	(0.054)	(0.030)
Years since migration (=0 for natives)	0.000	0.001**	0.000	0.000	0.000***	-0.001	-0.001*
	(0.001)	(0.001)	(0.001)	(0.001)	(0.001)	(0.001)	(0.000)
Health services (private sector)	Reference group						
Health services (public sector)	0.019**	-0.011	0.017*	0.113***	-0.147***	0.039***	-0.031***
	(0.010)	(0.007)	(0.010)	(0.013)	(0.005)	(0.012)	(0.005)

(Continued)

Table 5.4 (Continued)

	A. High symbolic analysts Δ Prob.	B1. Low public contact Δ Prob.	B2. Possibility of public contact Δ Prob.	C2–5. High in-person services Δ Prob.	C1. Nurses Δ Prob.	D. Low in-person service workers Δ Prob.	E. Manual workers Δ Prob.
Criminal justice	0.004	0.003	−0.021**	−0.007	−0.009***	0.030**	0.001
	(0.015)	(0.009)	(0.011)	(0.019)	(0.010)	(0.015)	(0.008)
Employed full-time (ref. employed part-time)	−0.040***	−0.016***	−0.021***	0.064***	−0.098***	0.128***	−0.017***
	(0.009)	(0.005)	(0.007)	(0.012)	(0.006)	(0.010)	(0.005)
Texas	Reference group						
Arizona	−0.012	0.005	−0.005	0.007	−0.009***	−0.008	0.022**
	(0.013)	(0.008)	(0.010)	(0.016)	(0.011)	(0.015)	(0.010)
California	0.009	0.023***	0.024***	−0.007	−0.031***	−0.031***	0.014**
	(0.010)	(0.007)	(0.009)	(0.013)	(0.008)	(0.011)	(0.007)
New Mexico	−0.005	0.000	0.006	0.003	−0.039***	0.027	0.009
	(0.017)	(0.011)	(0.014)	(0.022)	(0.012)	(0.021)	(0.012)

No. of observations: 7695

Pseudo $R2$: 0.22

***$p<0.01$; **$p<0.05$; *$p<0.1$; robust standard error in italics within parentheses.

Note: Fluent bilinguals are the reference group.

low symbolic analysts with high public oral interaction (B2) and high oral intensity occupations (C2–5). Fluent bilinguals were significantly more likely than English-only speakers to be represented in both of those occupational categories, at the strong $p < 0.05$ level. They were also more likely than limited English proficient speakers to be represented in those occupational categories (at the $p < 0.1$ level for B2 occupations and the $p < 0.01$ level for C2–5 occupations). In summary, fluent bilinguals do have elevated probabilities over other language backgrounds of occurring in occupations with extensive oral service to the public.

Hypothesis 1(c) suggested that nurses (occupation C1) would have elevated probabilities of English-only speakers over fluent bilinguals, despite their intensive and important spoken language service roles, because of the screening effect of credentials (education and licensing examinations) and the importance of symbolic communication to them. A high significance level ($p < 0.01$) supports this hypothesis and provides aggregate support of our case study findings.

Hypothesis 2 was discussed together with Hypothesis 1(a) above. In Hypothesis 3, we posited that limited English proficient speakers would have a greater probability of holding service jobs with minimal written and limited oral skills, and physical labor jobs. In fact, we found that limited English proficient speakers were significantly more likely to hold low intensity service jobs (D) and manual labor jobs (E) than fluent bilinguals ($p < 0.01$). One unexpected but significant result that we cannot explain is that monolingual English speakers are also more likely to have manual labor occupations than fluent bilinguals. Given the widely recognized disadvantages of having reduced English language skills in labor markets in the United States, including the US–Mexico borderlands (Daly, 2012), these occupational distributions are unsurprising.

Discussion of Overall Findings, Limitations and Future Directions

Our study of aggregate occupation and language distributions in the health and public safety sectors of the US–Mexico borderlands, a multilingual region, found an interesting pattern: fluent bilingualism tends to place its speakers above the disadvantaged occupations of low-skill services and manual labor, but partially below credentialed occupational sectors such as high symbolic analysts (who are mainly professionals and managers) and nurses, even when level of education is controlled. Fluent bilinguals are overrepresented in middle-tier oral public service roles, exemplified in our study by police officers and medical assistants. Language capabilities are an important variable affecting occupational location, and this is true not only for the expected effect of limited proficiency in the dominant language, but also, in a novel finding, in interesting and not entirely positive ways for high-level proficiency in two languages. This is consistent with our general hypotheses about the work productivity benefit of bilingualism in interactions with a multilingual public, and indicates that our qualitative findings about the advantages of bilingualism in the new service economy in El Paso can be generalized across the borderlands population.

However, we are careful not to claim causality; we do not argue that dealing with the public makes health and criminal justice organizations deliberately hire bilinguals. Such claims are beyond the scope of our data. Likewise, although we include standard labor market controls, other non-linguistic, non-work role factors (e.g. discrimination, social networks) may sort people by linguistic background, reflective of wider social groups, into occupations.

We suggest that with selection into workplace roles, we have captured one important part of the processes of selection for and against bilingualism in occupational sorting. Our previous qualitative research (Alarcón & Heyman, 2012, 2013, n.d.) suggests that Spanish–English bilingualism is often treated as a freely available, naturally occurring resource of the border social-cultural environment, a 'heritage language' rather than a learned skill, and it is infrequently treated as a high value skill requiring specific recruitment, retention, training and promotion (also see Villa & Villa, 2005).[16] It is likewise consistent with our findings that when bilingualism is a recruitment and retention target, it is usually for entry-level public interface jobs (such as receptionists and medical assistants), not necessarily managerial and professional roles (e.g. nurses, doctors, lawyers, public safety managers) that also require bilingual competency. For some of the latter positions, formal educational credentials based on work or examinations done in English overrode bilingual skills, even when such were needed.

Notably, our quantitative models did control for education, and we still see a reduced probability of fluent bilinguals holding high symbolic and nurse positions relative to monolingual English speakers. This brings us to an important suggestion for future research, which is the need to investigate whether 'ceilings' may exist for fluent bilinguals. The term 'glass ceiling' has been used for occupational distributions in which specific populations are well represented in all but the best paid, most powerful and most prestigious occupations. This is an apt description of our findings, although we should note that the highest occupations do include a substantial number of bilinguals, just a disproportionately low number relative to other occupations. Based on our qualitative work, we suggest a mechanism by which this glass ceiling occurs for professionals wherein Spanish–English bilinguals have fewer credentials needed for specific occupations. When jobs are filled, scarce credentials (e.g. for nurses) trump communication skills, regardless of the potential importance of these skills in the work place. However, the 'credential' explanation does extend to managers without special licenses, for whom a glass ceiling remains.

Furthermore, the US borderlands with Mexico have a profound history of discrimination against Mexican-origin people (see, e.g. Macías, this volume; Montejano, 1987; Richardson, 1999). This has included linguistic discrimination against Spanish, educational barriers and discrimination, highly unequal occupational placement (often deliberate) and extremely low capital accumulation. The last factor in turn results in limited access to and experience in managerial roles in the private sector. As Montejano (1987: 297–300) notes, explicit racism in the region has declined markedly, though residual discrimination does exist, but structural racial inequality (e.g. linguistic accent and register biases, differential social networks, etc.) remains important and is only gradually fading. This is the historical context in which bilinguals are moving, or not moving, into the occupational division of labor.

Our results, which affirm the value of bilingualism in production processes in the new information economy in multilingual societies, must be read carefully. The way that we identified some jobs as having focal components of spoken language services to the public should not be taken to isolate such functions to just those jobs. Bilingualism has wider workplace value, especially for top organizational levels with a public presence and professional service providers. Importantly, the quantitative data plus our qualitative work identify gaps in the presence of such useful language skills. Many workers in the high symbolic analyst occupations also deal extensively with the public (e.g. public safety executives, health executives, doctors, lawyers), as do nurses; yet monolingual English speakers are significantly more likely to fill these occupations than fluent bilinguals *or* limited English proficient individuals. Productivity benefits to the organization and society are lost when workers are not fluently bilingual in a multilingual setting. This reflects relative rates of occurrence; in the US–Mexico borderlands, many people in managerial and professional occupations are bilingual, as shown in our data.

We found common informal coping mechanisms for professionals and managers without Spanish language skills, such as having lower-ranking or less-educated bilingual staff interpret for monolingual staff. Such practices enable an incompletely functional work situation to cope with these weaknesses in the recruitment and development of bilingual professionals and managers, but the communicative quality of these coping strategies merits careful investigation.

The underrepresentation of fluent bilinguals in managerial and professional occupations is also significant insofar as such positions have more power, intraorganizationally and societally, have higher prestige and often pay better than the middle-tier occupations. In each regard, this may reproduce structural racial inequalities in the borderlands. Due to statistical limitations in our data, we cannot separate out linguistic background and ethnicity as channels to these stratified occupational positions.[17] A better understanding of existing education, recruitment, development, promotion and compensation processes is needed to ascertain how well our indirect inferences about these informalities and limitations actually hold in labor market and internal organizational realities.

We initially asked if bilingualism contributes to workplace productivity in more communication-intensive jobs, though we do not directly observe work processes. Rather, our findings highlight a greater concentration of bilinguals in some (though not all) occupations that involve intensive oral and written communication with the public in a multilingual setting; combined with our qualitative findings, this suggests a practical, important value of bilingualism. Questions remain, however, regarding selection by employers, self-selection by job seekers and the indirect effects of other societal and labor market processes. Future research might examine work activities directly, to investigate whether and how bilingualism might add to productivity in dealing with a multilingual public. We suggest that productivity enhancements may give meaningful value to language skills, especially in sectors where productivity affects the broad public good, such as health and public safety, as suggested by our findings.

Our study investigated Spanish–English bilingualism in a particular region (the US borderlands with Mexico) where the public is heavily Spanish–English bilingual or Spanish dominant. Future research should be extended to other language situations; either more complexly multilingual settings (e.g. New York or Los Angeles) or other concentrated bilingual settings (e.g. concentrated Chinese language areas in major US metropolitan areas). Future research might investigate regions in the US interior with a large Spanish-dominant public to determine if the public interaction occupations patterns exist there as they do in the borderlands.

Conclusion

Workers who deal with the public in a multilingual society are helped in their jobs by being able to use diverse languages. Doctors, nurses and medical assistants can understand and communicate more clearly with patients, improving health outcomes; lawyers, police officers, fire officers and government leaders gain similar benefits for public safety. Spanish–English bilingualism, like other forms of multilingualism, proves to be an asset in the performance of work duties that matter to the public good. As a public good, as well as a workplace asset, bilingualism merits consideration for cultivation, development and reward through deliberate policy within individual organizations and local, state and federal policies.

Likewise, research investigating the role of multilingualism in workplace productivity is vital. It offers a direction to explore the economic and social values of diverse language skills that runs counter to political movements toward English-only policies and a reduction in educational support for bilingualism and biliteracy.

Our findings suggest that Spanish–English bilingualism does occur in some, though not all, occupational roles that deal with the highly multilingual US borderlands with Mexico. We find that workplace bilingualism occurs through informal labor market and work role processes, and is often not the product of deliberate organizational or public policies. We also find that the use of bilingual personnel does not extend systematically to managerial levels or to educated professionals, even though they also need bilingual skills on the job, for the public good. Likewise, bilingualism is not encouraged or rewarded by added compensation, even though it represents a valuable asset. The US public is fortunate that so many excellent bilinguals offer this skill in performing their work; more explicit and stronger policies to identify, recruit, develop and reward multilingual skills should be considered.

Fluent Spanish–English bilinguals are broadly found in the middle, with more occupational prestige, power and pay than limited English proficient workers, but less than English monolinguals. We suggest that this may represent a 'glass ceiling', where individuals rise in the occupational hierarchy, but encounter barriers preventing entry into the top levels. Our data control for multiple factors, such that our findings are not just attributable to limits of education, citizenship, gender and so forth. This occupational limitation is primarily experienced by a linguistic group that draws predominantly from one ethnoracial group, Hispanics. We cannot make statements about whether this pattern will persist into the future, or is in a period of change as a history of systematic racism in the borderlands declines. It is, nevertheless, worth drawing attention to the underrepresentation of fluent bilinguals in the highest levels of organizational and professional hierarchies, a phenomenon that should be questioned in a context where multilingual public communication is vital in the leadership of society.

Notes

(1) See http://www.onetonline.org/find/descriptor/result/2.C.7.b (accessed 15 September 2013).

(2) The interior has more public linguistic complexity (e.g. our key argument might apply also to Chicago, but there the multilingual public might involve Spanish, Polish, Chinese languages and so forth, with small numbers and more complex statistical interpretations), and as a result, expected effects would be real but weaker.

(3)   The larger study had 115 interviews and two locations of participant observation (for more details, see Alarcón & Heyman, 2012, 2013, n.d.a). The health sector within that study consisted of 10 interviews at two sites (a surgical doctor's office and a large physical therapy office) and extensive, if unplanned, participant observation of daily work activities conducted in both English and Spanish. Three men and seven women across a range of occupations (as discussed in the main text), educational backgrounds and ethnic origins were interviewed. The public safety study was done later, in conjunction with writing this chapter (before data analysis, however), and was done rapidly. Prior to it, Heyman had extensive observation of and interaction with top executives of this organization (male and female, white non-Hispanic and Hispanic), in public presentations and personal conversations. The rapid study consisted of four qualitative interviews concerning language in hiring, promotion and compensation; work use of language; and personal language background and skills. These interviews were with two officers on street patrol, one supervisor and the head of human resources, all of them male, three Hispanic and one non-Hispanic white.

(4)   A misnomer as all jobs require language and communication.

(5)   Details of the construction of the sample can be found in the appendices located at http://faculty.utep.edu/jmheyman.

(6)   Details of the occupations in the ACS clustered in each linguistic occupation group can be found in the appendices located at http://faculty.utep.edu/jmheyman.

(7)   We ran additional multinomial logit models without the occupational subdivisions of B1 and B2, and C1 and C2–5, with similar if less informative results (results not reported here; available from the corresponding author).

(8)   Due to the region of our study and our topic of interest, as well as the small numbers involved, we eliminated all those who spoke a non-English, non-Spanish language at home ($n = 780$); no significant occupational concentrations were found in this population (results with this group included are available from the corresponding author).

(9)   The ACS asks if a person speaks a non-English language at home, and if so, which one; only for those people who reply yes does it ask about *spoken, but not reading or writing* ability in English. As the ACS first asks about non-English language use at home, it does not capture bilinguals who speak English at home. As a result, our category of monolingual English speakers is qualified with the term 'likely'.

(10)   We define limited English proficient individuals as those who speak Spanish at home and report speaking English well, not well or not at all. This is a conservative assumption. Since people may have a socially approved tendency to overstate their skill in the prestige language, English, we focus on the strongest case of bilingualism, fluent bilinguals, minimizing potential problems due to overstating English-speaking abilities. In exploratory multinomial analyses not shown, we also found a consistent break in occupational distribution (i.e. reversal of signs of coefficients) between fluent bilinguals and 'well' and 'not well' bilinguals and Spanish monolinguals.

(11)   See Note 8 for justification for limiting fluent bilinguals to this definition.

(12)   The results are invariant to our decision to exclude persons who speak non-English and non-Spanish languages at home, and are available upon request.

(13)   Details on the specific choices and construction of control variables can be found in the appendices located at http://faculty.utep.edu/jmheyman.

(14)   Details of these tests can be found in the appendices located at http://faculty.utep.edu/jmheyman.

(15) In order to simplify the interpretation of the estimates from the multinomial logit of occupational choices, we report the average marginal effects on the conditional predicted probabilities (see Long & Freese, 2006, Chapter 6).

(16) In Chapter 6, we address the real but sparse presence of additional stipends for language skills in public safety.

(17) A very strong colinearity occurs between speaking Spanish at home and ethnic self-identification as Hispanic (see the appendices located at http://faculty.utep.edu/jmheyman for technical details). This is unsurprising, but it means that we cannot add ethnicity as a separate variable in the models. The interesting implication for further research would be to look at the occupational placement of monolingual English Hispanics in the borderlands, to see if they do or do not manifest these advantages of overrepresentation in professional and managerial occupations.

References

Alarcón, A. (2007) Informationalism, globalisation and trilingualism: An analysis of the statistics of linguistic practices in small and medium companies in Catalonia. *Noves SL: Revista de Sociolingüística*, tardor-hivern (no volume, no pagination). See http://www6.gencat.net/llengcat/noves/hm07tardor-hivern/a_alarcon1_5.htm (accessed 12 August 2012).

Alarcón, A. and Heyman, J.McC. (2012) Limites socioeconomicos a la extensión de la lengua española en los Estados Unidos. *Revista Española de Investigaciones Sociológicas* 39, 3–20.

Alarcón, A. and Heyman, J.McC. (2013) Bilingual call centers at the US-Mexico border: Location and linguistic markers of exploitability. *Language in Society* 42, 1–21.

Aldashev, A., Gernandt, J. and Thomsen, S.L. (2009) Language usage, participation, employment and earnings – Evidence for foreigners in West Germany with multiple sources of selection. *Labour Economics* 16, 330–341.

Anderson-Mejías, P.L. (2005) Generation and Spanish language use in the lower Río Grande valley of Texas. *Southwest Journal of Linguistics* 24, 1–12.

Bills, G.D. (1989) The US Census of 1980 and Spanish in the Southwest. *International Journal of the Sociology of Language* 79, 11–28.

Bills, G.D., Hernández-Chavez, E. and Hudson, A. (1995) The geography of language shift: Distance from the Mexican border and Spanish language claiming in the southwestern United States. *International Journal of the Sociology of Language* 114, 9–27.

Boutet, J. (2001) Le travail devient-il intellectuel? *Travailler: Revue Internationalle de Psychopathologies et Psychodynamique du Travail* 6, 55–70.

Castells, M. (1998) *La era de la información*, Vol. II. Madrid: Alianza Editorial.

Cortina, J., Pinto, P. and De la Garza, R. (2008) No Entiendo: The Effects of Bilingualism on Hispanic Earnings. ISERP Columbia University Working Paper, 2008-6.

Charles, M. and Marschan-Piekkari, R. (2002) Language training for enhanced horizontal communication: A challenge for MNCs. *Business Communication Quarterly* 65 (2), 9–29.

Chiswick, B.R. (2008) The Economics of Language: An Introduction and Overview. IZA Discussion Paper 3568, Institute for the Study of Labor (IZA).

Chiswick, B.R. and Miller, P.W. (2010) Occupational language requirements and the value of English in the United States labor market. *Journal of Population Economics* 23, 353–372.

Cohen, D. (2009) *Three Lectures on Post-Industrial Society*. Cambridge, MA: Massachusetts Institute of Technology Press.

Daly, C. (2012) Immigration and education: Setbacks and opportunities for earnings along the Texas–Mexico border. *Journal of Borderlands Studies* 27, 287–298.

Gal, S. (1979) *Language Shift: Social Determinants of Linguistic Change in Bilingual Austria*. New York: Academic Press.

Glaser, B.G. and Strauss, A.L. (1967) *The Discovery of Grounded Theory: Strategies for Qualitative Research*. Chicago: Aldine Publishing Company.

Grin, F., Sfreddo, C. and Vaillancourt, F. (2010) *The Economics of the Multilingual Workplace*. New York: Routledge.

Heller, M. (2003) Globalization, the new economy and the commodification of language and identity. *Journal of Sociolinguistics* 7, 473–492.

Heller, M. (2010) The commodification of language. *Annual Review of Anthropology* 39, 101–114.

Hidalgo, M. (1993) The dialectics of Spanish language loyalty and maintenance on the US-Mexico border: A two-generation study. In A. Roca and J.M. Lipski (eds) *Spanish in the United States: Linguistic Contact and Diversity* (pp. 47–74). Berlin: Mouton de Gruyter.

Hidalgo, M. (2001) Spanish language shift reversal on the US-Mexico border and the extended third space. *Language and Intercultural Communication* 1, 57–75.

Jenkins, D.L. (2009) The cost of linguistic loyalty: Socioeconomic factors in the face of shifting demographic trends among Spanish speakers in the Southwest. *Spanish in Context* 6, 7–25.

Long, J.S. and Freese, J. (2006) *Regression Models for Categorical and Limited Dependent Variables Using Stata* (2nd edn). College Station, TX: Stata Press.

Martínez, G. (2009) Hacia una sociolingüística de la esperanza: El mantenimiento inter-generacional del español y el desarrollo de comunidades hispanohablantes en el sudoeste de los Estados Unidos. *Spanish in Context* 6, 127–137.

McCullough, R.E. and Jenkins, D.L. (2005) Out with the old, in with the new? Recent trends in Spanish language use in Colorado. *Southwest Journal of Linguistics* 24 (1-2), 91–110.

Mills, S. (2005) Acculturation and communicative need in the process of language shift: The case of an Arizona community. *Southwest Journal of Linguistics* 24, 111–125.

Montejano, D. (1987) *Anglos and Mexicans in the Making of Texas, 1836–1986*. Austin, TX: University of Texas Press.

Mora, M.T., Villa, D.J. and Dávila, A. (2006) Language shift and maintenance among the children of immigrants in the US: Evidence in the census for Spanish speakers and other language minorities. *Spanish in Context* 3, 239–254.

O'Hara-Devereaux, M. and Johansen, R. (1994) *Globalwork*. San Francisco: Jossey-Bass.

Peri, G. and Sparber, C. (2009) Task specialization, immigration and wages. *American Economic Journal: Applied Economics* 1 (3), 135–169.

Reich, R. (1991) *The Work of Nations*. New York: Alfred A. Knopf.

Richardson, C. (1999) *Batos, Bolillos, Pochos, and Pelados: Class and Culture on the South Texas Border*. Austin, TX: University of Texas Press.

Rivera-Mills, S. (2001) Acculturation and communicative need: Language shift in an ethnically diverse Hispanic community. *Southwest Journal of Linguistics* 20, 211–223.

Shin, H-J. and Alba, R. (2009) The economic value of bilingualism for Asians and Hispanics. *Sociological Forum* 24, 254–275.

Silva Corvalán, C. and Lynch, A. (2009) Los Mexicanos. In H.L. Morales (coord.) *Enciclopedia del Español en los Estados Unidos* (pp. 104–111). Alcalá de Henares: Instituto Cervantes-Santillana.

Tubergen, F. and Kalmijn, M. (2009) Language proficiency and usage among immigrants in the Netherlands: Incentives or opportunities? *European Sociological Review* 25 (2), 169–182.

Velázquez, I. (2009) Intergenerational Spanish transmission in El Paso, Texas: Parental perceptions of cost/benefit. *Spanish in Context* 6, 69–84.

Veltman, C.J. (1981) Anglicization in the United States: The importance of parental nativity and language practice. *International Journal of the Sociology of Language* 32, 65–84.

Villa, D., and Villa, J. (2005) Language instrumentality in a border region: Implications for the loss of Spanish in the Southwest. *Southwest Journal of Linguistics* 24, 169–184.

6 Returns to Spanish–English Bilingualism in the New Information Economy: The Health and Criminal Justice Sectors in the Texas Border and Dallas-Tarrant Counties

Amado Alarcón, Antonio Di Paolo, Josiah Heyman and María Cristina Morales[1]

Introduction

While human capital perspectives suggest that having additional skills, such as speaking Spanish in addition to English, should be an asset in the labor force, particularly in regions where there are many Spanish as well as English speakers, we have limited quantitative knowledge on this topic. In this chapter, we investigate whether Spanish–English bilingualism[2] is associated with increased earnings. While our source variable is earned income, our analysis excludes the self-employed so the income variable thus represents wages. In Chapter 5, this volume, we found that bilingual employees are overrepresented in jobs with high levels of public interaction; this confirmed findings from previous qualitative research on how Spanish is used in multilingual settings (Alarcón & Heyman, 2012, 2013). This suggests that there is a value to bilingualism relative to job access; however, we do not know whether this translates to favorable wages. Following the human capital framework, we expect Spanish bilingualism to be rewarded in terms of earnings, possibly through selective hiring into well-compensated jobs, higher compensation within job titles and/or selective promotions. However, we also consider an alternative hypothesis associated with the marginalization of the Spanish-speaking workforce. It is possible that Spanish bilingualism might not be economically rewarded, even when individuals speak English very well, due to the relatively low wages of Hispanics in the US labor market.

Investigation of returns to bilingualism occurs in the US context, where Spanish proficiency has historically been negatively associated with earnings and positively with low-skill labor, resulting in a shift from Spanish to English across generations. Two possible trends may change this: language shift reversal which hypothesizes greater Spanish retention across generations (Hidalgo, 2001; Mora *et al.*, 2005); and the intensification of the so-called new information economy, in which oral as well as symbolic communication has heightened roles in production processes (see literature review in Chapter 5). These two putative trends suggest the possibility that the historically negative returns to Spanish may have been reversed for bilinguals. Prior ethnographic research suggests that this would not be the case, at least in the US–Mexico borderlands, where the Spanish language is often treated in employment processes (hiring, compensation, promotion) as an uncompensated 'heritage' language freely available from the extensive Mexican-origin community (Heyman & Alarcón, 2012; see also Villa & Villa, 2005). Here, we explore that qualitative finding as a hypothesis in a quantitative fashion.

A preliminary quantitative inquiry found a statistically significant reduction in earnings of 5% for bilinguals who speak English very well in comparison to those who only speak English, even after controlling for key occupations and human capital factors along the length of the US–Mexico border (see Chapter 5). The negative association of bilingualism with earnings emerges in contrast to the human capital expectation of elevated earnings for bilinguals, though it is consistent with past research. Given the unique linguistic and geographic context of the study (US–Mexico border region), it is possible that this finding might be an artifact of the context, where there is an abundant supply of bilinguals (along with a high demand for English–Spanish bilingualism) engaged in public interaction. It is possible that on the border a wage bonus is not necessary to attract and retain bilinguals.

In this chapter, we use a paired comparison of two regions within the state of Texas, one border and one nonborder. We restrict the analyses to Texas in order to control for socioeconomic-political factors on the macro level that may influence wages. Thus, we utilize geographic sites with both substantial Spanish-dominant and English-dominant populations, meaning that public interaction roles should favor flexible bilingualism, although in one of the sites there are fewer bilingual individuals. Moreover, we focus specifically on two economic sectors characteristic of the new information economy, health and public safety, in which communication with a multilingual public is important. Consistent with this, we classify occupations by the role of language in the work process, which allows us to examine the possible returns to bilingualism in labor markets where we hypothesize the effects might be strongest.

Literature Review

Human capital, language skills and wages

Language skill is widely conceived as another form of human capital. Acquiring proficiency in a second or foreign language is costly in terms of time and effort; it represents an asset that is embodied in the individual and, in general, is productive in the labor market. Second or foreign language acquisition is thought to foster job opportunities and increase earnings, which should produce a premium in the labor market because of the usefulness of bilingualism for international trade and its relative scarcity in the labor force (Ginsburg & Prieto-Rodriguez, 2011). Indeed, bilingualism represents a valuable resource in a global economy, but not all languages are the same in the global language system. Williams (2011) calculates the returns of foreign languages in 15 countries of the European Union. While English proficiency has positive and significant returns in all countries, the only country where foreign language bilingualism does not have significant returns is the United Kingdom, an already English-dominant country. Indirectly, this informs the question of whether there are limits on returns for non-English languages in English-speaking settings, such as the United States.

Turning from returns to 'foreign languages' to the role of multiple languages inside nation-states, the economic literature has devoted substantial attention to the role played by limited proficiency in the host country's language among immigrant workers. The general lesson is that immigrants who are proficient in the language of the host country earn more than those who are not and this holds true for the US as well (Chiswick, 2008; Chiswick & Miller, 1995; González, 2005). The same framework can be applied to officially multilingual societies. In fact, internal multilingualism has been proven to be an economic advantage in terms of occupational sorting and/or earnings both for native and foreign-born. This is the case in Catalonia (Di Paolo & Raymond, 2012; Rendon, 2007), Switzerland (Cattaneo & Winkelmann, 2005; Grin, 1997; Grin & Sfreddo, 1998), Wales (Drinkwater & O'Leary, 1997), Canada (Albouy, 2008; Chiswick & Miller, 1988; Grenier, 1987; Shapiro & Stelcner, 1997; Vaillancourt, 1992) and Finland (Saarela & Finnäs, 2003, 2004). In each of these cases, internal multilingualism emerges from historical situations of linguistic diversity and is reinforced by cultural and political values. It provides economically valuable roles and opportunities for persons with such capabilities. Is the value of bilingualism in the US Southwest an exception?

Language as human capital is only one of the analogies used by economists. Another well-known analogy is the phrase 'language as currency' (Carr, 1985) with network externalities and monopolistic properties (Economides, 1996; Katz & Shapiro, 1986, 1994). Every new speaker adds value to a given language, with increasing returns associated with network externalities (Church & King, 1993). Here, it is not scarcity but relative abundance that gives value to a language. Intergroup relations are affected by macrostructure variables such as size, heterogeneity and segregation among groups (Blau, 1977). These variables are introduced in economic models in addition to individual-level variables in order to analyze the value of language in local markets.

From this perspective, the value of a second language can reflect the productivity added to the work process (Breton, 1978; Savoie, 1996). The lack of data regarding language use in the production process makes explaining evidence of irrelevant or negative economic returns for bilinguals relatively difficult, as we discuss below. Some recent research analyzes the links between language skills (mainly regarding English) and occupations. Peri and Sparber (2009) suggest that native and foreign-born workers with little formal education are imperfect substitutes in production. Immigrants are likely to have imperfect language skills, but they possess physical skills similar to those of native-born workers. Native and foreign-born workers specialize accordingly. According to Chiswick and Miller (2010), proficiency in English is associated more with intraoccupational increases in earnings than it is with interoccupation increases in earnings.

> For both birthplace groups, labor markets appear to sort workers appropriately, with those with high levels of English proficiency tending to work in jobs which require a high level of proficiency and in which English-language proficiency is important. Thus, there is a complementarity in occupational choice (i.e. English proficient workers tend to work in jobs requiring proficiency) and in generating earnings (i.e. English-proficient workers earn more than those not proficient, and this effect is greater the higher the level of proficiency required by the occupation). (Chiswick & Miller, 2010: 369)

However, this literature focuses on immigrants with an imperfect command of the dominant language; we add to this literature by considering occupational placement, income returns and, indirectly, productivity gains from high English skills and high non-English skills among *bilingual workers*; likewise, we not only investigate whether occupations benefit from English proficiency, but also from bilingual proficiency.

In this regard, Fry and Lowell (2003) consider that bilinguals could be important in some occupations, especially those requiring extensive public contact in locations with extensive non-English speakers, in the face of negative results regarding wage premiums for bilinguals in general. Some occupational studies centered on the health sector have focused on wage premiums for bilinguals. Spanish-speaking bilingual registered nurses earned premiums up to 5%, with the wage premium *falling* 0.5% for each 2% increase in the fraction of the population that spoke Spanish. Therefore, it seems that the supply effect (scarce vs nonscarce Spanish-speaking professionals) dominates over the linguistic demands of customers (Kalist, 2005: 115). A study of registered nurses by Coomer (2011) considered the demand for bilingual Spanish-speaking nurses by taking into account the proportion of the state population that speaks a language other than English at home, the percent Hispanic and their interactions. The results show neither positive nor significant interactions, but rather:

> suggest that the majority of the premium is due to accounting for levels of skill and availability that would otherwise be unknown to the firms. Bilingual nurses, by learning a second language, signal to the market that they have higher ability and skills. (Coomer, 2011: 281)

In this case, bilingual nurses have higher skill levels compared to nonbilinguals. We aim to generalize this study by examining a wider (but related) range of occupations and sectors and by examining two geographic settings, a comparison of which will help examine possible supply effects.

Marginalization of Spanish speakers

Since the value of language is mainly attached to communication in the human capital theory, bilingualism poses some challenges for the theory. In terms of investment, the language spoken at home in the United States could be considered an 'inherited' human capital, not an investment in the strict sense. Within the US Hispanic population there exist different degrees of disinvestment in the context of linguistic acculturation (Alba & Nee, 2003; Telles & Ortiz, 2008). In a perfect bilingual economy, communicative instrumentalism cannot explain itself through language choices, but symbolic reasons, including ethnic prejudices, will be key to explaining language preferences and use.

The question of economic returns to bilingualism occurs in the US context where speaking Spanish has historically been associated with negative effects on earnings and continues to be associated with low-skill labor. Previous quantitative research on the influence of being bilingual among Hispanics (Mexican, Cubans and Dominicans) did not find a positive association with wages. Shin and Alba (2009), for instance, found a negative association between bilingualism and wages among Mexican-origin workers. In particular, Shin and Alba (2009: 269) argued that the size of the mother tongue population shows substantial and statistically positive effects on earnings for Mexicans, Cubans and Filipinos. Their finding contradicts that of Chiswick and Miller (2002), who found that a concentration of mother tongue speakers is negatively associated with immigrants' earnings. Since Shin and Alba restrict their sample to native-born and 1.5 generations, they conclude that the effects of mother tongue co-ethnics differ by generation and that English-speaking bilinguals can serve in intermediate roles. Ethnic capital shows a significant positive effect on earnings only among Mexicans; however, socioeconomic status shows a positive effect for all groups.

The marginalization thesis, which would support an association between bilingualism and depressed wages, can be attributed in part to the correlation between nondominant languages and immigration. With the current growth in the immigrant population comes a corresponding upsurge in nondominant languages in a given society. In the US, bilingualism is associated with lower earnings among the foreign-born and limited primary language retention among the native-born (Chiswick, 2008; Chiswick & Miller, 2007; de la Garza *et al.*, 2000; Fry & Lowell, 2003; Shin & Alba, 2009). In spite of discourses about the increasing market value of Spanish in the US:

> among native-born adult men, those who report they speak another language at home but speak English 'very well' (the highest proficiency category) earn about 4 percent less than otherwise statistically similar men who are monolingual English speakers. (Chiswick, 2008: 22)

Cortina *et al.*, (2008) titled their paper on Spanish language and earnings with an illustrative 'No entiendo' [I do not understand] to stress the contradictions between human capital theory predicting value for bilingualism, and findings suggesting that bilingualism is penalized in some segments of the Hispanic labor market. And, as Shin and Alba (2009: 273) argue, the retention of the mother tongue could be a proxy for the maintenance of other aspects of ethnic culture 'that may invoke tensions with or prejudices from Anglos'. Thus, evidence to date suggests that Spanish–English bilingualism in the US may not yield any wage premium at least in part because the Spanish language is associated with a marginalized group.

It is also possible that the association between wages and bilingualism varies contextually among different geographical places. For example, the returns for acquiring English-speaking skills for immigrants are higher in areas with lower concentrations of immigrants and where the majority can speak English. Ethnic heterogeneous areas mean that communication is interethnic and intergroup, increasing the value of English as a lingua franca (Chiswick, 2008; Chiswick & Miller, 2002, 2008). Hwuang *et al.*,

(2010: 19–22) found that while the importance of English is weakened by the size and spatial segregation of the immigrant group, it is augmented by the linguistic heterogeneity of the community in which immigrants reside. This, however, focuses on language learning by immigrants, and does not address the value of having both excellent English and an excellent non-English language (such as among some native-born Hispanics). Is there any geographic pattern to the relative reward to bilingualism, or conversely to its marginalization?

Research on earnings along the US–Mexico border is in accord with the marginalization perspective. The US side of the border continues to be among the most economically depressed areas in the country (Dávila & Mattila, 1985; Sáenz & Ballejos, 1993; Sáenz et al., 2009). Thus, Mexican immigrants living along border metropolitan statistical areas (MSAs) tend to have higher levels of self-employment but lower wages than their counterparts in the interior. Accentuating the influence of the US–Mexico border on wages, Sáenz et al., (2009) found that being from the border is associated with a negative effect on the wages of Mexican immigrants even though they represent a significant portion of the workforce compared to the interior. Thus, researchers have questioned the human capital perspective and the positive influence of working in places with significant ethnic concentrations on wages. In prior ethnographic research, Alarcón and Heyman (2012, 2013) found that in the US–Mexico borderlands, the Spanish language is often rewarded for hiring purposes, but in terms of pay, speaking Spanish is an uncompensated 'heritage' language freely available from the extensive Mexican-origin community. Given what we know about the border, we expect either no extra reward to bilingualism, or reduced pay compared to the interior; however, discrimination may be more intense in the interior than at the border, reversing these expectations. Here, we examine these questions in terms of economic returns and in an aggregate, quantitative fashion.

Hypotheses

Building on the literature and our previous work, we develop two competing hypotheses:

H1: Fluent bilingualism[3] is associated with higher earnings than English monolingualism. A subhypothesis is that we will see the strongest added compensation in occupations where oral communication with the public is most concentrated.

vs

H2: Speaking Spanish, regardless of English skills, is associated with depressed earnings in comparison to monolingual English speakers. A key variant of this hypothesis is that the most qualified Spanish speakers, those who speak English *very well* (fluent bilinguals), have reduced earnings in comparison to monolingual English speakers. Lower compensation for limited English proficient speakers is expected and is of less interest.

H0: In each case, the null hypothesis (H0) suggests that no significant difference exists between monolingual English speakers and Spanish speakers of varying English ability (but particularly fluent bilinguals).

In addition, we consider a geographic hypothesis:

H3: Earnings for fluent bilinguals will be higher in Dallas-Tarrant counties than the Texas border counties.

Methods

Data set and dependent variable

We employ data from the 2006–2010 Public Use Microdata Sample (PUMS) of the American Community Survey (ACS). The sectoral selection is described in Chapter 5. We exclude all persons not in the labor force, the unemployed, self-employed persons and all those below 18 years old or over 70 years old. We exclude part-time workers and those who declared working more than 80 hours per week, aiming to obtain a consistent measure of hourly wages. Our dependent variable, (logged) hourly wages, is constructed from three variables: wages (adjusted) during the past 12 months; hours per week; and weeks per year. We exclude all workers with constructed hourly wage levels below $7.00 (i.e. approximately minimum wage), since there is a possibility that those cases include erroneous information. The natural logarithm of hourly wages is used to minimize outliers in the distribution and to facilitate the interpretation of regression coefficients. The log form of wages can be interpreted as the percentage change in wages in response to a unit change in the independent variables. For control variables, the estimates represent the percentage change in hourly wages associated with a switch of the respective variable from zero to one (not present to present).[4]

Geographic selection

The study uses Public Use Microdata Areas (PUMAs) clustered into two groups: (1) PUMAs that include most of the substantially populated areas of the Texas border, and (2) all Dallas and Tarrant Counties PUMAs, which includes the cities in the interior of Texas – Dallas, Fort Worth and their respective suburban areas.[5] We chose this geography carefully to contrast the value of bilingualism in and out of the border region, though other geographic approaches will be worth exploring in future studies.[6]

Background characteristics illustrate the contextual difference between border and nonborder counties in Texas. Of the populations of Dallas County and Tarrant County, 15.8% and 10.9%, respectively, speak Spanish at home and English very well, while the percentages for representative Texas border counties are 50.4% (Hidalgo), 42.9% (Cameron), 42.1% (El Paso) and 40.0% (Webb).[7] In terms of the supply of high-quality bilinguals for jobs, these background data illustrate that the border region should significantly surpass Dallas-Tarrant and, hypothetically, we would see more reward in the latter. On the other hand, demand for bilinguals should be robust in both regions, though clearly higher in the border region. Of the populations of Dallas County and Tarrant County, 17.0% and 9.8%, respectively, speak Spanish at home and have limited English proficiency, while the percentages for representative Texas border counties are 51.6% (Webb), 33.5% (Hidalgo), 30.1% (El Paso) and 29.6% (Cameron).[8] In this regard, we might see wage elevation for bilinguals to be higher in the border counties than in Dallas-Tarrant, though we expect positive reward in either setting, given a substantial multilingual public.

The reason for doing the two studies inside Texas is to better control for differences in income levels between states. For instance, there is considerable income difference by state along the border from the higher-income west (California) to the lower-income east (Texas). By restricting our sample to Texas, we avoid the confounding element of applying a state variable to one geographic sample and not the other. The border–nonborder comparison, while not perfect, is better controlled within a particular state.

Independent variable: Language background

The independent variable, language background, is discussed in Chapter 5 on occupations, including the definition and terminology of categories and the limitations of the ACS data. Following our hypotheses, we focus on the earnings of fluent Spanish–English bilinguals ('fluent bilinguals') mainly in comparison to monolingual English speakers, but also limited English-proficient speakers.

Language-augmented wage regressions

Our purpose is to analyze earning differences between fluent bilinguals and monolingual English speakers and how they vary by region. Therefore, in the empirical analysis, we follow the standard earnings equation proposed by Mincer (1974), augmented by linguistic and migration-related variables as is usually done in the literature about economic returns to language skills (e.g. Chiswick, 2008; Chiswick & Miller, 2007). As controls, we consider human capital variables, sociodemographic variables, national origin and time since migration (a proxy for potential acculturation), economic sector and location (since the border has lower earnings than Dallas-Tarrant).[9] Because Chapter 5 indicates important differences in occupational concentrations among language speakers, and because occupations have different earnings levels, we treat occupational categories as important controls. By controlling for these variables, we refine our understanding of the key relationship between language background and earnings. Table 6.1 presents the overall wage regression with controls.[10]

The model in Table 6.1 controls for occupational distribution, but it does not examine earnings patterns by language background within each occupational group. These are presented in Table 6.2, which provides five separate models for the controlled relationship between language background and earnings. Finally, because we are interested in comparing (and not just controlling for) geographic location, Table 6.3 sorts the model results into two separate geographic areas, border vs interior (Dallas-Tarrant). In all tables, the coefficients associated with language represent percent wage changes relative to fluent bilinguals (reference category); positive coefficients mean higher wages and negative coefficients mean lower wages. (Statistical significance levels are indicated with asterisks, with a key at the bottom of the table).

Table 6.1 Overall model of wages by language group

Dependent variable: Log (hourly wage)

Monolingual English	0.060***
	(0.014)
Fluent bilingual	Reference category
Limited English proficient	−0.097***
	(0.023)
A. High symbolic analysts	Reference category
B. Low symbolic analysts	−0.396***
	(0.015)
C. High in-person service workers	−0.115***
	(0.013)
D. Low in-person service workers	−0.426***
	(0.019)
E. Manual workers	−0.446***
	(0.027)
Female (ref. male)	−0.070***
	(0.019)
Children at home	0.045***
	(0.009)
Married (ref. single or other situations)	0.089***
	(0.021)
Female* children	−0.039***

(Continued)

Table 6.1 (Continued)

Dependent variable: log (hourly wage)

	(0.010)
Female* married	−0.036
	(0.024)
Years of schooling	0.094***
	(0.003)
Potential experience	0.025***
	(0.002)
Square of (Potential experience)	−0.000***
	(0.000)
Years since migration (=0 for natives)	0.014***
	(0.004)
(Years since migration)^2	−0.000***
	(0.000)
Criminal justice (ref. health services)	0.023*
US-born	Reference category
Latin America	−0.218***
	(0.059)
Puerto Rico, US Islands and other developed countries	−0.096
	(0.061)
Other developing countries	−0.140**
	(0.070)
Border	Reference category
Dallas-Fort Worth	0.054***
	(0.013)
Constant	1.498***
	(0.052)
No. of observations	8698
R2	0.425
Adjusted R2	0.424

***$p < 0.01$; **$p < 0.05$; *$p < 0.1$; robust standard error within parentheses.

Results

In the overall analysis (Table 6.1), the income for monolingual English speakers is 6% higher than for fluent bilinguals, even with extensive controls applied. Fluent bilinguals in turn earn 9.7% more than limited English proficient speakers. Both results are statistically significant at conventional levels. Further analysis[11] shows that uneven occupation distributions of language groups, as discussed in Chapter 5, have a substantial effect on earnings. Even when linguistic distribution is taken into account, as seen in Table 6.1, a significant disparity by language background remains.

Table 6.2 Model of wages by occupational group and language group

Dependent variable: Log (hourly wage)	A. High symbolic analysts	B. Low symbolic analysts	C. High in-person services	D. Low in-person service	E. Manual work
Monolingual English	0.038	0.039	0.076***	0.077*	0.004
	(0.034)	(0.024)	(0.020)	(0.040)	(0.069)
Fluent bilingual	Reference category				
Limited English proficient	-0.063	-0.098***	-0.025	-0.062	-0.161**
	(0.064)	(0.034)	(0.038)	(0.039)	(0.074)
Female (ref. male)	-0.087**	0.057	-0.052*	-0.078*	-0.142**
	(0.043)	(0.046)	(0.028)	(0.043)	(0.065)
Children at home	0.073***	0.048*	0.037***	0.013	-0.033
	(0.018)	(0.029)	(0.011)	(0.026)	(0.031)
Married (ref. single or other situations)	0.150***	0.148**	0.004	0.079	0.186***
	(0.046)	(0.065)	(0.029)	(0.053)	(0.067)
Female* children	-0.031	-0.062**	-0.043***	-0.029	0.035
	(0.021)	(0.030)	(0.014)	(0.028)	(0.039)
Female* married	-0.101*	-0.097	0.033	0.039	-0.208**
	(0.054)	(0.067)	(0.034)	(0.061)	(0.086)
Years of schooling	0.135***	0.055***	0.105***	0.049***	0.017**
	(0.006)	(0.006)	(0.005)	(0.007)	(0.008)
Potential experience	0.044***	0.019***	0.030***	0.013***	0.015**
	(0.004)	(0.003)	(0.002)	(0.003)	(0.007)
Square of (Potential experience)	-0.001***	-0.000***	-0.000***	-0.000**	-0.000*
	(0.004)	(0.003)	(0.002)	(0.003)	(0.007)

(Continued)

Table 6.2 (Continued)

Dependent variable: Log (hourly wage)	A. High symbolic analysts	B. Low symbolic analysts	C. High in-person services	D. Low in-person service	E. Manual work
	(0.000)	(0.000)	(0.000)	(0.000)	(0.000)
Years since migration (=0 for natives)	0.012	0.006	0.013**	0.007	0.016
	(0.012)	(0.007)	(0.006)	(0.008)	(0.014)
(Years since migration)^2	-0.000	-0.000	-0.000**	-0.000	-0.000
	(0.000)	(0.000)	(0.000)	(0.000)	(0.000)
Criminal justice (ref. health)	-0.035	0.105***	0.011	0.248***	0.156**
	(0.024)	(0.028)	(0.019)	(0.034)	(0.076)
US-born	Reference category				
Latin America	-0.148	-0.119	-0.269***	-0.177*	-0.266*
	(0.163)	(0.098)	(0.082)	(0.107)	(0.154)
Puerto Rico, US Islands and other developed countries	-0.011	-0.058	-0.130	-0.181	-0.070
	(0.172)	(0.110)	(0.080)	(0.154)	(0.096)
Other developing countries	-0.061	-0.077	-0.070	-0.302***	-0.034
	(0.169)	(0.119)	(0.105)	(0.111)	(0.367)
Border	Reference category				
Dallas-Fort Worth	0.078**	0.149***	0.000	0.066	0.123**
	(0.032)	(0.024)	(0.019)	(0.040)	(0.055)
Constant	0.577***	1.531***	1.277***	1.783***	2.082***
	(0.117)	(0.104)	(0.078)	(0.105)	(0.159)
No. of observations	2,170	1,387	3,803	1,020	318
R2	0.341	0.220	0.238	0.271	0.311
Adjusted R2	0.336	0.211	0.235	0.259	0.272

***$p<0.01$; **$p<0.05$; *$p<0.1$; robust standard error within parentheses.

Table 6.3 Model of wages by geographic location and language group

Dependent variable: Log (hourly wage)	Border	Dallas-Fort Worth
Monolingual English	0.059***	0.069***
	(0.021)	(0.019)
Fluent bilingual	Reference category	
Limited English proficient	−0.041*	−0.040
	(0.025)	(0.041)
Female (ref. male)	−0.098***	−0.048**
	(0.032)	(0.024)
Children at home	0.019	0.067***
	(0.012)	(0.013)
Married (ref. single or other situations)	0.088***	0.091***
	(0.032)	(0.029)
Female* children	−0.015	−0.059***
	(0.015)	(0.014)
Female* married	0.001	−0.053*
	(0.038)	(0.031)
Years of schooling	0.089***	0.099***
	(0.005)	(0.004)
Potential experience	0.021***	0.028***
	(0.003)	(0.002)
Square of (Potential experience)	−0.000***	−0.000***
	(0.000)	(0.000)
Years since migration (=0 for natives)	0.019***	0.007
	(0.006)	(0.006)
(Years since migration)^2	−0.000***	−0.000
	(0.000)	(0.000)
Criminal justice (ref. health services)	0.089***	−0.023
	(0.019)	(0.015)
A. High symbolic analysts	Reference category	
B. Low symbolic analysts	−0.437***	−0.370***
	(0.027)	(0.018)
C. High in-person services	−0.089***	−0.120***
	(0.024)	(0.015)
D. Low in-person service	−0.399***	−0.439***
	(0.031)	(0.023)
E. Manual work	−0.448***	−0.441***
	(0.045)	(0.034)

(Continued)

Table 6.3 (Continued)

Dependent variable: Log (hourly wage)	Border	Dallas-Fort Worth
US-born	Reference category	
Latin America	−0.302***	−0.082
	(0.083)	(0.083)
Puerto Rico, US Islands and other developed countries	0.009	−0.104
	(0.095)	(0.081)
Other developing countries	−0.136	−0.093
	(0.144)	(0.088)
Constant	1.577***	1.454***
	(0.083)	(0.065)
No. of observations	2,979	5,719
R2	0.423	0.420
Adjusted R2	0.419	0.418

***$p<0.01$; ** $p<0.05$; *$p<0.1$; robust standard error within parentheses.

In order to obtain finer-grained evidence about the effect of occupations on the language–earnings relationship, in Table 6.2 we divide the sample into five wage models according to occupation. We find a significant ($p < 0.01$) negative differential of 7.6% for fluent bilinguals compared to English-only speakers among one occupational category (C) – workers who provide in-person services with a high need for spoken interaction. A marginally significant negative relationship emerges for fluent bilingualism in occupational category (D) – low speech intensity service workers. These effects remain even when controlling for multiple background and labor market characteristics. The hypothesis that fluent bilinguals would receive added remuneration for their linguistic job skills in occupations with a high need for oral interaction with a multilingual public was not supported; indeed, the converse held true. No occupational category demonstrates a significant boost in income for the highest level of bilinguals (very well), rejecting the positive hypothesis (H1) for all occupations. Table 6.2 also reports significant lower levels of income across most occupations (except for managers/professionals, where the number is relatively small) for limited English proficient persons, a result that was expected following the literature.

Table 6.3 reports separate results for the two geographic areas, the Texas border and Dallas-Tarrant, respectively (that is, it sorts Table 6.1 by geography). In this specification, we consider occupation as a control variable, so we report results for all occupations combined. The estimated coefficients for fluent bilinguals compared to English monolinguals are negative in both regions, and do not differ greatly from each other (though the inequality is greater in the interior than the border). We can thus reject both the hypothesis that the two regions will differ and the hypothesis that Dallas will have higher earnings premium for bilinguals than the border; however, we cannot demonstrate whether the relative scarcity of fluent bilinguals in the interior results in their elevated compensation. In both areas, persons with limited English proficiency also had significantly lower earnings compared to fluent bilinguals and monolingual English speakers, but this was expected.

In summary, the hypothesis (H1) that fluent bilingualism would result in added reward is rejected overall, for both geographical regions and for all occupational groups. We find no evidence of positive compensation for fluent bilingualism in our analysis. Rather, the hypothesis that Spanish speakers (notably fluent bilinguals who speak English very well) would receive reduced compensation is supported in the overall data and for both geographic regions. Strikingly, this hypothesis proves true among occupation C workers (high in-person service), with high skill and intensive oral skill public interaction. Fluent bilinguals show a high concentration in sector C occupations where we expected higher rather than lower productivity, demand and compensation for bilingualism. H2 is also supported at a weak level of significance for fluent bilinguals in low oral skill service occupations and, unsurprisingly, for workers with lower skill levels in English. We reject the null hypothesis (H0), no significant differences in earnings between fluent bilinguals and monolingual English speakers, for the overall data and for both geographic regions; however, it is supported for all occupations except C and, weakly, D occupations. Finally, H3, the hypothesis that Dallas-Tarrant counties would have higher compensation than the Texas border for fluent bilinguals is rejected; both regions had reduced earnings relative to English-only speakers, but the border was somewhat less reduced than the interior.

Discussion and Future Directions

Our findings suggest that workers with the highest quality of bilingualism that our data can identify do not receive higher wages than monolingual English speakers, and in some occupations receive significantly lower wages. Notably, this pattern is most concentrated in occupations with the highest level of oral interaction with the public, occupations with the highest concentration of bilinguals. Our findings hold for both border and nonborder regions, reducing the likelihood of findings specific to geographic peculiarities.

Overall, we find that *Spanish speakers with very good skills in English* (to emphasize their high degree of linguistic human capital) experience a 6% decrease in wages in comparison to monolingual English speakers. The amount of the disparity is not large, but its very existence is notable and deserves explanation. It moves counter to the occupational advantages of bilingualism discussed in Chapter 5, and indeed it is concentrated in occupations where bilingualism should convey the most productivity benefits. Conventional human capital theory would predict an increase in earnings, not a decrease, all other factors being equal. We can imagine the base situation to be speaking English very well, whether as an English-only monolingual or as a bilingual. Speaking Spanish then should be an asset on top of speaking English very well. The absence of this human capital benefit is especially striking since we controlled for a number of other human capital factors that otherwise might have confounded the relationship between language and earnings: years of education, potential labor market experience, gender and family-related variables, country of origin, years since migration, etc. This is reinforced by our finding that the relative scarcity of Spanish speakers with fluent bilingual skills in the interior vs the relative abundance of such speakers at the border is not reflected in added compensation to attract them to employment in interior locales. We cannot say definitely that the overall earnings inequality comes from speaking Spanish, whatever the person's skill is in English, but a strong case can be made for this, which points to the marginalization perspective over the human capital perspective.

Given the constraints of the data and due to the limitations discussed below, we cannot explain these findings fully, but we propose several caveats about the data and then directions for further study and possible explanation. First, the language questions in the ACS have limits. As discussed in Chapter 5, the ACS questions refer only to oral skills at home (e.g. speaking Spanish to some family members), and we are making an inferential leap in translating them into an asset in the workplace (e.g. speaking Spanish for functional purposes to the public). Also, the English-language skill of bilinguals who report that they speak English 'very well' may not be as good on average as monolingual English speakers. However, that source of error may have been controlled for in our models by including years of education and number of years in the US, which should include education in American English. Moreover, our models eliminate Hispanics who speak English at home, but also speak Spanish; doing so, may have eliminated a group of more linguistically assimilated Hispanics who could have better labor market outcomes; this remains unknown.

Second, the role of language in productivity is addressed only inferentially (as in Chapter 5). Thus, a direct analysis of language use in the workplace must be done in order to understand precisely when and how the benefits of bilingualism are produced as well as what they might be (Grin *et al.*, 2010: 75). Hence, we do not fully understand the relationship between the productivity of bilingualism and worker compensation for it, though we have made progress in framing the topic.

Third, there may be unmeasured human capital factors, such as quality of education (the ACS only contains information about the highest educational attainment). Many possible occupational credentials are missing from the ACS. Likewise, individual career trajectories and personal decisions cannot be measured.

Fourth, perhaps English-only speakers have social network connections that provide income advantages and entry into professional and managerial positions, though not entry into public interface occupations. That brings us to the final possible explanation – discrimination. Discrimination cannot be proven with these data, but the case for its possible presence is strengthened by a study where (1) occupational concentration (e.g. in public interface occupations) runs in the opposite direction from compensation, when we would expect occupational demand for bilinguals to drive up wages; and (2) some degree of control for other causal factors is provided.

As we pointed out in Chapter 5, there is a long history of intense racism against Mexican-origin persons in Texas, both in the borderlands and in the Dallas-Tarrant region; while overt racial discrimination has declined (more definitively at the border than in the Dallas-Fort Worth region), structural racial inequality (e.g. unequal schooling), bias against Spanish as an immigrant, working-class and low-income language and some personal biases against Mexican-origin persons persist (Montejano, 1987: 297–300). It is interesting that our data apply specifically to persons who speak Spanish at home vs those who speak English at home; it may be that factors such as discrimination and unequal social networks emerge most clearly in data based on language at home rather than language used in public, even when the public setting logically has a greater effect on compensation at work. It is also interesting that the wage disparity of monolingual English speakers over fluent bilinguals is higher in Dallas-Fort Worth than along the border, since overt racial discrimination has persisted more in interior Texas and declined more along the border.

A number of future studies can follow from the present study. First, a larger geographic scope can examine if these patterns hold outside of Texas, with its intense history of racism against the Spanish-speaking community. For instance, it would be interesting to isolate the effects in areas in new immigrant destinations from regions with a long history of immigrant settlements. Likewise, studies might look for related patterns in other economic sectors than health and public safety; the new information economy extends across a variety of sectors and occupations. Our analysis is limited to Spanish–English bilingualism; it would be useful to examine other occupations and wages for other bilinguals (e.g. various Asian populations). The language variable in the ACS has serious limitations, which might be overcome by using other secondary or primary data sets. Finally, this study calls for qualitative and quantitative studies of hiring, classification, compensation and promotion processes. In particular, we need to understand how fluent bilingualism's negative returns emerge in these internal and external labor market processes, and the possible effects of wider dimensions of social–cultural inequality.

Conclusions

Among employees in the health and public safety sectors, fluent bilinguals receive lower average wages than monolingual English speakers, despite their added linguistic asset. This holds true for both the Texas border region and the Dallas-Tarrant counties, suggesting that the absence of a positive wage increment for bilingual skills is not specific to the saturated supply of bilinguals in the border region. There is a lower comparative wage for fluent bilinguals, specifically for workers in occupations involving high skill, intensive oral contact with the public, even though consideration of their work roles suggests that they would be most valuable in these activities and the occupational study elsewhere in this volume found them most concentrated there. All of these observations are statistically significant. Many alternative explanations are controlled for in the regression model.

An important societal good, bilingualism, is put at risk by being compensated less than English monolingualism. The ability to speak Spanish as well as English, or any other second, third, etc., language, is a valuable work asset contributing to the organizational and societal good. Not compensating it,[12] let alone rendering significant earnings penalties, will devalue good-quality bilingual skills in both material and prestige terms. That, in turn, may discourage its occurrence and cultivation (e.g. going from home-learned skills in Spanish to a command of oral and written workplace Spanish). That is a public and private sector loss, as well as a personal loss.

In our qualitative research in El Paso (a major border city), Texas, we found that Spanish is often brought into the workplace as a naturally occurring 'heritage language' (Alarcón & Heyman, 2012, 2013). Sometimes, absolutely no effort is made to recruit bilingual personnel; bilingualism is simply assumed to occur often enough in the local workforce that someone with these skills will be available when needs arise. In other cases, there is conscious effort to have at least some bilingual personnel in key public interface occupations, but they do not need to be rewarded for having that skill or for the specific language brokerage activities that they perform. We suggested, based on those studies, that Spanish–English bilingualism is unrecognized as an economic (human capital) asset or a specific factor of production. This quantitative, aggregate wage study, which builds on our qualitative case study research in a grounded theory process, cannot *prove* the heritage language analysis, but it adds important support to it.

Notes

(1) All four authors are equal; the authors' names are alphabetical.

(2) Throughout the rest of the chapter, we refer simply to bilinguals and bilingualism when discussing Spanish–English bilingualism, given the focus of our work. We do describe some specifications and limitations of this broad phenomenon in the text.

(3) Fluent bilingualism, monolingual English speakers and limited English proficient speakers are defined and justified in Chapter 5.

(4) Additional technical details can be found in the Appendices located at http://faculty.utep.edu/jmheyman.

(5) Additional technical details can be found in the Appendices located at http://faculty.utep.edu/jmheyman.

(6) We actually examined several other geographic options. These included a combination of PUMAs from sites with relatively recent increases in the Hispanic population within Texas (Tyler, Longview and Waco) and two sites outside Texas, metro Nashville and metro Portland, Oregon. This was an attempt to see if areas with few existing bilinguals (little historical depth of Hispanic population) but substantial recent Latin American immigration (a Spanish-speaking public) would have a wage premium for bilinguals in public interaction jobs, following the analysis in Kalist (2005). However, there were too few cases of bilinguals in health and public safety in these sites in the ACS Public Use Microdata Sample to provide adequate variability for the regression models.

(7) Calculated from data from http://factfinder2.census.gov/faces/nav/jsf/pages/index.xhtml, accessed 13 February 2013.

(8) Calculated from data from http://factfinder2.census.gov/faces/nav/jsf/pages/index.xhtml, accessed 13 February 2013.

(9) Details on the specific choices and the construction of control variables can be found in the Appendices located at http://faculty.utep.edu/jmheyman.

(10) In this chapter, we collapse several occupational subcategories into the large categories A–E (see Table 5.1 in Chapter 5). As a control variable, the subdistinctions within those categories are of reduced interest (as opposed to our analytical aim in Chapter 5), and collapsing the categories eliminates small cells. Our analysis here is invariant to this action; data are available from the corresponding author.

(11) Available from the corresponding author.

(12) Some Texas public safety organizations do provide a stipend for second language skills, including the City of Dallas Police Department ($1800) and the City of Fort Worth Police Department ($1200). The City of El Paso Police Department provides no added stipend (consistent with our initial expectation that fluent bilingualism is easier to obtain on the border than in the interior) (State Auditor's Office, 2010: 31). However, these specific policies do not appear to affect the aggregate earnings data provided in the ACS, even when public safety is split as a sector (available from the corresponding author).

References

Alarcón, A. and Heyman, J.M. (2012) La frontera del español. Límites socioeconómicos a la extensión social de la lengua española en los Estados Unidos. *Revista Española de Investigaciones Sociológicas* 139, 3–20.

Alarcón, A. and Heyman, J.M. (2013) Bilingual call centers at the U.S.-Mexico border: Location and linguistic markers of exploitability. *Language in Society* 42 (1), 1–21.

Alba, R. and Nee, V. (2003) *Remaking the American Mainstream: Assimilation and Contemporary Immigration*. Cambridge, MA: Harvard University Press.

Albouy, D. (2008) The Wage Gap between Francophones and Anglophones: A Canadian Perspective, 1970–2000. Canadian Journal of Economics/Revue canadienne d'économique 41: 1211–1238.

Blau, P.M. (1977) Inequality and Heterogeneity. A Primitive Theory of Social Structure. New York: The Free Press.

Breton, A. (1978) Nationalism and language politics. Canadian Journal of Economics 11, 656–668.

Carr, J. (1985) Le bilingüisme au Canada: l'usage consacre-t-il l'anglais monopole naturel? In F. Vaillancourt (ed.) Economie et langue (pp. 27–37). Québec: Documentation du Conseil de la langue française.

Cattaneo, A. and Winkelmann, R. (2005) Earnings differentials between German and French speakers in Switzerland. Swiss Journal of Economics and Statistics 2, 191–212.

Chiswick, B.R. (2008) The Economics of Language: An Introduction and Overview. IZA Discussion Papers 3568, Institute for the Study of Labor (IZA).

Chiswick, B.R. and Miller, P.W. (1995) The endogeneity between language and earnings: International analyses. Journal of Labour Economics 13, 246–288.

Chiswick, B.R. and Miller, P.W. (1988) Earnings in Canada: The roles of immigrant generations, French ethnicity, and language. In T.P. Schultz (ed.) Research in Population Economics (pp. 163–182). Greenwich, CT: JAI Press Inc.

Chiswick, B.R. and Miller, P.W. (2002) Immigrant earnings: Language skills, linguistic concentrations and the business cycle. Journal of Population Economics 15 (1), 31–57.

Chiswick, B.R. and Miller, P.W. (2007) The Economics of Language: International Analyses. London: Routledge.

Chiswick, B.R. and Miller, P.W. (2010) Occupational language requirements and the value of English in the United States labor market. Journal of Population Economics. 23 (1), 353–372.

Church, J. and King, I. (1993) Bilingualism and network externalities. Canadian Journal of Economics 26, 337–345.

Coomer, N.M. (2011) Returns to bilingualism in the nursing labor market – Demand or ability? The Journal of Socio-Economics 40, 274–284.

Cortina, J., Pinto, P. and de la Garza, R. (2008) No Entiendo: The Effects of Bilingualism on Hispanic Earnings. ISERP Columbia University Working Paper 2008-6.

Dávila, A. and Mattila, J.P. (1985) Do workers earn less along the U.S.-Mexico border? Social Science Quarterly 66 (2), 310–318.

de la Garza, R.O., Haynes, C.W. and Lee, J. (2000) The Impact of Bilingualism on Earnings. University of Texas Austin.

Di Paolo, A. and Raymond, J.L (2012) Language knowledge and earnings in Catalonia. Journal of Applied Economics XV (1-2012), 89–118.

Drinkwater, S.J. and O'Leary, N.C. (1997) Unemployment in Wales: Does language matter? Regional Studies 31, 581–591.

Economides, N. (1996) The economics of networks. International Journal of Industrial Organization 14, 670–699.

Fry, R. and Lowell, B.L. (2003) The value of bilingualism in the U.S. labor market. Industrial & Labor Relations Review 57 (1), 128–140.

Ginsburg, V. and Prieto-Rodriguez, J. (2011) Returns to foreign languages of native workers in the European Union. Industrial & Labor Relations Review 64 (3), 599–618.

González, L. (2005) Nonparametric bounds on the returns to language skills. Journal of Applied Econometrics 20 (6), 771–795.

Grenier, G. (1987) Earnings by language group in Quebec in 1980 and emigration from Quebec between 1978 and 1981. Canadian Journal of Economics XX (November), 774–791.

Grin, F. (1997) Langue et differentials de statut socio-conomique en Suisse. Bern: Bundesamt für Statistik.

Grin, F. and Sfreddo, C. (1998) Language-based earnings differentials on the Swiss labor market: Is Italian a liability? International Journal of Manpower 19, 520–532.

Grin, F., Sfreddo, C. and Vaillancourt, F. (2010) *The Economics of the Multilingual Workplace*. New York: Routledge.

Hidalgo, M. (2001) Spanish language shift reversal on the US-Mexico border and the extended third space. *Language and Intercultural Communication* 1, 57–75.

Hwang, S.S., Xi, J. and Cao, Y. (2010) The conditional relationship between English language proficiency and earnings among US immigrants. *Ethnic and Racial Studies* 39, 1620–1647.

Kalist, D.E. (2005) Registered nurses and the value of bilingualism. *Industrial and Labor Relations Review* 59 (1), 101–117.

Katz, M.L. and Shapiro, C. (1986) Technology adoption in the presence of network externalities. *Journal of Political Economy* 94, 822–841.

Katz, M.L. and Shapiro, C. (1994) System competition and network effects. *Journal of Economic Perspective* 8, 93–116.

Mincer, J. (1974) *Schooling, Experience, and Earnings*. New York: NBER Press.

Montejano, D. (1987) *Anglos and Mexicans in the Making of Texas, 1836–1986*. Austin, TX: University of Texas Press.

Mora, M.T., Villa, D.J. and Dávila, A. (2005) Language maintenance among the children of immigrants: A comparison of border states with other regions of the U.S. *Southwest Journal of Linguistics* 24, 127–144.

Peri, G. and Sparber, C. (2009) Task specialization, immigration, and wages. *American Economic Journal: Applied Economics* 1 (3), 135–169.

Rendon, S. (2007) The Catalan premium: Language and employment in Catalonia. *Journal of Population Economics* 20 (3), 669–686.

Saarela, J. and Finnäs, F. (2003) Unemployment and native language: The Finnish case. *The Journal of Socioeconomics* 32 (1), 59–80.

Saarela, J. and Finnäs, F. (2004) Interethnic wage variation in the Helsinki area. *Finnish Economic Papers* 17 (1), 35–58.

Sáenz, R. and Ballejos, M. (1993) Industrial development and persistent poverty in the Lower Rio Grande Valley. In W.W. Falk and T.A. Lyson (eds) *Forgotten Places: Uneven Development in Rural America* (pp. 102–124). Lawrence, KS: University Press of Kansas.

Sáenz, R., Murga, L. and Morales, M.C. (2009) Wage determinants of Mexican immigrant women along the Mexican-U.S. border. In M.T. Mora and A. Dávila (eds) *Labor Market Issues along the U.S. - Mexico Border: Demographic and Economic Analyses* (pp. 120–138). Tucson, AZ: University of Arizona Press.

Savoie, G. (1996) The comparative advantages of bilingualism in the job market: Survey of Studies. In *New Canadian Perspectives. Official Languages and the Economy* (pp. 65–88). Ottawa, Canadian Heritage: Minister of Public Works and Government Services Canada.

Shapiro, D.M. and Stelcner, M. (1997) Language and earnings in Quebec: Trends over twenty years, 1979–1990. *Canadian Public Policy/Analyse de Politiques* XXIII (June), 115–140.

Shin, H. and Alba, R. (2009) The economic value of bilingualism for Asians and Hispanics. *Sociological Forum* 2 (1), 254–275.

State Auditor's Office [Texas] (2010) Report on the State's Law Enforcement Salary Schedule (Salary Schedule C). SAO Report No. 10-707. See http://www.sao.state.tx.us/reports/main/10-707.pdf (accessed 20 August 2013).

Telles, E.E. and Ortiz, V. (2008) *Generations of Exclusion: Mexican Americans, Assimilation and Race*. New York: Russell Sage Foundation Press.

Vaillancourt, F. (1992) An economic perspective on language and public policy in Canada and the United States. In B.R. Chiswick (ed.) *Immigration, Language, and Ethnicity, Canada and the United States* (pp. 179–228). Washington DC: The AEI Press.

Williams, D.R. (2011) Multiple language usage and earnings in Western Europe. *International Journal of Manpower* 32, 372–393.

7 The Literal Cost of Language Assimilation for the Children of Immigration: The Effects of Bilingualism on Labor Market Outcomes

Orhan Agirdag

Introduction

Starting in the early 1980s, scholars have extensively examined the effects of immigrants' host-country language skills on their economic integration. These studies univocally conclude that immigrants who are more proficient in the dominant language of the host country earn higher wages (see Grin, 2003). However, this literature is dominated by a *deficit* perspective, as the emphasis is placed on what immigrants may *not* have, i.e. host-country language skills. What is generally missing in this literature is a *strengths* perspective, an investigation of immigrants' linguistic potential, i.e. native language proficiency. Hence, in this chapter, I focus on the relationship between bilingualism and immigrants' economic adaptation.

The lack of research on the effects of bilingualism on earnings is surprising because for half a century sociologists and sociolinguists have shown the benefits of bilingualism with respect to various cognitive, educational and socioemotional outcomes (Agirdag et al., 2013a; Bankston & Zhou, 1995; Bialystok, 1988; Cummins, 1978; Peal & Lambert, 1962; Portes & Hao, 2002; Rumbaut & Cornelius, 1995). However, research on the economic consequences of bilingualism is virtually nonexistent as labor market outcomes are mostly studied by economists who typically use standardized 'human capital theory' models in which skills in a minority language are rarely considered as a form of human capital (i.e. a source of economic advantage).[1] In various countries with high numbers of immigrants, fluency in another language is generally treated as a problem, rather than as an asset (see Agirdag, 2010; Agirdag *et al.*, 2013b; Rios-Aguilar & Gándara, 2012). Adopting an interdisciplinary approach, I incorporate sociological/sociolinguistic perspectives regarding the benefits of student bilingualism into an economic analysis of immigrants' integration in the labor market. More specifically, I examine whether student bilingualism in the long term is related to early career employment status and earnings. It should be noted that most of the economics studies cited above limit their analyses strictly to the foreign-born population; however, regarding the impact of immigrant languages, the assessment of the *children* of immigrants might be even more relevant because language assimilation plays an important role in their lives (see Portes & Rumbaut, 2001). Therefore, analyses are not limited to foreign-born individuals, but rather include data on both first- and second-generation young adults who have lived in the US since at least middle-school age and have grown up speaking a language other than English.

Literature and Theory

Immigrants in the economy

Regarding the literature investigating the economic situation of immigrants in the US, I distinguish between an 'optimistic' perspective, which focuses on the successful adaptation of immigrants, and a 'pessimistic' perspective, which emphasizes their failures (for reviews, see Alba & Nee, 1997; Portes & Rumbaut, 2001). Works by Chiswick (1977, 1978) are widely cited as pioneering studies that yielded very optimistic results. Chiswick (1978) showed that after 10–15 years, immigrants achieved the same levels – and eventually exceeded – the earnings of the native-born. He attributed this quick and successful adaptation process to the positive self-selection of immigrant workers in terms of motivation and abilities (Chiswick, 1977, 1978). A second 'optimistic' research tradition points to the success stories of immigrant workers in ethnic subeconomies (enclaves) and the achievements of those engaged in self-employment (Light, 1984; Portes & Jensen, 1989; Portes & Zhou, 1996; Zhou & Bankston, 1998; Waldinger, 1986). These researchers found that ethnic subeconomies provide stable working conditions and higher earnings for immigrant workers, and that self-employment plays an important positive role regarding the economic adaptation of immigrant families.

The optimistic perspective is challenged by a more pessimistic one. For instance – contradicting Chiswick's findings – Borjas (1985) argued that the earnings of more recent cohorts of immigrants did not gain parity with those of the native-born, which he attributed to the decline in 'immigrant quality' because of the Third-World origin of immigrants (Borjas, 1985). Other studies have also questioned the advantageous effects of ethnic subeconomies. This view holds that immigrants are instead 'trapped' in an ethnic enclave economy where earnings are lower than the broader competitive sector (Mar, 1991; Nee *et al.*, 1994) and that there is no evidence that immigrant entrepreneurs are particularly successful (Borjas, 1990). Apart from the optimistic or the pessimistic perspectives, a constant finding is that there is an enormous diversity among immigrant groups with respect to their adaptation to the US economy (see Portes & Rumbaut, 2001).

Language as a determinant of earnings

The significance of language for the economic adaptation of immigrants derives from the fact that language is assumed to be more easily *alterable* than other aspects of human capital such as educational attainment, even though it takes 5–7 years to become fluent in English (Hakuta *et al.*, 2000). According to Grin (2003), there are four types of empirical studies that examine the relationship between language and earnings. The first focuses on labor market *discrimination against language groups*. These studies investigate whether *membership* in a language group results in earning differences. Because of the strong intersections between ethnic and language groups, few studies focus explicitly on the latter. However, studies that do so have found differences among language groups even after controlling for their skills in the dominant language of the host country (see Grin & Sfreddo, 1998).

A second group of studies has focused on *the value of skills in the dominant language of a country*, for instance, the impact of English fluency on the earnings of immigrants in the US. This type of research has emerged from various parts of the world (for the US: Chiswick, 1991; Chiswick & Miller, 2002; Kossoudji, 1988; McManus *et al.*, 1983; for Germany: Dustmann, 1994; Dustmann & Van Soest, 2002; for Belgium: H'madoun & Nonneman, 2012; for Canada: Chiswick & Miller, 2003; for the UK: Dustmann & Fabbri, 2003; Leslie & Lindley, 2001; for international comparisons: Chiswick & Miller, 1995). Unsurprisingly, these studies conclude that proficiency in the dominant host-country language is related to higher wages.

Grin (2003) argues that a third type of study has investigated *the value of skills in a nondominant language in a region*. Typical examples are native French-speaking Canadians who have learned English or native French-speaking Belgians who have learned Dutch. Although there are variations across regions and gender, this type of research generally points to wage benefits for bilinguals (see Grin, 1999; Vaillancourt, 1996).

Fourth, there is a category of investigations that focuses on the *value of skills in an immigrant language*. However, Grin (2003) states that these 'exceedingly rare' studies have found that the economic value of being proficient in an immigrant language is very low. Nevertheless, he argues that immigrant language skills might be an asset instead of a hindrance, 'contrary to what seems assumed a *priori* by much of the research in group B [the second research type]' (Grin, 2003: 20). To my knowledge, *only one* study of this type has been conducted in the US: Fry and Lowell (2003) found that being bilingual has a positive impact on the earnings of foreign-born men, with this positive impact mostly explained by the educational background of these immigrants. For reasons of 'convention', the effects on women were not examined in this study.

While Grin's typology is very useful, it is still possible to distinguish a *fifth type* of research, where scholars might investigate the long-term effects of bilingualism and/or language assimilation on incomes for children of immigrants. While this type of research might be considered a specific form of the fourth type described above, it is distinct as the focus shifts from immigrants and immigration policy toward linguistic diversity and educational policy. The core question here is whether students' bilingualism should be valued in the educational system for the sake of economic benefits for individuals and society. Indeed, previous studies on immigrant students have found that there are several *metaphorical costs* associated with linguistic assimilation, such as a more problematic family and personality adjustment (e.g. Portes & Hao, 2002) and decreasing educational success (e.g. Feliciano, 2001). However, these outcomes are only short term, while language assimilation might also have *literal costs* in the long term. That is, student bilingualism might also have an impact on future earnings. Needless to say, the main goal of this study is to provide the first example of this type of research.

The value of linguistic skills: A Bourdieusian framework

Why are skills in a minority language expected to be positively associated with the earnings of immigrants and their children? To answer this question, I draw on the writings of Pierre Bourdieu, briefly sketching his theories about linguistic domination (Bourdieu, 1977b), using the concepts of field, doxa, heterodoxy and orthodoxy (Bourdieu, 1977a) and applying his notions of capital (Bourdieu, 1986).

In 'The economics of linguistic exchanges', Bourdieu (1977b) states that the value of being competent in a certain language – which he calls *linguistic capital* – is highly dependent on the social contexts in which these linguistic competences are used. Bourdieu called these social contexts 'linguistic markets' or 'fields': 'Linguistic competence functions as linguistic capital in relationship to a certain market' (Bourdieu, 1977b: 651). Any field or market primarily involves power relations between the dominant and the dominated groups, and therefore between the dominant and dominated languages. Bourdieu asserts that in a situation of bilingualism, a dominant and dominated language will emerge along social-class lines:

> A language is worth what those who speak it are worth, i.e. the powers and authority in the economic and cultural power relations ... the dominant language is the language of the dominant class. (Bourdieu, 1977b: 652)

As the dominant class has control over the educational system, it has the power to impose the rules that are followed within the field of economics, including those regarding the legitimacy and/or the value of a language. When the rules imposed on languages overtly favor the dominant group, linguistic dominance persists as long as the linguistically dominated group does not recognize it as a form of domination. Rather, the dominant *and* dominated groups are inclined to perceive this linguistic domination as something natural and obvious. Such collectively shared, taken-for-granted beliefs/opinions are called *doxa* (Bourdieu, 1977a). However, Bourdieu argues that each doxa might be challenged by competing actions. The dominated linguistic groups are more likely to behave in a *heterodox* way, meaning they will resist the doxa. This resistance involves, among other things, moving their (linguistic) competences to subfields in which they might function as (linguistic) capital. The dominant group, on the other hand, is more likely to behave in an *orthodox* manner, meaning they are more likely to reestablish the doxic tradition (Bourdieu, 1977a).

The application of this theory to the linguistic situation in the US is straightforward. It is clear that English monolingualism is a dominant ideology that favors the dominant monolingual class. As English monolingualism constitutes a quasi-doxa within the field of education, it is also a rule that is tacitly imposed in other fields such as the economy. Because this monolingual doxa is threatened by growing linguistic diversity, an orthodox position is taken by the English-only movement (e.g. ProEnglish or English First). The Bourdieusian framework also makes clear why the English-only movement opposes above all bilingualism in the field of education. On the other hand, the heterodox position is taken by the English Plus movement, which supports the preservation of bilingual education. Moreover, the linguistically dominated groups move to take up positions within subfields of the economy (submarkets) where their minority linguistic skills might function as linguistic capital. Some well-known examples of such subfields or submarkets are ethnic enclaves such as the many Chinatowns or the Cuban enclave in Miami.

How then is immigrants' linguistic capital converted to higher earnings? Let us conceptualize earnings as a form of economic capital, and consider the theoretical conversion process between the notions of cultural, social and economic capital (see Bourdieu, 1986). Bourdieu states that cultural capital exists in three different states. First, it can exist in *embodied* form, i.e. knowledge and skill that are incorporated by a social actor. Bourdieu (1986) states that linguistic capital is an example of embodied cultural capital. Second, it exists in *objectified* form, i.e. cultural objects that can be owned, such as books. Third, it can be *institutionalized* when it is officially recognized, mostly in the form of academic credentials. Finally, Bourdieu (1986) also distinguishes *social capital*, defined as 'resources which are linked to possession of a durable network'. All three forms of cultural and social capital can be converted to economic capital.

Minority linguistic capital (as embodied cultural capital) can be converted to higher earnings (economic capital) both *directly* and *indirectly*. Direct effects should be understood as bilinguals' ability to carry out duties that monolinguals cannot, such as interacting with customers who only speak the minority language. Bilingual persons might therefore be qualified for jobs with higher wages. Minority linguistic capital can also have an indirect effect, that is through conversion to other forms of capital. First, if bilingualism is positively related to educational outcomes (see Feliciano, 2001), minority linguistic capital might first be converted to *institutionalized cultural capital* (academic qualifications), which in turn, results in higher earnings. Secondly, minority linguistic capital might also give a person access to specific *objectified cultural capital* such as books or advertisements published in a minority language. To have access to such objects might give a boost to an entrepreneur's business. Thirdly, minority linguistic capital can be converted to social capital: that is, it might give an entrance to a social network in which the minority language prevails, access to which might result in higher earnings.

Nevertheless, it might be the case that the value of cultural and social capital that is specific to linguistic minorities is lower than the value of cultural and social capital within the English monolingual market because of linguistic racism. However, net of linguistic racism, bilinguals have access to *both* the English monolingual market *and* specific minority language subfields. In other words, all else being equal, I hypothesize that the earnings of bilinguals will be higher because they can take positions in specific linguistic minority subfields *in addition to* the regular market.

Methodology

Sample and design

Data for this study came from two different data sets: the NELS of 1988/2000, which is administered by the National Center for Educational Statistics, and the CILS of 1991/2003, which is administered under the supervision of Alejandro Portes and Rubén Rumbaut (see Portes & Rumbaut, 2005). For both data sets, the selection of participants was based on a two-stage stratified sample with schools as the first-stage unit and a sample of students within each selected school as the second-stage unit. The NELS survey was initiated in 1988 and included over 24,000 eighth-grade students across the US. The final follow-up with information about the employment status and income of the respondents was conducted in 2000, when most respondents turned 26. In contrast to the NELS, the CILS is not a nationally representative study, but it is specifically intended to investigate the adaptation process of the immigrant second-generation. The second-generation is broadly defined as children with at least one foreign-born parent or children born abroad but brought to the US at an early age. The original CILS survey was conducted in 1992 with 5000 children attending the eighth and ninth grades in schools in Miami/Fort Lauderdale and San Diego. In 2002, when most respondents turned 24, a final follow-up was conducted which included information about their employment status and income. To exclude a potential interfering effect of discrimination of linguistic minorities, analyses were limited to respondents who initially stated that another language than English is spoken at home (*hereafter* the native language) and for the sake of comparability between both data sets, the NELS data were additionally limited to respondents with immigrant roots.

Before analyzing earnings, I first examine whether bilingualism is related to respondents' employment status. More specifically, I conduct multinomial logistic regression analyses to predict full-time employment relative to either part-time employment or unemployment, comparing *balanced bilinguals*[2] to the *English-dominant* groups. The CILS and the NELS data are then limited to those who are employed full-time, to investigate the effects of bilingualism on earnings. Ordinary least-squares (OLS) regression analyses are employed for this purpose. The regression analyses are conducted with SPSS version 20. For the OLS regression, missing data are handled with the multiple imputation procedure: five imputations are requested and the pooled results are shown (Allison, 2002). Additionally, using only the CILS data, I examine whether noncognitive factors (self-esteem and family cohesion) account for the impact of bilingualism on earnings.

Outcomes

This study examines two distinct outcomes: employment status and earnings.

Information about *employment status* draws from the last follow-up of both the NELS and CILS. I distinguish between three categories: full-time employment, part-time employment and unemployment. For the CILS data, 1897 respondents were employed full-time (70.8%), 582 worked part-time (21.7%) and 199 respondents were unemployed (7.4%). Students, homemakers and disabled respondents of the final CILS follow-up are not included in the analysis. For the NELS data, 1371 respondents were employed full-time (80.8%), 109 worked part-time (6.4%) and 216 respondents were unemployed (12.7%). Respondents who were students during the final NELS follow-up are not included in the analysis.

Annual income. The annual earnings of the respondents were collected during the last follow-up of both the NELS and CILS. For the CILS, respondents were asked to state their monthly earnings from all sources. The NELS respondents were asked to state how much they earn before taxes and other deductions. They could report their earnings hourly, weekly, bimonthly, monthly or annually. I converted all earnings responses for both the NELS and CILS to annual earnings by multiplying by common full-time factors: hourly earnings by 2100, weekly by 52, bimonthly by 24 and monthly by 12 (see Table 7.1 for descriptive statistics on the NELS and CILS, after restriction of the sample to full-time workers). Most economists prefer to take the natural logarithm of earnings, i.e. log-linear form, for theoretical reasons regarding the statistical distribution of earnings. However, there are theoretical, practical and methodological reasons for avoiding this practice and staying with the linear form (for an elaborated discussion, see Portes & Zhou, 1996). Practically seen, the linear form yields coefficients that are directly interpretable as dollar gains per unit change in the independent variable, while the log-linear form is harder to interpret (i.e. as average percentage change in earnings). Theoretically, the log-linear form yields the *relative* impact of the independent variables, whereas the linear form gives us information about *absolute* earnings. Therefore, the log-linear form can obscure real differences between groups and as such is less preferable when the focus is on *actual* differences in earnings (see Portes & Zhou, 1996). Finally, methodologically, a statistical analysis on this issue has demonstrated that converting wages to the natural logarithm produces more bias than it reduces (Blackburn, 2007). Blackburn (2007: 95) concludes: 'While there is little to gain statistically from log-wage regression analysis, there is much to lose'. I find these arguments convincing and therefore stay with the absolute (linear) levels of earnings.

Explanatory variable: Multilingual proficiencies

The CILS and NELS respondents were asked to self-assess their proficiencies in their native language and English with respect to speaking, understanding, reading and writing. There were four response categories for all items: 'very well', 'well', 'not well' and 'not at all'. It should be noted that for the CILS, this information was collected during the baseline, whereas for the NELS the most recent data on language proficiency were collected in 1990 during the first follow-up. Latent class analysis (LCA) is

Table 7.1 Descriptive statistics for the CILS and the NELS after limiting the sample to full-time employed respondents

	NELS				CILS			
	n	Min	Max	Mean (SD)	n	Min	Max	Mean (SD)
Bilingualism	1556				1897			
Limited		0	1	21.72%		0	1	20.72%
Balanced bilingual		0	1	17.22%		0	1	25.62%
English dominant		0	1	61.05%		0	1	53.66%
Earning (year)	1575	1000	500,000	32,873 (23502)	1699	960	204,000	26,223 (16658)
Gender	1656				1897			
Male		0	1	51.09%		0	1	48.34%
Female		0	1	48.91%		0	1	51.66%
Education attainment	1639	-2	3	0.51 (1.32)	1867	-2	2	-0.49(0.93)
Ability	1434	-19.07	22.98	0 (8.66)	1672	-69.70	16.00	0 (5.53)
Parental SES	1544	-2.23	2.87	0 (0.87)	1897	-1.60	2.15	0 (0.73)
National origin	1656				1878			
Mexico		0	1	34.72%		0	1	14.00%
Cuba		-	-	-		0	1	28.49%
Other Hispanic		0	1	16.67%		0	1	28.43%
Filipino		-	-	-		0	1	13.58%
China		0	1	6.10%		-	-	-
Other Asian		0	1	18.30%		0	1	13.90%
Other		0	1	24.21%		0	1	1.60%
Region	1594				-			
North-East		0	1	17.13%		-	-	-

	n	Minimum	Maximum	Mean (SD) / Proportion
North-Central	—	0	1	12.17%
South	—	0	1	29.80%
West	—	0	1	40.90%
City	1987	—	—	—
Miami	—	0	1	59.67%
San Diego	—	0	1	40.33%
Self-esteem	1684	-2.36	.54	0 (0.50)
Family cohesion	1685	-2.63	1.37	0 (1.01)

Note: Number of observations (n), minimum, maximum, mean with standard deviations in parentheses (for continuous variables) and proportion (for categorical variables).

conducted to cluster the respondents into various linguistic groups. For this purpose, the eight categorical items of language proficiency are entered as indicators of potential clusters, *in casu* distinct linguistic groups. For both data sets, the results of the LCA show that there are three clusters that make theoretical and empirical sense.[3] More specifically, I distinguish between three groups: (1) *limited bilinguals*, (2) *balanced bilinguals* and (3) *English-dominant* individuals. For the NELS, 17.22% of the sample is categorized as *balanced bilingual*; for the CILS, 25.62% is categorized as *balanced bilingual* (see Table 7.1 for descriptive statistics). Table 7.2 provides the probability scales of the LCA. Here, it is shown that respondents who clustered as *English-dominant* or *balanced bilinguals* have high levels of English proficiency: more than 90% of respondents in both groups understand, speak, read and write very well. However, in contrast with the *English-dominant* group, balanced bilinguals have high scores on their native language proficiency as well. Hence, the only difference between *balanced bilinguals* and the *English-dominant* group is that the former has higher native language skills. Table 7.2 also demonstrates that individuals belonging to the cluster of *limited bilingual* have lower overall proficiency than the other two groups. For instance, only 6% of limited bilinguals write very well in English and only 21% write very well in the native language (see Table 7.2).

Control variables

First, I attempt to rule out selection effects by including various control variables that might have an effect on the dependent variable. With respect to effects on employment status, models control for respondents' gender and educational attainment. With respect to effects on earnings, models control for gender, educational attainment, cognitive ability, parental SES, national origin and regional location (see Table 7.1 for descriptive statistics for the NELS and CILS, after restricting the sample to respondents who are employed full-time).

In both data sets, the *educational attainment* of the respondents is measured by their highest educational degree. To make the analysis more straightforward, I will use this ordinal variable as if it were a metric variable in the analyses.

Scores on a standardized math achievement test serve as an indicator of respondents' *cognitive ability*. For the NELS, this test was conducted in the spring of 1988; for the CILS data, the Stanford math achievement test was administered by the schools and scores were provided to the researchers in 1991.

As a measure of *parental SES*, I use the composite SES scores calculated by both the NELS and the CILS administrators: the SES composite for the NELS is composed of five variables including family income, parents' education levels and parents' occupations; the SES composite for the CILS

Table 7.2 Results of the latent class analysis (LCA): Probability scales for a three-class solution

	Native				English			
	Understand (%)	Speak (%)	Read (%)	Write (%)	Understand (%)	Speak (%)	Read (%)	Write (%)
Limited bilingual								
Not at all	2	4	18	22	1	1	0	0
Not well	4	7	20	23	5	7	12	15
Well	45	45	37	34	73	77	82	80
Very well	49	43	25	21	22	15	6	6
Balanced bilingual								
Not at all	0	0	0	0	0	0	0	0
Not well	0	1	0	6	1	0	0	0
Well	3	13	32	39	1	1	1	2
Very well	97	86	68	54	98	99	99	98
English dominant								
Not at all	1	3	26	37	0	0	0	0
Not well	12	34	47	50	0	0	0	0
Well	56	48	26	13	1	2	2	6
Very well	32	16	1	0	99	98	98	94

Note: Results are shown for the CILS data. The results for the NELS data are almost identical.

is computed using father's and mother's education, occupations and family home ownership.

I was able to distinguish between seven categories of *national origin* with frequencies larger than 100: (1) Mexico, (2) Cuba (*only in CILS*), (3) other Latin America, (4) Philippines (*only in CILS*), (5) China (*only in NELS*), (6) Other Asian, (7) Others.

Finally, I controlled for the location of the respondents using a proxy variable taken from information about the location of the schools in the baseline data. For NELS, four census regions were distinguished and for the CILS, I distinguished between Miami/Fort Lauderdale in Florida and San Diego in California.

Noncognitive variables

To assess whether the impact of bilingualism on earnings can be explained by noncognitive characteristics, I examine the mediating role of self-esteem and family cohesion. Both variables come from the first follow-up of the CILS data. Self-esteem is assessed with 10 items of the Rosenberg's Self-Esteem scale (Rosenberg, 1979). Family cohesion is measured with three items from the Family Cohesion scale (Portes & Rumbaut, 2001). See Table 7.1 for descriptive statistics.

Results

Bilingualism and employment status

The relationship between bilingualism and employment status is first considered with bivariate analysis, then with multinomial logistic regression analysis. In both the CILS and NELS, full-time employment is more common among *balanced bilinguals* than among the *English-dominant* group, for whom unemployment was higher. For the CILS data, 74.47% of *balanced bilinguals* were employed full-time and 5.58% were unemployed, while 68.59% of the *English-dominant* group was employed full-time and 7.65% were unemployed. Similar figures are found for the NELS data.

Table 7.3 shows the results of the multinomial logistic regression demonstrating the relationship between bilingualism and employment status while controlling for gender and educational attainment. The results indicate that *balanced bilinguals* are significantly more likely to be employed full-time than to be unemployed, relative to the *English-dominant* group; this holds true for both the CILS ($b = 0.413$, $p = 0.03$) and the NELS data ($b = 0.415$, $p = 0.06$). The CILS data also show that *balanced bilinguals* are significantly more likely to be employed full-time than part-time compared with the *English-dominant* group ($b = 0.336$; $p = 0.004$), although this finding was not replicated with the NELS data ($b = -0.108$; $p = 0.693$).

Table 7.3 Multinomial logistic regression: Effects on employment status for CILS and NELS data

	Full-time vs unemployed			Part-time vs unemployed			Full-time vs part-time		
	b	(SE)	p	b	(SE)	p	b	(SE)	p
CILS									
Intercept	2.270	(0.133)	***	0.974	(0.149)	***	1.296	(0.088)	***
Bilingualism									
Limited bilingual	-0.146	(0.185)		-0.539	(0.211)	**	0.393	(0.134)	**
Balanced bilingual	0.413	(0.198)	*	0.079	(0.217)		0.336	(0.118)	**
English dominant	Ref			Ref			Ref		
Gender (1=female)	-0.119	(0.151)		0.166	(0.167)		-0.166	(0.098)	**
Education attainment	0.038	(0.083)		-0.158	(0.094)		2516	(0.056)	***
NELS									
Intercept	2.789	(0.181)	***	-0.037	(0.257)		2.826	(0.197)	***
Bilingualism									
Limited bilingual	-0.269	(0.182)		-0.509	(0.309)		0.241	(0.276)	
Balanced bilingual	0.450	(0.244)	°	0.558	(0.345)		-0.108	(0.273)	
English dominant	Ref			Ref			Ref		
Gender (1=female)	-1.544	(0.189)	***	-0.906	(0.277)	***	-0.638	(0.221)	**
Education attainment	0.394	(0.060)	***	0.058	(0.095)		0.337	(0.081)	***

° = 0.06; *p≤0.05; **p≤ 0.01; ***p≤0.001.
Note: Unstandardized regression coefficients (b), standard errors (SE) in parentheses and significance levels (p).

Bilingualism and earnings

The relationship between bilingualism and employment status is first considered with bivariate analysis, then with OLS regression. The CILS data suggest that *balanced bilinguals* earn $24,126 annually, while *English-dominant* individuals earn $22,188, i.e. a difference of $1938. In turn, the NELS data suggest only a small difference: *balanced bilinguals* earn $34,154 annually, while the *English-dominant* group earns $34,109. It should be noted that the mean income level is higher for the NELS data because the NELS asked for income *before* tax deduction while the CILS asked for net income.

Table 7.4 demonstrates the net effects of bilingualism. It is clear that among the NELS respondents, balanced bilinguals earn $3292 more at the beginning of their career than their English-dominant counterparts ($p = 0.03$). Similarly, the CILS results show that balanced bilinguals earn $2096 more than the English-dominant group ($p = 0.04$). Remarkably, no significant differences emerge between the earnings of limited bilinguals and the English-dominant group, even though the English proficiency level of the English-dominant group is much higher than that of limited bilinguals.

In the second CILS model, I include self-esteem and family cohesion as covariates. While self-esteem is significantly related to earnings, the significant relationship between balanced bilingualism and earnings does not change with the inclusion of these factors. Hence, it cannot be argued that noncognitive factors mediate the effect of bilingualism.

While the control variables in the models shown in Table 7.2 are not the primary concern of this study, the careful reader will note that women earn significantly less than men, and that parental SES, cognitive ability and educational attainment are all positively related to annual earnings. In addition, only Chinese American young adults earn significantly more than the reference group, 'other' children of immigrants.

In fact, the positive associations between balanced bilingualism and earnings are conservative estimates that might underestimate the actual impact of bilingualism as it relates to educational attainment. A Bourdieusian framework would suggest that bilingualism might be related to earnings *through* educational attainment. That is, bilingualism might be positively associated with educational attainment, which in turn, is positively associated with earnings. Indeed, the NELS data suggest that balanced bilingualism results in higher educational attainment ($b = 0.158$; $p = 0.03$; not shown in tables), and that educational attainment is positively associated with earnings ($b = 3073$; $p < 0.001$). In other words, above and beyond the direct effect of balanced bilingualism on earnings, there is a significant indirect effect of balanced bilingualism via educational attainment ($b = 485$; $p = 0.03$, not shown in tables). However, this finding

Table 7.4 OLS regression: Effects on annual earnings for NELS and CILS

	NELS			CILS			CILS+noncognitive		
	b	(SE)	p	b	(SE)	p	b	(SE)	p
Intercept	33913	(1583)	***	28163	(3613)	***	27877	(3624)	***
Bilingualism									
Limited	536	(1412)		-451	(1086)		-203	(1103)	
Bilingual	3292	(1536)	*	2096	(1014)	*	1959	(1021)	*
English dominant	Ref			Ref			Ref		
Gender (1=female)	-6498	(1059)	***	-3444	(817)	***	-3308	(813)	***
Education attainment	3073	(489)	***	2590	(488)	***	2516	(484)	***
Ability	387	(80)	***	186	(84)	*	165	(86)	*
Parental SES	3053	(817)	***	1108	(634)		1106	(636)	
National origin									
Mexico	-429	(1504)		916	(3687)		1097	(3691)	
Cuba	–			-2353	(3126)		-2424	(3146)	
Other Hispanic	-1838	(1701)		-4000	(3122)		-4075	(3138)	
Filipino	–			-1128	(3704)		-641	(3710)	
China	10421	(2551)	***	–			–		
Other Asian	102	(1744)		3389	(3632)		3793	(3636)	
Other	Ref			Ref			Ref		

(Continued)

Table 7.4 (Continued)

	NELS			CILS			CILS+noncognitive		
	b	(SE)	p	b	(SE)	p	b	(SE)	p
Region									
North-East	3476	(1657)	*	–	–		–	–	
North-Central	133	(1885)		–	–		–	–	
South	–2070	(1309)		–	–		–	–	
West	Ref			–	–		–	–	
City									
Miami	–	–		3643	(2216)		3776	(2213)	
San Diego	–	–		Ref			Ref		
Self-esteem	–	–		–	–		2215	(883)	***
Family cohesion	–	–		–	–		–200	(436)	

*$p \leq 0.05$; **$p \leq 0.01$; ***$p \leq 0.001$.
Note: Unstandardized regression coefficients (b), standard errors (SE) in parentheses and significance levels (p).

did not emerge with the CILS data where bilingualism was not significantly associated with educational attainment.

Noncognitive effects

Having established that balanced bilingualism is generally related to higher earnings, the reader might wonder whether this holds true for different groups. For this purpose, I include interactions between balanced bilingualism and both gender and national origin. While in general the results suggest that the positive relationship between balanced bilingualism and earnings is stronger among females and Mexican Americans, these differences were not statistically significant, potentially due to small sample sizes.

Discussion and Conclusions

Regarding the economic adaptation of immigrants in the United States, few topics are more studied than the relationship between immigrants' linguistic competencies and their earnings. However, this topic is primarily studied from a *deficit* perspective, that is, the emphasis among economists has almost exclusively been on the language skills that immigrants *lack* (i.e. English proficiency). Only rarely have scholars investigated the potential benefit of immigrants' *linguistic assets* (i.e. native language skills). In spite of the strong societal pursuit of *English only*, sociology and sociolinguistics research has been focused on the benefits of bilingualism and the *metaphorical* costs of linguistic assimilation. Inspired by this tradition, this study investigated the *literal* costs of linguistic assimilation for children of immigrants who speak an other-than-English langue.

Analyses using two independent data sets (NELS and CILS) demonstrate significant financial *costs* associated with linguistic assimilation. First, multinomial logistic regression analyses demonstrated that balanced bilinguals are more likely to be employed full-time than English-dominant individuals, who are also more likely to be unemployed than balanced bilinguals. Second, OLS regression results indicate that *balanced bilinguals* earn significantly more than the *English-dominant* group, even after controlling for cognitive ability, parental SES, region and educational attainment. More specifically, compared to English-dominant individuals, balanced bilinguals earn between $2000 and $3200 more annually. It should be noted that this is only a conservative estimate as the total impact of balanced bilingualism might be higher because the NELS data suggest that there is an additional indirect effect via educational achievement. Additional analyses with the CILS data suggest that noncognitive factors (self-esteem and family cohesion of students) do *not* account for the positive impact of balanced bilingualism.

Before I discuss the implication of these results, it is important to mention a limitation of this study. Given the nature of the NELS and CILS data, analyses were limited to the earnings of young adults in their mid-twenties. It might be the case that this positive relationship occurs only among people at the beginning of their careers. Future research may want to investigate how bilingualism functions for the whole population.

Several important political implications emerge with respect to these findings. First, student bilingualism is not only important with respect to socioemotional and educational outcomes (as previous studies have shown, e.g. Feliciano, 2001; Portes & Hao, 2002), but also its contrast, complete linguistic assimilation, is detrimental to the *economy*. Recognizing the cost associated with linguistic assimilation is critical given the labor market situation of some immigrant groups such as Mexican Americans. In short, linguistic assimilation policies do not merely *steal* from people, they steal from those who already have *less*. These results pose fundamental questions about the long-term consequences of educational *English-only* policies. Research has shown that English learners do not benefit from the restriction of bilingual education in terms of educational outcomes (Gándara & Hopkins, 2010). These findings suggest that English learners may be placed at an even greater disadvantage, given the negative association between monolingualism and earnings. The results of this study provide support for English language programs that develop native language proficiency, which provides tangible labor market benefits.

These findings have implications for the use of the Bourdieusian theory as well. More specifically, previous studies mainly used the notions of cultural capital and linguistic capital to denote competencies in dominant cultural forms and in the dominant language (*in casu* English proficiency). This lack of focus on the potential value of minority languages relates to the origins of the Bourdieusian theory itself, which does not indicate how cultural forms in a multiethnic society should be conceptualized (see also Erel, 2010), not surprising as Bourdieu's original writings reflect the ethnically homogeneous French society of the 1960s. However, findings clearly indicate that competency in a minority language might function as cultural capital as well. We might call this *multicultural capital*, a distinct type of cultural capital resulting from the retention of ethnic and linguistic cultural forms. Like cultural capital, multicultural capital has the potential to be converted into economic capital. Given the increasing importance of transnational economies, it is likely that *multicultural capital* will increase in value in the future. The notion of multicultural capital might enrich the Bourdieusian framework, which unfortunately is frequently used to reinforce deficit theories regarding ethnic minorities. A potential challenge for many scholars is then to examine to what degree the possession of multicultural capital (such as bilingualism) compensates for the alleged 'lack' of cultural capital (such as proficiency in the dominant language). Pursuing monolingualism (in the field of education and elsewhere) facilitates the destruction of multicultural capital and wastes economic capital on purely ideological grounds.

Notes

(1) Economists have only recently argued for including aspects of 'ethnic human capital' in their models (see Chiswick, 2009), while empirical economic studies that do so are still rare.
(2) Clearly, *balanced bilingualism* might be regarded as a problematic concept (see Baker, 2011). For instance, if we interpret 'balanced' literally, then an individual who demonstrates relatively undeveloped but equal proficiency in two languages would be categorized as a *balanced bilingual*; however, this is not the connotation employed by researchers in the field. The implicit idea is that *balanced bilingual* refers to someone who demonstrates an 'appropriate' competence in two languages. However, as noted by Baker (2011), the term has proved to be of value in research and theory, and will be applied in this study as well.
(3) The entropy value was 0.904 for the CILS and 0.745 for the NELS; entropy values approaching 1 indicate a clear delineation of latent classes (Celeux & Soromenho, 1996).

References

Agirdag, O. (2010) Exploring bilingualism in a monolingual school system: Insights from Turkish and native students from Belgian schools. *British Journal of Sociology of Education* 31, 307–321.

Agirdag, O., Jordens, K. and Van Houtte, M. (2013a) Speaking Turkish in Belgian schools: Teacher beliefs versus effective consequences. *Bilig*.

Agirdag, O., Van Avermaet, P. and Van Houtte, M. (2013b) School segregation and math achievement: A mixed-method study on the role of self-fulfilling prophecies. *Teachers College Record* 115 (3), 1–50.

Alba, R. and Nee, V. (1997) Rethinking assimilation theory for a new era of immigration. *International Migration Review* 31, 826–874.

Allison, P.D. (2002) *Missing Data.* Thousand Oaks, CA: Sage Publications.

Baker, C. (2011) *Foundations of Bilingual Education and Bilingualism* (5th edn). Bristol: Multilingual Matters.

Bankston, C.L. and Zhou, M. (1995) Effects of minority-language literacy on the academic achievement of Vietnamese youth in New-Orleans. *Sociology of Education* 68, 1–17.

Bialystok, E. (1988) Levels of bilingualism and levels of linguistic awareness. *Developmental Psychology* 24, 560–567.

Blackburn, McKinley L. (2007) Estimating wage differentials without logarithms. *Labour Economics* 14, 73–98.

Borjas, G.J. (1985) Assimilation, changes in cohort quality, and the earnings of immigrants. *Journal of Labor Economics* 3, 463–489.

Borjas, G.J. (1990) *Friends or Strangers: The Impact of Immigrants on the U.S. Economy.* New York: Basic Books.

Bourdieu, P. (1977a) *Outline of a Theory of Practice.* Cambridge: Cambridge University Press.

Bourdieu, P. (1977b) The economics of linguistic exchanges. *Social Science Information* 16, 645–668.

Bourdieu, P. (1986) The forms of capital. In J.G. Richardson (ed.) *Handbook of Theory and Research for the Sociology of Education* (pp. 241–258). New York: Greenwood.

Celeux, G. and Soromenho, G. (1996) An entropy criterion for assessing the number of clusters in a mixture model. *Journal of Classification* 13, 195–212.

Chiswick, B.R. (1977) Sons of immigrants – Are they at an earnings disadvantage? *American Economic Review* 67, 376–380.

Chiswick, B.R. (1978) Effect of Americanization on earnings of foreign-born men. *Journal of Political Economy* 86, 897–921.

Chiswick, B.R. (1991) Speaking, reading, and earnings among low-skilled immigrants. *Journal of Labor Economics* 9, 149–170.

Chiswick, B.R. and Miller, P.W. (1995) The endogeneity between language and earnings – International analyses. *Journal of Labor Economics* 13, 246–288.

Chiswick, B.R. and Miller, P.W. (2002) Immigrant earnings: Language skills, linguistic concentrations and the business cycle. *Journal of Population Economics* 15, 31–57.

Chiswick, B.R. and Miller, P.W. (2003) The complementarity of language and other human capital: Immigrant earnings in Canada. *Economics of Education Review* 22, 469–480.

Chiswick, C.U. (2009) The economic determinants of ethnic assimilation. *Journal of Population Economics* 22, 859–880.

Cummins, J. (1978) Bilingualism and the development of metalinguistic awareness. *Journal of Cross-Cultural Psychology* 9, 131–149.

Dustmann, C. (1994) Speaking fluency, writing fluency and earnings of migrants. *Journal of Population Economics* 7, 133–156.

Dustmann, C. and Van Soest, A. (2002) Language and the earnings of immigrants. *Industrial & Labor Relations Review* 55, 473–492.

Dustmann, C. and Fabbri, F. (2003) Language proficiency and labour market performance of immigrants in the UK. *Economic Journal* 113, 695–717.

Erel, U. (2010) Migrating cultural capital: Bourdieu in migration studies. *Sociology* 44 (4), 642–660.

Feliciano, C. (2001) The benefits of biculturalism: Exposure to immigrant culture and dropping out of school among Asian and Latino youths. *Social Science Quarterly* 82, 865–879.

Fry, R. and Lowell, B.L. (2003) The value of bilingualism in the US labour market. *Industrial & Labor Relations Review* 57, 128–140.

Gándara, P.C. and Hopkins, M. (2010) *Forbidden Language: English Learners and Restrictive Language Policies*. New York: Teachers College Press.

Grin, F. (1999) *Compétences et Récompenses. La Valeur des Langues en Suisse* [*Skills and Rewards: The Value of Languages in Switzerland*]. Fribourg: Universitaires de Fribourg.

Grin, F. (2003) Language planning and economics. *Current Issues in Language Planning* 4, 1–66.

Grin, F. and Sfreddo, C. (1998) Language-based earnings differentials on the Swiss labour market: Is Italian a liability? *International Journal of Manpower* 19, 520–532.

H'madoun, M. and Nonneman, W. (2012) Explaining differences in job retention between alien and nonalien workers after an in-company training. *Applied Economics* 44, 93–103.

Hakuta, K., Butler, Y.G. and Witt, D. (2000) *How Long Does It Take English Learners to Attain Proficiency? Policy Report 2000–1.* Santa Barbara, CA: University of California, Linguistic Minority Research Institute.

Kossoudji, S.A. (1988) English-language ability and the labor market opportunities of Hispanic and East Asian immigrant men. *Journal of Labor Economics* 6, 205–228.

Leslie, D. and Lindley, J. (2001) The impact of language ability on employment and earnings of Britain's ethnic communities. *Economica* 68, 587–606.

Light, I. (1984) Immigrant and ethnic enterprise in North-America. *Ethnic and Racial Studies* 7, 195–216.

Mar, D. (1991) Another look at the enclave economy thesis: Chinese Immigrants in the ethnic labor market. *Amerasia Journal* 17, 5–21.

McManus, W., Gould, W. and Welch, F. (1983) Earnings of Hispanic men – The role of English-language proficiency. *Journal of Labor Economics* 1, 101–130.

Nee, V., Sanders, J.M. and Sernau, S. (1994) Job transitions in an immigrant metropolis – Ethnic boundaries and the mixed economy. *American Sociological Review* 59, 849–872.

Peal, E. and Lambert, W.E. (1962) *The Relation of Bilingualism to Intelligence*. Washington DC: American Psychological Association.

Portes, A. and Jensen, L. (1989) The enclave and the entrants – Patterns of ethnic enterprise in Miami before and after Mariel. *American Sociological Review* 54, 929–949.

Portes, A. and Zhou, M. (1996) Self-employment and the earnings of immigrants. *American Sociological Review* 61, 219–230.

Portes, A. and Rumbaut, R.G. (2001) *Legacies: The Story of the Immigrant Second Generation*. Berkeley, CA: University of California Press.

Portes, A. and Hao, L. (2002) The price of uniformity: Language, family and personality adjustment in the immigrant second generation. *Ethnic and Racial Studies* 25, 889–912.

Portes, A. and Rumbaut, R.G. (2005) Introduction: The second generation and the children of immigrants longitudinal study. *Ethnic and Racial Studies* 28, 983–999.

Rios-Aguilar, C. and Gándara, P. (2012) (Re)conceptualizing and (re)evaluating language policies for English language learners: The case of Arizona. *Language Policy* 11 (1), 1–5.

Rosenberg, M. (1979) *Conceiving the Self*. New York: Basic Books.

Rumbaut, R.G. and Cornelius, W.A. (1995) *California's Immigrant Children: Theory, Research, and Implications for Educational Policy*: San Diego, CA: Center for US-Mexican Studies, University of California.

Vaillancourt, F. (1996) Language and socioeconomic status in Quebec: Measurement, findings, determinants, and policy costs. *International Journal of the Sociology of Language* 121, 69–92.

Waldinger, R.D. (1986) *Through the Eye of the Needle: Immigrants and Enterprise in New York's Garment Trades*. New York: New York University Press.

Zhou, M. and Bankston, C.L. (1998) *Growing Up American: How Vietnamese Children Adapt to Life in the United States*. New York: Russell Sage Foundation.

8 English Plus: Exploring the Socioeconomic Benefits of Bilingualism in Southern California

Rubén G. Rumbaut

Introduction

This chapter presents the results of a study carried out in Southern California with a multiethnic and multigenerational sample of young adults in their twenties and thirties. It merges data from two major surveys of adult children of immigrants: Immigration and Intergenerational Mobility in Metropolitan Los Angeles (IIMMLA) and the Children of Immigrants Longitudinal Study (CILS) in San Diego. Both surveys utilized the same measures for key variables, and they were carried out at about the same time in the six contiguous counties of Southern California with respondents who were of similar ages, ethnicities and generations. The analysis examines the independent effects of bilingualism (measuring multiple dimensions of linguistic ability), or 'English plus', on three socioeconomic outcomes: dropping out of high school, occupational status and earnings. The nation's largest regional site of immigrant incorporation over the past three decades, Southern California is home to the greatest diversity of immigrants (in both national and social-class origins) to have settled in the US over this period, as well as to their rapidly growing second generations, providing a strategic site for research. Indeed, of the region's 21 million residents, by 2010 about half spoke a language other than English at home while the other half spoke English only – a linguistic context that lends itself to an investigation of the potential socioeconomic benefits (or not) of bilingualism vs English monolingualism. The analysis focuses on young adults in their twenties and thirties, especially those who are the children of immigrant parents – both those who immigrated as children and those who were born in the US – in comparison with young adult children of US-born parents (third or higher generations).

Language Use Patterns in the United States, 1980–2010

The acceleration of international migration to the United States since the 1970s has been accompanied by renewed linguistic diversity (see Rumbaut & Massey, 2013). The 1970 census reported the lowest proportion of foreign-born in the country's history: only 4.7% of the population. A decade later, when the 1980 census began asking people aged 5 and older if they spoke a language other than English at home, it found that 11% (23 million) of those five years and older answered in the affirmative, and nearly half of them (11 million, or 5% of the total population) reported that they spoke Spanish. In 1990, 14% (32 million) of the population reported speaking a language other than English at home. These figures rose sharply again in 2000 to 18% (47 million). And as of 2010, more than 20% (60 million) of the population aged 5 and older reported speaking a language other than English. What is more, nearly two-thirds of those non-native English speakers (37 million) reported speaking Spanish; currently, Spanish speakers comprise 13% of the population.

Because the census never asked whether this was the 'usual' language spoken at home, or how frequently it was used relative to English, or how proficiently it was spoken, it probably elicited a considerable overestimate. With these data, it is impossible to measure or determine the extent and meaning of 'bilingualism', let alone determine its value, if any, in labor markets and the economy. Still, the data do point to the presence of a very substantial and growing minority of people who are not English monolinguals. Of the 60 million speakers of non-English languages in the US in 2010, 57% were immigrants, as were 49% of those who spoke Spanish. However, a sizable proportion of non-English speakers are native-born (see Chapter 2, this volume). These non-English speakers are not distributed randomly throughout the country, but are concentrated in states and metropolitan areas of principal settlement, above all in California – despite a diversification in patterns of settlement to 'new destinations' since the 1990s (Portes & Rumbaut, 2014; Rumbaut & Massey, 2013) – and within California, above all in Southern California. In 1990, fully a third of the total immigrant population of the United States resided in California; while their relative proportion has since declined, still more than a fourth of all immigrants live in California today. What are the levels of bilingualism of the people of Southern California? And in a country with a dubious reputation as a language graveyard (cf. Alba et al., 2002; Portes & Rumbaut, 2014; Rumbaut, 2009) – and in a world where the dominance of English as a global language has long been on the rise – are there measurable economic advantages of bilingualism in the region's labor market?

Southern California encompasses a six-county region, from the Mexican border through the coastal counties of San Diego, Orange, Los Angeles and

Ventura, to the 'Inland Empire' counties of Riverside and San Bernardino. Of its 21 million residents, just over half (52%) speak English only, while the other half (48%) speak a language other than English at home, including 7 million (34%) who speak Spanish at home. Each of the six counties is 'majority-minority', as California as a whole has been since 1999. Non-Hispanic whites account for 37% of the region's total population, blacks for about 7% and the diverse population of Asian origins for 13%. Hispanics comprise a plurality of 43% (nearly 9 million, 7.3 million of whom are of Mexican origin). Indeed, nearly a quarter of the total Mexican-origin population of more than 32 million in the United States in 2010 was concentrated in Southern California.

Immigrant Nationalities, Class Origins and Modes of Incorporation

The national and linguistic diversity of contemporary immigrants pales in comparison to the diversity of their social-class origins (for further discussion, see Chapter 2, this volume). By far the most educated *and* the least educated groups in the United States today are immigrants; the highest and lowest rates of poverty are likewise found among immigrant nationalities. These wide disparities reflect polar opposite types of migrations embedded in different historical contexts – and inserted in an 'hourglass-shaped' labor market, which attracts both immigrant professionals and low-wage laborers. Immigrants arrive with or without legal authorization, and some as state-sponsored refugees; these legal statuses interact with their human capital to shape distinct modes of incorporation. The undocumented tend to consist disproportionately of manual laborers, whose legal vulnerability (and intensified fears of detention and deportation) makes them economically exploitable and concentrates them in central cities; their children often grow up in neighborhoods and attend schools where they are exposed disproportionately to peer groups involved with youth gangs and intergroup violence, and where they are exposed to the weakest schools (Orfield & Lee, 2005). 'Brain drain' professionals mainly enter under the occupational preferences of US law, and some are also found among the first waves of refugee flows; they are more likely to become naturalized citizens and, usually within the first-generation, homeowners in the suburbs where their children have access to the best-resourced schools. Internal group characteristics interact in complex but patterned ways with external contexts of reception (e.g. government policies and programs, the state of the economy and employer preferences in local labor markets, the extent of racial discrimination and nativist hostility, the strength of existing ethnic communities) to form the conditions within which immigrants and their children adapt to different segments of American society. An analysis of the socioeconomic benefits of bilingualism in local labor markets needs to take these complex determinants into account in order to disentangle the independent relationship of fluent bilingualism to educational, occupational and economic outcomes.

What do we know about foreign-parentage young adults in this transformed national context, of their bilingual abilities and patterns of socioeconomic mobility? How do they fare vis-à-vis their native-parentage peers who are English monolinguals? Unfortunately, decennial census data on parental nativity, which had until 1970 permitted the identification of the foreign-born (the first-generation) from the US-born of foreign parentage (second-generation) and of native parentage (third and beyond generations), have not been collected since. Moreover, neither the decennial census nor now the annual American Community Survey (US Census Bureau, 2011) has ever collected language data on the level of proficiency, preference and use of non-English languages (see earlier discussion in Chapters 3 and 4, this volume); instead they have been concerned only with ascertaining the level of English ability of those persons who report that a language other than English is spoken at home. Scholarship on adult outcomes among the new generations spawned by the current era of immigration thus needs to rely on especially designed regional surveys, such as the third wave of the CILS-III, the Immigrant Second Generation in Metropolitan New York (ISGMNY) study and the IIMMLA survey. The merged IIMMLA and CILS-San Diego samples constitute a unique data set and they will be the focus of the analysis that follows.

Pan-ethnic categories such as 'Asians' and 'Hispanics or Latinos' (or 'black' or 'white' for that matter) are not homogeneous, but rather a combination of many different nationalities, migration histories, legal statuses, phenotypes, class and cultural backgrounds and local contexts of adaptation in the US. Table 8.1 begins to unpack these categories by examining the largest immigrant nationalities in the US and in California, and identifying three main immigrant types based on (1) legal status at entry as classified by the government (with or without authorization, or as state-sponsored refugees) and (2) human capital (indicated by their level of education, ranging from professionals to manual laborers). While each type is represented by several nationalities, each nationality may also include individuals representing different types. The first type is composed of a majority of unauthorized laborers with less than a high school education (e.g. Mexicans, Salvadorans and Guatemalans); the second type encompasses a majority of legal permanent residents with college degrees or more advanced credentials (e.g. Filipinos, Chinese, Koreans and Indians); and the third type represents those admitted with refugee status (and access to public assistance on the same basis as US citizens), albeit with a mixed (often low) human capital profile (e.g. Vietnamese, Cambodians, Laotians and Cubans). These nationalities

Table 8.1 Major immigrant nationalities in the US and California by legal status and education 2010

| Immigrant types | Foreign-born population in the US | | | | | | | California | |
| | Foreign-born total | | Undocumented | | | Education (ages 25–64) | | | |
Country of birth	n (000s)	%	n (000s)	%	% of group that is undocumented	% college graduate	% less than high school	% of all US immigrants in California	% in Southern California
All immigrants	39,956	100.0	10,790	100.0	27.0	27.3	31.9	25.6	15.8
I: Low education, irregular entry									
Mexico	11,711	29.3	6,640	61.5	56.7	5.5	59.2	36.9	23.8
El Salvador	1,214	3.0	620	5.7	51.1	6.7	54.7	35.1	27.0
Guatemala	831	2.1	520	4.8	62.6	7.3	56.6	31.8	26.0
II: High education, regular entry									
Philippines	1,778	4.4	280	2.6	15.7	51.9	5.2	45.7	25.7
China, Taiwan	2,167	5.4	130	1.2	8.1	54.3	16.9	35.4	18.2
Korea	1,100	2.8	170	1.6	15.5	54.4	5.3	31.0	23.8
India	1,780	4.5	200	1.9	11.2	77.8	5.9	18.4	6.1
III: Refugees, state sponsored									
Vietnam	1,241	3.1	160	1.5	12.9	24.9	29.0	39.6	23.7
Cambodia, Laos	355	0.9	NA	NA	NA	8.4	53.7	33.5	19.2
Cuba	1,105	2.8	NA	NA	NA	23.4	19.0	3.7	3.1

Sources: American Community Survey 2010 (US Census Bureau, 2011); Office of Immigration Statistics, DHS (Hoefer et al., 2011).

(the Indians and Cubans excepted) make up the bulk of the IIMMLA and CILS-III samples that provide the focus of analysis below.

While the 40 million foreign-born in the US in 2010 came from some 190 countries, 11.7 million (29%) came from only one: Mexico. As Table 8.1 shows, another 11.2 million (28%) came from China (including Taiwan), the Philippines, India, Vietnam, Korea, El Salvador, Guatemala and Cuba.[1] Thus, more than half (57%) of the foreign-born population of the US has come from these nine countries – all with close historical ties to the US, including prior neocolonial episodes and wars (India is a main exception in that regard). These countries are also the principal sources of international migration to California (except for Cuba), accounting for more than three-fourths of the state total. Indeed, while California is home to 10% of the native-born population of the US, it is also home to between a third and a half of each of the major foreign-born groups of interest to our study.

In 2011, data from the Department of Homeland Security estimated the unauthorized population of the US at 10.8 million – down from an estimated 11.8 million in 2007, but tripling since the early 1990s. Over a fourth (27%) of the foreign-born residing in the US may be undocumented. Legal status is a critical factor in shaping mobility trajectories; unauthorized status can affect virtually every facet of an immigrant's life. As Table 8.1 indicates, all of the principal sources of legal immigration to the US are also among the top sources of unauthorized migration. More than half of all Mexican, Salvadoran and Guatemalan immigrants in the US today lack legal status – together they account for nearly three-fourths of the unauthorized population – but so are nontrivial proportions of Filipinos (16%), Koreans (16%), Vietnamese (13%), Indians (11%) and Chinese (8%).

Given pronounced differences in migration histories and statuses, human capital, family backgrounds and contexts of exit and of reception in the United States among these nationalities, we can hypothesize possible mobility trajectories for their 1.5- and second-generation adult children as they acculturate and make their way in the Southern California economy and labor markets. However, since we cannot ascertain those mobility outcomes intergenerationally with the available official statistics, nor the effect of bilingualism on those outcomes (cf. Stevens, 1999), we turn to two specialized surveys, IIMMLA and CILS.

Sample, Data and Measures: The IIMMLA and CILS-III Surveys in Southern California

Data for the analysis that follows are drawn from two sources: the third wave of the CILS in San Diego, a decade-long panel study whose last phase of data collection ended in 2003; and the IIMMLA survey, a cross-sectional study whose data collection was carried out in 2004. (More detailed information about each study is presented in the Appendix.) Both surveys were conducted in the six contiguous counties comprising Southern California (San Diego, Orange, Los Angeles, Ventura, Riverside and San Bernardino), which include the largest communities of Mexicans, Salvadorans, Guatemalans, Filipinos, Taiwanese, Koreans, Vietnamese and Cambodians outside of their countries of origin. Adjacent to the Mexican border, Southern California has been the nation's largest net receiver of immigrants over the past three decades; by 2000, on the eve of these surveys, nearly one in every five US immigrants resided here.

For the purposes of this analysis the two data sets were merged, yielding larger sample sizes (n = 6135) for significant subgroups and greater precision and reliability in estimates of socioeconomic outcomes by group and generation. They are based on representative samples of respondents evenly divided by gender, of the same approximate age (28.6 years for IIMMLA respondents and 24.2 years for CILS) and national origins (Mexicans, Salvadorans, Guatemalans, Filipinos, Chinese, Koreans, Vietnamese, Cambodians and Laotians make up 76% of the merged sample, and other Latin American and Asian nationalities 10%), who were surveyed at about the same time (IIMMLA in 2004, CILS-III in 2001–2003) in the same metropolitan region (the six contiguous Southern California counties). The IIMMLA and CILS-III focused on patterns of adaptation of adult children of contemporary immigrants – both those who were born abroad but arrived in the US as children (the 1.5 generation) and those who were born in the US of immigrant parents (the second-generation); although in the IIMMLA, sizable random samples of native-parentage, white, black and Mexican-American respondents (third and higher generations) were added. Both surveys used identical measures of all relevant variables, including – among many others – language use, preference and proficiency (ability to understand, speak, read and write in that language), parental background (including immigrant parents' citizenship status, length of time in the US and English-language ability) and the respondents' educational, occupational and economic outcomes in adulthood.

Table 8.2 shows the number and distribution of IIMMLA and CILS respondents by gender and generational cohort (1.5, second, third and higher) for the main ethnic groups used in this analysis. Overall, their mean age was 27.5. Of the 6135 respondents in the merged sample, 80% were either 1.5 generation (n = 2356) or second-generation (n = 2566), and 20% were third or higher generations (n = 1213). Among the 1.5 and second-generations (n = 4922), Mexicans, Salvadorans and Guatemalans accounted for 1621; Filipinos, Chinese (including Taiwanese) and Koreans numbered 1824; and those from Vietnam, Laos and Cambodia

Table 8.2 Young adults in Southern California: Sample size by ethnicity, gender, age and generation (merged IIMMLA and CILS-III San Diego samples, $n = 6135$)

Ethnicity	Total (n)	Gender		Age (years)	Generation[1]		
		Female	Male		1.5	2nd	third-plus
Mexican	1642	855	787	27.5	423	818	401
Salvadoran, Guatemalan	380	193	187	26.8	181	199	0
Other Latin American	240	133	107	28.6	91	149	0
Chinese[2]	433	188	245	27.6	235	198	0
Korean	408	207	201	27.6	257	151	0
Vietnamese	590	296	294	26.0	434	156	0
Filipino	983	508	475	25.5	411	572	0
Other Asian[3]	329	183	146	25.3	232	97	0
Black (non-Hispanic)	432	239	193	30.5	11	24	397
White (non-Hispanic)	698	362	336	30.3	81	202	415
Total	6135	3164	2971	27.5	2356	2566	1213

[1]Generational cohorts: 1.5 = foreign-born, arrived in US in childhood; 2nd = US-born, with one or both parents foreign-born; 3rd or higher = US-born, both parents US-born. Of the 2566 classified as 2nd generation, 659 had one US-born parent ('2.5' generation). Of the 1213 classified as '3rd or higher' generations, half of the Mexican Americans (47%) had four US-born grandparents ('fourth-plus' generations), as did two-thirds (69%) of the non-Hispanic white respondents and almost all (95%) of the black respondents.
[2]Including Taiwanese.
[3]Including 200 Cambodians and Laotians (Lao and Hmong).

totaled 790. The 'Other Latin Americans' ($n = 240$) came from all of the other Spanish-speaking countries of Central and South America and the Caribbean. Other nationalities ($n = 447$) included respondents from Canada and dozens of countries from Europe, Asia, the Middle East and the non-Spanish Caribbean. For all groups except Mexicans and non-Hispanic whites and blacks, immigration was so recent that sampling was not feasible beyond the second-generation. (Indeed, for those groups without exception, more than 70% of their total population in the US is foreign-born, and of the remainder nearly all belong to the US-born second-generation.) Of the 2566 born in the US and classified as second-generation, 76% had two foreign-born parents (the '2.0' cohort), while 24% had one US-born parent (the '2.5' cohort). The immigrant parents in this Southern California sample were not recent arrivals: they had resided in the US for an average of 26 years (over 95% had been in the US for more than 10 years, and 75% for more than 20 years). Finally, of the 1213 respondents classified as third or higher generations (US-born persons with two US-born parents), half of the Mexican Americans (47%) had four US-born grandparents ('fourth-plus' generation), as did two-thirds (69%) of the non-Hispanic whites and almost all (95%) of the black respondents.

Linguistic Characteristics and Measures of Bilingualism

Table 8.3 summarizes the relevant survey evidence on bilingualism for our sample – comparing the percentage that grew up speaking a non-English language at home vs their current language preferences and level of proficiency in the non-English language. The data are broken down by ethnicity and detailed generational cohorts: in addition to the 1.5 and third-plus generations, the US-born second-generation is divided here into those with two foreign-born parents ('2.0') and those with one foreign-born and one US-born parent ('2.5'). Overall, among the foreign-parentage respondents, 94% of the 1.5 cohort and 87% of the '2.0' cohort grew up speaking a language other than English at home (somewhat less among Filipinos) – but the proportion dropped to 58% among the '2.5' cohort, suggesting that English rapidly becomes the sole language in homes where one parent is US-born. By the third-plus generations, only 14% reported speaking a language other than English at home while growing up. However, an examination of actual language preferences in adulthood shows a reversal; overall, more than half (52%) of the foreign-born 1.5 cohort now prefer to speak English only at home, as do more than two-thirds of the 2.0 (70%), 89% of the 2.5 and 98% of the third-plus cohort.

The rapid switch to English is accompanied by the rapid atrophy of respondents' speaking, reading and writing abilities in their non-English mother tongue. Without exception, respondents' English proficiencies are greater than those in their non-English language. Among the 1.5 cohort, less than half (47%) could speak their non-English language 'very well', and only a third could read it 'very well' (34%); by the 2.0 generation only a third (34%) could speak their non-English language 'very well', and only a quarter could read it 'very well' (25%); among the 2.5 cohort, those proportions decreased more sharply still to 16% and 13%, respectively; and the third-plus generations had become largely English monolinguals (less than 3% had either speaking or reading fluency in their non-English language, and less than 2% had writing fluency).

Of the four dimensions of language proficiency measured (each on a 4-item scale from 'very well' to 'well', 'not well' and 'not at all'), respondents reported greater ability in *understanding* a language, followed by *speaking*, then *reading* and then *writing* in that language. We present a dichotomous measure of *balanced bilingual* in the last column of Table 8.3, defined as the ability to understand, speak, read and write a non-English language 'very well' or 'well' on all four dimensions, for a combined score of 3.0 or higher on the 4-point scale. Balanced bilinguals in turn encompass *fluent bilinguals* (defined as having a proficiency of 'very well' on all four dimensions – a combined score of 4.0) and *moderate bilinguals* (who do 'well' on average on all four dimensions – for a combined score of between 3.0 and 4.0). By this measure, those who are not balanced bilinguals include *English monolinguals* as well as *limited bilinguals* (who understand, speak, read and write a non-English language 'not well' or poorly – who thus score 2 or less on all dimensions of proficiency).[2]

The patterns described above hold without exception across all of the ethnic groups and demonstrate the rapidity with which English is acquired and comes to be preferred by immigrants who arrive at a young age and especially by the US-born children and grandchildren of immigrants. As Table 8.3 also documents, all of the Asian-origin groups are much more likely than all of the Spanish speakers to lose their bilingual skills (especially literacy skills) by the second-generation, and to effectively become English monolinguals among the 2.5 cohort. Thus, among those of Mexican descent, between half and two-thirds of the 1.5 and 2.0 cohorts can still speak and read Spanish very well, but those proportions fall to between a quarter and a third in the 2.5 cohort, and decrease to single digits by the third-plus. Indeed, in a recent study of 'linguistic life expectancies' (Rumbaut *et al.*, 2006), also using the merged CILS-San Diego and IIMMLA data sets, we estimated the average number of generations a mother tongue can be expected to survive after the arrival of an immigrant in Southern California – home to the nation's largest concentration of immigrants, including Spanish speakers. The analysis showed that even among those of Mexican origin, the Spanish language 'died' by the third-generation; all other languages 'died' between the second and third-generations.

In sum, the proportion of those who have grown up speaking a non-English language at home plummets from over 90% in the 1.5 generation to just over 10% by the third-plus generations. At the same time, the preference for English increases rapidly, becoming nearly universal by the third-generation. The proportion of 'balanced bilinguals' (as previously defined) decreases generationally from just over 50% in the 1.5 generation, to about 25% in the 2.5 generation and 5% by the third-plus generations. Each of the measured dimensions of linguistic proficiency (understanding, speaking, reading and writing) clearly atrophies from generation to generation, with the most rapid decrease occurring in the 2.5 generation. Once a respondent is raised in a family where one parent is not an immigrant or native speaker of a non-English language, it becomes very difficult to sustain balanced bilingualism in the home. By the third-generation, the shift to monolingual English appears almost irreversible – even in a high-immigration region such as Southern California.

Table 8.3 Language spoken at home growing up, current language preference and bilingual proficiency by generation and ethnicity (merged IIMMLA and CILS-III San Diego samples, n=6135)

Ethnicity and generation[1]	Growing up spoke non-English language at home	Currently prefers to speak English at home	Current non-English language proficiency				Balanced bilingual[2]
			Understand 'very well'	Speak 'very well'	Read 'very well'	Write 'very well'	
Total (%)	72.3	70.8	40.0	30.7	23.0	17.3	37.0
Generation[1]							
1.5 (%)	94.1	52.4	54.8	46.6	34.3	25.8	50.6
2.0 (%)	87.3	69.6	49.1	33.8	25.3	19.1	44.5
2.5 (%)	58.4	88.9	24.5	15.9	13.3	10.5	24.5
third-plus (%)	13.7	98.4	5.4	2.8	2.6	1.6	5.3
Ethnicity							
Mexican (%)	77.2	60.7	52.9	43.3	40.0	31.5	55.1
Salvadoran, Guatemalan (%)	94.5	51.3	70.5	60.3	53.7	40.8	75.3
Other Latin American (%)	86.7	68.8	65.0	50.4	42.5	32.1	66.7
Chinese (%)	91.7	56.4	43.9	36.5	18.0	9.2	31.2
Korean (%)	89.2	63.7	36.3	31.4	21.8	15.9	40.2
Vietnamese (%)	96.3	53.4	41.5	33.7	14.7	11.4	35.6
Filipino (%)	78.3	88.8	31.6	14.4	12.1	9.4	23.8
Other Asian (%)	89.7	60.2	49.5	39.8	9.4	6.7	27.7
White (non-Hispanic) (%)	24.1	95.6	13.5	8.6	5.0	3.0	10.2
Black (non-Hispanic) (%)	8.8	98.8	3.0	0.9	1.9	1.2	3.0

[1]Generational cohorts: 1.5=foreign born, arrived in US in childhood; 2.0=US-born, both parents foreign-born; 2.5=US-born, one parent foreign-born, one parent US-born; 3rd or higher=US-born, both parents US-born.

[2]'Balanced bilingual'=understands, speaks, reads *and* writes a non-English language 'very well' or 'well' (on all four dimensions). Conversely, those who are not include English monolinguals and 'limited bilinguals' (who understand, speak, read and write a non-English language 'not well' or not at all). 'Balanced bilinguals' encompass 'fluent bilinguals' (proficiency of 'very well' on all four dimensions) and 'moderate bilinguals' ('well' on average).

Socioeconomic Characteristics of the Sample, by Gender, Age and Ethnicity

Education, and particularly the attainment of a college degree, increasingly determines the occupational and economic opportunities and payoffs available to young adults in the US, and hence their prospects for upward (or downward) mobility in relation both to their peers and to their parents. Access to and success in higher education, in turn, are shaped by a complex of factors, including all of those examined here – as well as by early school achievement. Before moving to a multivariate analysis of the effects of bilingualism on selected outcomes, including education, Table 8.4 presents a sketch of the key social and economic characteristics of the sample: parental socioeconomic status (SES), high school grade point average (GPA), years of education attained in adulthood, high school dropout status, college graduate status, part-time or full-time employment and annual earnings – broken down by gender, age and ethnicity.

Table 8.4 provides first an SES ranking of the groups in the sample, as measured by a composite index of father's and mother's education, occupational prestige and home ownership. Standardized z scores (mean = 0, standard deviation = 1) are here converted into a 0–1 scale for ease of interpretation. As the data show, the Chinese have the highest SES score (0.806), followed closely by non-Hispanic whites and Filipinos (0.798) and Koreans (0.789). At the bottom, with scores just above 0.500, are Vietnamese, Mexicans, Salvadorans and Guatemalans, and the 'other Asians' (mainly Cambodians, Lao and Hmong) lower still. Blacks and the 'other Latin Americans' are in between.

Four measures of educational attainment are also presented in Table 8.4 by gender, age and ethnicity: their average grades in high school[3] (during adolescence); their highest level of education attained (in adulthood), in years; the percentage of those who dropped out of high school; and of those who graduated from college (with a bachelor's or higher degree). There are very significant ethnic differences, observable both in their high school grades during adolescence as well as in the highest level of education completed in adulthood.

Intergroup differences in early achievement are clearly discernible in high school grades. Females had significantly higher GPAs than males. Getting mostly As in high school were Asian students (40%), followed by whites (31%), with Hispanics (15%) and blacks (13%) trailing well behind. Hispanics were more likely than other groups to get mostly Ds and Fs (10%), and blacks to get mostly Cs (34%). Mexicans in both the 1.5 and second-generations, as well as Cambodians and Laotians, were the groups most likely to get mostly Ds and Fs (14%) – but not the Salvadoran and

Guatemalans, the majority of whom (53%) were B students. At the other end of the scale, fully half of the Chinese (51%) and Koreans (50%) were A students, followed closely by the Vietnamese (45%), but only a third of the Filipinos (32%) received mainly As, slightly above the proportion for whites.

After leaving high school, a decade or so later on average, what was the highest level of educational attainment respondents had attained? Overall, 10% were high school dropouts, 17% had attained only a high school diploma and 41% had some college experience (but no college degree). At the other end, among those aged 25 and older, 27% had earned a bachelor's degree and 13% an advanced degree (or were enrolled in graduate or professional school). Virtually the same wide achievement gaps seen in high school are observable between groups in adulthood. Gender is an exception: female respondents significantly outperformed males in high school GPA, and in adulthood a slightly higher percentage earned college degrees (while a smaller proportion had dropped out of high school). However, women were significantly less likely to be working full-time, and reported significantly lower annual earnings than men (about $2500 less).

High school dropout rates were much higher among Hispanics (18%) and blacks (15%) than among whites (8%) and Asians (under 3%). Asians (41%) and whites (31%) were twice as likely as Hispanics (14%) and blacks (18%) to have earned a bachelor's degree, and in addition Asians (18%) and whites (17%) were more than twice as likely as Hispanics and blacks to have earned advanced degrees (or be in the process of earning them). (These results for a Southern California sample are only slightly more positive than those seen with national-level survey data, and the interethnic group rank order matches the results precisely; see Rumbaut [2008].)

Examining educational attainment and earnings more closely by national origin and generation reveals wider differences – suggestive of widening future socioeconomic inequalities segmented by ethnicity. By far the most outstanding level of achievement is observed among the Chinese, with the lowest high school dropout rate (a miniscule 0.7%), along with an extraordinarily high 33% who had earned or were earning an advanced degree, another 49% who had already earned a bachelor's degree, and the highest earnings of any group in the sample – even though, as can be seen in Table 8.3, the Chinese also had a low proportion of balanced bilinguals (less than a third). They were followed closely by the Koreans (27% earned or were earning an advanced degree, 51% earned a bachelor's and only 2% failed to complete high school) and then the Vietnamese (14% earned or was earning an advanced degree, 44% had a bachelor's and only 3% had dropped out of high school). The Filipinos most closely resembled majority-group whites and the Salvadorans and Guatemalans resembled minority-group blacks in their patterns of

Table 8.4 Educational attainment, labor force status and annual earnings by gender, age and ethnicity (merged IIMMLA and CILS-III San Diego samples, n=6135)

Gender, age and ethnicity	Parents' socioeconomic status[1]	GPA in high school (1–4)	Years of education attained	High school dropout (%)	College graduate (%)	Lives with parents (%)	Working part-time (%)	Working full-time (%)	Annual earnings ($) (n=4,554)
Total	0.655	2.93	14.2	9.6	31.8	44.1	20.4	52.2	19,339
Gender									
Female	0.647	3.05	14.3	8.7	33.6	41.6	21.9	45.9	18,112
Male	0.662	2.81	14.1	10.6	29.8	46.7	18.7	59.0	20,576
Age									
20–24	0.637	2.94	14.0	7.5	21.4	66.1	28.5	39.8	16,650
25–32	0.643	2.91	14.3	10.6	37.3	35.6	15.9	59.8	20,616
33–40	0.706	2.97	14.6	12.2	43.0	15.1	11.9	64.2	21,369
Ethnicity									
Mexican	0.538	2.59	13.1	19.6	13.9	36.8	16.8	58.1	17,009
Salvadoran, Guatemalan	0.509	2.79	13.5	15.5	16.3	50.5	20.0	51.1	15,313
Other Latin American	0.656	2.93	14.3	7.1	30.8	42.1	24.6	55.4	18,067
Chinese	0.806	3.40	15.8	0.7	63.0	54.3	21.0	49.0	25,680
Korean	0.789	3.39	15.5	2.2	59.6	55.9	18.9	44.9	22,566
Vietnamese	0.550	3.28	15.1	2.7	45.8	61.4	23.1	42.0	23,088
Filipino	0.798	2.96	14.7	2.3	33.0	55.5	25.8	50.9	20,103
Other Asian	0.484	2.90	14.0	7.0	27.4	51.4	18.5	56.8	20,331
White (non-Hispanic)	0.798	3.06	14.7	8.0	42.1	24.1	20.2	54.4	20,560
Black (non-Hispanic)	0.660	2.76	13.7	14.6	21.1	22.5	18.1	49.3	16,447

[1]Standardized SES measure of father's education, mother's education and homeownership (here on a 0–1 scale from lowest to highest SES).

educational attainment and earnings. The Mexicans, Cambodians and Laotians were at the bottom of the hierarchy, with the Mexicans having the highest dropout rates of any group.

In the Mexican case, data permit a more detailed analysis by generation, from the 1.5 to the second to the third-plus cohorts. Here the patterns are not linear, but reflect, first, a very significant improvement in high school dropout rates from the 1.5 to the second generation (in half from 30% to 15%) and a slight improvement in college graduation rates (from about 14% to 18%). But achievement peaks in the second generation: by the third-plus, high school dropout rates increase to 18%, while involvement in advanced-level education declines somewhat (cf. Telles & Ortiz, 2008).

Effects of Bilingualism on Dropping Out of High School

Dropping out of high school is a key turning point in the transition to adulthood, and a key predictor for future life chances, particularly in the labor market. Our prior research has shown (e.g. Rumbaut, 2005b, 2008), as has the prevailing research literature, that dropping out of high school is strongly linked to higher unemployment, the likelihood of being laid off or having never worked; with the lowest level of earnings and lifetime income; with being disabled and with worse health outcomes. High school dropouts are more likely to be divorced or separated, to not have been raised in an intact family with both natural parents present, to come from low-SES families and to have grown up in more dangerous neighborhoods. They are four to five times more likely to be incarcerated, to have had a teen pregnancy and a nonmarital birth (Rumbaut, 2005b, 2008). Given the strong link between dropping out of school and future economic outcomes, what is the relationship of balanced bilingualism to the likelihood of dropping out?

Table 8.5 presents a logistic regression analyzing the effects of balanced bilingualism and other key predictors on the likelihood of dropping out of school. English monolinguals (or limited bilinguals) and non-Hispanic whites are the primary reference groups. Both models control for age and gender, ethnicity, parental SES, family structure (growing up in a two-parent family) and an index of problems with drugs, gangs and crime in the neighborhood where the respondent grew up. The second model enters high school GPA, given the extremely strong influence of early achievement (as measured by high school grades) on dropping out (the Wald statistic is 231). In the equation on the left panel predicting the odds ratios of dropping out, the strongest (negative) determinant is parental SES (the Wald statistic is 169.8). Latinos, blacks and men are significantly more likely to drop out even after controlling for other predictors, while

Chinese and Vietnamese are less likely. Gender washes out of the equation once GPA is entered into the model (females had higher GPAs than men). However, in both models, the dichotomous measure of balanced bilingualism retains a strong and significant negative effect on dropping out; the odds ratio (0.603) can be interpreted to mean that English monolinguals and limited bilinguals are 66% more likely than balanced bilinguals to drop out of high school.

This finding confirms other research (*cf.* Portes & Hao, 2002; Portes & Rumbaut, 2001; Rumbaut, 2005a; Rumberger & Larson, 1998; but see also Mouw & Xie, 1999; Peal & Lambert, 1962) that illustrates the positive association of bilingualism with adolescent academic achievement, family cohesion, parent–child relations (including a lower incidence of parent–child conflict), self-esteem, aspirations and other factors that are protective against the decision to drop out of school. Feliciano (2001), for example, found that bilingual students are less likely to drop out than English-only speakers; students in bilingual households are less likely to drop out than those in English-dominant or English-limited households; and students in immigrant households are less likely to drop out than those in nonimmigrant households.

Effects of Bilingualism on Occupational Status and Annual Earnings

Table 8.6 provides a direct assessment of the effects of different levels of bilingualism (fluent, moderate and limited bilinguals, as previously defined) on (1) *occupational status* (as measured by the Duncan Socioeconomic Index (SEI), applied to respondents' current paid jobs) and on (2) *annual earnings* (measured in dollars). Multiple linear regressions are presented, each with the same set of predictors, and two models; in each equation, high school GPA (which serves in part as a proxy for cognitive ability) and total years of education attained in adulthood are entered into the second model. Again, English monolinguals are the reference group, as are non-Hispanic whites.

The first regression (left panels) focuses on occupational status (measured by the Duncan SEI). The strongest predictor in the first equation is parental SES: the higher the parental SES (a standardized composite measure of father's education, mother's education and home ownership), the higher the respondent's SEI score. In the second model, the respondent's years of education attained emerge as the main predictor. Once high school GPA and highest education attained are entered into the model, gender washes out, as does Vietnamese, Salvadoran and Guatemalan ethnicity. However, the multivariate analysis shows very strong and significant effects for fluent bilingualism (i.e. understanding,

Table 8.5 Odds ratios of dropping out of school: Effects of balanced bilingualism and selected predictors (merged IIMMLA and CILS-III San Diego samples, n=6135)

Model								
				Dropped out of high school				
	I				II			
Predictors	B	Wald[1]	Sig.	Odds ratio	B	Wald[1]	Sig.	Odds ratio
Balanced bilingual[2]	-0.506	23.40	***	0.603	-0.481	19.50	***	0.618
(Ref: English monolinguals and limited bilinguals)								
Age, gender								
Age (years)	0.039	22.90	***	1.040	0.044	26.91	***	1.045
Gender (male)	0.282	9.07	**	1.326	0.065	0.43	NS	1.067
Ethnicity								
Chinese	-1.796	9.30	**	0.166	-1.507	6.39	*	0.222
Vietnamese	-0.919	11.20	**	0.399	-0.0587	4.40	*	0.556
Mexican	1.218	105.29	***	3.382	0.987	64.82	***	2.684
Salvadoran, Guatemalan	0.895	23.72	***	2.446	0.898	22.32	***	2.454
African American	0.716	16.47	***	2.046	0.622	11.72	**	1.862
Parents' status/family contexts								
Parents' SES index[3]	-0.658	169.79	***	0.518	-0.557	111.39	***	0.573
Grew up in two-parent family	-0.338	12.29	***	0.713	-0.259	6.67	**	0.772
Neighborhood drugs, gangs, crime[4]	0.585	32.12	***	1.796	0.527	24.09	***	1.694
Early achievement								
Grades in high school (GPA)					-1.054	230.97	***	0.349
Constant	-3.903	219.85	***	0.020	-1.174	13.69	***	0.309

Significance: ***$p<0.001$; **$p<0.01$; *$p<0.05$; NS=not significant.
[1]Measure of strength of association (square of the logistic regression coefficient divided by its standard error).
[2]'Balanced bilingual' = understands, speaks, reads *and* writes non-English language 'well' or 'very well' (on all four dimensions).
[3]Standardized (*z* score) composite measure of father's education, mother's education and homeownership (mean = 0, SD = 1).
[4]Summed index of reported 'big problems' with drugs, gangs *and* crime in the neighborhood where the respondent grew up.

speaking, reading and writing a non-English language 'very well'), followed by moderate bilingualism (i.e. 'well'), on occupational status; the effects are attenuated but remain positive and significant even after entering high school GPA and years of education into the equation (*cf.* Feliciano & Rumbaut, 2005).

The second regression, predicting annual earnings, shows similarly strong and significant effects for the different levels of bilingualism, with the greater the level of bilingualism, the higher the annual earnings. Fluent bilingualism, net of other predictors in the equation, is associated with an annual gain of $2827; when GPA and years of education are entered into the second model, the effect is reduced but fluent bilinguals are still seen to earn $2234 more than English monolinguals. Even a lesser level of bilingual proficiency carries an economic payoff. Moderate bilingualism, net of other predictors in the equation, is associated with an added annual gain of $2425; once GPA and years of education are entered into the second equation, moderate bilinguals still earn $1876 more than English monolinguals. Indeed, even limited bilingualism shows a more modest but statistically significant annual earnings advantage. The models also show, as expected, that when controlling for other predictors, including educational attainment, women earn about $3000 less than men; Latinos and African Americans earn significantly less and Chinese and Vietnamese earn more than the reference group of non-Hispanic whites. Most unexpected, however, were the resilient and positive results for bilingualism.

Related research examining the effects of balanced bilingualism on earnings has reported parallel results based on two separate data sets: one is the National Educational Longitudinal Study (NELS), based on the final follow-up of a nationally representative sample when respondents were 26 years old on average; and the other is the full CILS-III study, with respondents from both the San Diego and South Florida samples, when they were in their mid-twenties (Agirdag, 2013). Regression analyses indicate that balanced bilingual individuals earned significantly more as young adults at the beginning of their careers than linguistic minorities who were dominantly proficient in English only. Even after controlling for cognitive ability, educational attainment and parental SES, the cost of monolingualism was estimated at $2100 to $3,300 annually – findings very much in line with those reported here for Southern California.

Discussion and Conclusion

These are remarkable findings. In all three distinct measures of socioeconomic outcomes examined here – educational, occupational and economic – even after controlling for age and gender, social class and other hypothesized predictors, and despite a substantial literature that has largely and solely focused on English ability as a human capital asset,

Table 8.6 Regressions of occupational status and annual earnings on bilingualism and selected predictors (merged IIMMLA and CILS-III San Diego sample)

| | Occupational status (SEI) | | | | | | Annual earnings ($) | | | | | |
| | I | | | II | | | I | | | I | | |
Predictors	B	t^1	Sig.	B	t	Sig.	B	t	Sig.	B	t	Sig.
Bilingualism[2]												
Fluent bilingual (very well)	2.35	4.23	***	1.21	2.35	*	$2,827	4.10	***	$2234	3.29	***
Moderate bilingual (well)	1.85	3.79	***	0.97	2.14	*	$2,425	3.96	***	$1876	3.12	**
Limited bilingual (not well)	1.10	2.42	*	0.85	2.02	*	$1,258	2.22	*	$1078	1.94	*
English monolingual	ref.			ref.			ref.			ref.		
Age and gender												
Age (years)	0.47	14.98	***	0.38	12.85	***	$200	5.12	***	$149	3.87	***
Gender (male)	-1.07	-3.29	***	-0.23	-0.75	NS	$2,572	6.34	***	$3192	7.89	***
Ethnicity												
Chinese	3.83	5.72	***	1.38	2.22	*	$4,056	4.51	***	$2263	2.53	**
Vietnamese	2.70	4.32	***	0.26	0.45	NS	$3,663	4.49	***	$2313	2.87	**
Mexican	-4.36	-10.27	***	-1.27	-3.13	**	-$3,579	-6.83	***	-$1860	-3.51	***
Salvadoran, Guatemalan	-2.32	-3.26	***	-0.21	-0.32	NS	-$5,146	-5.64	***	-$3778	-4.19	***
African American	-4.24	-6.10	***	-1.94	-3.00	**	-$4,386	-5.13	***	-$3202	-3.80	***
Parents' status												

Parents' SES index[3]	2.33	12.82	***	0.71	4.02	***	$1,217	5.41	***	$263	1.13	NS
Resides with parents	-2.30	-6.23	***	-1.92	-5.63	***	-$4,630	-10.18	***	-$4311	-9.65	***
Educational attainment												
Grades in high school (GPA)				0.96	4.35	***				$1110	3.78	***
Years of education attained				2.25	26.30	***				$1204	10.55	***
Constant	33.09	32.31	***	-0.10	-0.07	NS	$13,988	11.04	***	-$5510	-2.88	**

Significance: ***$p<0.001$; **$p<0.01$; *$p<0.05$; NS=not significant.

[1] Measure of strength of association (unstandardized regression coefficient B divided by its standard error).

[2] Bilingualism level measured on 4-item scale of ability to understand, speak, read and write non-English language (4=very well, 3=well, 2=not well, 1=not at all).

[3] Standardized (z score) composite measure of father's education, mother's education and homeownership (mean=0, SD=1).

the results presented above offer consistent, convergent and compelling evidence for the benefits of fluent bilingualism – and even of moderate or balanced bilingualism – in the labor markets and local economy of Southern California.

The research literature has largely focused on examining the workplace and economic benefits of English (or host-country language) fluency among immigrant workers (e.g. Chiswick, 1991; Chiswick & Miller, 2002; Dustmann & Van Soest, 2002), as illustrated in Chapters 3–6 of this volume. Proficiency in the host language is seen as a human capital variable, a resource in the labor market. The literature regularly finds that the more proficient immigrants are in the language of the host country, the higher their wages. However, fluency in a second language combined with English proficiency has been largely ignored as a competitive resource. Some new studies – including those in this volume – are now providing evidence of the economic benefits of bilingualism.

This study presented findings from Southern California on the mobility trajectories of foreign-parentage young adults, focusing on key ethnic groups (Mexican, Salvadoran and Guatemalan, Filipino, Chinese, Korean, Vietnamese, Cambodian and Laotian) with distinct modes of incorporation, compared to native-parentage peers (white, black and Mexican American). The outcomes examined are not reducible to a simple or single unilinear trend, but are complex, multidirectional and sharply segmented by class, ethnicity and gender. These highly stratified results are not accounted for by differences in English language acculturation. On the contrary, for all groups without exception, even in a region of extraordinarily high immigrant settlement such as Southern California, we showed that proficiency in and preference for English are well established by the second-generation, and are effectively completed by the third-generation among those of Mexican origin, with balanced bilingualism rapidly atrophying. What is novel is that fluent bilingualism is positively associated with educational, occupational and economic attainment, despite strong pressures toward English monolingualism by the third-generation.

That English is important for socioeconomic success in the US is axiomatic. Immigrants who come to the US with aspirations of a better life – for themselves but especially for their children – do so fully aware of the dominance of English. You cannot earn a college degree in the US without English proficiency, let alone advanced or professional degrees, or pass professional licensing examinations. Much the same applies to economic success in the labor market generally – aside from niches in ethnic enclaves or in subcontracted work where the clientele or the job may not require it. The question, rather, is whether there is value in *additive* as opposed to *subtractive* acculturation – i.e. in the case of language, in English plus vs English only. That is the core question this study has sought to address. The results of our analyses strongly suggest economic as well as social and cultural advantages for English plus, which paradoxically seem to be dissipated intergenerationally. In the absence of a sizable and economically potent co-ethnic community to support language maintenance, fluent bilingualism in the second-generation is likely to prove an elusive goal. But then, persistent economic advantage may yet turn an elusive goal into an enduring one.

Acknowledgment

The author gratefully acknowledges the support of the Russell Sage Foundation for the two surveys on which this research is based – IIMMLA (Immigration and Intergenerational Mobility in Metropolitan Los Angeles) and CILS-III (Children of Immigrants Longitudinal Study) San Diego – which were carried out in Southern California during 2001–2004.

Notes

(1) Cuba and the Dominican Republic ranked eighth and ninth in the size of their foreign-born populations in 2010 – but the Cubans and Dominicans are concentrated in Florida and New York, respectively.
(2) The surveys measure self-reported ability to understand, speak, read and write in both English and a non-English language, as was done in the CILS surveys in 1992, 1995 and 2001–2003. Longitudinal surveys employing the identical methodology carried out with large samples of Southeast Asian refugee adults from Vietnam, Laos and Cambodia in the 1980s, and studies of Southeast Asian youth from multiple ethnic groups, have been shown to produce valid and reliable results by, for example, correlating self-report survey data with objective test results of linguistic proficiency for the same dimensions measured (see Ima & Rumbaut, 1989; Portes & Rumbaut, 2001; Rumbaut, 1989; Rumbaut & Ima, 1988).
(3) High school grades were measured for CILS-San Diego respondents by official academic grade point averages calculated by the school district at the end of high school, on a 4-point scale (where A = 4). IIMMLA respondents provided self-reports.

References

Agirdag, O. (2013) The long-term effects of bilingualism on children of immigration: Student bilingualism and future earnings. *International Journal of Bilingual Education and Bilingualism* 17 (4), 449–464.
Alba, R., Logan, L., Lutz, A. and Stults, B. (2002) Only English by the third generation? Loss and preservation of the mother tongue among the grandchildren of contemporary immigrants. *Demography* 39 (3), 467–484.
Chiswick, B.R. (1991) Speaking, reading, and earnings among low-skilled immigrants. *Journal of Labor Economics* 9 (2), 149–170.
Chiswick, B.R. and Miller, P.W. (2002) Immigrant earnings: Language skills, linguistic concentrations and the business cycle. *Journal of Population Economics* 15 (1), 31–57.

Dustmann, C., and Van Soest, A. (2002) Language and the earnings of immigrants. *Industrial & Labor Relations Review* 55 (3), 473–492.

Feliciano, C. (2001) The benefits of biculturalism: Exposure to immigrant culture and dropping out of school among Asian and Latino youths. *Social Science Quarterly* 82 (4), 865–879.

Feliciano, C. and Rumbaut, R.G. (2005) Gendered paths: Educational and occupational expectations and outcomes among adult children of immigrants. *Ethnic and Racial Studies* 28 (6), 1087–1118.

Hoefer, M., Rytina, N. and Baker, B.C. (2011) Estimates of the unauthorized immigrant population residing in the United States: January 2010. Office of Immigration Statistics, Policy Directorate, US Department of Homeland Security. See http://www.dhs.gov/xlibrary/assets/statistics/publications/ois_ill_pe_2010.pdf (accessed 14 May 2013).

Ima, K. and Rumbaut, R.G. (1989) Southeast Asian refugees in American schools: A comparison of fluent English proficient (FEP) and limited English proficient (LEP) students. *Topics in Language Disorders* 9 (3), 54–77.

Mouw, T. and Xie, Y. (1999) Bilingualism and the academic achievement of first- and second-generation Asian Americans: Accommodation with or without assimilation? *American Sociological Review* 64 (2) 232–252.

Orfield, G. and Lee, C. (2005) *Why Segregation Matters: Poverty and Educational Inequality.* Cambridge, MA: Civil Rights Project www.civilrightsproject.ucla.edu.

Peal, E. and Lambert, W.E. (1962) *The Relation of Bilingualism to Intelligence.* Washington DC: American Psychological Association.

Portes, A. and Hao, L. (2002) The price of uniformity: Language, family and personality adjustment in the immigrant second generation. *Ethnic and Racial Studies* 25 (6), 889–912.

Portes, A. and Rumbaut, R.G. (2001) *Legacies: The Story of the Immigrant Second Generation.* Berkeley, CA and New York: University of California Press and Russell Sage Foundation.

Portes, A. and Rumbaut, R.G. (2014) *Immigrant America: A Portrait* (4th edn). Berkeley, CA: University of California Press.

Rumbaut, R.G. (1989) Portraits, patterns, and predictors of the refugee adaptation process: Results and reflections from the IHARP panel study. In D.W. Haines (ed.) *Refugees as Immigrants: Cambodians, Laotians and Vietnamese in America* (pp. 138–182). Totowa, NJ: Rowman and Littlefield.

Rumbaut, R.G. (2005a) Children of immigrants and their achievement: The roles of family, acculturation, social class, gender, ethnicity, and school contexts. In R.D. Taylor (ed.) *Addressing the Achievement Gap: Findings and Applications* (pp. 23–59). Charlotte, NC: Information Age Publishing.

Rumbaut, R.G. (2005b) Turning points in the transition to adulthood: Determinants of educational attainment, incarceration, and early childbearing among children of immigrants. *Ethnic and Racial Studies* 28, 1041–1086.

Rumbaut, R.G. (2008) The coming of the second generation: Immigration and ethnic mobility in Southern California. *The Annals of the American Academy of Political and Social Science* 620 (1), 196–236.

Rumbaut, R.G. (2009) A language graveyard? The evolution of language competencies, preferences and use among young adult children of immigrants. In T.G. Wiley, J. Sook Lee and R. Rumberger (eds) *The Education of Language Minority Immigrants in the United States* (pp. 35–71). Bristol: Multilingual Matters.

Rumbaut, R.G. and Ima, K. (1988) *The Adaptation of Southeast Asian Refugee Youth: A Comparative Study.* Washington DC: US Office of Refugee Resettlement.

Rumbaut, R.G., Massey, D.S. and Bean, F.D. (2006) Linguistic life expectancies: Immigrant language retention in Southern California. *Population and Development Review* 32 (3), 447–460.

Rumbaut, R.G. and Massey, D.S. (2013) Immigration and language diversity in the United States. *Daedalus: Journal of the American Academy of Arts and Sciences* 142 (3), 141–154.

Rumberger, R.W. and Larson, K. (1998) Toward explaining differences in educational achievement among Mexican American language-minority students. *Sociology of Education* 71 (1), 68–93.

Stevens, G. (1999) A century of U.S. censuses and the language characteristics of immigrants. *Demography* 36 (3), 387–397.

Telles, E.E. and Ortiz, V. (2008) *Generations of Exclusion: Mexican Americans, Assimilation, and Race*. New York: Russell Sage Foundation.

US Census Bureau (2011) American Community Survey. Washington DC: US Census Bureau. See http://www.census.gov/acs/www/ (accessed May 2013).

Appendix

The IIMMLA and CILS-San Diego Surveys

As explained in the text, the IIMMLA and CILS-III San Diego data sets were merged for this Southern California-based study. Both data sets with full documentation are available online:

IIMMLA: http://www.icpsr.umich.edu/icpsrweb/ICPSR/studies/22627

CILS: http://www.icpsr.umich.edu/icpsrweb/ICPSR/studies/20520

The IIMMLA Survey. The Immigration and Intergenerational Mobility in Metropolitan Los Angeles study was a computer-assisted telephone survey conducted in 2004 among targeted random samples of 1.5, second and selected third and higher generation adults in the five-county Los Angeles metropolitan area, which encompasses Los Angeles, Orange, Riverside, San Bernardino and Ventura counties (Rumbaut et al., 2003). For the purposes of sample design, eligible adult immigrants were defined as '1.5 generation' if they came to the US to live prior to the age of 15; as 'second generation' if they were born in the US and had at least one parent who was foreign-born; and as 'third-plus generations' if both they and their parents were US-born.

Prior to the start of interviewing, targeted quotas for 10 ethnic strata were established for eligible respondents between the ages of 20 and 40 in the five-county area, with an emphasis on the largest case – the Mexican-origin population. The IIMMLA project also sampled a strategic set of other large immigrant and refugee-origin groups that were expected to differ in their modes of incorporation into the US (the Filipinos, Chinese, Koreans, Vietnamese, and Salvadorans and Guatemalans taken together). All groups were assigned a separate sampling stratum for 1.5- to second-generation respondents, and targeted quotas for third-plus generation respondents were also established for Mexican Americans, non-Hispanic whites and non-Hispanic blacks, following the model of the New York Second Generation Study (Kasinitz et al., 2008). The final design called for completing approximately 4700 closed-ended telephone interviews with random samples of eligible respondents, about 3500 with 1.5- to second-generation respondents and around 1200 with third-plus generation respondents.

Multiframe sampling procedures were used to improve the chances of finding and interviewing members of the targeted populations. The first stage used random digit dialing (RDD) to sample and screen households in the five-county area; using this approach, the IIMMLA was able to complete sample quotas for Mexicans, whites and blacks of all generations. For other groups, samples were compiled using RDD until the incidence rates of eligible respondents became prohibitively low. At this point, more specific geographic and race–ethnic sampling frames were used, targeting RDD to households in high-density Asian residential areas and those on lists of Filipino, Chinese, Korean and Vietnamese surnames.

The surveys were administered in English or Spanish using a computer-assisted telephone interviewing system. A total of 4655 interviews were completed between the start of full-scale interviewing in April 2004 and its conclusion in October 2004. Of these, 2822 (61%) were derived from interviews using solely first-stage RDD sampling, while 1833 (39%) resulted from interviews using the augmented samples. To achieve this, a total of 263,783 different telephone numbers were dialed at least once, including 122,984 listings from the first-stage RDD sampling frame and 140,799 from the augmented samples. These calls resulted in the identification of 10,893 adults meeting the eligibility requirements of one of the 10 targeted sample subgroups. Efforts were made to complete interviews with 8815 of these adults (in 2078 cases the quota for the subgroup had already been filled).

The CILS Survey. For more than a decade, the Children of Immigrants Longitudinal Study followed the progress of a large panel of youths representing several dozen nationalities in two main areas of immigrant settlement in the US: Southern California (San Diego) and South Florida (the Miami and Fort Lauderdale metropolitan area). The baseline survey, conducted in Spring 1992, interviewed eligible students enrolled in the eighth and ninth grades of all the schools of the San Diego Unified School District ($n = 2420$). (A parallel sample was drawn from the Dade and Broward County Unified School Districts in South Florida.) The sample was drawn from the junior high grades, when dropping out of school is rare, to avoid the potential bias of differential dropout rates between ethnic groups at the senior high school level. Students were eligible to enter the sample if they were US-born but had at least one immigrant (foreign-born) parent, or if they themselves were foreign-born and had come to the US at an early age (before age 13). The resulting sample was evenly balanced between males and females, and between foreign-born and US-born children of immigrants. Reflecting the geographical clustering of recent immigration, the principal nationalities represented in the San Diego sample (as is largely the case in the IIMMLA sample) are Mexican, Filipino, Vietnamese, Laotian, Cambodian and Chinese and smaller groups of other children of immigrants from Asia (mostly Korean, Japanese and Indian) and Latin America (most of the Spanish-speaking countries of Central and South America and the Caribbean).

Three years later, a second survey of the same panel of children of immigrants was conducted. By this time the youths, who were originally interviewed when most were 14 or 15 years old, were now 17–18 years old and had reached the final year of high school (or had dropped out of school). The follow-up survey in San Diego succeeded in reinterviewing 2063 or 85.2% of the baseline sample, with almost identical proportions of males and females, of native-born and foreign-born youth, of US citizens and noncitizens and of main nationalities. There was a slight tendency for children from intact families (two parents present) to be overrepresented in the follow-up survey; other differences were statistically insignificant (Portes & Rumbaut, 2001).

During 2001–2003, a decade after the original survey, a final follow-up was conducted. The respondents now ranged from 23 to 27 years of age, and most had to be contacted individually in their places of work or residence. Mailed questionnaires (which included detailed questions on language use, proficiency and preference) were the principal source of completed data in this third survey. Respondents were also interviewed by telephone when possible; teams of trained interviewers visited respondents for whom no telephone numbers were available, but for whom their last known address or that of their parents was known. Over a period of more than 24 months of fieldwork, CILS-III in San Diego retrieved complete or partial information on 70% of the original sample and 82% of the first follow-up.

For our purposes here, we merged the 1480 cases from the San Diego sample for which complete survey data over the span of a decade were available. Unlike the first follow-up, where the effects of sample attrition were negligible, the time elapsed between the last two surveys and the significant sample mortality relative to the original one, suggested the need for adjusting the results for sample selection bias. Family composition and early academic performance were the principal predictors of presence/absence in CILS-III in San Diego. Subsequent analyses indicated, however, that adjusted averages did not differ significantly from those unadjusted for this source of error. (For details on CILS-III, see Portes and Rumbaut [2005].)

Section 3

Employment, Educational Attainment and Bilingualism

9 Bilinguals in the US and College Enrollment

Lucrecia Santibañez and Maria Estela Zárate

Introduction

While it is estimated that about half of the world's population speaks at least two languages, in the United States only 20% of the population is bilingual or multilingual (Grosjean, 2010). The many immigrant origins of most Americans and the ongoing influx of immigrants who speak languages other than English do not appear to slow the rapid English language assimilation that characterizes the linguistic experiences of most immigrants (Agirdag, Chapter 7, this volume; Alba, 2004; Rumbaut, 2007). In addition, loss of fluency in the native language sometimes coincides with rapid English acquisition.

This is unfortunate as significant evidence has emerged that attests to the cognitive benefits of learning two languages and the positive association between learning another language early on and success in academic subjects (Bialystok, 2001, 2008; Rumbaut, Chapter 8, this volume). For instance, studies show that bilingualism is associated with certain cognitive advantages, such as improved working memory in younger bilinguals, superior executive control and better selective attention (Bialystok, 2001; Bialystok et al., 2008). Working memory skills are positively associated with skills and knowledge in mathematics and reading comprehension (Alloway, 2007; Blair & Razza, 2007; D'Amico & Guarnera, 2005; Gathercole et al., 2006). Recent work by McClelland et al., (2008) also shows the transfer of working memory training to the comprehension of written material.

In addition, being bilingual demonstrates social benefits for youth that lead to more stable and successful academic trajectories (Feliciano, 2001; Valenzuela, 1999; Zárate & Pineda, 2014). Immigrant students who speak their parents' native language appear to be more adept at negotiating social networks with other adults, including teachers, have access to broader social networks and have more stable perceptions of ethnic identity (Stanton-Salazar & Dornsbusch, 1995; Valenzuela, 1999; Zárate et al., 2005). Several studies have further confirmed that the social benefits of speaking two languages yield positive academic and educational effects (Bankston & Zhou, 1995; Feliciano, 2001; Zárate & Pineda, 2014). Bilingual adolescents ultimately have access to broader social networks than their monolingual peers do, and these more expansive social connections can increase access to homework help, job, career and educational information (see Chapters 3–6 and 10 of this volume for labor market implications of this bilingualism).

Through the positive effects on test scores, grades and other cognitive functions, we would expect that knowing more than one language could also have a positive effect on college enrollment. To date, the relationship between learning and speaking two languages and college enrollment has not been fully examined. From Callahan (2008), we know that the relationship between language minorities' native language use at home and the likelihood of going to college differs between boys and girls. However, the context of native language use alone does not fully capture an individual's linguistic competencies, and we question whether more precise approximations of bilingualism are necessary to fully understand the impact of native language knowledge on college enrollment.

The principal focus of this chapter is to examine the relationship between language minority status, English proficiency, native language use and college enrollment. Using data from the Educational Longitudinal Survey (ELS) from 2000 to 2006, we constructed a model to estimate the determinants of college enrollment post high school. We built our model using the comprehensive framework of student access and enrollment to higher education suggested by Perna (2006). This model takes into account individual, family and institutional factors that have been found to affect college choice. Specifically, we investigate (1) students' bilingual status, narrowly defined by a native language other than English *and* English proficiency; and (2) students' language use with family members. With these two indicators, we conceptualize bilingualism as the *use* of a language other than English, not simply having had exposure to that language. We propose that the degree of bilingualism is related to college enrollment, a precursor to labor market access as other chapters in this volume attest. In addition, we estimate the relationship between college enrollment and immigrant generational status. State fixed effects remove fixed variation across states such as the unemployment rate and the availability of state-level higher education financial aid policies.

Conceptual Framework

We use a variation of the traditional model of student access and enrollment in higher education that is used to account for the individual and institutional factors related to college access (Perna, 2006). In Perna's model, four groups of factors impact college enrollment for students:

individual, school, institutional and state-level contexts. In this analysis, we examine the impact of individual factors on college enrollment while also controlling for state fixed effects. We are concerned mainly with the relationship between both native language use and English language proficiency and college enrollment. Many factors exist that describe individuals' competencies and use of English and the native language, all capturing different facets and influences of linguistic experiences. Here, we specifically examine the language an individual first learned as a child, English proficiency in high school and native language use at home and in high school, and their influence on college enrollment.

Early home language use

The existing literature on early home language is helpful to understand the mechanism by which an individual's first language can influence eventual college enrollment. Early home language is a commonly used indicator of acculturation (Phinney & Flores, 2002), and we specifically conceptualize early home language as an indicator of early parental acculturation. Admittedly, language indicators are only one dimension of the acculturation process, a process that is influenced by multiple contexts. As such, early home language is an imperfect indicator of early acculturation. For this reason, we employ language indicators at two different points in time (early and end of high school), as well as immigrant generation to provide another dimension of acculturation.

As an indicator of early parental acculturation, early home language use denotes parents' integration into the host country's social institutions and networks, including the US school systems (Hakuta & D'Andrea, 1992; LaFromboise et al., 1993). Existing research has shown that, even after controlling for educational level, less acculturated mothers are less knowledgeable of school activities, have lower perceptions of their parenting efficacy and are less likely to believe that they share responsibility with the teacher for their child's formal education, believing that teachers are accountable for solving issues like learning problems in school (Moreno & Lopez, 1999; Wong & Hughes, 2006). Spanish-speaking parents of elementary-age students often defer to a teacher's or administrator's authority, feel neglected or marginalized by schools and teachers, are unfamiliar with ways that they are expected to participate in school activities and generally lack English proficiency or knowledge of how to negotiate with US school personnel (Delgado-Gaitan, 1994; Klimes-Dougan et al., 1992; Moreno & Valencia, 2001; Valdes, 1996). Given the consistent evidence of the challenges faced by Spanish-speaking parents in navigating US schooling systems, we propose that early home language use provides an indicator of the relationship between parental acculturation and interactions with US schooling practices.

Ultimately, less acculturated parents of elementary-age children are less likely to advocate for their children if it requires familiarity with US school systems. For example, early academic exposure among Latino students is a pivotal determinant of college preparation tracking in high school (González et al., 2003). However, less acculturated parents who may not be part of a privileged information-sharing network, or who are unaware of their right to contest school authority may not request higher track placement that could benefit their children (Auerbach, 2002).

English proficiency in high school

It is a reasonable expectation that English proficiency is a necessary condition for enrolling in a college degree program in the US. In fact, baccalaureate-granting institutions typically have minimum standards for English proficiency before admitting undergraduate students. While some colleges, particularly community colleges, may offer English as second language (ESL) programs targeting limited English proficient (LEP) students, these programs are typically not baccalaureate degree programs (Kuo, 1999) nor do 'remedial English' or ESL courses typically confer credit toward a degree (Kibler et al., 2011). In this study, students who are not English fluent in high school are likely recent immigrant arrivals, transnational students (who come and go) or longer-term immigrant students who have not received adequate language support (Menken et al., 2007). Unfortunately, being labeled LEP (or English language learner [ELL]) in high school, regardless of whether the label reflects actual English proficiency levels, has been identified as a factor limiting students' preparation for college (Callahan et al., 2010; Swail et al., 2004). For students in any of these groups, gaining access to a degree program or transfer program at a community college is a challenging feat.

Native language use at home

While early native language use is useful in interpreting *parents'* early acculturation, it is not necessarily useful in understanding their *children's* acculturation, as students' integration into US institutions and practices can vary widely from parents' acculturation trajectories (Portes & Rumbaut, 2001). Instead, we use students' native language use with family members to approximate students' proximity to parents' home culture. The explicit or implicit mechanism for linking native language use to acculturation is that its use contributes, among other factors, to native language maintenance (Portes & Rumbaut, 2001; Yeung et al., 2000). Considered a dimension of various acculturation models, native language maintenance can indicate the degree to which immigrant families (parents and children) have adapted culturally, politically or socially to a new country (LaFromboise *et al.*, 1993). Acculturation processes, in turn, have implications for schooling outcomes.

One of the ways that acculturation might confer benefits to academic outcomes is that native language maintenance may facilitate access to family and co-ethnic academic or social support networks which buffer the effects of negative schooling experiences often faced by Latino students (Callahan, 2008; Portes & Rumbaut, 2001; Valenzuela, 1999; Zhou, 1997). Native language maintenance at home and with peers demonstrates a positive effect on high school academic performance and college enrollment for Latino boys (Callahan, 2008; Lutz & Crisp, 2009). In contrast, when adolescents do not maintain parents' native language, disruption to intergenerational relations and communication can occur and cause parent–child conflict (Portes & Rumbaut, 2001; Zhou, 1997). In turn, conflict in parent–child relationships or disconnect with other co-ethnic peers can hinder positive academic achievement and jeopardize school engagement (Portes & Rumbaut, 2001; Valenzuela, 1999; Zhou, 1997).

Student background variables

Many factors influence who goes and who does not go to college after high school. Academic achievement, as early as elementary school, certainly plays a very important role in determining who goes to college (Hamrick & Stage, 2004; Hurtado *et al.*, 1997; Zárate & Gallimore, 2005). Standardized test scores have also been associated with an increased probability of enrolling in college (Perna & Titus, 2005). Similarly, student expectations have also been associated with college enrollment (Perna, 2000), although this association is not as consistent for students of color as it is for white students (Hurtado *et al.*, 1997; Zárate & Gallimore, 2005). Finally, models predicting college enrollment generally include background characteristics in order to account for the unique gender and racial schooling experiences of students in US schools. Gender is particularly relevant at a time when females are enrolling at higher rates in postsecondary education than males (Freeman, 2005; Peter *et al.*, 2005). Race is another explanatory variable also typically examined in models of college enrollment.

The relevance of parental and familial factors is also evident in research identifying high school indicators of college preparation and college enrollment (Hamrick & Stage, 1998; Hurtado *et al.*, 1997; Perna, 2000; Perna & Titus, 2005). These studies have found that families' socioeconomic status (SES), largely captured by parental education and family income, is a strong predictor of college enrollment (Berkner & Chavez, 1997; Hamrick & Stage, 1998; Hurtado *et al.*, 1997; Perna, 2000; Perna & Titus, 2005; Riegle-Crumb, 2010). Parental expectations for college also comprise one of the most examined predictors of college enrollment; most research has found a positive association between parental college expectations and college enrollment (Perna, 2000; Perna & Titus, 2005; Riegle-Crumb, 2010; Swail *et al.*, 2004). Here again, the association is inconsistent for students of color (Perna, 2000; Zárate & Gallimore, 2005).

In addition to parental expectations and parents' SES, parents' involvement in their child's education has been associated with college enrollment. This body of research has examined different forms of parental involvement and participation to understand which forms of parental involvement influence college preparation and enrollment (Crosnoe, 2001; Desimone, 1999; McNeal, 1999; Perna & Titus, 2005; Riegle-Crumb, 2010; Valadez, 2002). Parental involvement has been measured by the frequency of certain parental activities, including whether parents attended school events and activities and were involved with parent/teacher organizations (PTO/PTA). Using these forms of parental involvement, studies relying on aggregated samples mostly confirm the positive role of parental involvement in college-related outcomes (Jeynes, 2007; Perna & Titus, 2005). However, in disaggregated samples, some of the activities that contribute to white students' academic achievement prove insignificant among students of color (Desimone, 1999; McNeal, 1999; Perna, 2000; Valadez, 2002).

Methods, Data and Variables

This study seeks to answer the following research questions:

(1) Does college attendance vary between bilingual students and monolingual English-speaking students?
(2) Does four-year college attendance vary between bilingual students and monolingual English-speaking students?
(3) Does the relationship between bilingualism and college attendance hold among different Spanish bilinguals?

Data

To answer these questions, we use data from the Educational Longitudinal Study (ELS:2002)[1] administered by the National Center for Education Statistics (NCES). The ELS:2002 is designed to monitor the progression of a national sample of students from tenth grade into young adulthood. In the base year of data collection (2002), the ELS collected information on students' academic achievement in mathematics and reading standardized tests, it collected demographic information, and it obtained information about students' and parents' college expectations and parents' participation in school activities. Subsequent waves of data collection took place in 2004, 2006 and most recently in 2012. In the third round of data collection in 2006, information was collected about students' college decisions, financial aid considerations, enrollment in postsecondary education, employment and earnings and living situation. In addition, high school completion status was updated for those who had not completed high school as of the 2004 follow-up. This study makes use of the first and third waves of data for respondents who completed the base-year survey (2002) as well as the second follow-up (2006) survey.[2]

Methods

We employ logistic regression models to estimate whether tenth graders ever attended college. In some models, we include a state-level fixed effect to capture fixed differences across states, such as the costs of higher education and the availability of statewide financial aid policies. We include numerous control variables to account for the background characteristics of the students and other factors that could affect going to college in this population. All models are estimated using sample ELS:2002 weights.[3]

Variables

To estimate college enrollment, we use the students' SES, gender, race, high school graduate status and academic achievement indicators as control variables. A continuous composite variable of the student's SES at base year is included. This variable, constructed by the NCES, is based on the father's occupation and education, the mother's education, the family income and material possessions, and is a simple average of the non-missing components after each component score has been standardized. High school graduate status is also a dummy variable documenting having graduated from high school by the third wave of data collection (two years post-high school) or having obtained a general education development (GED) certificate. We control for racial background by using four dummy variables: African American, Asian and Pacific Islander,[4] Hispanic and white (the reference group). To control for academic preparation, we use students' tenth-grade standardized test scores in reading and mathematics. We also include a set of dummy variables related to parental influence: parent participation in a parent–teacher association (PTA), parental attendance at school activities at tenth grade and parental expectation for the tenth grader to enroll in college. In addition, we include a dummy variable indicating whether the tenth grader expects to go to college.

Two dummy variables for immigrant status are included. *First-generation* students are those who were foreign-born (born outside the US). *Second-generation* refers to students who were US-born with at least one foreign-born parent.[5]

Language constructs: Bilingualism

In our sample, close to 14% of tenth graders in 2002 indicated that English was not the first language they learned to speak as a child, i.e. their native language. Minority language speakers are predominantly concentrated among Latino and Asian/Pacific Islander students; 52% of Latino and 63% of Asian/Pacific Islander students first spoke a language other than English.[6]

In the base-year survey, students who responded that they learned to speak a language other than English as a child were asked to rate their English proficiency by indicating how well they understood, spoke, wrote and read English (1 = very well, 2 = well, 3 = not well, 4 = not all). We used a principal component factor analysis to create a factor score that approximated overall English proficiency using these self-reports. We used a threshold of 0.84 to designate an individual as *English proficient* to capture those students who spoke, read and understood English well or very well. It also includes people who reported that they wrote English 'not well.' We reason that writing skills capture quality and length of education, whereas speaking, understanding and reading are better indicators of proficiency. Because the ELS does not ask directly about native language fluency, we consider any student to be '*bilingual*' who reported a native language other than English *and* self-reported being English proficient. We do, of course, acknowledge the limitations inherent in the use of any self-reports of language proficiency (Oller & Perkins, 1978).

We extend the definition of bilingual to account for frequency of use of the native language, as well. It is difficult to ascertain the degree of dual language skills or true bilingualism by the time the student is in the tenth grade because the ELS does not include any measure of fluency in the native language. To approximate native language fluency, we employ a measure of native language frequency. Language minority students were asked to rate the frequency of use of their native language with mother, father and siblings (i.e. 1 = never, 2 = sometimes, 3 = about half of the time, 4 = always or most of the time). The assumption in using a variable that captures frequency of native language use to construct bilingual indicators is that use of the native language contributes, among other factors, to its maintenance (Portes & Rumbaut, 2001; Yeung *et al.*, 2000).

We used a principal component factor analysis to measure the overall frequency of native language use. In this factor score, native language use with mother, father and siblings (not with friends) is loaded at a threshold that would designate an individual who regularly speaks the native language with at least two out of three family members.[7] This indicator largely captures language minority students who spoke their native language with parents and/or siblings sometimes, about half the time and always.[8] Factor analysis results can be found in Appendix A.

Table 9.1 Language constructs

Construct name	Native language other than English?	Self-report: English proficient	Frequency of native language use with family
English-only	No	–	–
PL dominant	Yes	No	–
Bilingual	Yes	Yes	–
High-use bilingual	Yes	Yes	High

We expand on these basic definitions of bilingualism, native language use and English proficiency from the base-year wave of data collection (tenth grade) to build our language constructs shown in Table 9.1. Language constructs result in three mutually exclusive groups: (1) *English only*, (2) *primary language* (PL) *dominant* and (3) *bilingual*. The bilingual group also includes a subgroup, *high-use bilinguals*.

Limitations

Like other authors in this volume (notably Chapters 3, 4, 7 and 8), we are keenly aware of the strengths and limitations of the linguistic indicators offered us in ELS:2002. One clear limitation that we face is the lack of a true measure of native language fluency, which we approximate by measuring both the frequency and context in which native language is used. Clearly, more precise indicators of oral and written skills in different contexts would be most desirable; however, such detailed measures are generally not available in nationally representative data sets.

In addition, in order to capture English skills and abilities, we draw on an indicator of self-reported English proficiency, also not entirely ideal. We are well aware of the limitations of self-reports of language proficiency (Oller & Perkins, 1978), much like native language fluency; therefore, we use the strongest possible indicators available in the ELS data set. In addition, we measure college enrollment as an absolute indicator independent of whether students actually persisted to graduation; future research should investigate whether the language constructs employed here are associated with college persistence.

Exploratory analysis

Table 9.2 shows the descriptive statistics for the final analytic sample, which includes individuals who responded to the survey in both the base year and the second follow-up, resulting in approximately 16,000 observations in 2002.[9] The sample is 50% female; nearly two-thirds white (61%), 15% Hispanic, 14% black and 4% Asian. Seven percent of the respondents are first-generation and 12% are second-generation. Eighty-six percent of respondents in our sample are native English speakers and nearly 14% are language minorities (non-native English speakers). Bilinguals comprise 9% of the overall sample, and PL dominant are 5% of the total sample. High-use bilinguals, a subset of bilinguals, comprise 6% of the overall sample.

As mentioned previously, one limitation of our bilingual constructs is that the ELS does not directly measure fluency in the native language. We assume in this analysis that native speakers of languages other than English will be at least orally fluent in their native language to be considered a bilingual. To examine this assumption, we employ Rumbaut's (2007) argument that the earlier an immigrant acquires English, the more likely she or he is to lose the native language. We propose that after age 5, young immigrants would be exposed to formal education in English, possibly hastening linguistic assimilation. In our analytic sample, bilingual, first-generation immigrants came to the US when they were 7 years old on average. High-use, first-generation bilinguals came to the US older, at 8 years of age. Students classified as PL dominant (those whose native language is not English, but who do not self-report as being English proficient) arrived at 10 years, on average.

Together, these characteristics suggest that the first-generation bilingual students in our sample arrived after commencing formal education in their country of origin and likely cementing some degree of native language fluency. In recent years, most migrants to the US have come from Mexico, China, India, the Philippines and Central America[10] where kindergarten is compulsory; by age 7, most children would have had at least one if not two years of formal schooling prior to arriving in the US, lending credence to the assumption that respondents' native language proficiency will be at least adequate.

Results

As described in Table 9.2, the vast majority of students in our sample attended some type of college at least for some time after high school graduation (71%), and 41% attended a four-year college as their first institution. In addition, students overwhelmingly completed high school (92%).

Predicting college going for all

Bilingualism and college enrollment

Table 9.3 presents the results from estimating a logistic model of college enrollment post high school. We estimated four different models. Columns 1 and 2 present the results for bilinguals and columns 3 and 4 show the

Table 9.2 Means and proportions for full sample and language groups

	Full sample (n=16,197)*	Native English speakers (n=12,658)	Bilinguals (n=1,632)	High-use bilinguals (n=1,029)	PL dominant (n=954)
Language constructs					
Native English speaker	0.864				
Non-native English speaker	0.136				
Language minorities					
PL dominant	0.050				
Bilingual	0.085				
High-use bilingual	0.055				
Bilingual (Spanish)	0.050				
High-use bilingual (Spanish)	0.040				
Immigration characteristics					
First-generation	0.070	0.019	0.348	0.405	0.486
Age upon US arrival	n/a	5.1[1]	7.0	7.4	10.2
Grade upon US arrival	–	–	4.5	4.7	6.4
Second-generation	0.115	0.077	0.409	0.410	0.264
Race/ethnicity					
Hispanic	0.153	0.08	0.556	0.620	0.645
Asian	0.039	0.15	0.204	0.192	0.167
Black	0.141	0.154	0.053	0.037	0.065
White	0.611	0.688	0.144	0.131	0.087

(Continued)

Table 9.2 (Continued)

	Full sample (n = 16,197)*	Native English speakers (n = 12,658)	Bilinguals (n = 1,632)	High-use bilinguals (n = 1,029)	PL dominant (n = 954)
Native language					
Spanish	0.077	–	0.599	0.644	0.653
Chinese	0.021	–	0.161	0.140	0.151
Education background and SES					
High school graduate	0.922	0.931	0.889	0.894	0.828
Socioeconomic index	0.00	0.07	-0.30	-0.41	-0.66
College going					
Ever attended college	0.707	0.716	69.9%	70.9%	56.1%
Four-year institution initially	0.409	0.428	34.3%	34.5%	18.7%

Source: ELS:2002, sample of tenth graders who answered the second follow-up survey.

*Sample sizes for each of the language constructs (columns 2–5) are calculated using the ELS variable ('bystlang'), measuring native language use. Percentages in these columns may differ from what they would be using the full sample (column 1) because of weights applied to that sample and non-response (or other responses) in some cases.

†This proportion includes only native English speakers who were born outside the US (first-generation immigrants).

Note: In all cases, English proficiency is self-reported and based on a composite score; use of the primary language is based on a composite frequency of use.

results for high-use bilinguals, a subgroup of bilinguals. The dependent variable is any postsecondary enrollment (either community or four-year college) within two years after completing high school. For simplicity of interpretation, in all models the reference group includes English-only monolinguals.

All models include control variables that have been found in the existing literature to have a significant relationship with college enrollment.[11] The following variables prove positively and significantly related to college enrollment in all of our models: being a high school graduate, female, Asian/Pacific Islander and black all increase the odds of college enrollment, as does expecting to go to college in tenth grade. In addition, SES and tenth-grade mathematic and reading test scores are also positively associated with college enrollment. Parental expectations of college also had a significant and positive, although relatively modest, relationship with college enrollment. Parental participation in the PTA and school activities was also significantly associated with an increase in the odds of enrolling in college.

The results in Table 9.3 suggest that once we control for all of the above characteristics, bilinguals have some advantage over the reference group (English monolinguals), while high-use bilinguals have even higher odds of college going. Results for high-use bilinguals with state fixed effects are similar, suggesting that even within states these differences persist. In addition, we found that the odds of going to college are significantly higher for first- and second-generation students compared to third-plus generation students (i.e. those with no immediate immigrant background). In fact, being second-generation offered an advantage (nearly doubled the odds) of enrolling in college, compared to being third-plus generation.

Bilingualism and four-year college going

Table 9.4 presents the results from a model estimating initial enrollment at a four-year college (i.e. the first postsecondary institution attended) for all students. In this model, only high-use bilinguals appear to have higher odds of going to a four-year college, relative to the reference group (English monolinguals).

The results also suggest that second-generation students have higher odds of attending a four-year college relative to all other students; first-generation status also appears to increase the odds within states, but the relationship is not significant at conventional confidence levels. All results are robust to the inclusion of an additional control variable, the age at which the student came to the US (if first-generation).[12] This suggests that preimmigrant education experiences are not a major force behind any of these results.

Table 9.3 Logistic regression model predicting any college enrollment (full sample)

Outcome: Ever attended college	Model 1: Bilinguals	Model 2: Bilinguals	Model 1: High-use bilinguals	Model 2: High-use bilinguals
Bilingual	1.44**	1.42**		
	(0.243)	(0.241)		
High-use bilingual			1.61**	1.60**
			(0.307)	(0.309)
Immigration controls				
First-generation	1.36*	1.42**	1.39*	1.45**
	(0.235)	(0.246)	(0.262)	(0.274)
Second-generation	1.79**	1.81**	1.83**	1.87**
	(0.258)	(0.257)	(0.272)	(0.274)
n	13,176	13,176	12,773	12,773
Population (weighted)	2,659,015	2,659,015	2,588,030	2,588,030
State fixed effects	No	Yes	No	Yes
Controls	Yes	Yes	Yes	Yes

Source: ELS:2006 data.
*Significant at 10%; **significant at 5%. Standard errors in parentheses.
Note: All models are estimated with the following additional controls: family SES composite, test scores in reading and math. Constant is included in model. All models are weighted using sample weights provided in the ELS.

Predicting college going for Spanish bilinguals

To test for differences between language groups, we reran the previous models using bilingualism constructs for Spanish. We focus only on Spanish, because sample sizes are very low for other languages. In this model, the reference group is, as previously, English monolinguals. All of the language constructs are defined as in the previous discussion. Table 9.5 shows the descriptive statistics for the Spanish bilingual population. Here, we note that Spanish-speaking bilinguals are more likely to be recent immigrants and, on the whole, demonstrate lower SES than the larger aggregate bilingual population. Their parents are less likely to have either graduated from high school or attended college. In addition, Spanish-speaking bilinguals tended to immigrate at a slightly younger age than the larger, recent immigrant population; and they are primarily Latino.

Spanish bilinguals and college enrollment

The results for models predicting enrollment in any type of college two years post high school for Spanish bilinguals are shown in Table 9.6, and suggest that Spanish bilinguals are more likely to enroll in college than English monolinguals, all else held equal. Results are significant at the 95%

Table 9.4 Logistic regression model predicting initial four-year college enrollment (full sample)

Outcome: First attended four-year institution	Model 1: Bilinguals	Model 2: Bilinguals	Model 1: High-use bilinguals	Model 2: High-use bilinguals
Bilingual	1.22	1.27		
	(0.173)	(0.193)		
High-use bilingual			1.38*	1.43**
			(0.230)	(0.249)
Immigration controls				
First-generation	1.19	1.22	1.18	1.24
	(0.198)	(0.212)	(0.213)	(0.236)
Second-generation	1.28**	1.42**	1.30**	1.44**
	(0.150)	(0.173)	(0.159)	(0.185)
n	13,159	13,159	12,758	12,758
Population (weighted)	2,654,347	2,654,347	2,583,637	2,583,637
State fixed effects	No	Yes	No	Yes
Controls	Yes	Yes	Yes	Yes

Source: ELS:2006 data.
*Significant at 10%; **significant at 5%.
Note: All models are estimated with the following additional controls: family SES composite, test scores in reading and math. Constant is included in model. All models are weighted using sample weights provided in the ELS.

confidence level for bilinguals and high-use bilinguals. This holds for the state fixed effects model as well.

Spanish bilinguals and four-year college going

Table 9.7 presents the coefficients predicting four-year college enrollment. These results suggest that the odds of going to a four-year college are significantly higher for high-use Spanish bilinguals relative to English monolinguals, clearly highlighting the bilingual advantage. The results remain unchanged when we include a control for the age at which the student came to the US. Even though Spanish bilinguals are more likely to be recent immigrants, and differ demographically and socioeconomically from the full sample (see Table 9.5), our models take these differences into account. Therefore, the language 'advantage' persists even when holding these other variables constant. Together, these results suggest that preserving the native language translates into an advantage for Spanish bilinguals.

Conclusions

In order to examine the relationship between bilingualism and college enrollment, we based our model on Perna's (2006) concept of student

Table 9.5 Means and proportions for Spanish bilinguals

	Bilinguals (n=676)	High-use bilinguals (n=477)
Immigration characteristics		
First-generation	0.327	0.385
Age upon US arrival	6.4	6.9
Grade upon US arrival*	4.8	4.8
Second-generation	0.481	0.464
Race/ethnicity		
Hispanic	0.976	0.990
Asian	0.003	0.003
Black	0.006	0.000
White	1.0%	0.0%
Education background and SES		
High school graduate	0.859	0.862
Socioeconomic index (ELS composite)	−0.57	−0.67
College going		
Ever attended college	0.636	0.639
Four-year institution initially	0.259	0.270

Source: ELS:2002 sample of tenth graders who answered the second follow-up survey.
*This is estimated at the average grade a new immigrant was placed in, assuming that he or she came to the US after the age of 7 (inclusive).
Note: In all cases, English proficiency is self-reported and is based on a composite score of four questions that report skills in reading, writing and speaking in English. Use of the other language is based on a composite score of questions that report use with family (parents and siblings). Frequently includes those answering 'sometimes, almost always and always'. Very frequently includes those answering 'Almost always and always'.

access and enrollment in higher education. We found a positive and statistically significant relationship between the odds of going to college and being bilingual, affirming the positive educational (Chapter 8) and labor market (Chapter 7) outcomes recently discussed. These results held after we disaggregated our analysis for the Spanish language group. Moreover, the association between being bilingual and attending a four-year college was more consistently observed for high-use bilinguals, where the level of native language use had implications for first-time enrollment at a four-year college, lending nuance to the discussion of native language maintenance.

Among Spanish speakers, the most consistent advantage of bilingualism exists among Spanish-language bilinguals who frequently speak the native language with family members. Our results suggest that high-use Spanish bilinguals have significantly higher odds of ever attending college, as well as first attending a four-year college right after

Table 9.6 Logistic regression predicting any college enrollment (Spanish bilinguals only)

Outcome: Ever attended college	Model 1: Bilinguals	Model 2: Bilinguals	Model 1: High-use bilinguals	Model 2: High-use bilinguals
Bilingual (Spanish)	1.53**	1.54**		
	(0.319)	(0.322)		
High-use bilingual (Spanish)			1.68**	1.70**
			(0.378)	(0.386)
Immigration controls				
First-generation	1.26	1.30	1.26	1.29
	(0.232)	(0.241)	(0.248)	(0.254)
Second-generation	1.73**	1.77**	1.80**	1.84**
	(0.253)	(0.254)	(0.271)	(0.273)
n	12,440	12,440	12,440	12,440
State fixed effects	No	Yes	No	Yes
Controls	Yes	Yes	Yes	Yes

Source: ELS:2006 data.
**significant at 5%.
Note: All models are estimated with the following controls: high school graduate, female, race/ethnicity, individual and family college expectations, parental involvement in PTA and school in general, family SES composite, test scores in reading and math and immigration status. Constant is included in model. All models are weighted using sample weights provided in the ELS.

high school than the reference group (mostly native English speakers). We posit that *high-use bilinguals* are those students who are most likely to be fully bilingual and thus reap the most rewards associated with native language maintenance. It is beyond the limits of our data to determine whether these high-use bilinguals are bilingual because they live in contexts where opportunities to speak Spanish are more prevalent, or if instead they use Spanish frequently because they developed their bilingual skills early on. The causal order is beyond our scope; however, we find the relationship to be strong and compelling.

These results suggest that, among Spanish bilinguals, simply having learned Spanish as a child and achieving English proficiency alone does not translate into the same linguistic or human capital advantage that we find among high-use Spanish bilinguals. Students who speak the native language regularly with family members might actually have a human or social capital advantage that translates into higher college-going rates (see Agirdag, Chapter 7, this volume for greater discussion of language as human capital). We propose that not only is being bilingual (learning a native language as a child and being English proficient) not *harmful*, but being bilingual *and* maintaining and using the native language frequently with family also

Table 9.7 Logistic regression predicting initial four-year college enrollment (Spanish bilinguals only)

Outcome: Attended four-year institution as first postsecondary institution	Model 1: Bilinguals	Model 2: Bilinguals	Model 1: High-use bilinguals	Model 2: High-use bilinguals
Bilingual	1.29	1.32		
	(0.259)	(0.277)		
High-use bilingual			1.81**	1.85**
			(0.390)	(0.418)
Immigration controls				
First-generation	1.15	1.16	1.10	1.13
	(0.202)	(0.216)	(0.203)	(0.220)
Second-generation	1.32**	1.47**	1.34**	1.48**
	(0.162)	(0.189)	(0.170)	(0.200)
n	12,425	12,425	12,425	12,425
State fixed effects	No	Yes	No	Yes
Controls	Yes	Yes	Yes	Yes

Source: ELS:2006 data.
**significant at 5%.
Note: All models are estimated with the following controls: high school graduate, female, race/ethnicity, individual and family college expectations, parental involvement in PTA and school in general, family SES composite, test scores in reading and math and immigration status. Constant is included in model. All models are weighted using sample weights provided in the ELS.

appears to increase the odds of going to college among Spanish-language speakers. Native language use with family members during high school, which both promotes and is facilitated by native language maintenance, should be widely supported in order to obtain the educational benefits of having learned a native language early on, and potentially an economic advantage as well (Agirdag, Chapter 7, this volume).

The existing body of work on immigrant students illustrates the mechanisms by which native language use yields benefits. One body of work suggests that youth who both maintain their native language and are English proficient have wider social networks offering more resources and supports (Stanton-Salazar & Dornsbusch, 1995; Valenzuela, 1999; Zhou & Bankston, 1994). In contrast to English monolinguals, high-use bilinguals are able to include both English monolinguals and co-ethnic individuals in their social and support networks. Native language use with parents also lessens the cultural dissonance that may result when youth acculturate to US cultural norms faster than their parents (Portes & Rumbaut, 2001). Minimizing potential cultural conflict between parents and children is associated, in turn, with higher academic achievement (Portes & Rumbaut, 2001).

It is also important to point out that the observed significant effects of immigrant generation align with the existing body of work on immigrant students. Like us, others have found that immigrant students do better than their third-plus generation peers (Han, 2012; Kao & Tienda, 1995; Zárate & Pineda, 2014). The theory of immigrant optimism suggests that immigrant students' expectations and school performance reflect foreign-born parents' optimistic expectations of their children – above and beyond what might be expected given racial and social background characteristics (Kao & Tienda, 1995). Together, the immigrant optimism theory, combined with our findings on the effects of bilingualism, point to the need to cautiously manage immigrant youths' linguistic assimilation. Reiterating Agirdag's findings (Chapter 7, this volume), we argue that the urgency to divest immigrant youth of their parents' native language, often intimated in public debates, may cause more harm than benefit in the long run. In fact, the pressure of linguistic assimilation may cause more harm than benefit, by reducing the chances that these young people have to gain the advantage of a college education, which increases their economic value in the US labor market.

Notes

(1) For more information, see http://nces.ed.gov/surveys/els2002/.
(2) This sample is equivalent to 16,197 students.
(3) We use the weights for students that respond in both the baseline year (BY) and at the second follow-up (F2).
(4) The ELS composite race/ethnicity variable classifies Asians as those who reported 'Asian, Hawaii/Pacific Islander, non-Hispanic'.
(5) Puerto Rico-origin is considered as 'foreign-born'.
(6) Results not shown, but are available upon request.
(7) This cutoff threshold was -1.07 for sometimes, about half of the time, most of the time or always with two out of three family members (mother, father and/or siblings). For those reporting that they speak the non-English language with two out of three family members always or almost always, the cutoff was -1.30.
(8) We left 'speaking with friends' out of the composite score as factor loadings suggested this question was not part of the 'speaking with family' construct.
(9) The second follow-up of ELS:2002 includes 16,197 respondents.
(10) From 2000 to 2010, 53% of immigrants came from Latin America (Mexico, Central America, South America and the Caribbean). The top immigrant-sending countries between 2000 and 2010 were Mexico, India, China, the Philippines, El Salvador and Guatemala (source: Center for Immigration Studies, available at http://www.cis.org/2012-profile-of-americas-foreign-born-population#execsum).
(11) For brevity, we do not show these coefficients, but they are available upon request.
(12) To avoid the issue of small cell sizes in some ages, this variable is coded as 1 if the person came to the US at age 7 or younger, and 0 otherwise.

References

Alba, R. (2004) Language assimilation today: Bilingualism persists more than in the past, but English still dominates. Working Paper no. 111. Center for Comparative Immigration Studies, University of California, La Jolla, CA.

Alloway, T.P. (2007) What can phonological and semantic information tell us about the mechanisms of immediate sentence recall? *Memory* 15, 605–615

Auerbach, S. (2002) "Why do they give the good classes to some and not to others?" Latino parent narratives of struggle in a college access program. *Teachers College Record* 104 (7), 1369–1392.

Bankston, C.L. (1995) Effects of minority-language literacy on the academic achievement of Vietnamese youths in New Orleans. *Sociology of Education* 68 (1), 1–17.

Berkner, L. and Chavez, L. (1997) Access to postsecondary education for the 1992 high school graduates (p. 108). US Department of Education, Office of Educational Research and Improvement, Washington DC.

Bialystok, E. (2001) *Bilingualism in Development: Language, Literacy, and Cognition.* New York: Cambridge University Press.

Bialystok, E., Craik, F.I.M. and Luk, G. (2008) Cognitive control and lexical access in younger and older bilinguals. *Journal of Experimental Psychology: Learning, Memory and Cognition* 34, 859–873.

Blair, C. and Razza, R.P. (2007) Relating effortful control, executive function, and false-belief understanding to emerging math and literacy ability in kindergarten. *Child Development* 78, 647–663

Callahan, R.M. (2008) Latino language-minority college going: Adolescent boys' language use and girls' social integration. *Bilingual Research Journal* 31 (1–2), 175–200.

Callahan, R.M., Wilkinson, L. and Muller, C. (2010) Academic achievement and course taking among language minority youth in US schools: Effects of ESL placement. *Educational Evaluation and Policy Analysis* 32 (1), 84–117.

Crosnoe, R. (2001) Academic orientation and parental involvement in education during high school. *Sociology of Education* 74 (3), 210–230.

D'Amico, A. and Guarnera, M. (2005) Exploring working memory in children with low arithmetical achievement. *Learning and Individual Differences* 15, 189–202. doi:10.1016/j.lindif.2005.01.002

Delgado-Gaitan, C. (1994) "Consejos": The power of cultural narratives. *Anthropology & Education Quarterly* 25 (3), 298–316.

Desimone, L. (1999) Linking parental involvement with student achievement: Do race and income matter? *The Journal of Educational Research* 93 (1), 11–30.

Feliciano, C. (2001) The benefits of biculturalism: Exposure to immigrant culture and dropping out of school among Asian and Latino youths. *Social Science Quarterly* 82 (4), 865–879.

Freeman, C.E. (2005) Trends in educational equity of girls & women (NCES 2005-016). US Department of Education, National Center for Education Statistics. Washington DC: US Government Printing Office.

Gathercole, S.E., Lamont, E. and Alloway, T.P. (2006) Working memory in the classroom. In S. Pickering (ed.) *Working memory and Education.* London: Academic Press.

González, K.P., Stoner, C. and Jovel, J.E. (2003) Examining the role of social capital in access to college for Latinas: Toward a college opportunity framework. *Journal of Hispanic Higher Education* 2 (2), 146–170.

Grosjean, F. (2010) *Bilingual: Life and Reality.* Cambridge, MA: Harvard University Press.

Hakuta, K. and D'Andrea, D. (1992) Some properties of bilingual maintenance and loss in Mexican background high school students. *Applied Linguistics* 13 (1), 72–99.

Hamrick, F.A. and Stage, F.K. (1998) High minority enrollment, high school-lunch rates: Predispositions to college. *The Review of Higher Education* 21 (4), 343–357.

Hamrick, F.A. and Stage, F.K. (2004) College predispositions at high-minority enrollment, low-income schools. *The Review of Higher Education* 27 (2), 151–168.

Han, W. (2012) The bilingualism and academic achievement: Does generation status make a difference? In C. Garcia Coll and A.K. Marks (eds) *The Immigrant Paradox in Children and Adolescents: Is Becoming American a Developmental Risk?* (pp. 161–184). Washington DC: American Psychological Association.

Hurtado, S., Inkelas, K.K. and Briggs, C. (1997) Differences in college access and choice among racial / ethnic groups: Identifying continuing barriers. *Research in Higher Education* 38 (1), 43–75.

Jeynes, W.H. (2007) The relationship between parental involvement and urban secondary school student academic achievement: A meta-analysis. *Urban Education* 42 (1), 82–110.

Kao, G. and Tienda, M. (1995) Optimism and achievement: The educational performance of immigrant youth. *Social Science Quarterly* 76 (1), 1–20.

Kibler, A.K., Bunch, G.C. and Endris, A.K. (2011) Community college practices for U.S.-educated language-minority students: A resource-oriented framework. *Bilingual Research Journal* 34 (2), 201–222.

Klimes-Dougan, B., Lopez, J.A., Nelson, P. and Adelman, H.S. (1992) Two studies of low income parents' involvement in schooling. *The Urban Review* 24 (3), 185–202.

Kuo, E.W. (1999) English as a second language in the community college curriculum. *New Directions for Community Colleges* 1999 (108), 69–80.

LaFromboise, T., Coleman, H.L. and Gerton, J. (1993) Psychological impact of biculturalism: Evidence and theory. *Psychological Bulletin* 114 (3), 395–412.

Lutz, A. and Crist, S. (2009) Why do bilingual boys get better grades in English-only America? The impacts of gender, language and family interaction on academic achievement of Latino/a children of immigrants. *Ethnic and Racial Studies* 32 (1), 346–368.

McClelland, M.M., Cameron, C.E., Connor, C.M., Farris, C.L., Jewkes, A.M. and Morrison, F.J. (2008) Links between behavioral regulation and preschoolers' literacy, vocabulary, and math skills. *Developmental Psychology* 43 (4), 947–959.

McNeal Jr., R.B. (1999) Parental involvement as social capital: Differential effectiveness on science achievement, truancy, and dropping out. *Social Forces* 78 (1), 117–144.

Menken, K., Kleyn, T., Chae, N., Funk, A. and Rafal, J. (2007) Meeting the needs of long-term English language learners in high school. Report submitted to New York City Department of Education, Office of English Language Learners.

Moreno, R.P. and Lopez, J.A. (1999) Latina parental involvement: The role of maternal acculturation and education. *The School Community Journal* 9 (1), 83–101.

Moreno, R.P. and Valencia, R. (2001) Chicano families and schools: Myths, knowledge, and future directions. In R. Valencia (ed.) *Chicano School Failure and Success: Past, Present, and Future* (2nd edn, pp. 227–250). New York: RoutledgeFalmer.

Oller, J.W. and Perkins, K. (1978) A further comment on language proficiency as a source of variance in certain affective measures. *Language Learning* 28 (2), 417–423.

Perna, L.W. (2000) Differences in the decision to attend college among African Americans, Hispanics, and Whites. *The Journal of Higher Education* 71 (2), 117–141.

Perna, L.W. (2006) Studying college access and choice: A proposed conceptual model. In J.C. Smart (ed.) *Higher Education: Handbook of Theory and Research*, Vol. XXI (pp. 99–157). Springer: Dordrecht, The Netherlands.

Perna, L.W. and Titus, M.A. (2005) The relationship between parental involvement as social capital and college enrollment: An examination of racial/ethnic group differences. *The Journal of Higher Education* 76 (5), 485–518. doi:10.1353/jhe.2005.0036

Peter, K., Horn, L.J. and Carroll, C.D. (2005) Gender differences in participation and completion of undergraduate education and how they have changed over time. Postsecondary Education Descriptive Analysis Reports. NCES 2005-169. US Department of Education, Washington, DC.

Phinney, J.S. and Flores, J. (2002) Unpacking acculturation: Aspects of acculturation as predictors of traditional sex role attitudes. *Journal of Cross-Cultural Psychology* 33 (3), 320–331.

Portes, A. and Rumbaut, R.G. (2001) *Legacies: The Story of the Immigrant Second Generation*. Berkeley, CA: University of California Press.

Riegle-Crumb, C. (2010) More girls go to college: Exploring the social and academic factors behind the female postsecondary advantage among Hispanic and White students. *Research in Higher Education* 51 (6), 573–593.

Rumbaut, R.G. (2007) The evolution of language competencies, preferences, and use among immigrants and their children. US Department of Education, National Center for Education Statistics. Washington DC: US Government Printing Office.

Stanton-Salazar, R.D. and Dornbursch, S.M. (1995) Social capital and the reproduction of inequality: Information networks among Mexican-origin high school students. *Sociology of Education* 68 (2), 116–135. See http://www.jstor.org/stable/10.2307/2112778 (accessed 5 May 2013).

Swail, W.S., Cabrera, A.F. and Lee, C. (2004) Latino youth and the pathway to college (p. 56). Washington DC: Pew Hispanic Center.

Valadez, J.R. (2002) The influence of social capital on Latino high school students. *Hispanic Journal of Behavioral Sciences* 24 (3), 319–339.

Valdes, G. (1996) *Con respeto: Bridging the Distance Between Culturally Diverse Families and Schools*. New York: Teachers College Press: Columbia University.

Valenzuela, A. (1999) *Subtractive Schooling: U.S.-Mexican Youth and the Politics of Caring*. Albany, NY: State University of New York Press.

Wong, S.W. and Hughes, J.N. (2006) Ethnicity and language contributions to dimensions of parental involvement. *School Psychology Review* 35 (4), 645–662.

Yeung, A.S., Marsh, H.W. and Suliman, R. (2000) Can two tongues live in harmony: Analysis of the national education longitudinal study of 1988(nels88) longitudinal data on maintenance of home language. *American Educational Research Journal* 37 (4), 1001–1026.

Zárate, M.E., Bhimji, F. and Reese, L. (2005) Ethnic identity and academic achievement among Latina/o adolescents. *Journal of Latinos and Education* 4 (2), 95–114.

Zárate, M.E. and Gallimore, R. (2005) Gender differences in factors leading to college enrollment: A longitudinal analysis. *Harvard Educational Review* 75 (4), 383–489.

Zárate, M.E. and Pineda, C.G. (2014) The effects of early home language and school-related language contexts on high school graduation. *Teachers College Record*.

Zhou, M. (1997) Growing up American: The challenge confronting immigrant children and children of immigrants. *Annual Review of Sociology* 23 (1), 63–95.

Zhou, M. and Bankston III, C.L. (1994) Social capital and the adaptation of the second generation: The case of Vietnamese youth in New Orleans. *International Migration Review* 28 (4), 821–845.

Appendix A

Factor loadings and calculations for English proficiency

Survey item	Factor loading	Mean factor score	
		Very well	Well
a. How well do you understand spoken English?	0.87	−0.52	1.09
b. How well do you speak spoken English?	0.93	−0.63	0.89
c. How well do you read spoken English?	0.93	−0.65	0.84
c. How well do you write spoken English?*	0.90	−0.69	0.66

*Not included in designation of English proficient.
Note: Survey scale is 1=very well, 2=well, 3=not well and 4=not at all. Mean cutoff is 0.84.

Factor loadings and calculations for frequency of native language use

Survey item	Factor loading	Mean factor score		
		Sometimes	Half the time	Always
a. How often do you speak your native language with your mother?	0.86	−1.18	−0.33	0.69
b. How often do you speak your native language with your father?	0.85	−1.07	−0.21	0.73
c. How often do you speak your native language with your brothers and sisters?	0.84	−0.23	−0.23	0.97
c. How often do you speak your native language with your friends?*	0.67			

*Not included in calculation of factor scores.
Note: Survey scale is 1=never, 2=sometimes, 3=about half of the time and 4=always or most of the time. Mean cutoff is −1.07.

10 Employer Preferences: Do Bilingual Applicants and Employees Experience an Advantage?

Diana A. Porras, Jongyeon Ee and Patricia Gándara[1]

As the nation's population continues to grow, its racial, ethnic and *linguistic* landscape is also transforming. More than 60 million people over the age of five speak a language other than English at home in the US (US Census Bureau, 2013), accounting for one of every five residents. Nearly two-thirds (62%) of these individuals speak Spanish, followed at a distant second by Chinese (4.8%, almost 3 million speakers). There are also nearly 2 million or more speakers of French, German, Korean, Vietnamese and Tagalog in the US (US Census Bureau, 2013). While the traditional immigrant gateway states (i.e. California, Texas, Florida and New York) continue to have the largest concentrations, other states have actually experienced more growth among speakers of other languages. The 'new South' (i.e. Alabama, Arkansas, Georgia, North Carolina) has experienced an explosion of Spanish speakers over the last two decades, often in communities where virtually none existed before. Maine and Louisiana have seen an increase in the number of French speakers while the number of German speakers has grown in North Dakota and South Dakota. In Illinois, New York, New Jersey and Connecticut, the number of Slavic language speakers has also increased (US Census Bureau, 2010). Furthermore, the nation's linguistic diversity has developed at a rapid pace.

Since 1980, the number of speakers of other languages has increased by 158% while the population has grown by only 38% (US Census Bureau, 2013). This increasing linguistic diversity would suggest that people who speak these languages might have an advantage in the labor market, especially in jobs that require high levels of client interaction (e.g. sales, marketing and social and health services), particularly in areas with high concentrations of non-English languages. However, relatively little research has investigated this question, and the research that has been conducted has not resulted in a clear consensus.

It seems intuitive that having dual or multiple language skills would translate into economic and social benefits. If one were to ask college graduates in the US if being bilingual provides an advantage in the labor market, most would probably answer 'yes'. The ability to communicate effectively with co-workers, clients and business contacts in multiple languages seemingly would enhance a workplace. Using their second language skills to address customer needs, bilingual employees can help businesses enhance their bottom line. On the other hand, if people in the US who *are* bilingual by virtue of coming from an immigrant family, are asked about these same advantages, many might say, 'No, only English matters'. To some extent, both opinions might be right, as we have seen in earlier chapters in this volume.

From restaurant kitchens and factory floors, to hospitals and schools, to high-level international business and policy meetings and every place in between, multilingual people can be observed playing key roles in local and global economies. Whether completing a simple transaction at a cash register with a customer or training a patient in the proper uses of a home oxygen tank, multilingual employees are using their communication skills to deliver critical information on a daily basis. How do factors such as language, industry and job type impact the value of these individuals in the labor market? With relatively few studies conducted on the topic, the extent to which employers value and compensate employees for their second language skills is unclear. However, what is apparent is a growing interest among parents to raise bilingual children; presumably, these parents believe that there is a social and economic advantage to speaking more than one language.

The increasing demand of middle-class parents in particular, especially to educate their children in English and another world language has contributed to the rise of two-way immersion programs across the country (Palmer, 2009). According to Yang Su (2012), the California Department of Education estimates that 318 two-way immersion programs exist in the state, up from just 201 in 2006. These programs are designed to teach school-age children both English and another language (Lieu & Berestein Rojas, 2013). In many of these schools, more than half of the students enrolled come from middle-income families (Palmer, 2009). While national leaders such as Arne Duncan, the current Education Secretary tout the economic advantages of bilingualism (Maxwell, 2013), California, New York, Texas and at least five other states had made it official by implementing a State Seal of Biliteracy (SSB) by the time this volume went to press.

In 2012, California became the first state in the nation to issue a SSB [1].[1] To be awarded an SSB, students must complete a series of assessments and coursework that demonstrate their mastery of standard academic English and another world language [2].[2] During the first year it was offered, more than 10,000 high school seniors graduated with the SSB designation, certifying their high level of proficiency in reading, writing and speaking English and another world language (Jung, 2012). At the end of its second year, nearly 20,000 students had earned the SSB. Recognizing the importance of cultivating a linguistically diverse student population, Tom Torlakson, the current California State Superintendent stated, 'Fluency in a second language helps our students be well-prepared to compete in a global marketplace. The gold seal on their high school diploma recognizes and celebrates a second language as an asset not just for themselves, but for our state, nation, and world' (Jung, 2012, para. 6).

Attaining the SSB designation is a truly important accomplishment for these California (and other) graduates, as research suggests it will provide them with social, psychological and cognitive advantages (see, for example, Bialystok, 2001; Bialystok & Craik, 2010; Lee, 2008; Vom Dorp, 2000). However, the 'market value' of both the Seal and bilingual and biliteracy skills remains unclear. Language contained in the SSB legislation asserts that there is an increasing demand for multilingual employees in California (California State Legislature, 2011), and the data bear this out. A recent report by the US Census Bureau finds that nearly half of the metropolitan areas in the US with 50% or more speakers of other languages are located in California, including more than 7 million persons age 5 years and older (US Census, 2013).

Given the nation's changing demographics as well as its increasing global economic interests, do employers seek out bilingualism as a trait when hiring? Are there specific sectors or job categories where bilingualism is a plus factor? What languages are most valued and what advantages do employers perceive bilingual speakers to hold? Are employees paid more for using their specialized language skills to accomplish their job duties? Also, does possession of the SSB confer any particular advantage on the job seeker? In sum, do bilingual people have any real advantage in the labor market?

To answer these questions, we conducted a survey of 289 public and private sector employers mostly based in California. Although not necessarily random or representative, this survey included a great diversity of organizational size, industry type and location. While heavily representative of the Los Angeles/Long Beach metropolitan area (home to the highest proportion of non-native English speakers nationally), employer surveys were also conducted in the San Francisco/San Jose area, Monterey County, Fresno County and the Sacramento region. The participants in this study included companies from California's five largest private industries: leisure/hospitality, retail, health care, professional/scientific/technical services and administrative/

support services (Kleinhenz *et al.*, 2013). All these sectors have recently experienced considerable growth and are representative of the emerging 'new economy'.

In a 2013 study commissioned by the Los Angeles County Economic Development Corporation, Kleinhenz *et al.* found that of the 248,000 new jobs created in California in the prior year, 80% originated in these five sectors. Moreover, these new jobs ranged from lower-skilled, entry-level positions to highly skilled, highly compensated positions (Kleinhenz *et al.*, 2013). Capturing the impressions of hiring managers in these sectors highlights the potential importance that bilingual skills will play in the recovering job market and a new era of increased linguistic diversity.

Government employers comprised another 11% of our sample. Although not growing at the rapid rate of the five sectors listed above, at both the national and state levels, government jobs continue to make up a significant portion of the employment sector. In 2010, nearly 20% of all nonfarm jobs across the country were in federal, state or local government (US Bureau of Labor Statistics, 2012). In fact, a substantial portion of every state's employment sector is made up of government positions, ranging from 38% in Washington DC, to 12% in Ohio (Morales, 2010). In California, 16.5% of all wage and salary jobs in the state are public sector positions. Even during the downturn in economy, the public sector has continued to be a leading employer in the state and across the country (Kleinhenz *et al.*, 2013); in response, we include a cross section of these employers in the survey.

Literature Review

Most research into the labor market benefits of bilingualism has centered on the value of non-English speakers learning to speak English – a characteristically American framing of bilingualism. Historically, this work finds that stronger English language capabilities lead to better job market prospects and earnings (see Chiswick, 2009; López & Mora, 2008). As Agirdag (Chapter 7, this volume) points out, studies that look at the benefits of bilingualism in the US from the perspective of having high levels of proficiency in *two* languages (or more) are scant and often suffer from both conceptual problems and data limitations. For example, using US Census data, Chiswick and Miller (2007) attempted to determine if Spanish–English bilinguals in the US earned more than English monolinguals. They found that, even controlling for education, Spanish–English bilinguals actually earned less on average than monolinguals, a finding echoed by Robinson in Chapter 4 of this volume. Chiswick and Miller explained this by noting that Spanish-speaking bilinguals tend to cluster (or be segregated) in areas where job prospects are more limited. Moreover, Spanish-speaking bilinguals in the US population are usually minorities with all the attendant disadvantages of minorities in US society, including lower-quality formal education. It is notable that earlier research by Chiswick (1978) had found more positive results for bilinguals, but these findings included many different language groups and were not limited to Spanish speakers.

Similarly, López (1999) asked whether speaking a second language affected labor market outcomes. Using a different data set – the 1992 National Adult Literacy Study (NALS) – López's findings contradict those of Chiswick and Miller (2007). López found that bilingual individuals earn a slight premium compared to English monolinguals. In testing for differences by region, he further found that 'individuals residing in states with English Only laws do not see this premium mitigated' (1999: 1). It is important to note that the NALS data set allows for the evaluation of different levels of language proficiency (which census data do not) and López's findings are associated with speaking English *and* a second language 'proficiently'. López (1999: 1) argues 'since there is a return associated with bilingualism, policies that seek to make English the official language of the US or emphasize English proficiency over other languages may inadvertently minimize the development of important human capital, namely bilingualism'.

Following López's study and using the same data source as López – the 1992 NALS – Fry and Lowell (2003) also asked what the value of bilingualism is in the US labor market. They took a somewhat different analytic approach and also concluded that bilingual workers receive higher pay, but found that this reflects the higher educational attainment they bring to the labor market rather than their bilingualism. Once observable characteristics were controlled, there did not appear to be any statistically significant wage payoffs to competency in second languages. The fact that self-reported bilinguals had acquired higher levels of education than the monolinguals in the sample is, however, an interesting finding in itself, which is echoed in the study by Santibañez and Zárate (Chapter 9, this volume). Thus, while bilingualism may not directly increase earnings, these findings suggest that its effect on educational attainment may indirectly increase earnings, at least for Spanish speakers.

Turning to the corporate executive level, a 2011 *Forbes Insights* survey underscored the important role that bilingualism plays in an increasingly global economy. Their study included over 100 executives from US firms with annual revenues of over $500 million (Forbes Insights, 2011). In addition to the advantages that multilingual executives experienced in terms of promotions and salary increases, the Forbes findings also showed 'that organizations with a high degree of multilingualism – not to mention, an understanding of and respect for other cultures – will commit fewer mistakes and increase efficiency, productivity, and quality. Language proficiency may also promote a safer work environment, an issue of significant importance for many firms that have opened overseas and domestic manufacturing facilities employing foreign-born workers' (Forbes Insights, 2011: 1).

Linking productivity to multilingualism, the *Forbes Insights* survey found that language barriers (where managers did not speak the languages of their employees) had led to a multiplicity of challenges with overseas operations. They found that rank and file workers did not fully respect management, offered lackluster customer service, had an inability to collaborate effectively with coworkers and negatively affected overall company inefficiency (Forbes Insights, 2011). The respondents reasoned that some employees may have felt too intimidated to speak with a manager who spoke only English. In fact, 80% of the respondents agreed that workers were more productive when their managers communicated with them in their native language.

The Forbes findings also showed that 70% of companies regarded an overseas assignment as an essential component of an executive's professional growth. In addition, more than 50% of the companies that issued overseas assignments required their employees to take cultural competency, foreign language and business etiquette training (Forbes Insights, 2011). On the flipside, the *Forbes Insights* survey also found 'three-quarters of survey respondents agreed that it was easier for foreign nationals to work in the US than for US nationals to work overseas because they were more likely to be multilingual' (Forbes Insights, 2011: 8). Findings from the Forbes survey appear to be at odds with those of Alarcón and his colleagues (Chapter 6, this volume) who found no premium for multilingualism among managers in the Southwest. Alarcon and colleagues conclude that education level or specialization trumps language skills in the upper tiers of the employment structure in this region of the US. However, the Forbes study focuses on multinational corporations, which can explain the differences the investigators found.

Given the limited and sometimes conflicting findings among the disparate studies (e.g. López, 1999; Chiswick, 1978; Fry & Lowell, 2003; Santibañez & Zárate, Chapter 9, this volume; Forbes Insights, 2011; Alarcón *et al.*, Chapter 6, this volume), our goal was to clarify whether advantages exist for bilingual job seekers, especially in a linguistically diverse context like California. Coupling our survey with insights from 10 personal interviews, we found that employers as well as employees spoke to the cultural connections established between bilingual personnel and an organization's clients. We also found that most industries hire numerous bilingual employees – whether this was intentional or simply good fortune was not always clear – and that many are in fact compensated for their linguistic skills.

Methods

Survey development

As with any survey, our primary challenge was obtaining a robust number of participants, but this survey harbored unique obstacles. We wanted to hear directly from human resources (HR) directors, hiring managers and recruiters from an array of industries across California. Since we would be cold-calling most businesses, we would have to develop a persuasive argument to connect us with the right person. We would also need a reliable call sheet and partners to publicize our study online. From the outset, we knew that our survey would not only have to be relatively brief, but also capture key attitudes and characteristics about bilingualism in a job setting. Trying to achieve this balance, we developed multiple drafts of our survey questions over a three-month period and received valuable feedback and input from colleagues intimately familiar with HR practices. Our final survey consisted of 19 employment-related questions with mostly closed, and a few open-ended responses that took approximately 5–7 minutes to complete after the initial introductory conversation.

Sampling

Our initial call sheet drew from the *Los Angeles and San Francisco Business Journals 2012 Book of Lists*. These lists contain the top 100 employers in various industries across the state, including hospitality, health care and nonprofit, and the largest regional employers. We considered that obtaining their input would help strengthen the generalizability of the study findings. Beginning with a list of over 300 businesses, our early attempts to reach HR directors proved daunting. Many organizations were reluctant to go on record, even anonymously, and share information about their hiring practices regarding bilinguals; large companies were especially careful to shield their HR directors. Over time, our call list grew to include employers listed on California's Employment Development Department website. We reached out to organizations such as the UCLA Labor Center, the Los Angeles Area Chamber of Commerce and MBDA business centers located across the state. The UCLA Career Center was especially helpful in facilitating the surveying of hiring managers and recruiters during two on-campus career fairs. In addition, we conducted general internet searches and several research team members personally visited businesses located throughout the state, while others reached out to former colleagues and other contacts. As our list of respondents grew, we sought to 'fill in' respondents in labor sectors that were underrepresented in our survey.

After nearly six months, our team of 13 graduate and undergraduate students had completed 289 surveys, 183 in-person and over-the-phone and

106 online. Survey respondents represented an array of industry sectors, company sizes and locations; some were from small businesses with a presence only in California, while others were from large corporations with multiple locations in numerous states. In addition, some respondents provided services to a national customer base via their business centers in California.

Classification of respondent businesses

Following data collection, we grouped respondents into 10 overarching industry sectors based on the standard used by federal agencies (North American Industry Classification System, 2013). These sectors included (a) manufacturing and construction; (b) retail trade; (c) transportation and warehousing; (d) finance, insurance, real estate and rental and leasing; (e) professional, scientific and technical services and information; (f) management of companies and enterprises, administrative and support, waste management and remediation services; (g) educational services; (h) health care and social assistance; (i) arts, entertainment, recreation, accommodation and food services; and (j) public administration, utilities and other services.

As Table 10.1 demonstrates, the survey respondents ($n = 289$) represented a diverse group of industries. They also varied in size, ranging from small businesses to large organizations. Forty-two percent of participants represented companies that had fewer than 100 employees. More than 25% of participants were from companies that had between 100 and 499 employees. Approximately 6% had between 500 and 999 employees. The remaining 27% represented companies with 1000 or more

Table 10.1 Number and share of companies by industry

Industry	No.	%
Professional, scientific and technical services/information	65	22.5
Public administration and utilities/other services	54	18.7
Health care and social assistance	35	12.1
Educational services	28	9.7
Arts, entertainment and recreation/accommodation and food services	26	9.0
Finance and insurance/real estate and rental and leasing	23	8.0
Manufacturing and construction	16	5.5
Retail trade	15	5.2
Management of companies and enterprises/administrative and support and waste management and remediation services	15	5.2
Transportation and warehousing	12	4.2
Total	289	100

employees. However, not every respondent replied to every question in the survey so the N of respondents is included in each figure/table that follows.

Interviews

To deepen our understanding of how bilinguals function and are utilized in the workplace, we also conducted interviews with 10 employees in different industries. Interviewees were selected to represent different sectors of the economy. One worked in the medical equipment industry in the Sacramento region and another supervised at a Central Coast federal social service call center. We interviewed two Central Valley teachers as well as a teacher and an administrative assistant working at Central Coast elementary schools. The remaining four interviewees were from the Los Angeles area: a general clerk for an airline catering company; a branch manager for a national commercial bank; a caseworker employed in the district office of a Member of Congress and a county social services office worker. All interviewees spoke English and most spoke Spanish as well, but one spoke Hmong, and another spoke Farsi and Arabic.

Survey Findings

Desirability of bilingual workers

Almost all the survey respondents reported having at least one bilingual employee. Over 80% reported that their bilingual employees use their language skills while at work, with half reporting this use between 75% and 100% of the time. When asked about their hiring practices, most employers reported that they seek out bilingual candidates. Nearly 92% reported that their company planned to hire additional employees during the upcoming fiscal year, and 56% reported that they would seek out bilingual candidates for at least some of those positions. Fewer than 20% responded that for no positions would bilingualism be a desired trait.

Looking at the desirability of bilinguals illustrated in Figure 10.1, it is clear that in every industry bilingualism was a desirable trait for some or all positions. In the sectors with the highest levels of interpersonal interaction (retail, health and education), not surprisingly employers reported few, if any positions that would not benefit from bilingual abilities. As the congressional caseworker interviewed for this study explained, in some organizations and in some job positions, being bilingual is simply a requirement. Working in an office where more than 70% of the constituents were limited English speakers, he viewed bilingualism as a necessity to effectively support the needs of the community (F.C., May 28, 2013).

In contrast, in sectors that require minimal human interaction, bilingualism was less likely to be considered necessary (e.g. scientific and technical, management and administration). Industries that were least

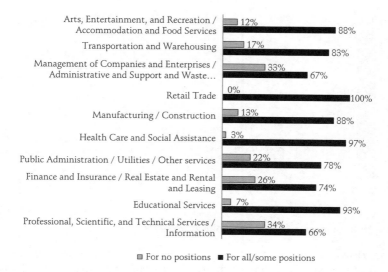

Figure 10.1 graph content:

Arts, Entertainment, and Recreation / Accommodation and Food Services — 12% / 88%
Transportation and Warehousing — 17% / 83%
Management of Companies and Enterprises / Administrative and Support and Waste... — 33% / 67%
Retail Trade — 0% / 100%
Manufacturing / Construction — 13% / 88%
Health Care and Social Assistance — 3% / 97%
Public Administration / Utilities / Other services — 22% / 78%
Finance and Insurance / Real Estate and Rental and Leasing — 26% / 74%
Educational Services — 7% / 93%
Professional, Scientific, and Technical Services / Information — 34% / 66%

▨ For no positions   ■ For all/some positions

Figure 10.1 Does a company look for bilingualism as a desired trait? (by industry). Note: Percentages were rounded to the nearest whole number. Percentage may vary by job and regions (N=288)

likely to find bilinguals particularly desirable tended to be in the areas of management and technical skills, where highly skilled individuals could presumably rely on lower-skilled employees to provide translation services when necessary, or where interactions with non-English speakers were less likely to occur, consistent with the findings of Alarcón and colleagues (Chapter 5, this volume). Our findings complement those of the Forbes management study mentioned earlier, suggesting that bilingualism can always be seen as additive – that is, there is no downside to being multilingual. However, in many managerial and administrative positions, bilingualism is not viewed as necessary as in other positions.

Preferred languages

Our survey also asked employers which language or languages other than English were most valued at their workplaces. Figure 10.2 shows the breakdown of these responses. (Respondents could name as many as applied, so responses do not sum to 100%.) It is hardly surprising that about three-quarters of respondents named Spanish, but it is interesting that nearly half of respondents also named Chinese (Mandarin and Cantonese) and that fully 15% sought Korean. In addition, 83% took the time to note one of the less frequently spoken languages as well.

Analyzing the individual industries in Table 10.2, Spanish and Chinese emerged as the two most commonly named languages for every

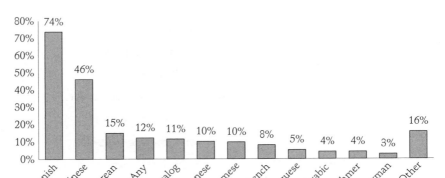

Figure 10.2 Languages sought by employers (N=271)

sector. However, some languages were more or less desirable than others according to the sector. The desirability of languages other than Spanish and Chinese reflects the linguistic diversity of California and the industries that serve its population, as well as the growing linguistic diversity that is emerging throughout the nation. For example, French was desirable to one-third of respondents in the management of companies and enterprises/administrative industry. It is also worth noting that several employment sectors named 'any language' in third place, but for almost all sectors there was considerable interest in a variety of Asian languages. This no doubt reflects California's position in the Pacific Rim and the amount of economic activity that the nation has with Asian countries, and clients who prefer to conduct business in their native languages.

Do bilingual employees earn more?

Exploring the issue of compensation, we asked employers if there were any job titles in which their company would pay someone with multilingual skills more than someone who is monolingual. Given three options (yes, no, don't know), more than half of the respondents (54%) replied that they did not know. We do not know how to interpret this. In some cases, we knew that companies did not want to go on record about discrepancies in wages paid to different employees – this was a highly sensitive issue for some and one that may have kept some potential respondents from filling out the survey. But the extent to which this applied to all the 'don't know' responses is not clear. Of our sample of 289 respondents, 131 gave a clear 'yes' or 'no' answer to this question. Thus, we show the responses for this reduced sample, acknowledging that there may very well be unknown bias in these numbers. It is important to note that the 'don't know' responses were not evenly distributed across the sectors.

Table 10.2 Languages sought after by employers by job sector (N=271)

Employer Labor Market Sector	First Preferred Language	Second Preferred Language	Third Preferred Language	Fourth Preferred Language
Professional, scientific and technical services/information	Spanish (68%)	Chinese (41%)	Any (15%)	Korean (11%)
Educational services	Spanish (79%)	Chinese (50%)	Korean (21%)	Other (21%)
Finance and insurance/real estate and rental and leasing	Spanish (74%)	Chinese (52%)	Any (17%)	Korean (13%) Japanese (13%)
Public administration/utilities/other services	Spanish (83%)	Chinese (44%)	Korean (15%) Vietnamese (15%)	Khmer (11%)
Health care and social assistance	Spanish (71%)	Chinese (62%)	Vietnamese (26%)	Korean (14%)
Manufacturing/construction	Spanish (63%)	Chinese (25%)	Japanese (13%)	Any (13%)
Retail trade	Spanish (73%)	Chinese (34%)	Any (27%)	Korean (13%) Japanese (13%) Tagalog (13%)
Management of companies and enterprises/administrative and support and waste management and remediation services	Spanish (47%)	Chinese (40%)	French (33%)	Japanese (20%)
Transportation and warehousing	Spanish (75%)	Chinese (75%)	Korean (50%)	Japanese (25%)
Arts, entertainment and recreation/accommodation and food services	Spanish (88%)	Chinese (38%)	Other (23%)	French (19%) Korean (19%) Japanese (19%)

For example, almost three-quarters of employers in finance/insurance and management/administration replied 'don't know'. About 60% of employers in professional services, education, arts/entertainment and health also responded 'don't know' and approximately 40% of employers in each of the remaining sectors (transportation, retail, manufacturing and public sector) replied 'don't know'. So, while we provide the findings here, we caution using the results of this question to generalize beyond this subsample.

Most (56%) of those who responded noted that their company did pay more for bilingual skills, at least in some cases; 44% said they did not. As one might expect, Figure 10.3 shows that many of those job sectors with a great deal of public interface – health, social services, public services such as utilities, education and real estate – were much more likely to pay a salary differential for bilingual skills. The perhaps surprising omission from this list is retail; however, store clerks and other low pay, minimum wage and nonunionized workers are typically not offered salary differentials for any particular skill. Again, management and professional/technical sectors did not typically pay a differential for bilingualism, consistent with our earlier discussion about the importance of specialized skills and education over language.

In regard to the public sector, California law drives some of the pay differentials provided for workers in government positions. Adopted in 1973, the Dymally-Alatorre Bilingual Services Act in California requires

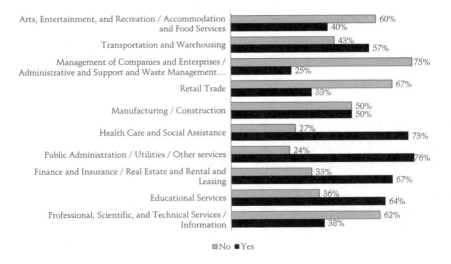

Figure 10.3 Responses to the question: Are there any job titles in which your company would pay someone with dual language skills more than someone who is monolingual? (by industry) (N=131)

that bilingual services be provided at any state or local government agency where at least 5% of the public served is limited English speakers. The state offers a bilingual pay differential to individuals in certified bilingual positions. This pay differential ranges from $100 to $250, and is determined by an employee's pay grade, assignment, department and collective bargaining agreement (California Department of Human Resources [CalHR], 2012). Moreover, some state employees are eligible for supplemental pay if they work in a 'certified' bilingual position. Many state government social service and health-care positions are listed in this category, as are some law enforcement positions. For example, California Highway Patrol (CHP) officers are eligible for supplemental pay if they are bilingual, earning an additional $100 per pay period (California Highway Patrol, 2013). A 2001 survey by the City and County of San Francisco found that a number of local police departments around the state paid a bilingual differential to police department employees, ranging between 2.75% and 5% of base pay (Cabrera, 2001).

The county social services caseworker interviewed for this study was a recipient of the state stipend. He described the written and oral testing process he underwent to qualify for the certified bilingual position, which included translating documents and having a conversation with a testing panel (L.A.C., June 7, 2013). Other states such as Oregon (Oregon Department of Administrative Services, 2009), Illinois (Illinois Department of Central Management Services, 2012) and Texas (Texas Comptroller of Public Accounts, 2004) also provide a stipend for some certified bilingual employees.

Perceived added value of bilingual employees

Turning to questions related to the contributions made by bilingual staff, only 6% of respondents said that employees with dual language skills would not add value to their workplace. Moreover, 64% of employers said a bilingual worker would provide more effective customer service than a monolingual, and 51% said a bilingual might be better able to translate documents, write letters or help advertise to diverse clients. In addition, 41% of employers replied that a bilingual person might be better able to work with diverse coworkers, and 25% said that she or he might be better equipped to create a more welcoming work environment. Interviewees illustrated these positive contributions, describing how their language skills helped them connect with their clients and gain their trust. As the federal call center supervisor said:

> Sometimes you make them feel so much more at ease because a lot of times people are afraid to call us because they hear the rumors of having to deal with our type of agency and they feel more at ease. They get a

different experience because there was a connection there. ... They feel that we're there as well to help. (S.S.C.; June 16, 2013)

More opportunities for advancement

While it seemed that a majority of employers across the industries in our study sought out bilingual candidates and recognized the value they added to their companies, only 45% said there were some job categories in which bilinguals would have more opportunities for advancement, and only 6% said that bilingual employees would have an advantage in promotion in all job categories. Upon closer inspection, our data suggest that in 6 of the 10 industries, bilingual employees would have more opportunities for advancement in some, if not all, job categories.

A majority of employers in transportation/warehousing (80%), retail (71%), manufacturing/construction (69%), finance/insurance/real estate (64%), arts/entertainment (63%) and education (63%) said that someone with bilingual language skills would have more opportunities for advancement than their monolingual counterparts. Health-care respondents were evenly split; 50% reported that bilingualism would be an advantage for some or all job categories and 50% said there were no jobs in which it would help in advancement. Interestingly, the kinds of jobs in which bilinguals would have an advantage were evenly divided across the hierarchy. Again echoing Alarcón and colleagues' findings (Chapter 5, this volume), approximately 32% of respondents indicated that bilingualism would provide an advantage in lower-skilled jobs that required either direct contact with the public or working with diverse coworkers. Another 33% indicated that the advantage would be in mid-level, customer service positions and, supporting the Forbes management study, nearly 31% said bilingual skills would benefit top and middle management positions. In fact, in health care, finance/insurance/real estate and manufacturing/construction, more employers said the advantage would be in top and middle management positions than in lower-skilled jobs.

Do bilinguals have an advantage in hiring?

Finally, we asked employers, when considering two otherwise equally qualified candidates for the same position, would they be more likely to hire the bilingual candidate. A full 66% responded 'yes', while only 27% said 'no'. Careful inspection of the individual industries revealed that in every sector more employers would hire the bilingual candidate over the monolingual candidate (Figure 10.4).

Interestingly, employers in the administrative management sector unanimously reported that they would be more likely to hire bilinguals even

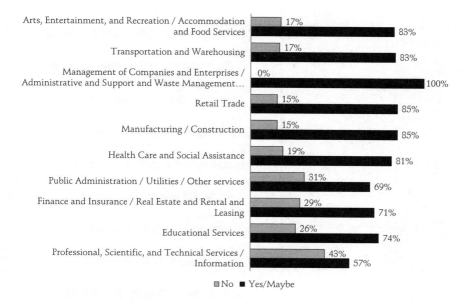

Figure 10.4 Do bilinguals experience a hiring advantage? (N=249)

though one-third had said there were no positions in which bilingualism was a desirable trait. It is also worth noting that 26% of employers in education said a bilingual candidate would not have an advantage in a hiring decision. This seems to conflict with the 93% that regarded bilingualism a desirable trait and the important role held by bilingual teachers, administrators and staff. Particularly given the demographics of California, school districts must be able to communicate effectively with all parents and students, including limited English speakers. These contradictory findings suggest ambivalence among some respondents with respect to their perceptions of the value of multilingualism in the workplace.

Will Seal of Biliteracy holders benefit in the future?

Although the state certification is new and most respondents were not familiar with it, we wanted to know if SSB award holders would be more likely to receive a job offer than their monolingual counterparts. Over three-quarters of employers in our survey replied yes or maybe, affirming their preference for hiring bilinguals. Figure 10.5 shows that as with the previous question, employers voiced opinions that appeared to be inconsistent with respect to the value of the SSB. For example, approximately one-third of health-care/social assistance employers

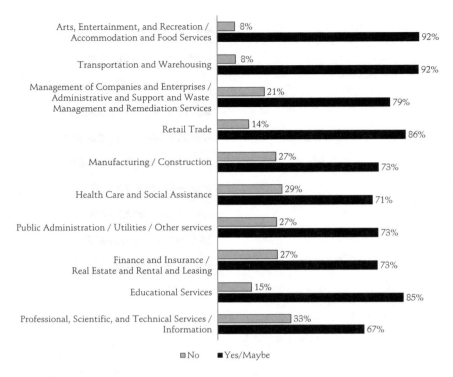

Figure 10.5 Will Seal of Biliteracy holders potentially benefit? (N=274)

said the SSB holder would not have an advantage in hiring, but almost 100% of these employers said bilingualism was a desirable trait for all or some positions.

The results also indicate that employers in four sectors would more often give the job offer to SSB award holders than bilingual candidates without the seal. For example, 57% of employers in professional/scientific/technical services said they would be more likely to hire a bilingual candidate over a monolingual one; in addition, the likelihood of hiring a bilingual jumped by 10% in this sector when the SSB was mentioned. Sixty-seven percent of employers in professional/scientific/technical services said SSB candidates would be offered the job over a monolingual candidate. As employers become more familiar with the SSB award, perhaps holders in more sectors will experience a clearer advantage in the hiring process. Especially in positions that require some kind of certification involving a test of language skills, it would appear that the SSB could be an efficient and money-saving alternative to some current assessment practices.

What do interviewees say?

Although the survey results tell an interesting story, the lived experiences of those interviewed for the study provided a deeper understanding of how bilingualism affects workplace dynamics. One theme that ran across the majority of the interviews was the link between bilingualism, cultural competency and trust. For example, a bank manager in an affluent part of Los Angeles noted that while he spoke both Farsi and Arabic, this would have served him little if he did not also understand these cultures. 'If I look directly into the eyes of an Arabic woman when we are speaking, this is offensive. If I don't understand this, even being able to communicate in the same language won't help' (B.M., May 14, 2013). When asked how this cultural connection assisted him in the workplace, he noted,

> I am not paid more for being multilingual, but as a banker, I make more money than the monolinguals because I have more clients that come to me and have faith in me. They want to invest their money with me. (B.M., May 14, 2013)

In fact, in an informal survey of a number of banks in the Los Angeles area, all had multilingual tellers and bankers. And in each branch, employees spoke several languages.

A teacher in the California Central Valley explained how important she felt it was to understand her students' culture in order to create a bond of trust with them and their families:

> It is very helpful to also have cultural competence, we see it with our families from Yemen, we have to address their needs culturally; when they are fasting, going through celebrations, those are things that you have to be aware of. I had two siblings from Yemen last year, that's how I became aware of their fasting. When the celebration was over they would come back to school with tattoos on their hands. It is important to be aware of their culture a little bit more. (C.V.S., June 20, 2013)

While the teacher quoted above did not speak Arabic, the Hmong-speaking teacher asserted that being bilingual in any languages was still an asset. She argued, 'People who speak more than one language understand diversity. They connect with each other', suggesting that multilingualism fosters this sensitivity. She went on to explain that although her principal spoke Spanish, if the principal also spoke Hmong, support would grow among Hmong parents as they would feel more comfortable and connected with the school (C.V.H., June 24, 2013).

Similarly, other interviewees spoke at length about the trust that comes about from speaking the language – and understanding the culture – of a customer or a coworker and how this trust facilitates working conditions and customer satisfaction. A young Spanish-speaking interviewee who works at the middle management level of a catering company remarked,

> The fact that I can express to them in Spanish that I understand their concerns regarding a missing diagram, or an unfair write up, allows for me to build a relationship of trust with the employees. Once this relationship is built employees actually begin to work better and feel like their work is actually being appreciated. (A.I.R., May 23, 2013)

This same employee talked about the importance of bilingualism for 'creating trust at both ends' and helping the company to be more productive,

> My role as middle man has placed me as an 'essential commodity' in the eyes of the company, and the more fluent and proficient I become in both languages the better my chances of generating more money for the company, creating a better chain of communication between employee and management, and also getting promoted. It's a constant struggle but there is no doubt speaking both languages allows me to build trust on both ends, a very valuable asset to possess. (A.I.R., May 23, 2013)

This 'middle manager' explained that while she wasn't paid any more for this skill as a bilingual, management knew she was invaluable and this had resulted in promotions, which meant a bigger paycheck.

Access to services was mentioned by all of the bilingual individuals who worked in social services and education. For them, speaking the language of the client or student or parent was critical to helping them receive the services they needed. One Hmong-speaking teacher asserted,

> Being bilingual is a great benefit. It means students have equal access to the curriculum. Plus it helps create a bridge, a connection, an understanding with EL students and their parents. (C.V.H., June 24, 2013)

The Spanish-speaking congressional caseworker explained that being bilingual was a necessity. But he clarified that his language skills must go beyond the basics and include the specialized jargon adopted by each federal agency. Navigating bureaucracy for constituents is a complex process and each agency requires its own forms to be completed correctly. In order to fully support limited English-speaking constituents, he asserted that staff must know the jargon well, both in English and other languages (F.C., May 28, 2013).

Another theme that ran across the interviews was the extent to which many of the bilinguals in these companies (which included schools, social service organizations, banks, legislator's office, medical supply and transportation businesses) often found themselves providing very critical, even life or death information and services for people. A medical supply deliveryman who received no extra pay for being bilingual noted how, nonetheless, he was often called from one delivery to another because of his language skills. Assisting a monolingual coworker, the bilingual delivery person would be called out to explain something critical such as how to use a home oxygen tank to a Spanish-speaking patient or caregiver. Misuse of the equipment could result in death or an explosion in the home. A customer service agent working in a federal social service information center recounted how she frequently received calls from suicidal individuals,

> Actually, lately more than often people state that they're going to commit suicide, that they're going to harm themselves, and there have been times when they're Spanish speaking and thank goodness that we have our agents that are Spanish speaking because they can act on it. They understand what the person is saying to them to act on the situation fast, get police out to the residents, or do whatever it is that we got to do to get them the necessary help. (S.S.C., June 16, 2013)

About a third of the people we interviewed were actually paid a salary differential for their bilingual skills – and these were individuals in social service jobs, but several others noted that they actually made more money through promotions (because they were viewed as being very valuable) or because they were able to generate more business. Others mentioned that they would not have gotten the job if they were not bilingual, and all seemed to feel a sense of satisfaction that they were able to do their jobs well because they could help people who otherwise would have been marginalized or in the worst cases would have actually suffered harm without someone to assist and explain things in a language they understood. These individuals also noted that speaking people's language also made them 'feel more comfortable, like you understand them' (S.S.C., June 16, 2013).

Discussion

Earlier chapters in this volume found that jobs that require specialized skills and that command more authority and pay are the least likely to be filled by bilinguals. In Chapters 5 and 6 of this volume, Alarcón and his colleagues explain that at the top of the job hierarchy there is a perception that lower-level employees can provide the translation services that may be required. To some extent our data, including the interviews we conducted, tend to reinforce this finding. Respondents from professional, technical and management sectors were the least likely to say they sought bilingual employees or would give them the benefit of employment where two candidates were equally qualified. This would appear to be a vestige of a time before the major demographic shifts that are underway in this country as a result of immigration and globalization. As the *Forbes Insights* survey showed, increasingly managers of businesses that operate internationally are and will be multilingual and increasingly business is seeing this as, if not a requirement, a significant added advantage. To be competitive, businesses must seek clients from outside their region.

As the country continues to diversify linguistically and companies become more multinational, ultimately multiple language skills will likely hold a larger premium. Findings from the present survey suggest that process is already well underway among industries and agencies hoping to serve clients whose primary language is not English. As our findings demonstrate, every industry is seeking out bilingual candidates and these bilingual candidates as well as the SSB awardees will compete with monolinguals for the same job. While 44% of respondents reported that their companies do not pay bilingual staff more, as an HR director at an advertising agency explained, the economic benefit to a candidate with dual language skills may not be expressed through more pay, but rather in the hiring process.

Moreover, the diversity of linguistic needs across organizations in our survey demonstrates that companies continue to value Spanish to support their clientele, but many also value Chinese. Other languages such as Korean, Japanese, French, Vietnamese and Tagalog are also sought by hiring managers in various sectors. These findings support the recent US Census report on the changing linguistic landscape of the nation as well as the implications of the *Forbes Insights* report about growing international business interests.

Conclusion

This study was conducted with a focus on California employers, a purposeful choice as the state has more immigrants and speakers of other languages than any other state. In this sense, one could conclude that the findings of this survey might be relevant to California, but perhaps to nowhere else. However, many other states look if not the same, startlingly similar to California, as a massive demographic shift is changing the face of the entire nation. As the new US Census report makes clear: linguistic diversity is our future. In a globalizing world, the ability to speak the languages of the world can only be a benefit.

Many communities are seeking to attract immigrants because of the economic stimulus they provide. A recent *Wall Street Journal* story (Peters & Nicas, 2013) interviewed the city leaders of Pittsburgh, Pennsylvania, a city marked by net population loss over time. Pittsburgh now runs ads in Spanish and other languages targeted to immigrants who might consider making Pittsburgh their home. The city leaders understand that without population growth, their city is doomed to economic decline, and the entrepreneurial spirit of many immigrants has revitalized dying areas in the East and Midwest. To make immigrants feel welcome, however, it is important to speak their language, and as our interviewees suggest, it isn't just about communication, it is also important because it makes people feel comfortable, 'like maybe you understand me' (S.S.C., June 16, 2013). Whether functioning to attract entrepreneurial immigrants, negotiating international business deals or fostering trust in a potential client or consumer, multilingual skills play a significant role in the contemporary economy. Moreover, as the US economy continues to restructure, many economists project an ongoing crisis of underemployment, especially among younger job seekers. Our data suggest that being multilingual will provide an important advantage in the labor market, which over time, will result in higher earnings.

Acknowledgments

The authors would also like to acknowledge the invaluable assistance they received from Natasha Amlani, Tolu Bamishigbin, Dinah Dominguez, Valerie Gomez, Amelia Gonzalez, Lauren Ilano, Andrew Kang, Melody Liao, Kfir Mordechay, Charlene Unzueta, Evelyn Vasquez and Jenny Vasquez.

Notes

(1) Assembly Bill 815 (AB815) was introduced by then Assemblyperson Julia Brownley and signed into law by Governor Jerry Brown. AB815 became effective on 1 January 2012.
(2) To be eligible for the SSB designation, students must:
   1. Complete all English language arts requirements for graduation with a GPA of 2.0 or higher, and
   2. Pass the California Standards Test in English language arts in the eleventh grade with at least a 'proficient' score, and
   3. Demonstrate proficiency in a language other than English by:
      a. Passing an AP exam with a score of 3 or higher, or
      b. Passing the IB exam with a score of 4 or higher, or
      c. Completing a four-year high school language course of study with a GPA of 3.0 or higher, or
      d. Passing a district's foreign language exam with at least a proficient score, or
      e. Passing a foreign government's approved language exam, or
      f. Passing a SAT II foreign language exam with a score of 600 or better.

If the primary language of a student is a language other than English, the student must meet requirements 1, 2 and 3, and achieve an Early Advanced Proficiency Level on the California English Language Development Test (CELDT).

References

Bialystok, E. (2001) *Bilingualism in Development. Language, Literacy and Cognition.* New York: Cambridge University Press.

Bialystok, E. and Craik, F. (2010). Cognitive and linguistic processing in the bilingual mind. *Current Directions in Psychological Science* 19, 19–23.

Cabrera, G. (2001) Bilingual police services. Report of the legislative analyst, city and county of San Francisco. See http://www.sfbos.org/index.aspx?page=1226 (accessed 16 August 2013).

California Department Human Resources (2012) About Salaries. See http://www.calhr. ca.gov/state-hr-professionals/Pages/about-salaries.aspx (accessed 22 May 2012).

California Highway Patrol (2013) CHP Recruiting. See http://www.calhr.ca.gov/state-hr-professionals/Pages/about-salaries.aspx (accessed 6 August 2013).

California State Legislature (2011) AB 815 Assembly Bill – Chaptered. See http://www. leginfo.ca.gov/pub/11-12/bill/asm/ab_0801-0850/ab_815_bill_20111008_chaptered. html (accessed 17 February 2011).

Chiswick, B. (1978) Effect of Americanization on earnings of foreign-born men. *Journal of Political Economy* 86, 897–921.

Chiswick, B. (2009) The economics of language for immigrants: An introduction and overview. In T. Wiley, J.S. Lee and R. Rumberger (eds) *The Education of Language Minority Immigrants in the United States* (pp. 72–91). Bristol: Multilingual Matters.

Chiswick, B. and Miller, P. (2007) *The Economics of Language: International Analyses.* London: Routledge.

Forbes Insights (2011) *Reducing the Impact of Language Barriers.* See http://www.forbes. com/forbesinsights (accessed July 2011).

Fry, R. and Lowell, B.L. (2003) The value of bilingualism in the US labor market. *Industrial & Labor Relations Review* 57,128–140.

Illinois Department of Central Management Services (2012) Pay Plan: Effective for Fiscal Year 2013 (1 July 2012 edition). See http://www2.illinois.gov/cms/Employees/ Personnel/Documents/emp_payplan.pdf (accessed 1 July 2012).

Jung, T. (2012) State schools chief Tom Torlakson announces more than 10,000 student earn new State Seal of Biliteracy. See http://www.cde.ca.gov/nr/ne/yr12/yr12rel68. asp (accessed 5 July 2012).

Kleinhenz, R., Ritter-Martinez, K. and Guerra, F. (2013) 2013–2014 Economic Forecast and Industry Outlook: California and Southern California Including National and International Setting. See http://cdn.laedc.org/wp-content/ uploads/2012/04/2013-14EconomicForecastandIndustryOutlook.pdf (accessed February 2013).

Lee, J.W. (2008) The effect of ethnic identity and bilingual confidence on Chinese youth's self-esteem. *Alberta Journal of Educational Research* 54, 83–96.

Lieu, A. and Berestein Rojas, L. (2013) Why raise a child bilingual? Parents on language, culture, and roots (video). See http://www.scpr.org (accessed 4 March 2013).

López, H. (1999) Does speaking a second language affect labor market outcomes? Evidence from the National Adult Literacy Survey of 1992. School of Public Affairs, University of Maryland. See http://pweb.jps.net/~lsbonnin/mark/docs/ seclangoct99.pdf (accessed 28 July 2013).

López, M.H. and Mora, M. (2008) Bilingual education and labor market earnings among Hispanics: Evidence using High School and Beyond. Association for Public Policy

Analysis and Management (APPAM) 19th Annual Research Conference, University of Maryland Labor Seminar, and Princeton University.

Maxwell, L.A. (2013) Arne Duncan touts advantages of bilingualism. *Education Week.* See http://blogs.edweek.org/edweek/learning-the-language/2013/05/arne_duncan_touts_advantages_o.html (accessed 30 May 2013).

Morales, L. (2010) State of the States. See http://www.gallup.com/poll/141785/gov-employment-ranges-ohio.aspx?version=print (accessed 6 August 2010).

North American Industry Classification System (2013) North American Industry Classification System (NAICS) main page. See http://www.census.gov/eos/www/naics/index.html (accessed 1 August 2013).

Oregon Department of Administrative Services (2009) Pay Practices. See http://www.oregon.gov/DAS/CHRO/docs/advice/p2000510.pdf (accessed 31 August 2013).

Palmer, D.K. (2009) Middle-class English speakers in a two-way immersion bilingual classroom: Everybody should be listening to Jonathan right now.... *TESOL Quarterly* 43 (2), 177–202.

Peters, M. and Nicas, J. (2013) Rust-belt reaches for immigrant tide: Aim is to reverse population decline and revive businesses. *Wall Street Journal.* See http://online.wsj.com/article/SB10001424127887323687604578467134234625160.html (accessed 12 May 2013).

Texas Comptroller of Public Accounts (2004) Texas Payroll/Personnel Resource. See https://fmx.cpa.state.tx.us/fm/pubs/paypol/index.php (accessed 1 August 2004).

US Bureau of Labor Statistics (2012) Employment by major industry sector. See http://www.bls.gov/emp/ep_table_201.htm (accessed 1 February 2012).

US Census Bureau (2013) *Language Use in the United States: 2011.* See http://www.census.gov/library/publications/2013/acs/acs-22.html (accessed 17 August 2013).

US Census Bureau (2010) New census bureau report analyzes nation's linguistic diversity: Population speaking a language other than English at home increases by 140 percent in the past three decades. See http://www.census.gov/newsroom/releases/archives/american_community_survey_acs/cb10-cn58.html (accessed 27 April 2010).

Vom Dorp, I.E. (2000) Biliteracy, monoliteracy and self concept in native Spanish-dominant and native English dominant fifth graders. Unpublished doctoral dissertation, University of New Mexico.

Yang Su, E. (2012) Dual language programs growing in popularity, *California Watch*, Center for Investigative Reporting, March 12. Accessed June 24, 2014 http://californiawatch.org/dailyreport/dual-language-lessons-growing-popularity-15424.

Section 4

Policy Options: Fostering Bilingualism in the Market Place

11 The International Baccalaureate: A College Preparatory Pathway for Heritage Language Speakers and Immigrant Youth

Ursula Aldana and Anysia Mayer

Introduction

Despite the steady flow of immigrants to the US and the richness of the languages they bring with them, American schools often adopt an English-only approach to instruction for students from immigrant homes (Gándara et al., 2010; García, 2009). As a consequence, the languages spoken by immigrants from Latin American and Asia often fall into the 'language graveyard' (Rumbaut & Massey, 2013: 153); by the third-generation, these groups are likely to speak only English (Rumbaut et al., 2006). While there has been no evidence supporting a negative effect of multilingualism, abundant evidence suggests cognitive (Barac & Bialystok, 2012; Bialystok, 2009; Bialystok & Craik, 2010), social (Genesee & Gándara, 1999; Morales & Aldana, 2010) and now economic benefits (see Chapters 7–10 of this volume) for those who maintain their heritage language. The promise of bilingualism may be especially important for Latinos who currently demonstrate the lowest academic outcomes of any subgroup in the US, and are expected to comprise one in five American residents by 2025 (Tienda & Mitchell, 2006).

Recognizing the need to successfully educate language minorities in the US, this chapter investigates an educational program with the potential to improve the academic trajectories of immigrants and heritage speakers,[1] especially Latinos. We examine the potential of the International Baccalaureate (IB) program to leverage the linguistic capital of immigrant youth and heritage speakers to realize the academic potential of these typically marginalized students.

Social Reproduction in Schools and the Practice of Sorting Students for Instruction

Economists have long argued that investment in human capital through education can improve a country's economic growth by increasing earnings and productivity (Reardon & Bischoff, 2011). In 2008 in the US, 25–34 year olds with a college degree earned up to 70% more than those with only a high school diploma (Baum *et al.*, 2013). Yet Latino students, who now comprise 22% of the school-age population, are the least likely to graduate from high school or college (Gándara & Contreras, 2009; Goldrick-Rab, 2006). Given the potential benefit of a college education to both individuals and society, it is troubling that these students are so seriously underrepresented in college completion. Perhaps even more troubling is how American schools reproduce these outcomes across generations, particularly for Latinos (Bourdieu, 1990; Telles & Ortiz, 2008). A number of studies now show that third-plus generation Latinos fare worse than earlier generations in the US educational system (see, for example, Rumbaut, Chapter 8, this volume).

Multiple factors in the lives of ethnic minority immigrant children contribute to disparities in their academic performance relative to more privileged white and Asian students. While immigrant families from Southeast Asia, Mexico and Central America have rich linguistic and cultural heritages, most do not have access to the types of social and cultural capital that translate into additional resources in the US economy (Grant & Sleeter, 2011), resulting in low educational attainment among some immigrant youth (Aud *et al.*, 2010; Gándara & Contreras, 2009; Ngo & Lee, 2007). Many immigrant students face additional challenges as they enter and seek to participate in US schools, including immigration status (Passel, 2005), racial and ethnic stereotyping (Steele, 1997), limited access to qualified teachers and well-resourced schools (Gándara & Contreras, 2009), as well as family and friends who are not able to help them navigate a foreign school system (Valenzuela, 1999).

In addition to family background, the structure of schools can also limit students' access to both academic and social resources in ways that further reinforce social reproduction (Lewis *et al.*, 2008). Studies find that both minority and English language learners (ELL) are overrepresented in urban schools and low-track classes, while affluent, white and Asian students tend to be overrepresented in high-track (college prep) courses (Ngo & Lee, 2007; Noguera, 2003; Oakes, 1992; Talbert-Johnson, 2004). In addition, ELL students often lack access to rigorous coursework as a result of their ELL identification (Callahan & Gándara, 2004; Callahan *et al.*, 2010). Even after controlling for individual, family and school background and achievement, language minority students experience a significant negative effect of placement in English as a second language (ESL) coursework on their likelihood to enroll in science and social science courses compared to their language majority peers not enrolled in ESL coursework (Callahan et al., 2010). By limiting access to academically rigorous, developmentally appropriate content courses, educators fail to prepare ESL students for postsecondary education, and often even for high school graduation (Callahan et al., 2010). However, several innovative programs have emerged to provide a rigorous college preparatory curriculum for heritage language speakers (Hopkins et al., 2013). We argue that one of the most important is the IB program.

IB programs offer a potential solution to the educational dilemma of heritage language speakers. IB programs reframe the student's primary language as an asset through the provision of an internationally prestigious curriculum based on rigorous academic standards. This chapter examines eight representative schools that offer the IB Diploma Programme (IB DP) to heritage language speakers in their final years of high school. The IB DP strives to prepare all students for college, regardless of their perceived proficiency in English.

The International Baccalaureate

The International Baccalaureate Organization (IBO) has authorized 3589 schools worldwide in 145 countries to offer the Primary Years Programme (PYP), the Middle Years Programme (MYP), the Diploma Programme (DP) and the Career-related Certificate (CC) to over one million students aged 3–19. The first IB program in the US, established in 1971, was the United Nations International School in New York City. Currently, there are 1528 IB World Schools in the US offering one or more of the three IB programs: 416 schools offer the IB PYP, 517 schools offer the IB MYP and 800 schools offer the IB DP. Approximately 90% of IB schools in the US are public. In 2012, the majority of IB diploma candidates (59%) identified as white, while 15% identified as Asian/Pacific Islander, 12% as Hispanic and 10% as black/non-Hispanic (4% identified as other). Only 21% of IB Diploma candidates qualified for free and reduced lunch; in 2012, a small group of 265 students self-identified as ELL (IBO website, retrieved from www.IBO.org, June 18, 2014; IBO, 2011).

Rigorous curriculum

The IB DP is a comprehensive two-year curriculum that is both vertically and horizontally aligned to promote students' critical thinking skills and deep content knowledge development. The overarching goals of the curriculum are for students to gain both depth and breadth in each area of knowledge, for students to think critically about how all six areas of knowledge[2] fit together and for students to become engaged global citizens (IBO, 2011). Additionally, the IB DP includes an extended essay requirement that is similar to the capstone or senior projects offered in some US schools, a community service requirement and a theory of knowledge course, similar to that of a college-level philosophy course that guides students through epistemological traditions across academic disciplines.

Multilingualism

The IB program's language policy across the PYP, MYP and DP is to promote multilingualism among all students. The IB educational philosophy incorporates additive bilingualism (Cummins, 1994), i.e. learning both the mother tongue and another language simultaneously. Both languages are viewed as a right and a resource:

> Students learning in a language other than their mother tongue should no longer be framed as a 'problem'; a multilingual view recognizes diversity in language profiles as the norm. Whole-school practices that honour this, however, need to be put in place if all students, including those who are learning in a language other than their mother tongue, are to have equal access to the IB programs. Isolating English as a Second Language (ESL) students from the mainstream, in an attempt to teach them the language they need separately from the subject areas, is not a practice that honours multilingualism. (IBO, 2011: 13)

From a curricular and policy perspective, the IB programs offer a particularly attractive alternative for meeting the needs of heritage Spanish speakers, supporting bilingual language development. As a truly international program, the IB does not privilege any particular language; it simply requires that students demonstrate a competency in at least two. These heritage language speakers can meet the IB language course requirement by taking these classes in their native language.

A global perspective

According to their mission statement, the 'International Baccalaureate aims to develop inquiring, knowledgeable and caring young people who help to create a better and more peaceful world through intercultural understanding and respect' (IBO, 2011: 12). In this manner, the IB philosophy aims to develop students' ability to respect sociocultural identity, understand differences, tolerate ambiguity, serve the community and take an individual role in creating a more peaceful world. The following excerpt from an IB teacher's Language and Literature course syllabus illustrates this point:

In the view of the international nature of IB courses, this course does not limit the study of literature to the achievements of one culture or the cultures covered by any one language. In this class the study of world literature is important because it helps students to gain a global perspective. This perspective offers students the opportunity of the various ways in which cultures influence and shape life experiences common to all humanity. (Spanish Teacher, Granada High)

Adoption of an IB program does more than facilitate multilingualism; it encourages 'students across the world to become active, compassionate and lifelong learners who understand that other people, with their differences, can also be right' (IBO, 2011: 15). For language minority students in particular, implementing an IB program has the potential to improve their educational experience not only via rigorous instruction in two languages, but also through a culture of learning whereby reducing prejudice and valuing diversity is a major tenet of the program.

Unique aspects of the IB DP

Becoming an authorized IB DP school is a multistep process that can take up to five years from the time an administrator first considers implementing an IB DP until the first students enroll. Buy-in from key stakeholders is an important aspect of the application process. During a preauthorization site visit, IB administrators look for evidence that: faculty think it is worth the extra effort to be a part of the IB, students demonstrate an interest in the program, parents think it is important and the superintendent or school board agrees to fund the program.

The IB relies on active and retired teachers for the everyday operation of IB programs around the world. Experienced IB teachers score student exams, participate on international curricular review committees, run site visits for schools seeking authorization and teach all of the professional development courses for minimal remuneration. In general, teachers perceive that teaching for IB means 'a lot of extra work' (Mayer, 2006). The process creates a sense of ownership among teachers, resulting in a willingness to accept the myriad of IB rules and regulations for the operation of its programs (Mayer, 2006). The payoff for teachers is the opportunity to be recognized for excellent practice and to exercise leadership in places with very flat career ladders (Hallinger & Lee, 2012). And for students, the payoff is that coursework and exams are validated externally, affording them special consideration in college admissions.

Colleges and universities across North America and throughout the world have come to recognize the level of preparation provided by the DP. This recognition comes in the form of scholarships and substantial credit for college courses to students who successfully complete the DP or pass individual DP examinations. Unfortunately, most US language education programs and policies do not view the mother tongue as a resource (Ruiz, 1984). The IB philosophy directly counters this perspective and provides the opportunity to build on students' heritage languages and cultures, as well as on their differing sociocultural perspectives.

Our Research

Having identified several US IB DPs that have adopted this more additive philosophy, the authors of this chapter sought to understand how these schools came to the decision to establish an IB program for heritage language speakers, and what lessons might be learned from their experiences. Specifically, we designed the present study to explore the driving forces in schools that not only adopt an IB program, but also do so in order to serve language minority students. In particular, we sought to answer:

- How did these eight schools come to the decision to adopt the IB DP?
- What are some of the challenges schools faced when implementing the IB DP as educators sought to integrate low-income Spanish heritage students?
- How is the IB language philosophy understood in schools serving low-income Spanish heritage students?

Methodology

We employed a case study approach (Yin, 2003) to examine how and why eight public schools chose to implement and sustain an IB DP targeting low-income Spanish heritage speakers. Our sample selection first drew from national data, as well as school-level student reports collected when graduates complete their IB examination each spring. We searched for schools whose group of IB DP graduates met two criteria for inclusion: a majority or near majority Latino students and at least 30% free and reduced lunch participants. We also looked for other indicators that would signal the presence of Spanish heritage students. Given that many ELL students are redesignated by high school, we looked for other measures such as the number of Spanish exam takers (Abedi, 2008).

We engaged in a multisite case study (Yin, 2003) to enable us to explore similarities and differences among the final sample of eight high schools that offered low-income Spanish heritage speakers enrollment in the IB DP. To this end, our study provides a multifaceted view of IB program implementation that varied according to social context, geographic location, size and type of public school, among other factors. Our use of case study methodology allowed us to interrogate common themes across

IB programs serving a relatively underrepresented group of students: low-income Spanish heritage students.

Sample selection

Of the 777 US schools offering the IB DP, 24 schools located in 14 states appeared to meet the two initial criteria. Still, a review of the published data was insufficient to determine if the IB program (oftentimes a strand within a larger public school) in fact served low-income Spanish heritage speakers. The research team engaged in follow-up communications with the 24 schools via both email and phone, contacting the IB coordinator. We asked who the program served at each site, what kinds of IB coursework supported Spanish heritage speakers and whether low-income students had access to the IB program. These conversations narrowed our focus to 12 schools, from which we identified eight sites that represented a range of school settings and student experiences (Creswell, 2008). Given that California is home to more than 10 million immigrants, and half of California schoolchildren have at least one immigrant parent (Johnson & Mejia, 2013), we included a heavier sample from this region. The eight schools listed in Table 11.1 comprise the final sample and reflect a range of contexts to help us explain the conditions under which such programs may be implemented and thrive. Four of the schools are in California, and four are in other states.

Data collection and analysis

After identifying the sample schools, we visited each school and interviewed key educators, observed classroom instruction and collected student demographic and achievement data. We interviewed the IB coordinator, school principal and an IB teacher; when possible, we interviewed other relevant educators at the school site, including but not limited to counselors and classroom teachers. Interviews were recorded and transcribed by a professional transcribing agency. We observed classroom instruction in IB Spanish classrooms utilizing a common observation guide. The observation guide focused on the curriculum and instruction of the classroom. The IB coordinator at each site provided us with student demographic data from the IB DP, including IB exam scores and diploma recipients.

We employed Dedoose (2013), a qualitative data analysis program, to organize and later analyze the interview data. At the initial stages of data analysis, one researcher developed a list of themes based on the current literature and coded the interviews. Both researchers then reviewed these initial codes and participated in data discussions to share a common understanding and interpretation of the data (Saldana, 2009). We engaged in a second review of the data, but this time each researcher coded only for

Table 11.1 Demographic data of IB schools 2011–2012

	San Juan High Academy	Naranja High School	International Studies Academy Westside High School	Granada Senior High School	Roosevelt High School	Las Flores High School	Mariposa High School	Collegiate Academy
No. of students	1150	1600	273	3000	1160	1500	1500	50
School characteristics								
Region	West	Southwest	Northwest	Southeast	Midwest	West	West	West
State	CA	AZ	OR	FL	WI	CA	CA	CA
Context	Urban	Urban	Rural	Suburban	Suburban	Urban	Suburban	Urban
School type	Comp.	Comp.	Small school	Comp.	Comp.	Comp.	Comp.	Charter
Student body characteristics								
Free and reduced lunch	0.68	0.80	0.79	0.54	0.67	0.72	0.80	0.69
Hispanic	0.78	0.95	0.96	0.87	0.51	0.95	0.86	0.49
ELL	0.27	0.04	0.38	0.10	0.08	0.25	0.40	0.12

Source: Arizona Department of Education; California Department of Education; Florida Department of Education; Oregon Department of Education; Wisconsin Department of Public Instruction websites.

a specific set of codes and in some cases recoded the data that allowed the team to generate themes from the data, such as rigor, reputation, college preparation, perceptions of the school community and linguistic capital. We used these data themes to help us understand how and why school leaders chose to implement and develop an IB program, and to uncover the challenges that school leaders faced in framing the program for low-income Spanish heritage students.

Findings

Local contexts and the decision to offer IB

All but one of the target schools served majority Latino populations (Table 11.2); however, each school came to adopt the IB program under distinct circumstances. Some adoptions were spearheaded by superintendents or principals, others by teachers or parents. Before the implementation of the IB DP, some schools were mandated to desegregate while others were charged with restructuring to improve academic outcomes, especially for Latinos. Nonetheless, in all cases the IB program served as a vehicle that allowed the schools to improve the instructional program for their Spanish heritage students.

San Juan High Academy (CA). In the mid-1980s, San Juan High School was closed down due to underperformance. It was reconstituted and reopened as an IB World School in July 1986 under a federal desegregation order. The school was given magnet status with the IB program serving to strengthen the academic culture of the school as well as attracting some middle-class students. The school draws mostly from low-income Mexican immigrant communities despite its proximity to Silicon Valley and other more affluent communities, but it has achieved some level of voluntary integration as a result of the IB program. School leaders maintain that the staff continuously works toward a college-going culture, their primary focus.

Collegiate International Academy (CA). Two teachers with more than 35 years of combined public school teaching experience founded the Collegiate International Academies. The founders purposefully located the schools in former office buildings in the heart of downtown Portville to ensure easy accessibility via public transportation. Their educational mission is captured on their website:

> We passionately believe that the children of Portville are capable and enthusiastic learners and that they deserve the opportunity for a broad, high quality, integrated and concurrent liberal arts education. We desire to serve interested students in Portville Unified School District and in neighboring districts by offering a quality program that is free, public, and open to all students. (Mission Statement, PUSD website)

Table 11.2 Means and proportions of IB program enrollment by high school

	San Juan High Academy	Naranja High School	Westside High School	Granada Senior High School	Roosevelt High School	Las Flores High School	Mariposa High School	Collegiate Academy
IB exam candidates (*n*)	131	35	154	183	193	88	124	35
Free and reduced lunch	0.82	0.91	1.00	0.30	0.54	1.00	0.90	0.89
Hispanic	0.62	0.97	0.73	0.75	0.43	0.98	0.84	0.51
Primary language: Spanish	0.05	0.00	0.64	0.01	0.02	0.34	0.07	0.14
Spanish exam takers	0.21	0.20	0.41	0.21	0.14	0.00	0.22	0.20

Source: International Baccalaureate Organization: Diploma Programme Examinees [Data File].

The founders of Collegiate decided to transition to a charter school because they found that the traditional bureaucratic organizational systems in the public school were not amenable to effective operation of the three IB programs.

Westside High School (OR). In 2001, a superintendent who believed strongly in the IB academic program approached a Westside High counselor and asked her to develop and submit an application. After an initial failed attempt, the application was revised and resubmitted, this time with the support of the school leadership, resulting in the establishment of an IB program at Westside. The district subsequently established elementary and middle school bilingual programs to prepare students for the secondary IB program. Later, when Westside High was converted to five small schools, a group of teachers interested in establishing a bilingual school founded the International Studies Academy (ISA), whose mission is 'to cultivate community and global relationships in a bilingual environment of academic excellence that inspires and promotes social justice' (Westside High website).

Las Flores High School (CA). Discussions and planning for the IB program at Las Flores began in 2007, and the first courses were implemented in the 2008 academic year. Opened in 2006, Las Flores was dubbed the 'jewel of the district' for its rigorous college preparatory curriculum. Students and their families had to apply to enroll, which initially created parent controversy over open access. With district support, the school principal, the first IB coordinator and a few faculty members sought to convert Las Flores High into an IB World School to prepare students for careers and college in the global economy.

Naranja High School (AZ). The Naranja High IB program, which has been in place for about 20 years, grew out of the community's desire to provide the best possible program options for students. It was established by the current assistant superintendent in reaction to faculty and parent complaints regarding a lack of college preparatory rigor. Both advanced placement (AP) and the IB DP were instituted at the same time; community pride in these programs is evidenced by annual votes in favor of budget overrides in order to support these programs. As in many small communities, high school athletics and other school events are key entertainment for the whole town. As the principal noted, 'The school is at the center of our town'.

Mariposa High School (CA). Discussions and planning for the IB DP at Mariposa began in 2007, and the first courses were implemented in the 2008–2009 academic year. In the year prior to planning the IB DP, Mariposa High was identified as a program improvement school, and underwent an overhaul designed to address underperformance. Previously, Mariposa High had a poor reputation in the community where it was perceived to be the 'ghetto school' due to its location, social-class composition and history of low achievement. During the school reform process, all faculty, counselors and school administrators were asked to resubmit employment applications and were evaluated by district personnel. Faculty were then transferred, asked to resign or asked to return to their Mariposa assignment depending on the district advisors' final recommendations.

Roosevelt High School (WI). To improve the academic achievement of their underperforming schools, the Milwaukee School District chose a market-based portfolio model that assumes parents will choose the school that best suits their family's needs, and that good schools will thrive by attracting the most students. As a result, district office administrators began the Roosevelt High IB DP in 2003, in a heavily Latino area, as a strategic plan to replicate the successful IB program at M.L. King High School[3] in a heavily African American area. Roosevelt's IB DP has largely succeeded in this effort, growing in eight years from a school with 127 students and 6 staff, to over 1100 students and 60 staff. According to program documents, Roosevelt operates a whole-school IB model:

> At Roosevelt, all regular and most special education students participate exclusively in IB classes. IB philosophy mandates that classes focus on global implications and applications of content being learned. We have worked together to create a school culture of success, consistency and safety that is conducive to learning. We are accomplishing this through the use of a variety of learning safety nets that include: tutoring during and after school, a credit recovery program, and 'double dosing' the freshmen who enter lacking proficiency in math and/or English. (Program Brochure, March 2013)

Roosevelt characterizes itself as a data-driven school (e.g. daily attendance is posted in the front of the school); a full IB school; and a Professional Learning Community (PLC) school. Maintaining an elite status in the city, the campus manifests a positive learning environment with student activities adorning walls and IB DP students' work in display cases.

Granada High School (FL). Like Roosevelt, Granada High was created by the district as a magnet school to help desegregate the district. The district is supportive of bilingualism as is state policy, supporting K-12 Spanish for Native Speakers courses. Latino students at Granada High are a mix of first- and second-generation immigrants from South and Central America.

Generally, the literature on IB programs focuses on their rigor and selectivity; students from marginalized communities are typically absent from the discussion of these programs (Tarc, 2009). However, the evidence suggests that IB programs are able to serve low-income Spanish heritage speakers and Latino students successfully. Our data suggest that the schools that integrated heritage Spanish speakers faced similar programmatic challenges, including shifting the academic culture on campus, addressing financial deficits and changing the deficit perceptions of students. And yet the eight schools also shared similar strengths in meeting these challenges. In particular, educators at all eight schools share an asset-based approach to educating immigrant heritage Spanish-speaking students and express high expectations through the implementation of a rigorous college preparatory curriculum.

Working against the odds: Programmatic issues

As schools attempted to implement the IB program and encourage historically under-enrolled students, three issues emerged. First, IB educators were often met with a perceived culture of disengagement in school. Teachers and IB coordinators recounted how students hesitated to enroll in IB classes because they feared the work would be too difficult; a lack of self-confidence inhibited students from enrolling in IB classes. In response to this trend, the IB coordinator at Las Flores established an IB club and used current IB students to disseminate information to underclassmen about the DP. In this manner, potential students heard about the benefit and accessibility of the program from other students. San Juan and Mariposa shared a similar experience and word of mouth from students and alumni eventually worked to make the IB program grow in popularity.

As schools increased the number of diploma candidates as well as program offerings, a second issue emerged: cost. Schools struggled to pay for the increasing number of students and the program costs (e.g. professional development) as school district budgets were cut across the state. Both teachers and administrators indicated that staffing and IB training were an issue because of the expense, as well as staff turnover. Additionally, every school faced the issue of paying for the IB program and tests, especially as the number of students from families who could not help pay for the exams increased. In response, principals either prioritized the funding of the IB program or enlisted IB program coordinators to fundraise.

Based on interview data with teachers and administrators, we also discovered that as schools made attempts to serve more English learners and newcomer students, several faced resistance from members of the school community who held deficit perceptions of these students. During our interviews with staff at Westside High School, ISA teachers shared a common desire to build on newcomer students' knowledge of Spanish while they learned English. In fact, the staff at ISA developed the small school with the intention of enrolling a higher proportion of heritage Spanish speakers. The bilingual focus ultimately attracted mostly a Latino student demographic separate from the other small schools on campus. In doing so, the school was characterized as the 'paisa[4] school', reflecting the disdain for the immigrant students on the part of some members of the school community. In response, the ISA teachers at Westside made attempts to counter these negative stereotypes by maintaining rigor in their coursework and establishing a reputation for being the 'hardest' of the five small schools. To their credit, students from ISA received the highest IB exam scores in all disciplines in comparison to the other IB students enrolled at Westside small schools.

After the establishment of the IB program at San Juan High Academy, two camps of educators emerged: those who believed that all students could participate in rigorous IB classes, and those who expressed lower expectations for ELL and poor Latino students. Because San Juan High Academy was under pressure to ensure that its students pass the California High School Exit Exam (CAHSEE), some teachers expressed frustration at the placement of Spanish-speaking students who had not passed the CAHSEE in IB English classes. In an effort to ameliorate their concerns, the IB office continued to recruit a range of diverse students, but allowed English teachers to make final decisions about IB enrollment.

Educators at these schools did not treat these programmatic challenges as insurmountable. Rather, the teachers, administrators and coordinators shared the common belief that there is always a solution to a problem. Generally, we found that these issues were not impediments to the development of the IB program at these schools. Instead, these schools made every attempt to uphold the integrity of the IB academic program and its language philosophy.

Seeing language as an asset

IB teachers and coordinators shared a language-as-resource ideology (Ruiz, 1984). That is, rather than seeing the speaking of a primary language as a problem to be solved, IB teachers shared an assets-based approach. Staff argued that speaking Spanish was not an impediment to learning, but rather a starting point in the classroom. A principal explained:

A lot of them speak Spanish, they're very fluent. They may not be able to write it or read it at a higher level but they speak it well enough that we can use that and build on that skill. And so we have been talking about that in trying to get the students to [receive] a certificate in English, high level – HL, and we're trying to make it so that most of them also get it in Spanish because a lot of them were 90% Latino, pretty much, most of them speak Spanish already, so we're trying to capitalize on that. (Principal, Las Flores High School)

For these administrators, potential bilingualism was a resource to be developed in these traditionally marginalized students. At both Roosevelt and ISA at Westside High School, teachers successfully lobbied their principals to create an IB Spanish course focused on the needs and strengths of native Spanish speakers – in some cases, newly arrived immigrants. At many of these schools, Spanish teachers wanted not only to capture students' Spanish language skills, but also to develop bilingual, biliterate graduates. These IB DP students participated in writing and oral assignments that mirrored college-level foreign language classes. The creation of IB native Spanish speaker courses allowed these schools to offer a rigorous course that challenged their heritage Spanish language students.

In terms of practice, the staff at these IB schools not only welcomed language minority students, but also looked for ways to bring more of these students to their schools. At Roosevelt, the IB coordinator indicated that the school actively tried to recruit Latino Spanish speakers for their IB DP, even though it was difficult to get an actual gauge of students' Spanish skills prior to enrollment. IB educators and administrators believed strongly that these students would be an asset to the school and continuously engaged with feeder schools to recruit Latino Spanish speakers. Not only did school staff share a positive view of Latino students' bilingual skills, but they also reported how their IB program sought to promote and build on these language skills.

For example, at Naranja, the IB history teacher, a young man from Minnesota who spoke no Spanish when he arrived at the school, learned the language in order to support his students who were more comfortable speaking and writing in Spanish. He allowed his students to write their exams in Spanish if they chose to, which allowed some students to excel in the subject matter.

The educators in these IB programs conveyed a sense of urgency to meet the needs of their Spanish heritage students, often indicating it was unjust to make students sit in classes where they learned nothing. One teacher noted,

You don't want to mix non [Spanish] speakers with the [Spanish] speakers because I think both get frustrated. If you want to push the [Spanish] speakers farther, the non-speakers hate it and resent that. This is not fair. If you put the [Spanish] speakers in with the non-[Spanish] speakers and you translate everything to English …then the [Spanish] speakers are falling behind. They're frustrated like why is she talking to us and giving the instructions in English? (Spanish Teacher, Granada High School)

Moving beyond an additive approach, these IB educators called on their school to develop rigorous classes to teach bilingual Latino students in Spanish. In reaction to the new Latino diaspora in the Midwest (Millard & Chapa, 2004; Wortham *et al.*, 2002), an IB Spanish teacher related, 'As our demographic got heavier and heavier toward Hispanic, it was like, okay. Well, wouldn't it be great if we could have a class where they were learning something new?'. Even in a region of the country with few bilingual teachers, the IB Spanish teacher called on the principal to create a rigorous course of study for Spanish heritage students. Observations in this Spanish teacher's classroom suggest that bilingual Latino students had the opportunity to develop meaningful writing assignments and respond to difficult readings in Spanish. In the sample IB DP schools, students with Spanish language skills were not only perceived to be 'good' students, but their linguistic skills made them a good fit for the IB program. For the IB teachers and staff, the language-as-resource approach to Spanish allowed them to engage students in rigorous academic work in a non-English language.

Additionally, the IB program allowed teachers to engage in a more holistic assessment of Latino students' linguistic abilities. One administrator explained how the IB program helped teachers understand that all languages are a tool for learning:

> I think IB helps teachers realize that we are – that all teachers are language teachers and that we help foster languages regardless of what level or where they are at, and we want to validate where they come from, validate their language and also foster the languages that we have here, which is English and Spanish. …I think it's important that we don't see things black and white that we seek the color the students come with because it's important that we validate who they are, their culture and their background. (Principal, Las Flores High School)

Given the IB DP's multilingual focus, students' writing, cognitive and academic abilities are monitored and assessed in two languages. IB English and Spanish teachers lauded the IB design in which students received double doses of language support in two languages and classrooms. The IB coordinator from Portville Collegiate highlighted the various writing genres the IB program asked students to produce. This IB coordinator reported that this genre focus allowed students to transfer writing skills from one language to another: 'I mean, essentially language is language. It's not, this is in Spanish. You're simply doing these things in Spanish, but it would be very parallel to what you're doing in English'. The IB teachers in our sample consistently reported that the strength of the IB DP was its intentional provision of double language blocks, one in Spanish and the other in English, to reinforce students' academic language and writing skills in both languages.

Bilingual assessment allows IB teachers to become acutely aware of bilingual students' needs and strengths in two languages. Particularly important, we learned that students' ability was not reduced to their skills in one language or the other; rather an emphasis was placed on cognitive skill development across both languages.

Spanish teachers were particularly motivated to leverage the Spanish language skills that seemed to have been completely overlooked by a monolingual educational system. Because Spanish speakers were able to fully demonstrate their cognitive skills in the IB Spanish class, these teachers were more aware than others of the students' strengths. They were uniquely able to deeply assess the students' skills in their primary language and, as a result, they often played the role of advocate for the Spanish speakers. They were a powerful voice on behalf of retaining and growing the programs for these students. One Spanish teacher shared,

> Well, you use the language. We speak as much as we can only in Spanish, and the HLs, the higher level students, their writing is just – is very – reveals how much proficiency they have in the language. And they get very creative, and they're able to expand because we're using a language that they're stronger in. (Spanish Teacher, Mariposa High School)

The IB program at these schools seemed to give license to teachers to move beyond a deficit orientation of Spanish heritage students and instead challenge these students academically. Spanish teachers across the eight schools spoke highly of their Spanish heritage language students and pointed to the rigorous work they often asked of these students. And despite the move toward this level of rigor, allowing Spanish heritage students to use their entire language repertoire was an important scaffold that seemed to be missing before the establishment of the IB programs. A principal explained:

> And part of the reason that we encourage IB and that we believe in IB is that it does value that second language. As much as people sometimes see second language students as struggling; to be able to meet those high expectations in other ways, the richness of their language is part of what makes them ideal IB students. If you look at our IB Language A, Language B scores, our Language B scores are pretty phenomenal. (Principal, Westside High)

The ISA school community at Westside was by far one of the best examples of a school that aimed to serve newcomer students through an IB program. The IB program allowed students frequently perceived through a subtractive lens (Valenzuela, 1999) to be valued for talents that would go unrecognized in a mainstream American classroom.

Offering college preparatory curriculum

In this era of testing and accountability, with school leaders feeling the constant pressure to improve academic outcomes, the IB program provides an avenue for school improvement. While not all of the schools in our sample were labeled 'in need of improvement', all of the administrators reported that they adopted the program with the potential to improve student academic achievement and postsecondary attainment through the program. For example, one principal reported on the cultural shift that her school experienced with IB:

> I was a student when they started the movement to bring the IB Program to Naranja and it was basically because we didn't have any – back then I remember we used to have regular classes and college bound classes, that was it and we used to have honors English. That was one of the only honors classes that we had but we didn't have anything else to motivate those high achieving students and I remember that, that was one of the reasons why they brought it over just to try to promote academic excellence. We have the potential and that was the reason why and they looked at both programs so we could have more options for the students. (Principal, Naranja High)

Our interview data also suggest that IB offered schools the opportunity to develop rigorous courses in a variety of content areas (including Spanish). Expanding the variety of courses offered allowed a wider, more diverse group of students than ever before to enter a college preparatory course of study. A Spanish IB teacher in Florida reported that her recent immigrant students benefit from IB:

> Some kids, they are taking, like remedial classes sometimes. They come and suddenly they're taking ESL classes and content classes in English. The ESL classes are not challenging academically. And in the English only content classes they feel like they're not the brightest in that class because of the language, but when they come to [IB Spanish] class, they can be the best they can be. Actually they are the best because they're the ones who know more than the rest. So I think their self-esteem [is heightened.] They can say things like I'm taking AP, when everyone expects them to be taking ESL and remedial content classes because of their language skills. IB classes help their GPA because they get an extra point – and you know, it helps motivate them to go to college. … I believe FIU gave them six credits for my AP Lit class. And six credits for AP Language. So they go with 12 units of credits already. (Spanish Teacher, Granada High School)

Given the IB focus on multiple language development, schools are able to provide upper-level language courses for students who enter high school with low levels of English. Furthermore, educators reported that IB classes were better able to prepare their students for college than mainstream coursework. An IB counselor explained that:

> (My) primary goal [for students] is just to not only get into college but complete college .... a large portion of our students ...go to college but don't have the skills. They're stuck in remedial. ... So one of the biggest goals that I have for the IB students is ... struggle through high school with IB courses, the rigor and all that. (Coordinator, Mariposa)

Many of the counselors and IB coordinators we interviewed tried to keep in touch with the graduates of their IB programs, reporting that these students overwhelmingly reported that the rigor of the IB program prepared them for college so well that some of their introductory courses were easier than they had anticipated. The Westside High IB counselor shared:

> I really believe the biggest thing...(was) that this program prepares kids for college. And the proof is when those kids come back and tell me, whether they're at a small selective liberal arts college or they're at a large state institution; that is the common message: 'Freshman year has not been that hard for me because I felt like I've already been doing this for two years'... And it's a message that I receive from colleges too. We have a big group at Willamette University, one of the selective liberal arts colleges about 20, 25 miles away from here. They get a few of our students every year and say things like, '[Westside] students are unbelievable. They're so prepared'. ...And I think, with the majority of these kids being Latino kids as well, I think that also adds to the diversity and to the perspective to those [college] campuses, which I think is what they want to see as well. (IB Counselor, Westside High)

School leaders shared that the nature of IB coursework challenged their students to think critically and ultimately would best prepare them for college. One school principal reported that the IB school experience helped prepare his students for college:

> They have to write a 4,000 word essay and a lot of the students come back saying, 'I'm glad I did that because it really helps me in college'. And the theory of knowledge [course] is really exploring and questioning things that they thought were true and learning how to learn and I think it allows the kids to kind of understand you know how important it is to kind of continually be critical of our learning and to ask questions

and never to accept things as a fact through face value, and to always probe and find the answers for themselves to be informed, so I think those parts of the program help our students. (Principal, Las Flores)

Various teachers, coordinators and principals discussed the high expectations that came with participating in IB classes and course assignments. For the IB school leaders, the program offered students an intellectual challenge that was not always present in other courses. The IB curriculum requires students to think critically, which is integral to college success.

In addition to highlighting the college preparatory nature of the IB DP, site leaders promoted their school and students' success. Many schools had experienced years of failure and low achievement prior to the IB program. Educators often reported the development of a college-going culture (Oakes et al., 2000) with the introduction of the IB program. The counselor at Mariposa High School observed the surge in college acceptances since the addition of the IB program:

> In my family, we're all counselors. My brother's a counselor. My sister-in-law is a counselor. My wife's a counselor, so we always go home bragging. Oh, I got this [student] in here. My sister-in-law works in a district where money's not an issue. ... so for her, getting [students] into UCLA is like, 'we get them in all the time'. But yet we're beating them. ... My brother does work in Santa Ana where the demographics are very similar [to Mariposa HS], and I tell him, I got 11 [students] in to UCLA. And he's like, 'Oh, wow, I got six' or something like that. And even his school has a bigger population where they're financially, they're very stable and stuff like that. So I just – I try to compare it. ... And we are blowing things out of the water with *our* [low-income and Latino] population, with the culture that we have here. (Counselor, Mariposa High School)

In particular, educators related how the IB DP helped students prepare for college and earn academic distinctions. Two principals spoke with pride about their school's Gates Scholars (a minority/economically disadvantaged student program), whose success they attributed to the power of the IB curriculum to prepare Latino students for college. Several people we interviewed at Naranja were eager to share that the prior year's valedictorian, an IB student now attending a very prestigious university, had delivered her final IB oral presentation in Spanish. This was, in many ways, the greatest validation the program could receive. The student had excelled in both English and Spanish to the extent that she was able to gain admittance to one of the most selective institutions in the US, and she was also able to address the school and the community in a moving speech delivered in perfect Spanish. Interviewees recounted how people in the audience cried. Of course, it was a validation of the community as well, of what they were capable of producing.

Although these schools ranged in size, organization and location, we found that each site chose to implement the IB DP to improve the academic program and reputation of the school. Whether they were being pressured by outside forces or they simply felt that they could be doing a better job of educating their Latino and heritage language speakers, administrators described their schools as *underserving* their students. But, before schools could improve the way that they served their students, we conclude that educators' perspectives needed to change from a deficit-based to an asset-based orientation. An IB coordinator and teacher explained,

> I think we're our worst enemy in the classroom. We put the limits on our students like, well, they can't do this so I'm not going to bother. ...And I think, again, with the standards that IB has, it's like, okay. I have to teach this curriculum. This is what the end product should be. (Coordinator, San Juan High Academy)

We also found that the IB program was strategically implemented as a vehicle for both ideological and practical change. Educators involved with these IB programs framed the heritage language as an educational resource and coupled this with the rigor of a college preparatory program. Our respondents argued that the IB DP allowed schools to better serve language minority students by harnessing their linguistic capital to improve both their critical thinking and analytical skills. However, we also found that not all teachers were ready to shift their mindset and in some cases schools lost many faculty members when they established the program. But for those who remained, teachers and leaders shared the importance of both the ideological shift and the academic structure provided by the IB DP as they attempted to change their school's culture toward one of excellence.

Discussion and Conclusions

While each school in this study utilized the IB DP for a slightly different reason, one key commonality emerged: stakeholders' positive attitudes toward additive bilingualism. A focus on additive bilingualism was especially prevalent among the Spanish language teachers. While we can't make causal arguments about the origin of these attitudes, we can say that they shaped educators' decisions about how they would construct the educational experience for the students they served. For example, during preliminary screening interviews with coordinators at schools that were later excluded from our final sample, we learned that teaching students English was their first educational goal. In contrast, the IB educators in our sample perceived language as a means to communicate content rather than as an end in and of itself. As a result, the IB DP schools we studied ensured access to college preparatory academic content through students' primary language.

As pathbreaking as these schools are, a great deal of untapped potential remains to be developed in these programs. We learned that the schools in our study could be doing much more to help develop their students' content and dual language proficiency. With the exception of ISA at Westside, most of these schools could do more to enroll Spanish heritage students, especially ELLs. The IB's additive language philosophy includes the belief that every child has the right to maintain and acquire content knowledge in his or her mother tongue. In the case of Naranja or Granada, where most students speak Spanish, the Spanish-bilingual history teachers could provide their students with reading materials in both Spanish and English. Likewise, a teacher could choose to instruct her or his chemistry course in Spanish one year and in English the next, based on the students' needs. DP schools in French-speaking Canada offer a number of content courses in both French and English. Courses in both languages are equally recognized as students work toward earning their high school diplomas. In Finland, IB students learn most of their content in English, their second language, and schools offer content courses in Finnish as well. All IB students are allowed to take exams in the language they choose, regardless of the language of instruction.

For more US schools to adopt the IB DPs and the practices that we have described would require a major shift in language ideology in schools and the communities they serve. For some, this shift might feel as drastic as the move toward racial and ethnic integration in education during the Civil Rights era (May, 2012). Teacher educators, teachers and community groups in the US can begin this ideological shift by framing the learning of one's mother tongue as a basic human right, consistent with the IB philosophy. If linguistic civil rights were to be recognized more widely and students' linguistic assets nurtured, we could expect to see disparities in achievement shrink in response, and the economic benefits described in other chapters increase.

Those schools identified as serving substantial numbers of low-income Spanish heritage speakers that have taken advantage of the IB DP are few in number. It is unfortunate that education policy remains fixated on a 'closing the gap' approach rather than turning to focus on expanding the high end of the achievement continuum. Considerable research finds that a high-quality curriculum, delivered consistently over a long period of time can have a significantly positive impact on academic outcomes for low-income and ethnic minority students (Culross & Tarver, 2011; Mayer, 2008). IB programs appear to offer this option and point the way to seeing immigrant students in a whole new light – as potential high achievers.

Notes

(1) We acknowledge the complexity and the pitfalls of the term 'heritage language speaker', which, in fact, can be ascribed to different speakers under different conditions, but we adopt this term in this and other chapters of this volume to describe individuals who have 'been raised in a home where a language other than English is spoken' and 'who speak[s] or merely understand[s] that language, and who is to some degree bilingual in English and the heritage language' (Valdés, 2000, as cited in Wiley, 2014: 25).

(2) IB DP students must choose one subject from each of five groups (1–5), ensuring breadth of knowledge and understanding in their best language, additional language(s), the social sciences, the experimental sciences and mathematics. Student may choose either an arts subject from Group 6, or a second subject from Groups 1 to 5. See http://www.ibo.org/diploma/curriculum/.

(3) The M.L. King IB DP, one of the oldest in the country, is extremely well regarded in the community and serves as a point of integration, drawing white, middle-class families to the school and away from private schools.

(4) 'Paisa' is a derogatory term that refers to a Mexican immigrant from a rural or remote area who is characterized as ignorant, unsophisticated or uncouth.

References

Abedi, J. (2008) Classification system for English language learners: Issues and recommendations. *Educational Measurement: Issues and Practice* 27 (3), 17–31.

Aud, S., Fox, M. and Kewal-Ramani, A. (2010) *Status and Trends in the Education of Racial and Ethnic Groups (NCES 2010-015)*. US Department of Education, National Center for Education Statistics. Washington DC: US Government Printing Office.

Barac, R. and Bialystok, E. (2012) Bilingual effects on cognitive and linguistic development: Role of language, cultural background, and education. *Child Development* 83 (2), 413–422.

Baum, S., Ma, J. and Payea, K. (2013) *Education Pays, 2013: The Benefits of Higher Education for Individuals and Society. Trends in Higher Education Series*. New York: College Board Advocacy & Policy Center.

Bialystok, E. (2009) Bilingualism: The good, the bad, and the indifferent. *Bilingualism: Language and Cognition* 12 (1), 3–11.

Bialystok, E. and Craik, F.I. (2010) Cognitive and linguistic processing in the bilingual mind. *Current Directions in Psychological Science* 19 (1), 19–23.

Bourdieu, P. (1990) *Reproduction in Education, Society and Culture*. London: Sage Publications.

Callahan, R. and Gándara, P. (2004) On nobody's agenda: Improving English language learners' access to higher education. In M. Sadowski (ed.) *Teaching Immigrant and Second Language Students: Strategies for Success* (pp. 107–127). Cambridge, MA: Harvard Education Publishing.

Callahan, R., Wilkinson, L. and Muller, C. (2010) Academic achievement and course taking among language minority youth in U.S. schools: Effects of ESL placement. *Educational Evaluation and Policy Analysis* 32 (1), 84–117.

Creswell, J. (2008) *Educational Research: Planning, Conducting, and Evaluating Quantitative and Qualitative Research* (3rd edn). Upper Saddle River, NJ: Prentice Hall.

Culross, R. and Tarver, E. (2011) A summary of research on the International Baccalaureate Diploma Programme: Perspectives of students, teachers, and university admissions offices in the USA. *Journal of Research in International Education* 10 (3), 231–243.

Cummins, J. (1994) The acquisition of English as a second language. In K. Spangenberg Urbschat and R. Pritchard (eds) *Kids Come in All Languages: Reading Instruction for ESL Students* (pp. 36–62). Newark, DE: International Reading Association.

Dedoose Version 4.5 (2013) Web application for managing, analyzing, and presenting qualitative and mixed method research data. Los Angeles, CA: SocioCultural Research Consultants, LLC. See www.dedoose.com.

Gándara, P. and Contreras, F. (2009) *The Latino Education Crisis: The Consequences of Failed Social Policies.* Cambridge: Harvard Education Press.

Gándara, P., Losen, D., August, D., Uriarte, M., Gómez, M.C. and Hopkins, M. (2010) Forbidden language: A brief history of U.S. language policy. In P. Gándara and M. Hopkins (eds) *Forbidden Language: English Learners and Restrictive Language Policies* (pp. 20–33). Multicultural Education Series. New York: Teachers College Press.

García, O. (2009) *Bilingual Education in the 21st Century: A Global Perspective.* Malden, MA: Wiley-Blackwell.

Genesee, F. and Gándara, P. (1999) Bilingual education programs: A cross national perspective. *Journal of Social Issues* 55 (4), 665–685.

Goldrick-Rab, S. (2006) Following their every move: An investigation of social-class differences in college pathways. *Sociology of Education* 79 (1), 67–79.

Grant, C. and Sleeter, C. (2011) *Doing Multicultural Education for Achievement and Equity.* New York: Routledge.

Hallinger, P. and Lee, M. (2012) A global study of the practice and impact of distributed instructional leadership in International Baccalaureate (IB) schools. *Leadership and Policy in Schools* 11 (4), 477–495.

Hopkins, M., Martinez-Wenzl, M., Aldana, U.S. and Gándara, P. (2013) Cultivating capital: Latino newcomer young men in a U.S. urban high school. *Anthropology & Education Quarterly* 44 (3), 286–303.

IBO (2011) *Language and Learning in the IB Programmes.* Cardiff: International Baccalaureate.

Lewis, C.W., James, M., Hancock, S. and Hill-Jackson, V. (2008) Framing African American students' success and failure in urban settings: A typology for change. *Urban Education* 43 (2), 127–153.

May, S. (2012) *Language and Minority Rights: Ethnicity, Nationalism and the Politics of Language.* New York: Routledge.

Mayer, A.P. (2006) *Interrupting Social Reproduction: The Implementation of an International Baccalaureate Diploma Program in an Urban High School.* Davis, CA: University of California.

Mayer, A.P. (2008) Expanding opportunities for high academic achievement: An international baccalaureate diploma program in an urban high school. *Journal of Advanced Academics* 19 (2), 202–235.

Millard, A.V. and Chapa, J. (2004) *Apple Pie and Enchiladas: Latino Newcomers in the Rural Midwest.* Austin, TX: University of Texas Press.

Morales, P.Z. and Aldana, U.S. (2010) Learning in two languages: Programs with political promise. In P. Gándara and M. Hopkins (eds) *Forbidden Language: English Learners and Restrictive Language Policies* (pp. 159–174). New York: Teacher College Press.

Neumark, D., Johnson, H. and Mejia, M.C. (2013) Future skill shortages in the US economy? *Economics of Education Review* 32, 151–167.

Ngo, B. and Lee, S.J. (2007) Complicating the image of model minority success: A review of Southeast Asian American education. *Review of Educational Research* 77 (4), 415–453.

Noguera, P. (2003) *City Schools and the American Dream: Reclaiming the Promise of Public Education* (Vol. 17). New York: Teachers College Press.

Oakes, J. (1992) Can tracking research inform practice? Technical, normative, and political considerations. *Educational Researcher* 21 (4), 12–21.

Oakes, J., Rogers, J., Lipton, M. and Morrell, E. (2000) The social construction of college access: Confronting the technical, cultural and political barriers to low income students. In W.G. Tierney and L.S. Haggedorn (eds) *Extending our Reach: Strategies for Increasing Access to College*. Albany, NY: State University of New York Press.

Passel, J.S. (2005) *Estimates of the Size and Characteristics of the Undocumented Population*. Washington DC: Pew Hispanic Center.

Reardon, S.F. and Bischoff, K. (2011) Income inequality and income segregation. *American Journal of Sociology* 116 (4), 1092–1153.

Ruíz, R. (1984) Orientations in language planning. *NABE Journal* 8 (2), 15–34.

Rumbaut, R.G., Massey, D.S. and Bean, F.D. (2006) Linguistic life expectancies: Immigrant language retention in Southern California. *Population and Development Review* 32 (3), 447–460.

Rumbaut, R.G. and Massey, D.S. (2013) Immigration & language diversity in the United States. *Daedalus* 142 (3), 141–154.

Saldana, J. (2009) *The Coding Manual for Qualitative Researchers*. London: Sage Publications.

Steele, C. (1997) A threat in the air: How stereotypes shape intellectual identity and performance. *American Psychologist* 52, 613–629.

Talbert-Johnson, C. (2004) Structural inequities and the achievement gap in urban schools. *Education and Urban Society* 37 (1), 22–36.

Tarc, P. (2009) *Global Dreams, Enduring Tensions: International Baccalaureate in a Changing World*. New York: Peter Lang.

Telles, E.E. and Ortiz, V. (2008) *Generations of Exclusion: Mexican Americans, Assimilation and Race*. New York: Russell Sage Foundation.

Tienda, M. and Mitchell, R. (2006) E plurbis plures or e plurbis unem? In M. Tienda and F. Mitchell (eds) *Multiple Origins, Uncertain Destinies: Hispanics and the American Future* (pp. 2–13). Washington DC: National Academies Press.

Valdés, G. (2000) Introduction. In *Spanish for Native Speakers* (pp. 1–20). AATSP Professional Development Series Handbook for Teachers, K-16. Orlando, FL: Harcourt College Publishers.

Valenzuela, A. (1999) *Subtractive Schooling: US-Mexican Youth and the Politics of Caring*. New York: SUNY Press.

Wiley, T. (2014) The problem of defining heritage and community languages and their speakers. In T. Wiley, J. Peyton, D. Christina, S.C. Moore and N. Liu (eds) *Handbook of Heritage, Community, and Native American Languages in the United States: Research, Policy, and Educational Practice* (pp. 16–26). New York: Routledge/Washington DC: Center for Applied Linguistics.

Wortham, S., Murillo, E. and Hamann, E.T. (2002) *Education in the New Latino Diaspora: Policy and the Politics of Identity*. Westport, CT: Ablex Publishing.

Yin, R.K. (2003) *Case Study Research: Design and Methods* (3rd edn). London: Sage Publications.

12 Looking Toward the Future: Opportunities in a Shifting Linguistic Landscape

Patricia C. Gándara and
Rebecca M. Callahan

Globalization has changed the world in radical ways. Today, every developed country is the recipient of immigrants and with them, their languages; yet, nowhere have we seen a response to this phenomenon that is truly forward thinking. Europe, for all its comfort with multiple languages, is in many ways like the US with its monolingual obsession. At the beginning of the decade, Rotterdam's population was 45% immigrant and Amsterdam's is expected to exceed 50% by 2015 (Suárez-Orozco & Páez, 2002). Despite these numbers, the schools in Rotterdam and Amsterdam are hardly more prepared than American schools to incorporate these new students into their classrooms. We have seen signs posted in front of Dutch schools reading, *We speak Dutch, how about you?*; but the Dutch are not alone in their anxiety over these demographic shifts. The Russians worry about the Uzbekistani migrant students whose Russian isn't up to par, and urban Chinese worry about rural students with their indigenous dialects and weak Mandarin literacy moving into the central cities. In Hong Kong, they complain that the South Asians fall behind academically because of their lack of familiarity with Cantonese and English. Everywhere, immigrant languages are disparaged and native-speaking parents navigate the system to ensure that their children attend schools where they will not mix with immigrant students and their languages. In short, the achievement gap is global, growing and increasingly defined along linguistic lines (Suárez-Orozco & Páez, 2002).

As we searched for more progressive models of linguistic incorporation, we found hope in the European Union's (EU) *mother tongue plus two* language policy (European Commission, 2004). Here, the EU certainly reflects a more expansive view of linguistic diversity than the US; however, this policy, in fact, is not very progressive with respect to immigrant languages. Only those languages with roots on the European continent are considered to be of educational value, but Europe's immigrants increasingly come from outside of the EU, and as a result, their children encounter many of the same prejudices and barriers as immigrant students in the US.

Seizing the Opportunity in a Globalizing World

The United States has the unique opportunity to be at the forefront of a more visionary, but also more practical, language policy. The nation is host to most of the world's languages due to trends in immigration flow. In fact, the three most spoken languages in the US are also the three most spoken languages in the world: English, Spanish and Chinese. The US is home to literally hundreds of thousands of bilingual and biliterate youth (as discussed in Chapter 10) who *could* become the bilingual teachers of tomorrow. However, the nation must actively seize the opportunity rather than squander it. The US is poised to take the lead in the global marketplace, but to do so, it must first acknowledge the tremendous, unique resource that exists in its cultural and linguistic diversity.

While research has been building that demonstrates the social and cognitive benefits of bilingualism, it was, until now, still possible to make the argument that no real economic benefit to multilingualism existed. In the global marketplace, nothing speaks louder than money and the consensus in the field had converged around a finding that multilingualism was not a remunerated asset. Now, however, with data sets that allow us to track the educational and occupational trajectories of a new generation of children of immigrants and others who are entering into the labor market with proficiency in more than one language, a new picture has begun to emerge.

The initial chapters in this book first outline the nation's predominantly monolingual historical context and the role of restrictive language policies in undermining the economic value of languages other than English. Chapter 2 also shows that *literacy* in both English and other languages is sometimes used as a further means of excluding some and including others whose language is privileged. We then turn to traditional US labor market analyses that document little economic value associated with being multilingual. Our contributors then move on to innovative analyses that incorporate different variables (e.g. gender and age) with newer data sets (e.g. Children of Immigrants Longitudinal Study [CILS] and the Educational Longitudinal Survey [ELS]). Together, more comprehensive variables and finer-tuned data allow researchers to not only answer questions about a younger population of bilinguals, but also incorporate more sophisticated methods than were previously possible. The combination of new variables, new data and new analytical methods has yielded quite different findings than past studies. However, not all studies, even those using the same data sets, arrive at the same conclusions. We find this both intellectually challenging and illuminating of the difficulties inherent in extrapolating the meaning of language and literacy from data that are never perfect, and often barely adequate to the task. In Chapter 5, Alarcón and colleagues allude to the 'black box' of language in the labor force that all of the research in this volume attempts to address, in one way or another. In fact, several chapters of the book (Chapters 7–10 especially) make significant contributions to the literature in prying open that black box and speculating about the role of language *as it is used* in a variety of contexts, including among family, peers and work colleagues, and adding important information about literacy in both English and Spanish, to help understand the role of bilingualism in the economy.

We have also seen how the definition of variables (e.g. the difference of one rather arbitrarily defined age group vs another) can make a considerable difference in the study outcomes. The assumptions that are made about fluency and literacy and the ways that both English and other languages are used in the workplace can result in different conclusions. Chapter 10 investigates bilingualism and employment, and begins to provide some insights into how multilingualism may sometimes be officially overlooked as a labor market asset, and yet indirectly rewarded. It also reaffirms that the most salient value of multilingualism may be in getting a job in the first place, something that most of the large data sets are not able to discern. Thus, while not all of the studies presented here align perfectly with each other, as the analyses become more fine-grained a clear conclusion can be drawn: multilingualism matters in the present-day labor market.

Despite the methodological innovations presented in this volume, and in the field in general, the absence of a unifying theoretical frame to explain the role of language in the US labor market is notable. Several of the chapters in this volume incorporate different theoretical perspectives, yet no one unifying theory rises to the forefront. Macias (Chapter 2) alludes, albeit indirectly, to sociolinguistic identity theory (Norton, 1997) as well as sociopolitical and economic subordination theories to explain the robust legacy of English-only policies in the United States. A desire to create a singular American identity (Mertz, 1982) out of the myriad of immigrants that comprise America drives populist discourse to position English as the one and only language of the land. Likewise, a nationalistic perspective provides a particularly generous explanation for the failure of employers to acknowledge, if not reward, the multilingual skills of their employees. Agirdag (Chapter 7) introduces a Bourdieusian perspective, positioning language as human capital and questioning why multilingualism would not consistently yield labor market rewards. Yet, conflicting interpretations of the intent of language policies persist.

Ultimately, an overarching theory to explain the uniquely American relationship with language(s) remains elusive. Currently, a variety of theories reflect the multiple, often conflicting, approaches of the nation to the languages in its midst. Some suggest that linguistic assimilation, with its rejection of non-English languages, is the inheritance of a nation of immigrants. The English-only American identity is manifested in the 'polyglot boarding house' that President Theodore Roosevelt, who presided over the largest immigration in the nation's history, so abhorred[1] and believed had to be avoided at all costs. In contrast, an ecology of languages approach (Haugen, 1972) critically examines the influence of multiple languages on one another in a shared environment, also mirroring the peculiar history of language(s) in the US (cf. Macias, Chapter 2). Indeed, adopting a 'language as human capital' approach, Agirdag suggests that the cost of lost linguistic competence has been high, both to the individual and to society as a whole. Others theorize that racial and ethnic discrimination have gone hand in hand with linguistic discrimination (see Alarcon et al., Chapter 6), again reflecting a linguistic ecology perspective (Wurm, 1991), which takes into account linguistic loss through social conflict. Historically, this social and linguistic rejection of the 'other' has translated into a devaluation of the human capital inherent in linguistic skills (Chiswick & Miller, 2003), redefining multilingualism instead as 'an inherited trait' with no particular economic value (cf. Alarcón et al., Chapter 6).

As this volume set out to reanalyze old data and introduce new data to answer a very grounded, practical question, we did not attempt to forge a theory that could explain the ways in which multilingualism is treated. Analyses in this volume investigate whether being multilingual in contemporary US society holds any value in the labor market; in the process, however, multiple theoretical perspectives began to emerge. Ultimately, we believe that the beginnings of a unifying socio-politico-linguistic theory are inherent in the chapters of this book; we can only hope that future authors will find fertile ground here for its development.

From the studies presented in this volume, we have seen a new generation of bilingual and multilingual Americans enter the workforce in an era of global competition and ever-greater linguistic diversity at home. Bilinguals in the new generation will more readily find jobs and many will make more money over their lifetimes as a result of their linguistic skills. When a nation's youth become more economically competitive, so does its economy. These new studies converge around a conclusion that it is simply in the economic self-interest of the US to nurture and value the languages that immigrant populations and their progeny have bequeathed to the national patrimony.

Nor is bi- or multilingualism any longer a phenomenon restricted to US coastal ports of entry or border regions; rather, linguistic awareness, competence and diversity now encompass great swaths of the country. Linguistic diversity has spread into rural and suburban America, in the Midwest and the Deep South, and in pockets dotting virtually the entire US landscape (Millard & Chapa, 2004; Wortham et al., 2002). Today, these new destination regions, all previously untouched by immigration and largely unfamiliar with 'accented' English (Lippi-Green, 2012), are not only host to any number of the 381 languages now estimated to be spoken by 21% of the US population (Ryan, 2013), but also reflect a heightened awareness of linguistic and cultural diversity (Dondero & Muller, 2012). Recently, both The Washington Post[2] and The New York Times[3] ran articles drawing on Census 2010 data to illustrate the linguistic diversity in US homes and schools. The Washington Post map showed that one in four US counties reported that more than 10% of residents speak a language other than English at home. In turn, The New York Times indicated that all 50 states have experienced an increase in language minority students (those whose primary language is not English), with several showing greater than 200% growth.

Macias (Chapter 2) argues in his description of America's long-standing, yet strained relationship with bilingualism that a hierarchy of languages may help to explain a history fraught with contradictions. The implications of this two-tiered system rise to the forefront with the unprecedented growth of the relatively young (read: labor market-oriented) Latino population (Durand et al., 2006; Pew Hispanic Center, 2009), while the white and monolingual English-speaking baby boomers cede their cultural stronghold and edge into retirement. An increasingly multilingual domestic context, coupled with a global marketplace, awaits bilingual youth entering the labor market in the 21st century. The bilingual youth of today will encounter a different world than that described in the first chapters of this volume.

While Robinson-Cimpian (Chapter 4) and Alarcón and colleagues (Chapters 5 and 6) approach bilingualism in the labor market through relatively traditional analytic lenses, their work also suggests that the use of broadly drawn models may miss important changes to the context of bilingualism: gender, region and age cohort. The labor market entry of a 24-year-old bilingual today differs markedly from that of her or his predecessor in 1974 or even 1994, and it almost certainly varies across regions of the US. Casting a broad net, we find little tangible evidence of an income advantage; it is only when analyses focus on the current generation entering into the 21st century workforce, as do Agirdag (Chapter 7), Rumbaut (Chapter 8) and Santibañez and Zárate (Chapter 9), and where much more is known about the literacy skills of these young workers, that the returns to bilingualism begin to solidify. In addition, the benefits may not always be in immediate salary premiums. Alarcón and his colleagues (Chapters 5 and 6) as well as Porras and her colleagues (Chapter 10) suggest that the bilingual benefit occurs most often at hiring. Likewise, and with a larger net, Robinson-Cimpian (Chapter 4) finds that bilingual females are more likely to be employed than their nonbilingual peers.

Not all languages, however, have equal value in the labor market. While some employers in the Porras *et al.* survey said that they valued any additional languages among their employees, there are clearly language market niches. These niches are composed of a concentration of particular language speakers, such as the Farsi and Arabic speakers in some high-income areas of the Los Angeles region referenced by the authors. Overwhelmingly, however, Spanish followed by Chinese, were the most highly sought after languages in that survey.

The New Latino America

Since 1990, the US has experienced unprecedented demographic change, driven largely by immigration from Mexico and Central and South America (Pew Hispanic Center, 2009). Not only have Latino immigrants arrived in large numbers, but their fertility rate has surpassed that of the white and native-born populations (Passel & Cohn, 2008). Latino immigrants and their children, the new second-generation (Hernández *et al.*, 2009), are changing the face of US schools, causing educators to rethink pedagogy (Dondero & Muller, 2012) and whole communities to reconsider race relations (Marrow, 2011). Unfortunately, shortsighted educational policies have often not only held the children of immigrants back, but have also stripped them of important assets: the language and culture of their home. Developing linguistic proficiency as well as the ability to comfortably navigate both the home and host culture may allow the new second-generation to build bridges all across the Americas; but forced into English-only instruction and assimilative curricula, these students' best opportunity to become biliterate world citizens is often denied them. In US English-only environments, those Latino students whose first language is Spanish are typically the stragglers, struggling to master the content area curriculum while simultaneously learning English at academically proficient levels. Even those Latino students who begin school speaking English often come from communities where the academic English of the classroom is never spoken. To no one's surprise, Latino students are frequently labeled 'slow learners', and represent a threat to the advancement of the rest of the class. Native-born, native English-speaking parents lobby to keep their children out of classrooms with these English learners so that the Latino language minority students find themselves isolated in low-track classrooms where both teachers' and students' expectations are frequently very low.

Perhaps most damaging is the increasing segregation and isolation that so many Latino language minority students experience. In 2005–2006, approximately 78% of Latinos attended predominantly (50% to 100%) minority schools; nationally, about 40% of Latinos attend hypersegregated schools in which 90% to 100% of their classmates are non-white. The situation is even worse in the central cites of the West, where over 60% of Latinos were attending hypersegregated schools at the middle of the decade (Orfield & Frankenberg, 2008). As a result, Latino students frequently experience triple segregation – by ethnicity, poverty and language (Gándara, 2010). In these highly segregated contexts, it is difficult to become truly biliterate due to insufficient exposure to naturally occurring academic English. At the same time, native English speakers also lose out on the opportunity to develop cross-cultural and linguistic competence and skills, isolated in socially, linguistically and culturally homogenous contexts as well. Yet importantly, Santibañez and Zárate (Chapter 9) tell us that those Latino graduates who do manage to develop strong proficiency in two languages – Spanish and English – are more likely to go to college than those who lose their heritage language. This should be a very strong message for both policymakers and educators.

Dual language programs provide a viable model for the integration of students from different social and linguistic backgrounds while also providing the advantage of a rigorous curriculum in two languages. Two-way dual language classrooms are comprised of both native English speakers and language minority youth; most often, the non-English language is Spanish, but not always. Initially, the program promotes a heavy dose of the target language (Spanish, Chinese, etc.) and less English. As students develop a stronger dominance of the target minority language, more English is added. The research on these programs has consistently found them to result in superior academic outcomes for both the English speakers and the speakers of other languages (Genesee et al., 2007; Umansky & Reardon, forthcoming), as well as increased respect for the other culture and increased interest in having friends from that culture (Genesee & Gándara, 1999). However, the caveat remains that without careful attention paid to students' social integration and the development of academic hierarchies, dual language education can easily prioritize the foreign language learning of native English speakers over the academic development of language minority youth (Palmer, 2007; Valdés, 1997).

Aldana and Mayer (Chapter 11) introduce us to another option for providing highly rigorous, culturally enriching instruction to Latino students: the International Baccalaureate Programme (IB). This program, based in Geneva, offers a rigorous curriculum, primarily in the latter half of high school, in which students must demonstrate a high level of competence in at least two languages. Because the program does not privilege any one language, students whose strongest language is Spanish may take core courses in that language while they also continue to develop their English. Aldana and Mayer describe the way in which a number of schools across the US have adapted the IB to accommodate the needs of Latino students who are capable of taking a rigorous, college preparatory curriculum, but would not have had access to it otherwise because of a perceived deficit in English. If Latino students are to thrive academically and continue to develop the linguistic and cultural assets that they bring to school, it will be necessary to identify and implement programs like these that take an assets-based approach to the education of the Latino population.

Considering the Life Course: Considering the Era

We have posed the question as to *when* it would be relevant to consider bilingualism as a labor market factor. This question is critical from two perspectives: an individual's age and the era in which she or he first enters the labor market. In their chapter, Moore and colleagues break down their analyses by age cohort, separating out the 16- to 29-year-old cohort; similarly, Agirdag (Chapter 7), Rumbaut (Chapter 8) and Santibañez and Zárate (Chapter 9) all analyze data sets that target young adults as they enter the labor market, in an effort to better understand when proficiency in a non-English language may prove to be an asset. The historical context in which an individual enters the workforce matters as well; global forces drive the current economy and the onset of the internet has brought us firmly into an age of easily accessed information. No longer is the American isolationism that prevailed between World Wars I and II an option, as Macias (Chapter 2) clearly argues. Not only are Americans increasingly global citizens, but the domestic market is now filled with multilingual, multicultural consumers whose needs must be met.

Language in a New Era: Will it Matter?

Today's newspapers are full of stories about the growing linguistic diversity in the US. Facts and figures from the 2010 US Census drive home the fact that the nation is increasingly bilingual; yet the question remains, will immigrant children's bilingualism be framed as a resource, or will it remain a problem to be eradicated? In fact, the *US News and World Report*[4] recently argued that maintaining and teaching languages other than English will be critical to the success of the nation's schools in the coming century. The costs of primary language loss are becoming increasingly real; while Agirdag (Chapter 7) measures the costs to the individual in terms of lost wages, we argue the need to measure the cost of a *no-longer-bilingual* workforce to the country's economy. The US cannot remain a nation of isolationists in an era of social media and globalization. Previously, US neighbors existed only on either side of the nation's physical borders; now, opportunities for collaboration extend far beyond the physical borders. Global 'neighbors' can be anywhere. While these same economic, social and political opportunities have changed how Americans think about language and bilingualism, we refer to Ruiz's (1984) problematizing of language in the US as either a resource or a problem. Bilingualism among the children of immigrants in the US represents a previously untapped national resource; what the country will do with that potential remains to be determined.

Today's young language minority population is unique; their experiences have made them distinct from previous generations and not only with respect to their access to social media and entrance into a global economy. Children of immigrants today are coming of age in a majority-minority era. Their linguistic and cultural caché is increasingly common, rather than 'othered', among their peers. For today's youth, language is not just lexicon and grammar, but rather represents interpersonal ties – social and economic, as Porras and colleagues (Chapter 10) aptly illustrate. Entering into a new millennium, employers increasingly prefer employees who can reach a wider client base and work collaboratively with coworkers across racial, ethnic and cultural lines. This new generation needs interpersonal skills to deal with a wider variety of colleagues, customers and coworkers in a way that previous generations simply did not.

Looking Forward: Framing Language as a Resource

As we look forward with respect to both policy and practice, we ask how we can best tap into the linguistic potential of bilinguals – especially bilingual children from immigrant communities. These children represent both an economic and an educational resource for the nation. The surge in popularity of dual language education programs demonstrates native English-speaking parents' recognition of language as an important resource they want to cultivate in and for their children. At an individual level, these forward-facing parents call attention to the needs of the nation. In California, the immense popularity of the recently adopted Seal of Biliteracy[5] on the high school diploma (more than 21,000 students earned this recognition in 2013) has prompted a proposal for a national seal of biliteracy.[6] This linguistic phenomenon represents both a societal and an institutional recognition of the value of bilingualism in our youth. An extension of dual language education, the IB programs can also work to develop national linguistic resources as well as a more global perspective.

The question of language as part of the national identity, however, poses another set of issues. Macias (Chapter 2) clearly presents an American history of dual linguistic streams, with Spanish and Spanish speakers squarely occupying a lower status. As the Latino population grows and increasingly enters the mainstream, these dual streams of language valuation appear to be converging. Across the country, German and French classes in high school and college go begging for students while the Spanish classes are overenrolled. Not only are increasing numbers of Latino students seeking to study their heritage language, but the population as a whole has come to realize that Spanish will serve them better in a nation in which nearly 40 million people already speak it (Gónzalez-Barrera & López, 2013). Historically, the US has continuously reverted to an English-only, isolationist stance, which is evident today in our expanding criteria for citizenship, including a 2012 proposal to include a Test of English as a Foreign Language (TOEFL)-like test of English proficiency.[7] However, as recent census data on linguistic diversity suggest, this perspective may literally be dying out.

Perhaps more important, however, in a capitalist economy, the customer is always right; ultimately, employer preferences will prevail, driven by an increasingly linguistically diverse consumer base. Several analyses in this volume indicated an emerging pattern of employer preference to hire and to promote bilinguals although they were often not paid any more than their monolingual coworkers. This pattern suggests that in the future, bilinguals may be more competitive for higher-level jobs and have greater earning power, changing the face of the workplace. We call attention to the case in point, the banker interviewed in Chapter 10, who reported that while he didn't get paid more, he actually earned more because he generates more business as clients gravitate to him for his linguistic and cultural aptitude. Likewise, the *Forbes Insights* study reported in Porras *et al.* found that two-thirds of the executives surveyed at large businesses (more than $500 million in revenues) reported that their companies suffered from communication barriers caused by the inability of management and workers to communicate effectively. However, these leaders did not see demanding that workers strengthen their English skills as the solution. Rather, leaders in these large businesses reported an increase in the requirement that managers know the languages of their workers in order to better interact with them and their clients. This study suggests that the days of simply finding interpreters and translators for managers and executives (cf. Alarcón *et al.*, Chapter 5) may be numbered.

As a nation, the US is changing in response to shifting internal and external power structures. Internally, immigration and the new Latino diaspora have changed the consumer base across the country. Even the smallest, most remote Midwestern towns now lay claim to at least one *taqueria* (Millard & Chapa, 2004). Externally, the US is increasingly linked to and dependent on the strength of the global economy. The *Forbes Insights* study cited earlier quoted one of its interviewees as saying, '[T]here needs to be more dialogue between the education and business worlds to create the mutual understanding necessary to improve and match the supply and demand' of languages (*Forbes Insights*, 2011: 2). Clearly, it is time for American educators to realize that English-only instruction is a vestige of another era and the new economy calls for a multilingual approach to educating America's children.

Notes

(1)   Roosevelt, in a period of intense immigration to the US, is often quoted as taking a strong stand against multilingualism in the US, arguing that it was divisive to the nation. The 'polyglot boarding house' comment is cited in L.N. Hines, *Proceedings and Papers of the Indiana State Teachers Association*, 31 October and 1 November 1917, 350.

(2)   http://www.washingtonpost.com/wp-srv/special/national/us-language-map/?wpisrc=nl_politics

(3)   http://www.nytimes.com/interactive/2009/03/13/us/ELL-students.html?_r=1&

(4)   http://www.usnews.com/opinion/articles/2013/09/19/3-ways-to-combat-boredom-and-close-the-global-education-gap

(5)   http://www.cde.ca.gov/sp/el/er/sealofbiliteracy.asp

(6)   http://juliabrownley.house.gov/media-center/press-releases/brownley-puts-the-california-seal-of-biliteracy-on-the-national-stage

(7)   http://www.schumer.senate.gov/forms/immigration.pdf

References

Chiswick, B.R. and Miller, P.W. (2003) The complementarity of language and other human capital: Immigrant earnings in Canada. *Economics of Education Review* 22, 469–480.

Dondero, M. and Muller, C. (2012) School stratification in new and established Latino destinations. *Social Forces* 91 (2), 477–502.

Durand, J., Telles, E. and Flashman, J. (2006) The demographic foundations of the Latino population. In M. Tienda and F. Mitchell (eds) *Hispanics and the Future of America* (pp. 66–99). Washington DC: National Academies Press.

European Commission (2004) *Promoting Language Learning and Linguistic Diversity: An Action Plan 2004–06*. Brussels: Office for Official Publications of the European Communities.

Forbes Insights. (2011) Reducing the impact of language barriers. Forbes & The Rosetta Stone. See http://resources.rosettastone.com/CDN/us/pdfs/Biz-Public-Sec/Forbes-Insights-Reducing-the-Impact-of-Language-Barriers.pdf (accessed 1 February 2014).

Gándara, P.C. (2010) Overcoming triple segregation. *Educational Leadership* 68 (3), 60–64.

Genesee, F. and Gándara, P.C. (1999) Bilingual education programs: A cross-national perspective. *Journal of Social Issues* 55 (4), 665–685.

Genesee, F., Lindholm-Leary, K., Saunders, W. and Christian, D. (2007) *Educating English Language Learners: A Synthesis of Research Evidence*. New York: Cambridge University Press.

González-Barrera, A. and López, M.H. (2013) *Spanish is the Most Spoken non-English Language in U.S. Homes, Even Among Non-Hispanics*. Washington DC: Pew Hispanic Center.

Haugen, E.I. and Dil, A.S. (1972) *The Ecology of Language: Essays by Einar Haugen. Selected and Introduced by Anwar S. Dil*. Stanford: Stanford University Press.

Hernández, D., Denton, N. and Macartney, S. (2009) School-age children in immigrant families: Challenges and opportunities for America's schools. *Teachers College Record* 111 (3), 616–658.

Lippi-Green, R. (2012) *English With an Accent: Language, Ideology and Discrimination in the United States*. New York: Routledge.

Marrow, H.B. (2011) *New Destination Dreaming: Immigration, Race, and Legal Status in the Rural American South*. Stanford, CA: Stanford University Press.

Millard, A.V. and Chapa, J. (2004) *Apple Pie and Enchiladas: Latino Newcomers in the Rural Midwest*. Austin, TX: University of Texas Press.

Norton, B. (1997) Language, identity, and the ownership of English. *TESOL Quarterly* 31, 409–429.

Orfield, G. and Frankenberg, E.D. (2008) The last have become first: Rural and small town America lead the way in desegregation. Los Angeles, CA: UCLA Civil Rights Project/Proyecto Derechos Civiles.

Palmer, D. (2007) A dual immersion strand programme in California: Carrying out the promise of dual language education in an English-dominant context. *International Journal of Bilingual Education and Bilingualism* 10 (6), 752–768.

Passel, J.S. and Cohn, D.V. (2008) *U.S. Population Projections: 2005–2050*. Washington DC: Pew Research Center.

Pew Hispanic Center. (2009) *Statistical Portrait of the Foreign-Born Population in the United States, 2007*. Washington DC: Pew Research Center.

Ruiz, R. (1984) Orientations in language planning. *NABE: The Journal for the National Association of Bilingual Education* 8 (2), 15–34.

Ryan, C. (2013) *Language Use in the United States: American Community Survey Reports* (Vol. ACS-22). Washington DC: US Census Bureau.

Suárez-Orozco, M. and Páez, M. (eds) (2002) *Latinos: Remaking America*. Berkeley, CA: University of California Press.

Umansky, I. and Reardon, S.F. (forthcoming) Reclassification patterns among Latino English learner students in bilingual, dual immersion, and English immersion classrooms *American Educational Research Journal*.

Valdés, G. (1997) Dual-language immersion programs: A cautionary note concerning the education of language-minority students. *Harvard Educational Review* 67 (3), 391–429.

Wortham, S., Murillo, E. and Hamann, E.T. (2002) *Education in the New Latino Diaspora: Policy and the Politics of Identity*. Westport, CT: Ablex Publishing.

Wurm, S.A. (1991) Language death and disappearance: Causes and circumstances. *Diogenes* 39, 1–18.

Index